The Word Order
of the Gospel of Luke

Its Foregrounded Messages

Ivan Shing Chung Kwong

t & t clark

Published by T&T Clark
A Continuum imprint
The Tower Building, 11 York Road, London SE1 7NX
15 East 26th Street, Suite 1703, New York, NY 10010

www.tandtclark.com

British Library Cataloguing-in-Publication Data
A catalogue record for this book is available from the British Library

Typeset by Free Range Book Design & Production
Printed on acid-free paper in Great Britain by MPG Books Ltd, Bodmin, Cornwall

ISBN 0567030512   (hardback)

LIBRARY OF NEW TESTAMENT STUDIES
˅ 298

formerly the Journal for the Study of the New Testament Supplement series

Editor
Mark Goodacre

Studies in New Testament Greek
12

Contents

Acknowledgements

The current work is a slightly modified version of a doctoral thesis submitted to the University of Surrey (UK) in 2003. I wish to express my deep thanks to Professor Stanley E. Porter, my main thesis supervisor, who has guided my studies and has given me invaluable suggestions and comments. Deep thanks also need to be expressed to Dr John Jarick, the Director of Studies and also my supervisor, who consistently demonstrates his patience to me and has given many encouragements to me. Without their participations and efforts, this work could never be finished.

I am also deeply indebted to my two external examiners, Professor Loveday Alexander and Dr Mark Goodacre, for their insightful observations.

I also wish to thank the Ming Yee Theological Education Foundation, who generously financially supported me in the years that I studied in London.

Above all, my wife, Florence, and my son, Titus, who was born in London while I studied there, have endured the entire journey with me. It is to them that I owe the most.

Abbreviations

AB	The Anchor Bible
ABRL	The Anchor Bible Reference Library
ACL	Amsterdam Classics in Linguistics, 1800-1925
ADP	Advances in Discourse Processes
ANTC	Abingdon New Testament Commentaries
AJP	*American Journal of Philology*
ASCP	Amsterdam Studies in Classical Philology
ASTHLS	Amsterdam Studies in the Theory and History of Linguistic Science
ASV	American Standard Version
AV	Authorized Version
BETL	Bibliotheca Ephemeridum Theologicarum Lovaniensium
BI	*Biblical Interpretation*
Bib	*Biblica*
BibSac	*Bibliotheca Sacra*
BECNT	Baker Exegetical Commentary on the New Testament
BILS	Berkeley Insights in Linguistics and Semiotics
BIS	Biblical Interpretation Series
BLG	Biblical Languages: Greek
BR	*Bible Review*
BTB	*Biblical Theology Bulletin*
CB	*Classical Bulletin*
CBNTS	Coniectanea Biblica New Testament Series
CBQ	*Catholic Biblical Quarterly*
CC	Concordia Commentary
CHLS	Croom Helm Linguistics Series
CILT	Current Issues in Linguistic Theory
CJ	*Classical Journal*
ClQ	*Classical Quarterly*
CQNS	*Classical Quarterly New Series*
CR	*The Classical Review*
CRNS	*The Classical Review New Series*
CSL	Cambridge Studies in Linguistics
CTIL	Current Trends in Linguistics
CTL	Cambridge Textbooks in Linguistics
DUPS	Dublin University Press Series
ELS	English Language Series
ETL	*Ephemerides Theologicae Lovanienses*

ExpTim	*Expository Times*
FGS	Functional Grammar Series
FN	*Filología Neotestamentaria*
GHA	Göteborgs Högskolas Arsskrift
Glotta	*Glotta: Zeitschrift fur Griechische und Lateinische Sprache*
GTJ	*Grace Theological Journal*
HDC	Harvard Dissertations in Classics
HS	*Historische Sprachforschung*
HSCP	Harvard Studies in Classical Philology
HTS	Harvard Theological Studies
ICC	The International Critical Commentary
Int	*Interpretation*
IF	*Indogermanische Forschungen*
JB	Jerusalem Bible
JBL	*Journal of Biblical Literature*
JCP	*Jahrbücher für Classische Philologie*
JD	*Jian Dao*
JIES	*Journal of Indo-European Studies*
JIESM	Journal of Indo-European Studies Monograph
J Ling	*Journal of Linguistics*
JLT	*Journal of Literature and Theology*
JLSMaj	Janua Linguarum Series Major
JLSMin	Janua Linguarum Series Minor
JLSP	Janua Linguarum Series Practica
JOTT	*Journal of Translation and Textlinguistics*
JQL	*Journal of Quantitative Linguistics*
JR	*Journal of Religion*
JSNT	*Journal for the Study of the New Testament*
JSNTSup	*Journal for the Study of the New Testament, Supplement Series*
JSOTSup	*Journal for the Study of the Old Testament, Supplement Series*
KJV	King James Version
KRL	Kregel Reprint Library
KTR	*King's Theological Review*
Lang	*Language*
LII	Luke the Interpreter of Israel
Ling	*Linguistics*
Lingua	*Lingua: International Review of General Linguistics*
Ling Inq	*Linguistic Inquiry*
Link	*The Link: A Review of Mediaeval and Modern Greek*
LIM	Linguistic Inquiry Monographs
LLC	*Literary and Linguistic Computing*
LV&C	*Language Variation and Change*
LXX	Septuagint

MnemosyneSup	Mnemosyne Supplement Series
MNTC	The Moffatt New Testament Commentary
MSL	Monographs in Systemic Linguistics
NAC	The New American Commentary
NEB	The New English Bible
NCBC	New Century Bible Commentary
Neot	*Neotestamentica*
NHLS	North Holland Linguistics Series
NIGTC	The New International Greek Testament Commentary
NIDNTT	C. Brown (ed.), *The New International Dictionary of New Testament Theology*
NKJV	New King James Version
NovT	*Novum Testamentum*
NovTSup	*Novum Testamentum* Supplements
NOT	*Notes on Translation*
NRSV	New Revised Standard Version
NT	New Testament
NTC	New Testament Commentary
NTS	*New Testament Studies*
NTTS	New Testament Tools and Studies
ODL	Outstanding Dissertations in Linguistics
OPSL	*Occasional Papers in Systemic Linguistics*
OPTAT	*Occasional Papers in Translation and Textlinguistics*
OT	Old Testament
QALS	Quantitative Analysis of Linguistic Structure
REB	The Revised English Bible
RevExp	*Review and Expositor*
RSV	Revised Standard Version
SBG	Studies in Biblical Greek
SBLDS	Society of Biblical Literature Dissertation Series
SBLMS	Society of Biblical Literature Monograph Series
SBLSP	Society of Biblical Literature Seminar Papers
SBLSCS	Society of Biblical Literature Septuagint and Cognate Studies Series
SBTSS	Studies in Biblical Theology, second series
SCL	The Semiotics of Culture and Language
SCS	Scottish Classical Studies
SGS	Studia Graeca Stockholmiensia
SGG	Studies in Generative Grammar
SILPL	Summer Institute of Linguistics Publications in Linguistics
SJOT	*Scandinavian Journal of the Old Testament*
SL	*Studies in Language*
SLSc	*Studies in the Linguistic Sciences*
SNTG	Studies in New Testament Greek
SNTSMS	Society for New Testament Studies Monograph Series

SPS	Sacra Pagina Series
SSEJC	Studies in Scripture in Early Judaism and Christianity
START	*Selected Technical Articles Related to Translation*
SUA	Studia Uralo-Altaica
TAPA	*Transactions of the American Philological Association*
TB	*Tyndale Bulletin*
TDNT	G. Kittel and G. Friedrich (eds.), *Theological Dictionary of the New Testament*
TILSM	Trends in Linguistics: Studies and Monographs
TPI	Trinity Press International
TPS	*Transactions of the Philological Society*
TR	*Te Reo: Journal of the Linguistic Society of New Zealand*
TSL	Typological Studies in Language
UHL	Universals of Human Language
WAR	*West African Religion*
WBC	Word Biblical Commentary
WCA	Written Communication Annual
Word	*Journal of the International Linguistic Association*
WUNT	Wissenschaftliche Untersuchungen zum Neuen Testament
ZNW	*Zeitschrift für die neutestamentliche Wissenschaft*

PART I

INTRODUCTION

The scope of this work is to investigate the word order of all the clauses in the Gospel of Luke and some of its related foregrounded messages. The classification of the constituents of the Lukan clauses to be studied is functional; that is, the constituents of the clauses are classified as Subject, Predicate, Complement and Adjunct, rather than Subject, Verb, Object as many other works classify grammatically. This work not only investigates the orders of the three main constituents: Subject, Predicate and Complement, but also the one which has seldom been tackled in Greek language: Circumstantial Adjunct; while studying the orders of these four types of constituents, the tense form of the Predicate is also taken into consideration. The result of this work provides a framework of the general tendencies of the constituent orders in the Gospel, and some marked word orders related to some foregrounded messages of the Gospel.

Part I of the thesis includes Chapter 1 which surveys the recent works on the topic of word order in linguistic studies, and the topic in Greek language; the next is Chapter 2 which provides the criteria and methodology of the study. Part II is the result and data of the unmarked word orders of the Gospel; this includes Chapter 3 which presents the relative positions of the three main constituents, and Chapter 4 which presents the unmarked positions of different types of circumstantial adjunct relative to predicate. Part III is studies of the foregrounded messages of some Lukan passages carrying marked word orders; the prominent messages of these passages are studied mainly based on some marked word order patterns obtained from the framework of Lukan word orders in Part II, and linguistic theories from Hallidayan Functional Grammar. The studies in Part III include Chapter 5 regarding the failure of the disciples' understanding of Jesus, Chapter 6 regarding Pilate's crime of handing over Jesus, Chapter 7 regarding Jesus' parents' failure of understanding him, and Chapter 8 regarding Jesus' predictions of his future sufferings and Peter's future failure.

Chapter 1

RECENT STUDIES ON THE TOPIC OF WORD ORDER

This chapter introduces recent significant works on the topic of word order. These include linguistic studies on the area of word order typology, works focused on Classical Greek language and works on the language of New Testament Greek.

Significant Recent Linguistic Studies on Word Order

Word order is an important subject being discussed in the area of modern linguistics. Conferences, monographic studies and collective papers devoted to the topic are numerous. Basically there are two approaches to this topic. The first is the grammatical and syntactic approach; the second is the functional and pragmatic approach.[1] Rather than giving a detailed survey of studies on word order typology, it is appropriate to mention works of several significant authors in the area in this section.

H. Weil

H. Weil's work is an important starting point in this area of study.[2] Despite word order long being a subject of discussion in Europe since the eighteenth century,

---

1.　Cf. M. Karali, 'Aspects of Delphic Word Order' (DPhil thesis, University of Oxford, 1991), pp. 2–7; T. Vennemann, 'Topics, Subjects and Word Order: From SXV to SVX via TVX', in J.M. Anderson and C. Jones (eds.), *Historical Linguistics. I. Syntax, Morphology, Internal and Comparative Reconstruction. Proceedings of the First International Conference on Historical Linguistics, Edinburgh, 2–7 September 1973* (NHLS, 12a; Amsterdam: North Holland, 1974), p. 342. The grammatical and syntactic approach mainly considers constituents of a clause grammatically: subject, verb, object and indirect object, etc. For example, in the clause *John gave an apple to his son*, 'John' is the subject (the subject here is considered grammatically), 'gave' is the verb, 'apple' is the object and 'his son' is the indirect object. The functional and pragmatic approach considers constituents pragmatically, which classifies constituent elements such as topic and comment, theme and rheme, given and new. See B. Comrie, *Language Universals and Linguistic Typology: Syntax and Morphology* (Oxford: Basil Blackwell, 2nd edn 1989), pp. 104–23; cf. A. Siewierska, *Word Order Rules* (New York: Croom Helm, 1988), pp. 64–75; and C.N. Li (ed.), *Subject and Topic* (New York: Academic Press, 1976).

2.　H. Weil, *The Order of Words in the Ancient Languages Compared with that of the Modern Languages* (ASTHLS, I; ACL, 14; Amsterdam: John Benjamins, new and reprint edition 1978). This is a new reprint edition of Super's translation in 1887 (H. Weil, *The Order of Words in the Ancient Languages Compared with that of the Modern Languages* [trans. C.W. Super; Boston: Ginn & Company, 1887]).

this work is one of the first attempts to study the topic in general instead of concentrating on a particular language.[3] Weil studies the word orders of seven languages: English, French, German, Classical Greek and Latin, Chinese and Turkish. He tries to lay out the interaction between two independent levels: order of ideas and order of words, or in other terms, progression of thought and progression of syntax. Weil considers these two levels are independent and thus differences between the two occur,[4] and the situation between ancient and modern languages is different.[5] Weil concludes that there is always a great difference between the two orders in ancient languages, and thus ancient languages have free word orders; while modern languages have fixed word orders since these two orders (ideas and syntax) tend to be the same in modern languages. The most important contribution of Weil's work is paying attention to word orders of 'languages', rather than to word orders of one particular language.[6] Although the number of languages he has included in his studies is only seven, his work stimulates the works of other scholars on the topic.

J.H. Greenberg

J.H. Greenberg's work on word order universals is widely agreed to be significant in the field.[7] He approaches this topic by studying the interrelationships between different order types in languages, and he concludes that word order universals are related to each other implicationally; that is, if a language has a tendency in a particular order type, then it would have a tendency in another particular order type.[8] Based on the data from studying 30 languages grammatically, Greenberg proposes 45 universals. These 45 universals are classified into three main categories: basic order typology (universals 1-7), syntax (universals 8-25) and morphology (universals 26-45). In the first category, Greenberg mainly argues the interrelationships between three order types: a) orders of main constituents (VSO, SVO and SOV),[9] b) positions of adpositions: prepositions and postpositions (Pr and Po) and c) adjectives preceding nouns and nouns preceding adjectives (AN and NA). Some conclusions have been drawn that in certain degrees the order types are implicationally related. For example, prepositions are harmonic with VS and disharmonic with SV; postpositions are harmonic with SV and disharmonic with VS; OV is harmonic with postposition and VO is harmonic with preposition.[10]

---

3.   P.K. Anderson, *Word Order Typology and Comparative Constructions* (ASTHLS, 4; CILT, 25; Amsterdam: John Benjamins, 1983), p. 2.

4.   Weil, *The Order of Words in the Ancient Languages*, p. 28.

5.   Weil, *The Order of Words in the Ancient Languages*, p. 35.

6.   Cf. Comrie, *Language Universals and Linguistic Typology*, pp. 1–2.

7.   J.H. Greenberg, 'Some Universals of Grammar with Particular Reference to the Order of Meaningful Elements', in *idem* (ed.), *Universals of Language* (Cambridge: MIT Press, 2nd edn 1966), pp. 58–93.

8.   Greenberg, 'Some Universals of Grammar', p. 58.

9.   There are supposed to be six main constituent orders: SVO, SOV, VSO, VOS, OSV, and OVS (S stands for subject, V for verb, and O for object at here), but only the first three are taken into consideration by Greenberg, because he finds they are obviously predominant and the last three are 'excessively rare' (Greenberg, 'Some Universals of Grammar', p. 61).

10.   Greenberg, 'Some Universals of Grammar', p. 77.

The second category is mainly regarding harmonies between other syntactic structures, and also harmonies of other order types with the three order types stated above (main constituent orders [VSO, SVO and SOV], prepositions and postpositions [Pr and Po], adjective preceding noun and noun preceding adjective [AN and NA]).[11] The third category is mainly regarding harmonies between morphological items. Greenberg's grammatical study is important to the area of word order typology, it is an attempt to work on the topic based on a wide range of languages; its conclusions serve as a starting point for later works on implicational relations of word order universals.

W.P. Lehmann

W.P. Lehmann basically modifies Greenberg's universals.[12] He thinks the subject does not play a significant role in typological studies, but believes the construction formed by object and verb is the fundamental syntactic pattern in a language.[13] This leads Lehmann simply to classify languages into two types: VO languages and OV languages, and treat the relative orders of verb and object to be the most fundamental aspect of typological studies.[14] Lehmann proposes 'The Principle of Placement for Modifiers' which can be presented as follows:

VO languages: Q V (N obj) (N mod)
OV languages: (N mod) (N obj) V Q

11. For example, initial particle against final particle for yes-no questions (universal 8), question word (interrogatives) first against question and statement order identical (universal 10), auxiliary precedes verb against auxiliary follows verb (universal 15), the order of demonstrative and noun, numeral and noun (universal 17), order of adverb and adjective (universal 20), adjective-marker-standard against standard-marker-adjective (universal 21) (e.g. 'taller than John' is adjective [tall]-marker [er]-standard [John]), common noun-proper noun against proper noun-common noun (universal 22) (e.g. 'Sir Edward' is common noun-proper noun) (cf. P.K. Andersen's objection on this universal: 'On Universal 22', *J Ling* [1982], pp. 231–43), relational expression precedes noun against noun precedes relational expression (universal 23) (e.g. 'The box which I bought yesterday' is noun precedes relational expression).

12. Based on the assumption that the essential constituents of a sentence are the verb and its object, and the role of subject is secondary, Lehmann thinks the object-verb construction is usually not disrupted by other elements such as modifiers of nouns and verbs. See W.P. Lehmann, 'The Great Underlying Ground-Plans', in *idem* (ed.), *Syntactic Typology: Studies in the Phenomenology of Language* (Sussex: The Harvester Press, 1978), pp. 1–55.

13. W.P. Lehmann, 'From Topic to Subject in Indo-European', in Li (ed.), *Subject and Topic*, pp. 447–56 (447).

14. Lehmann, 'The Great Underlying Ground-Plans', pp. 6–8. Lehmann's position on the two main language types (VO and OV) and their implicational relations with other word order types can best be presented by these words: 'Nominal modifiers, such as relative constructions, descriptive adjectives and genitives, are placed on the side of the object opposite the verb; in OV languages these constructions are placed before nouns, in VO languages after them... In an OV language the interrogative and negative markers would be aligned after the verb, and nominal modifiers before the object or other nouns. In an optimum VO language the alignment would be reversed.' (Lehmann, 'From Topic to Subject', p. 447; cf. *idem*, *Historical Linguistics* [London:

Lehmann mainly proposes the general locations of verbal modifiers (Q) and nominal modifiers (N mod) in consistent VO and OV languages. In consistent VO languages, verbal modifiers tend to be located before verbs, and nominal modifiers tend to be located after nouns. In consistent OV languages, verbal modifiers tend to be located after verbs, and nominal modifiers tend to be located before nouns.[15] Lehmann's important contributions to typological studies relate many of Greenberg's implicational universals through his theory of two main language types (VO and OV).[16] In Lehmann's position, the object and verb construction of a language is so fundamental that the other orders are only dependent on this. Greenberg shows word order rules are not independent of each other; they are in certain degrees implicationally related to each other. Lehmann takes a further step on this and concludes these implicational rules are all related to a main VO/OV rule.

T. Vennemann

T. Vennemann's work draws extensively on that of W. Lehmann.[17] Vennemann tries to reformulate and explain Greenberg's universals, and gives a theory of word order change. Vennemann's work is based firstly on Lehmann's results, which reduces Greenberg's three way typology (VSO, SVO and SOV) to two basic verb positions: VO (or VX, X is verb complement) and OV (or XV),[18] and classifies all of Greenberg's constituent elements into a syntactic and semantic relation of operand and operator.[19] Vennemann modifies Lehmann's proposal and states there

Routledge, 3rd edn 1992], pp. 96–113, 237–53; D. Mitchell, 'Lehmann's Use of Syntactic Typology', in C.F. Justus and E.C. Polomé [eds.], *Language Change and Typological Variation: In Honor of Winfred P. Lehmann on the Occasion of his 83rd Birthday.* II. *Grammatical Universals and Typology* [JIESM, 31; Washington: Institute for the Study of Man, 1999], pp. 437–43).

15. W.P. Lehmann, 'A Structural Principle of Language and its Implications', *Lang* 49 (1973), pp. 47–66 (48–49); cf. *idem*, *Proto-Indo-European Syntax* (Austin: University of Texas Press, 1974), p. 12; and also *idem*, 'Converging Theories in Linguistics', *Lang* 48 (1972), pp. 266–75 (267–69); cf. Andersen, *Word Order Typology and Comparative Constructions*, pp. 14–15.

16. Greenberg's universals suggest if a language has 'x' order type, then it has 'y' order type. Lehmann's work divides language orders into two main types: VO and OV. In his theory, if a language has 'x' order, then it has 'A', 'B', 'C', 'D'...order types. For example, if a language has a VO order type, then it has NG (dependent genitive located after its governing noun), NA (adjective located after its modifying noun), AdV (adverb located before its modifying verb), etc; if a language has a OV order type, then it has GN (dependent genitive located before its governing noun), AN (adjective located before its modifying noun), VAd (adverb located after its modifying verb), etc.

17. T. Vennemann, 'Analogy in Generative Grammar: The Origin of Word Order', in L. Heilmann (ed.), *Proceedings of the Eleventh International Congress of Linguistics* (Bologna: Societa editrice il Mulino, 1974), II, pp. 79–83.

18. T. Vennemann, 'An Explanation of Drift', in C.N. Li (ed.), *Word Order and Word Order Change* (Austin: University of Texas Press, 1975), pp. 269–306 (288).

19. The criteria of Vennemann defining operator and operand can best be shown by his words ('Analogy in Generative Grammar', p. 81):

is only one single word order rule as follows, all other word order rules are then classified as exceptions to this general rule.[20]

XV languages: (Operator [Operand])
VX languages: (Operand [Operator])

Lehmann's work mainly concerns locations of modifiers of verbs and nouns, but it is much limited by its only two aspects: verb and noun (subject is not put into consideration in Lehmann's work). Vennemann's work much widens this limitation and broadens it to a relation of operator and operand. His work proposes relative locations of operator and operand in VX and XV languages. VX languages have operator located after operand. XV languages have operator located before operand.

J.A. Hawkins

J.A. Hawkins incorporates Greenberg's sample as a starting point. He expands the language samples to some 350 languages and modifies Greenberg's implica-

The criteria are that, semantically, the application of an operator results in a specification of the operand predicate, and syntactically, that the application of an operator to an operand results in a constituent of the same general syntactic category as that of the operand.

Vennemann tries to define operator and operand semantically and syntactically, his given examples further explain his syntactic criterion ('Analogy in Generative Grammar', p. 81):

Adverbials are operator in verbs because the result of the operation is a complex verb rather than a complex adverbial. Main verbs, which are infinitives, are operators on finite modals and auxiliaries, which are finite verbs, because the result of the operation is a finite verb rather than an infinitive. And noun phrases are operators on prepositions, which are transitive adverbials, because the result of the operation is a prepositional phrase, i.e. an adverbial, rather than a noun phrase…object-verb relationship is itself an operator-operand relationship, with the object as operator and the verb as operand, because, semantically, object application delimits the extension of a transitive verb, and syntactically, the operation of applying an object noun phrase to a transitive verb results in a verb rather than a noun phrase.

The other operator-operand relationships include adjective-noun, relative clause-noun, numeral-noun, genitive-noun, determiner-noun, adjective stem-comparison marker, standard-comparative adjective, noun phrase-adposition (preposition and postposition) (Vennemann, 'Analogy in Generative Grammar', p. 79; cf. *idem*, 'Topics, Subjects and Word Order', p. 345).

Besides the syntactic consideration, Vennemann considers operator and operand as equal to function and argument (e.g. adjective and noun is function and argument) (Vennemann, 'Topics, Subjects and Word Order', pp. 344–47). However, his equating operator and operand as function and argument is rejected by J.A. Hawkins (*Word Order Universals* [QALS, 3; New York: Academic Press, 1983], pp. 37, 47), where he criticizes: 'for which he sets up the operator-operand distinction is NOT that of the function-argument relation, but corresponds instead to the more traditional distinction between a modifier and its head', Hawkins' position on this can well be represented by his modifier-head classification in his works (which is discussed below; for list of the specific typological characteristics governed by operator-operand proposed by Vennemann, see Andersen, *Word Order Typology*, pp. 16–18).

20.   Vennemann, 'Analogy in Generative Grammar', p. 82; *idem*, 'An Explanation of Drift', p. 288.

tional universals to much more complicated implicational universals: if a language has word pattern of A, and if it has B, then it has C pattern.[21] Hawkins states three main reasons which determine the preferred types of the multi-implicational universals. The first one is heaviness hierarchy (or called heaviness serialization principle). This heaviness hierarchy helps to predict leftward-rightward asymmetry and is much more applicable in prepositional languages than postpositional languages. Hawkins finds 'lighter' constituents (morphologically and syntactically shorter) are more likely to be placed to the left of the head, and 'heavier' ones (morphologically and syntactically longer) are more likely to the right. This means light modifiers prefer leftward positioning, heavy modifiers prefer rightward positioning. For example, the heaviness of a relative clause is greater than or equal to a genitive's, and the heaviness of a genitive is heavier or equal to a descriptive adjective's, and a descriptive adjective is heavier or equal to demonstrative and numeral determiners.[22] The second one is the consideration of constituent mobility (or is called the mobility principle). This mobility principle suggests adjective, demonstrative and numeral determiners exhibit greater or equal mobility than relative clause and genitive. This means the first category (adjective, demonstrative and numeral determiners) can usually move around their head more easily.[23] The third one is the preferred positions of modifier and head in prepositional and postpositional languages (or is called modifier-head theory). Figures from Hawkins' language examples suggest a majority of prepositional languages have postposed noun modifiers and a majority of postpositional languages have preposed noun modifiers. These three principles (heaviness serialization principle, mobility principle and modifier-head theory) contribute to the explanation of the word order types of Hawkins' multi-implicational universals.[24] Hawkins' work

21. J.A. Hawkins, 'On Implicational and Distributional Universals of Word Order', *J Ling* 6 (1980), pp. 193–235 (200–10); *idem*, *Word Order Universals*, pp. 63–88; cf. *idem*, 'Implicational Universals as Predictors of Language Acquisition', *Ling* 25 (1987), pp. 453–73; *idem*, 'A Parsing Theory of Word Order Universals', *Ling Inq* 21 (1990), pp. 223–61.

22. The heaviness of a constituent is considered morphologically and syntactically. They are determined by the length and quantity of the related morphemes, quantity of words and syntactic depth of branching nodes. For example, an adjective contains a single descriptive predicate, which may be morphologically and syntactically shorter than a genitive, because a genitive may consist of a noun phrase or a prepositional phrase; a genitive is syntactically shorter than a relative clause, because the number of branching nodes of a relative clause is relatively larger than a genitive's (which may only consist of a noun phrase or a prepositional phrase) (Hawkins, *Word Order Universals*, pp. 89–91, 98–106; Hawkins' heaviness hierarchy is much based on his leftward–rightward asymmetry; for his further discussions on this asymmetry, see. J.A. Hawkins and A. Cutler, 'Psycholinguistic Factors in Morphological Asymmetry', in J.A. Hawkins [ed.], *Explaining Language Universals* [Oxford: Basil Blackwell, 1988], pp. 280–317 [281–94]; also J.A. Hawkins and G. Gilligan, 'Prefixing and Suffixing Universals in Relation to Basic Word Order', in J.A. Hawkins and H.K. Holmback [eds.], *Papers in Universal Grammar: Generative and Typological Approaches* [*Lingua* 74 (special issue); Amsterdam: Elsevier, 1988], pp. 219–59; and J.A. Hawkins, *A Performance Theory of Order and Constituency* [CSL, 73; Cambridge: Cambridge University Press, 1994], pp. 321–41).

23. Hawkins, *Word Order Universals*, pp. 93–95, 107–12.

24. Hawkins, *Word Order Universals*, pp. 97–98.

modifies Greenberg's implicational universals to a more complicated multi-implicational universal, which also represents his position of modifying Vennemann's operator-operand theory to a modifier-head relationship.[25]

Others

The works of the authors mentioned above have stimulated many others' works in the area. For example, Tomlin's work includes a list of 1063 languages and their basic constituent orders.[26] His main work is his proposal of three principles explaining causes behind basic word orders. Although the title of his book indicates his functional approach, he actually works on the topic both functionally (the theme first principle represents an idea of 'old' information tending to precede 'new' information; the animated first principle demonstrates that a more 'animated' noun phrase tends to precede a less 'animated' noun phrase in a transitive clause [the most animate is human, then other animate, the least is inanimate]) and syntactically (verb-object bounding principle, which represents an idea of verb and object bounding; Tomlin shows generally the object of a transitive clause is syntactically and semantically more tightly 'bound' to the verb than the subject of a transitive clause; the principle is in fact more in a syntactic approach).[27] Based on four models of grammar: Functional Grammar (FG), Word Grammar (WG), Lexical Functional Grammar (LFG) and Generalized Phrase Structure Grammar (GPSG), Siewierska tackles the question of word order rules in several aspects: grammatical and thematic relations (by FG), dependency relations (by WG) and constituency relations (by LFG and GPSG).[28] Dezső studies the topic from a contrastive approach with application to Russian and Hungarian; Andersen takes a more grammatical approach focusing the topic on comparative constructions; Cheng studies the movement of Wh-elements in direct and indirect questions from a transformational approach, which is then particularly considered in Mandarin Chinese; Radics studies the positions of prefix and suffix person markings grammatically.[29] Other authors taking a grammatical approach to their works include Friedrich and Flynn.[30] Other authors taking a pragmatic approach to their work include Zubizarreta, Gergely (who

25. Hawkins, *Word Order Universals*, p. 137.

26. R.S. Tomlin, *Basic Word Order: Functional Principles* (CHLS; London: Croom Helm, 1986).

27. Tomlin, *Basic Word Order*, pp. 102–4 (for his functional approach); and pp. 73–74 (for his syntactic approach).

28. Siewierska, *Word Order Rules*.

29. L. Dezső, *Studies in Syntactic Typology and Contrastive Grammar* (trans. I. Gombos and B. Hollósy; JLSM, 89; The Hague: Mouton, 1982); Andersen, *Word Order Typology*; L.L.S. Cheng, *On the Typology of Wh-Questions* (ODL; New York: Garland, 1997); K. Radics, *Typology and Historical Linguistics: Affixed Person-Marking Paradigms* (SUA, 24; Szeged: Attila József University Press, 1985).

30. P. Friedrich, *Proto-Indo-European Syntax: The Order of Meaningful Elements* (JIESM, 1; Washington: The Institute for the Study of Man, 1975); M.J. Flynn, *Structure Building Operations and Word Order* (New York: Garland, 1985).

works on Hungarian in an approach of topic-focus structure [the number of works on one particular language is actually numerous; one example is Brody's work, which particularly considers the matter on Tojolabal]),[31] Hamitouche (whose work is mainly a study on the word order of Berber-Kabyle based on Dik's theory of functional grammar), Ross (a study based on generative grammar), Givón, Foster and Hofling (a study based on a 30-language sample comparing a number of aspects of word order in two main types of languages: SVO languages and verb-object languages), Ard (a short study on word order and ergative languages), and Vande Kopple (who considers the matter of ordering in terms of 'Given' and 'New').[32]

Besides the above mentioned works by individual authors, collective works on the area are also vast in number. Most of them are collective papers from conferences on the topic. These include works mainly representing positions from the grammatical and syntactic approach,[33] and works from the functional and pragmatic approach,[34] or both.[35]

---

31. J. Brody's work: 'Some Problems with the Concept of Basic Word Order', *Ling* 22 (1984), pp. 711–36.

32. M.L. Zubizarreta, *Prosody, Focus, and Word Order* (LIM; Cambridge, MA: MIT Press, 1998); G. Gergely, *Free Word Order and Discourse Interpretation* (Budapest: Akadémiai Kiadó, 1991); F. Hamitouche, 'Studies in Word Order: A Functional Pragmatic Approach' (PhD thesis, University of Essex, 1988); J.R. Ross, 'Gapping and the Order of Constituents', in M. Bierwisch and K.E. Heidolph (eds.), *Progress in Linguistics: A Collection of Papers* (JLSMaj, 43; The Hague: Mouton, 1970), pp. 249–59; T. Givón, *Syntax: A Functional-Typological Introduction* (2 vols.; Amsterdam: John Benjamins, 1984–1990), pp. 187–237; J.F. Foster and C.A. Hofling, 'Word Order, Case and Agreement', *Ling* 25 (1987), pp. 475–99; J. Ard, 'Word Order Templates in Ergative Languages', *Ling Inq* 9 (1978), pp. 297–99; W.J. Vande Kopple, 'Given and New Information and Some Aspects of the Structures, Semantics, and Pragmatics of Written Texts', in C.R. Cooper and S. Greenbaum (eds.), *Studying Writing: Linguistics Approaches* (WCA, 1; Beverly Hills: Sage Publications, 1986), pp. 72–111 (80–89).

33. For example, N. Corner and H. van Riemsdijk (eds.), *Studies on Scrambling: Movement and Non-Movement Approaches to Free Word-Order Phenomena* (SGG, 41; Berlin: Mouton de Gruyter, 1994); Lehmann (ed.), *Syntactic Typology*; M. Hammond, E.A. Moravcsik and J.R. Wirth (eds.), *Studies in Syntactic Typology* (TSL, 17; Amsterdam: John Benjamins, 1988), esp. pp. 77–169.

34. For example, J. Nuyts and G. de Schutter (eds.), *Getting One's Words into Line: On Word Order and Functional Grammar* (FGS, 5; Dordrecht: Foris, 1987), a model of word order typological studies based on S. Dik's theory of functional grammar; J.E. Grimes (ed.), *Sentence Initial Devices* (SILPL, 75; Dallas: Summer Institute of Linguistics, 1986), which represents papers from two seminars; the approaches of the papers are more on pragmatics, especially papers from pp. 7–44 and pp. 103–200; Li (ed.), *Subject and Topic*.

35. For example, P. Downing and M. Noonan (eds.), *Word Order in Discourse* (TSL, 30; Amsterdam: John Benjamins, 1995); B. Palek (ed.), *Proceedings of LP'94. Proceedings of the Conference: Item Order in Natural Languages* (Prague: Charles University Press, 1995); D.L. Payne (ed.), *Pragmatics of Word Order Flexibility* (TSL, 22; Amsterdam: John Benjamins, 1992); N.E. Enkvist and V. Kohonen (eds.), *Reports on Text Linguistics: Approaches to Word Order* (Abo: Text Linguistic Research Group, 1976); Li (ed.), *Word Order and Word Order Change*.

Summary
Various authors' works contribute significantly to the area of word order typological studies. Weil offers an attempt to study the topic based on a range of languages. Greenberg extends the number of languages to be studied, and explains word order universals implicationally. His work sets an important starting point showing the dependencies of different word order universals. Lehmann modifies Greenberg's results and proposes the relative positions of verbal and nominal modifiers with their heads in VO and OV languages. His works put many of Greenberg's unrelated universals into a relationship of dependency. Vennemann develops Lehmann's works by proposing the operator-operand relationships and concludes their relative positions on VX/XV languages. Lehmann's result is limited by only two categories (noun and verb); Vennemann's proposal of operator-operand leads Lehmann's results to a much wider range. Hawkins much expands Greenberg's language samples as a starting point; his work not only relates word order universals multi-implicationally, but also attempts to explain causes behind word order universals.[36] Works of these authors contribute much to the studies of word order and stimulate many others' works in the area such as works from Tomlin, Siewierska, Andersen and others.

Recent Studies on Word Orders of Classical Greek

Many scholars have already observed the importance of the issue of word order in the Ancient Greek language.[37] Most scholars agree that there is a certain degree of freedom in Greek word orders (there are languages which can even be classified as having 'free word order', e.g., Hungarian, a non-Indo-European language).[38] The

---

36. Although these authors' ideas may not be appreciated by all (e.g. J. Jepson, 'Holistic Models of Word Order Typology', *Word* 40 [1989], pp. 297–314; F. Parker, 'Typology and Word Order Change', *Ling* 18 [1980], pp. 269–88; D.L. Payne, 'Hawkins: Word Order Universals', *Lang* 61 [1985], pp. 462–66), their contributions to the area of word order studies are apparently significant (e.g. cf. R. Jeffers, 'Review of Lehmann: Proto-Indo-European Syntax', *Lang* 52 [1976], pp. 982–88, esp. p. 987).

37. For example, W.R. Roberts ('A Point of Greek and Latin Word-Order', *CR* 26 [1912], pp. 177–79) and J.D. Denniston (*Greek Prose Style* [Oxford: Oxford University Press, 1952], pp. 41–59).

38. See Gergely, *Free Word Order and Discourse Interpretation*. It is now a widely accepted opinion that the degree of freedom in Ancient Greek is much higher than it is in English (cf. R.S. Cervin, 'Word Order in Ancient Greek: VSO, SVO, SOV, or All of the Above?' [PhD thesis; University of Illinois at Urbana-Champaign, 1990], p. 5; Cervin has classified several languages according to their degree of rigidness and freedom: English, German, Hindi, Greek and Warlpiri, in which he states English is the most rigid and Warlpiri is the most free [though Cervin has not shown any evidence for his classification; this situation occurs again in his work, e.g., he later states word order in Greek poetry is much more free than it is in prose; this statement also lacks sufficient evidence by only showing three examples as demonstrations (pp. 8–9)] [for works particularly relating to word order and Classical Greek poetry, cf. C.W. Conrad, *From Epic to Lyric: A Study in the History of Traditional Word-Order in Greek and Latin Poetry* (HDC; New York: Garland, 1990); and B.L. Fraser, 'Word Order, Focus, and Clause Linking in Greek Tragic Poetry' (PhD thesis, University of Cambridge, 1999)]).

matter of Greek word order's freedom has already been observed by scholars as early as Dionysius of Halicarnassus.[39] In fact, scholars have long noticed that different positions of Greek words represent different syntactic and semantic features in a piece of Greek writing. For example, in the area of NT Greek, Middleton notices the importance of positions of an article, adjective and substantive; Moeller and Kramer, Reed, and Cheung have observed the significance of positions of two accusative cases in a NT Greek infinitival clause; Wallace has considered double accusative construction in non-infinitival clauses; Porter has noticed the position of a participle in a clause.[40] Ancient Greek language is recognized to have a certain degree of freedom in its word order, thus there is also a degree of natural Greek word patterns.[41] Order represents expression of thought, and carries meaning.[42] A degree of freedom may carry a certain degree of ambiguity,[43] which may be varied among different genres.[44] The matter of word order in Classical Greek language has drawn many scholars' attentions and thus works on the topic are numerous. These are being introduced as follows:

39. See Karali, 'Aspects of Delphic Word Order', pp. 7–10.

40. T.F. Middleton, *The Doctrine of the Greek Article: Applied to the Criticism and Illustration of the New Testament* [rev. J. Scholefield; Cambridge: J. & J.J. Deighton, 2nd edn 1828], pp. 141–48; H.R. Moeller and A. Kramer, 'An Overlooked Structural Pattern in New Testament Greek', *NovT* 5 (1962), pp. 25–35; J.T. Reed, 'The Infinitive with Two Substantival Accusatives: An Ambiguous Construction?', *NovT* 33 (1991), pp. 1–27; P.W. Cheung, 'Revisiting the Case of an Infinitive with Two Substantival Accusatives', *JD* 13 (1999), pp. 69–101; D.B. Wallace, 'The Semantics and Exegetical Significance of the Object-Complement Construction in the New Testament', *GTJ* 6 [1985], pp. 91–112); S.E. Porter, *Idioms of the Greek New Testament* [BLG, 2; Sheffield: Sheffield Academic Press, 2nd edn 1994], pp. 187–90.

41. Scholars have long observed some natural Greek word patterns. For example, D.B. Monro, *A Grammar of the Homeric Dialect* (Oxford: Clarendon Press, 2nd edn; 1891), pp. 335–38; C.E. Bishop, 'The Greek Verbal in TEO. Part III', *AJP* 20 (1899), pp. 241–53 (252–53); J.D. Denniston, *The Greek Particles* (Oxford: Oxford University Press, 2nd edn 1954), pp. lviii–lxi, and his ongoing discussions of positions of different particles throughout his work (e.g. pp. 22–23, 41–42, 146–52 etc.) (cf. A. Morpurgo-Davies, 'Article and Demonstrative: A Note', *Glotta* 46 [1968], pp. 77–85 (77 n. 3, 81–82); A.C. Moorhouse, *The Syntax of Sophocles* [MnemosyneSup, 75; Leiden: E.J. Brill, 1982], pp. 152–53 and 158–62 on the positions of article and demonstratives; and M.E. Thrall, *Greek Particles in the New Testament* [NTTS, 3; Leiden: E.J. Brill, 1962], pp. 34–40 for the change of positions of certain particles from Classical period to Koine period). This can be seen not only from works of modern scholars, but also from works of ancient copyists: changes such as transposed orders made by copyists may reflect natural or usual word orders (see W. Headlam, 'The Transposition of Words in MSS', *CR* 16 [1902], pp. 243–56; G. Thompson, 'Simplex Ordo', *CQNS* 15 [1965], pp. 161–75, esp. pp. 164–66).

42. T.D. Goodell, 'The Order of Words in Greek', *TAPA* 21 (1890), pp. 5–47 (5).

43. Roberts, 'A Point of Greek and Latin Word-Order', pp. 177–79.

44. For example, K.J. Dover recognizes the bigger percentage of postponement of γάρ and δέ in Attic comedy than in tragedy and prose ('Abnormal Word Order in Attic Comedy', *CQNS* 35 [1985], pp. 324–43 (325) [reprinted in K.J. Dover, *Greek and the Greeks: Collected Papers*. I. *Language, Poetry, Drama* (Oxford: Basil Blackwell, 1987), pp. 43–66]). Postponement of postpositives is not infrequent in Classical and Hellenistic Greek. The situation varies greatly between different authors and texts, see J. Blomqvist, *Greek Particles in Hellenistic Prose* (Lund: Berlingska Boktryckeriet, 1969), pp. 108–27.

B. Giseke

The matter of different positions of a verb is the main concern in B. Giseke's work.[45] Giseke focuses his studies on some selected samples of Homer's works, and he particularly works on one aspect: subordinate clauses. Giseke's conclusion is that verbs tend to be located at the end in subordinate clauses. Although Giseke's studies are only focused on one author (Homer), and are limited to one aspect (subordinate clauses), his work is an important starting point in the area.[46]

C. Short

C. Short mainly selects works of Xenophon, Thucydides, Aeschines, Demosthenes, Plato and some other Attic orators, and provides an extensive study of word order in different aspects of the Greek language: from article, adjectives and pronouns to different moods of verbal forms, adverbs, prepositions and particles.[47] Short mainly represents the usual orders of different combinations of the above categories (i.e., the order of adjective and noun, verb and adverb, preposition and noun, etc.); each stated pattern is regularly followed with lots of related citations of different

45. B. Giseke, 'Über die Wortstellung in abhängigen Sätzen bei Homer', *JCP* 31 (1861), pp. 225–32.

46. A later work on the same topic (Homeric Greek word order) agrees with Giseke's position: after studying samples of different types of Homeric writings (not only subordinate clauses as Giseke does), H. Ammann states that verbs in Homeric clauses are usually located at the end, and proposes the marked initial positions of verbs in clauses are mainly due to emphatic purpose (see H. Ammann, 'Untersuchungen zur homerischen Wortfolge und Satzstruktur', *IF* 42 (1924), pp. 149–78, 300–22; *idem*, 'Wortstellung und Stilentwickelung', *Glotta* 12 (1922), pp. 107–11.

Both Giseke and Ammann's findings favour an unmarked final position of Homeric verbs; this may be Homer's unique word order (cf. some other much later works: J. Aitchison finds when a Homeric Greek clause only has subject and verb, or verb and object, the order tends to be SV and OV, where the verb tends to be in the final position ['The Order of Word Order Change', *TPS* (1979), pp. 43–65]; J.L. Houben's findings favour an OV structure in Homeric subordinate clauses: 'Word-Order Change and Subordination in Homeric Greek', *JIES* 5 [1977], pp. 1–8), and is different from writings of other Classical authors (E. Kieckers states the unmarked position of a verb in a Greek clause is medial [especially in subordinate clauses] after studying samples from Herodotus, Thucydides and Xenophon [*Die Stellung des Verbs im griechischen und in den verwandten Sprachen* (Strassburg: K.J. Trübner, 1911)]; cf. *idem*, 'Die Stellung der Verba des Sagens in Schaltesätzen im Griechischen und in den indogermanischen Sprachen', *IF* 30 [1912], pp. 145–90; also cf. criticisms about his works by other scholars: e.g. P. Fischer challenges Kiecker's conclusion after examining further extended samples, and he proposes a verb tends to be located after its subject and object ['Zur Stellung des Verbums im Griechischen', *GL* 13 (1924), pp. 1–11, 189–205]; and also cf. Karali's criticism ['Aspects of Delphic Word Order', pp. 19–21]; for studies also suggesting a change from an essentially verb-final structure in Homeric Greek to both verb-final and verb-medial structures in Herodotean Greek, see A. Taylor, 'The Change from SOV to SVO in Ancient Greek', *LV&C* 6 [1994], pp. 1–37).

47. Short's work is an article prefixed in an English-Greek Lexicon (C. Short, 'The Order of Words in Attic Greek Prose: An Essay', in C.D. Yonge, *An English Greek Lexicon: With Many New Articles, an Appendix of Proper Names, and Pillon's Greek Synonyms* [ed. H. Drisler; New York: Harper & Brothers, 1870], pp. i–cxv).

authors' works. Short says in his preface that his work 'is rather to find the laws of order than to discuss them',[48] thus he does not tackle the elements which determine the orderings except one: emphatic condition. Short regularly states one major factor which affects a normal order pattern is emphasis.[49]

Short cites lots of examples from works of Greek authors to support his arguments,[50] but he does not have concrete numeric data to support his statements, and thus it is difficult to demonstrate to his readers that his work is convincing and has enough evidence. Short's work at least shows us that Greek word order carries a certain degree of freedom, since many of its patterns have a preferred pattern alongside varieties of alternatives.

T.D. Goodell

T.D. Goodell does not provide usual patterns of Greek word order, but instead proposes determinants which affect Greek word order of which he has included:[51] (1) syntactic—clear grammatical relations are necessary in a language, and thus the degree of Greek word order freedom is naturally limited in order to have clear grammatical relations; for example, a noun and its related article cannot be widely separated to avoid ambiguity;[52] (2) being partly influenced by Weil's work,[53] Goodell proposes rhetoric as the second factor: elements of communication are presented to readers/listeners in a desire that they would conceive them with the least possible effort and get the relative weight and importance intended by the author; and this influences order;[54] and (3) euphonic.[55] Goodell's work contributes to the area of study which has not been tackled by his predecessors: determinants which are behind the usual patterns of Greek word order.

---

48. Short, 'The Order of Words in Attic Greek Prose', p. ii.

49. For example, in the section mentioning the infinitive, the view of emphasis constantly appears: 'If the infinitive is emphatic, it stands before the leading word' (p. xli), 'If the subject of infinitive be emphatic, it may follow the infinitive' (p. xli), 'If the subject accusative be very emphatic, it may stand before the leading word' (p. xli), 'If both the infinitive and its subject be emphatic, they are both put before the leading word, the more emphatic commonly preceding...' (p. xlii), 'If the subject of the infinitive be emphatic, it may follow the infinitive' (p. xliv), 'If the subject be very emphatic, it may stand before the leading word' (xliv), 'If the infinitive be very emphatic, it may stand before the leading word' (p. xliv), 'If both the infinitive and its subject be emphatic, they are both put before the leading word, the more emphatic commonly preceding...' (xlv), 'For the sake of emphasis, the above order is sometimes reversed' (p. xlvi), 'But if the infinitives are severally emphatic, the article may be repeated and stand with each other' (p. xlviii).

50. Actually this work is only mainly a collection of examples, as Goodell has rightly said: '...is a learned collection of examples, but so arranged as to be of little use, even as a collection of material, and bringing to light no such general principles and practical precepts as the learner wants' (Goodell, 'The Order of Words in Greek', p. 7).

51. Goodell, 'The Order of Words in Greek', pp. 5–47.

52. Goodell, 'The Order of Words in Greek', pp. 13–14.

53. Weil, *Order of Words in the Ancient Languages*.

54. Goodell, 'The Order of Words in Greek', pp. 14–15.

55. Goodell, 'The Order of Words in Greek', p. 44.

H.L. Ebeling

H.L. Ebeling's work covers relative positions of copula and predicate,[56] and the three main components: subject, verb and object.[57] After examining Xenophon's Anabasis I, Plato's Protagoras, Gorgias and Isocrates I, II, III, IV, Ebeling claims that SOV is a more usual order than SVO,[58] and this SOV is the most frequent figure in the six combinations,[59] especially in Plato's and Isocrates' works. Ebeling further claims the subject tends to precede the verb; this is mainly based on the figures of his analysis of Protagoras and the first book of Anabasis, where the percentages of the subjects preceding their verbs are 65 per cent and 66 per cent respectively.[60] Although Ebeling's work is based on selected works from only three authors, his results based on concrete numeric data demonstrate a good challenge to previous statements simply based on observations such as Short's work.[61]

G. Thompson

G. Thompson mainly studies orders of the copula verb εἰμί, its subject and predicate.[62] The first part concentrates on Attic Greek, which is based on Plato's Apology, Crito and Phaedo, and states that the word that carries highest emphatic value tends to be placed first, or words tend to be postponed to let the significant part of the sentence to be placed initially, and thus position indicates emphasis.[63] The second part is Hellenistic and is based on the Gospel of Matthew, which Thompson concludes is different from Attic Greek. The initial part of a Hellenistic sentence is not necessary to be an emphatic element; it may be an emphasis, or it may not show any significant force of the word.[64] Thompson's work is disappointing, and his conclusion is strange and surprising, because his work does not show how the first part (Plato) of his work indicates that the initial element of a sentence carries emphasis, and also fails to show why this linguistic feature is absent in the second part (Matthew). Although Thompson's argument is not convincing,[65]

---

56. The 'predicate' mentioned here is the complement of a copula verb (which is different from one of the three main constituent elements [predicate] discussed in this work [see Chapter 2 of this work]). For work particularly on this topic, see A.W. Milden, *The Limitations of the Predicative Position in Greek* (Baltimore: John Murphy, 1900).

57. H.L. Ebeling, 'Some Statistics on the Order of Words in Greek', in *Studies in Honor of Basil L. Gildersleeve* (no stated editor; Baltimore: The Johns Hopkins Press, 1902), pp. 229–40.

58. The number of SOV in Anabasis I, Protagoras, Gorgias and Isocrates are 45, 62, 74 and 73 respectively; while SVO are 42, 24, 32, 17 (Ebeling, 'Some Statistics on the Order of Words in Greek', p. 234).

59. SOV, SVO, OSV, OVS, VSO, VOS.

60. Ebeling, 'Some Statistics on the Order of Words in Greek', p. 238.

61. The results of his studies based on his collected data are to a certain degree contradictory to Short's work ('The Order of Words in Attic Greek Prose', see Ebeling, 'Some Statistics on the Order of Words in Greek', pp. 234–37).

62. G. Thompson, 'On the Order of Words in Plato and Saint Matthew', *Link* 2 (1939), pp. 7–17.

63. Thompson, 'On the Order of Words in Plato and Saint Matthew', p. 16.

64. Thompson, 'On the Order of Words in Plato and Saint Matthew', p. 16.

65. Thompson's other work on position of interrogatives is more appreciable ('The Postponement of Interrogatives in Attic Drama', *ClQ* 33 [1939], pp. 147–52). Since interrogative

his work is still significant because it is the first attempt to compare the Greek word order of works from two different periods of time (Attic and Hellenistic); it also raises an important question in this field of studies: features of Greek word orders may be different in different periods of time.

H. Frisk

H. Frisk firstly studies orders between subject and predicate, and predicate and object in main clauses, which he bases on a wide range of material: selected samples from works of Herodotus, Thucydides, Xenophon's Anabasis and Hellenika, Plato, Antiphon, Lysias, Demosthenes, Polybius, Plutarch, Philostratus, Matthew, and papyri of the Ptolemaic period.[66] Frisk's statistical data consistently show that about 70–80 per cent of subjects precede the predicate in all examined works,[67] and most of the works have about 50–70 per cent of objects preceding the predicate, with exceptions of samples from Matthew and papyri, which have a tendency to have predicates located before the object.[68] Frisk secondly studies the above orders in subordinate clauses, and he increases his range of material by including selected samples from the other three Gospels and Acts, and separately studies the order of subject/predicate and predicate/object in three categories: relative clauses, temporal clauses and conditional clauses. These results show that the word orders of works from the Koine period significantly differ from the word orders of works from other periods.[69]

Frisk regularly states that initially located elements are being emphatic, but does not show how the elements which he treats as emphatic can be seen as significant

elements are usually placed at the front of a clause, Thompson proposes when an interrogative element of a clause is postponed that it normally indicates that the new initial word of the clause carries emphatic force (or it can be said that an emphatic word forces a postponement of an interrogative element in a clause) ('The Postponement of Interrogatives', p. 147).

66. H. Frisk, *Studien zur griechischen Wortstellung* (GHA, 39.1; Göteborg: Wettergren & Kerbers Förlag, 1933).

67. Frisk, *Studien zur griechischen Wortstellung*, p. 16; Matthew is the lowest, which is 64.5 per cent.

68. Frisk, *Studien zur griechischen Wortstellung*, p. 16; predicates located before their object in samples of Matthew and papyri is 77.8 per cent and 66.7 per cent respectively.

69. For relative clauses, Matthew, Mark, John and Acts tend to have equal distributions of SP and PS, Luke and papyri tend to have PS rather than SP, the samples from other works tend to have SP rather than PS; the samples of the five New Testament books significantly tend to have PO rather than OP, which is different from the majority of other works' samples. For temporal clauses, the four Gospels and Acts tend to have PS (about 70–80 per cent) rather than SP, while the others tend to have SP rather than PS; the five New Testament books tend to have PO rather than OP, while some of the other works do not have great difference in distributions of PO and OP, and some others tend to have OP rather than PO (e.g. the percentages of OP in samples from Demosthenes and papyri are 80 and 85 respectively). For conditional clauses, there is not much difference in the percentages of SP and PS between the five NT books and the other works, but the NT books still show their tendency to have PO rather than OP (except the Gospel of John, which has 55 per cent in OP); while all other works have a favor in OP (Frisk, *Studien zur griechischen Wortstellung*, pp. 28–31).

from the texts of the writings; in fact, considering an element to be emphasized or not can easily be subjective.[70] What Frisk's work contributes most is providing a solid figure which is based on statistical data from much more extensive sources than the ones of his predecessors, which cover a wide range from Classical to Koine Greek; his work indicates that there is a major difference in syntactic order between Classical and Hellenistic Greek.[71]

A. Loepfe

A. Loepfe's work is a pragmatic approach,[72] which examines the order of theme and rheme from passages of Plato's Lysis and Menander's Epitrepontes. Although Loepfe's work may be disputable because of the difficulty in avoiding subjectivity in identifying theme and rheme in Greek clauses,[73] his work is important in the area of these studies, because it sets a good attempt in working on Greek word orders pragmatically, and this approach is completely different from his predecessors.

K.J. Dover

Instead of studying usual Greek word orders, K.J. Dover proposes three main determinants which affect Greek word order: lexical and semantic, syntactical and logical determinants.[74] For the lexical and semantic determinant, Dover has classified two main types of lexical items: mobile words and words with limited mobility;[75] his classification shows several categories of lexical items tend to

70. It can be arguable on the matter of considering certain clause elements being emphasized or not. For example, Denniston finds there is a number of instances which he thinks are being emphatic, but they are treated as unemphatic in Frisk's classification (J.D. Denniston, 'Review of H. Frisk, *Studien zur griechischen Wortstellung*', CR 47 [1933], pp. 18–20 (20)).

71. Thompson's work shows different Greek word order patterns may occur between different periods of time. Frisk's much more solid statistical data can confirm this proposal much further; cf. some much later works by A. Taylor, which also support Greek word order changes through different periods of time: from OV (or verb-final) structure in the Homeric period to VO (or verb-medial) structure in some later periods ('Clitics and Configurationality in Ancient Greek' [PhD thesis, University of Pennsylvania, 1990]; 'The Change from SOV to SVO in Ancient Greek', pp. 1–37).

72. A. Loepfe, *Die Wortstellung im griechischen Sprechsatz, erklärt an Stücken aus Platon und Menander* (Paulusdruckerei: Freiburg in der Schweiz, 1940).

73. Karali, 'Aspects of Delphic Word Order', pp. 26–27. In fact, some of Loepfe's identifications of theme and rheme are rejected by others; for example, K.J. Dover, *Greek Word Order* (Cambridge: Cambridge University Press, 2nd edn 1968), p. 39 n. 2; H. Dik, *Word Order in Ancient Greek: A Pragmatic Account of Word Order Variation in Herodotus* (ASCP, 5; Amsterdam: J.C. Gieben, 1995), pp. 272–73; cf. A.C. Moorhouse, *Studies in the Greek Negatives* (Cardiff: University of Wales Press, 1959), pp. 76–82.

74. Dover, *Greek Word Order*.

75. The class of mobile words is symbolized as M, which can be placed at the beginning of a clause, at its end, or in the middle. This type of mobile words can further be divided into two groups: preferential mobile (*Ma*) (certain categories of words tend to occur at the beginning of a clause, such as interrogatives, negatives, demonstrative pronoun and some other particular lexical items being tested from samples of Herodotus, Plato, Lysias) and ordinary mobile (*Mb*);

occur at the beginning and the end of clauses. Dover's first proposed determinant well illustrates that the freedom of Greek word order is limited by certain lexical items. Dover's second proposed determinant is based on syntactic considerations, and it shows preferences of certain constituent positions.[76] Dover's studies on his third determinant approach the topic logically.[77] Dover's work is significant in the area, it is a work in studying the determinants behind Greek word orders; moreover, it does not approach the topic in one aspect, but in three different aspects: lexical, syntactic and pragmatic.[78]

P. Friedrich
Friedrich's work includes a large section on discussing orders of three main Greek clause elements (subject, verb and object).[79] Friedrich focuses on a piece of Homeric work (lines 1-296 of book V of Iliad) and finds the unmarked patterns are SVO, SOV and OVS,[80] a more marked one is OSV, and the very marked one

the limited mobile words are postpositives (symbolized as *q*, which usually do not occur at the beginning of a clause) and prepositives (symbolized as *p*, which are not usually located at the end of a clause) (Dover, *Greek Word Order*, pp. 12–14, 20–24; cf. a later work stimulated by Dover's studies on his first determinant: M.H.B. Marshall, *Verbs, Nouns and Postpositives in Attic Prose* [SCS, 3; Edinburgh: Scottish Academic Press, 1987], in which Marshall gives a more extensive studies on the positions of postpostives relative to verb and nouns in a clause by studying samples from Thucydides, Plato and Demosthenes [also samples of Herodotus in the Appendix of Marshall's work]).

76. Again studying samples from Herodotus, Plato and Lysias, Dover works on relative positions of two main aspects syntactically: subject and verb, verb and object, where he concludes a marked preference for SV, and a less marked preference for OV.

77. The third determinant classifies clause elements into nucleus (N) (which cannot be predicted from the preceding element and is indispensable) and concomitant (C). This classification is actually similar to other pragmatic approaches, such as 'psychological or cognitional subject and predicate, or determinand and determinant, or thema and rhema' (Dover, *Greek Word Order*, p. 34).

78. Although Dover's work is significant in the area, his work actually has its own limitations and his arguments may be disputable (for example, interrogatives, negatives, personal and demonstrative pronouns are classified as lexical and semantic determinants as to the category of *Ma* [the mobile words having a tendency to be located at the beginning of a clause]). Dover's position on these words is rejected by H. Dik. Dik claims these words should be treated as pragmatic or logical rather than lexical and semantic: 'They are likely to play an important role in a clause, be it to help placing utterances in the text as a whole, or presenting contrastive or otherwise essential information to the [structure of a] text' (Dik, *Word Order in Ancient Greek*, pp. 260–61). In the second determinant, Dover concludes subject and object tend to precede their verbs. In fact, Dover's results are based on samples of only three authors, and thus they may not rightly represent the general patterns of Classical Greek word order (Dover himself also admits this limitation: 'very far indeed establishing for Classical Greek' [*Greek Word Order*, p. 31]). In the third determinant, it is apparent that it is easy to be subjective in deciding nucleus (N) and concomitant (C) (cf. Karali, 'Aspects of Delphic Word Order', p. 36). It is a common problem to be easily subjective in dealing with the matter pragmatically.

79. Friedrich, *Proto-Indo-European Syntax*. Though Friedrich's work is titled as 'Proto-Indo-European Syntax', this work is mainly focused on Homeric Greek and thus it is well worth mentioning in this section.

80. Friedrich, *Proto-Indo-European Syntax*, p. 21.

is VOS. This leads him to conclude that a Homeric verb almost never locates initially when all the three constituents (S, V, O) are present.[81]

G. Dunn

G. Dunn mainly works on the word orders of the writings of Herodotus with an approach of dependency model (Head/Modifier).[82] His work is based on a detailed classification of different Heads and Modifiers,[83] and further relies on theories of statistics, which provide insight to the topic of studies.[84]

R.S. Cervin

R.S. Cervin's work chiefly covers examples of the Greek language in the Classical and Hellenistic periods.[85] Cervin not only works on the order of the three main constituents (S, V, O), but also tries to study the pragmatic factors which affect the orders. Cervin works on the topic through some movement processes such as fronting (moving an element to the beginning of a clause or sentence) and extraposition (moving an element to the end of a clause or sentence), and investigates the landing sites (usually the initial and final positions of a clause or a sentence) which are associated with these movements.[86]

---

81. Friedrich, *Proto-Indo-European Syntax*, p. 23. Friedrich's results do not totally agree with Giseke and Ammann's findings regarding the usual final position of Homeric verbs. Friedrich's work may not be able to represent an accurate picture of Homeric word order, since his sample size is apparently too small (only less than 300 lines of one of Homer's work is studied).

82. Dunn has done a series of work related to the word order of the Greek of Herodotus ('Ancient Greek Order and the Lehmann Hypothesis', *TR* 28 [1985], pp. 81–94; 'Syntactic Word Order in Herodotean Greek', *Glotta* 66 [1988], pp. 63–79; 'Greek Word Order: Three Descriptive Models', *TR* 33 [1990], pp. 57–63) following his doctoral studies on the same topic ('Syntactic Word Order in Herodotus' [PhD thesis; University of Canterbury, 1981]).

83. Dunn's dependency model is mainly based on a relationship of Head and Modifier (e.g. noun phrase: noun is head and adjective is modifier; verb phrase: verb is head and object is modifier; prepositional phrase: preposition is head and noun is modifier). This type of classification is studied in several aspects: main and subordinate clauses, main and participial clauses, noun phrases and prepositional phrases.

84. One interesting feature Dunn has got from his search is that he finds the order of Head and Modifier gradually changes in different periods of time ('Ancient Greek Order and the Lehmann Hypothesis', in which Dunn has based his work on selected samples from a wide period of time [about 800 years]: from Homer [eighth century BCE], Herodotus [fifth century BCE] to Matthew [first century CE]; in this work Dunn finds a steady changing tendency moving away from MH to HM [Homer: more on MH; Herodotus: more on HM; and Matthew: more on HM]).

85. Cervin, 'Word Order in Ancient Greek'.

86. Cervin strongly criticizes other methods of studying the topic: statistical and typological studies and their results ('Word Order in Ancient Greek', pp. iii, 30–31), but strangely he also relies on them to create conclusions: 'the proposal that Greek is a VSO language may be confidently abandoned on the grounds that several Greek grammars and all of the previous statistical studies unanimously agree that the subject precedes the predicate. This leaves only SVO and SOV are serious candidates for a basic order' (p. 142). In fact, his conclusion of basic Ancient Greek order is SVO and SOV (p. 145), which Cervin agrees is parallel to previous statistical and

Cervin concludes that the orders of SOV and SVO are equally frequent in non-finite structures (infinitives, participles and genitive absolutes), and that is also true in an overall view: the basic word order in Ancient Greek is SVO and SOV. Cervin also proposes topicalization and emphasis are mainly the discourse factors which affect the constituent orders: the pragmatic factors of moving elements to initial are topicalization, contrastive focus and emphasis, and the pragmatic factors of moving elements to final positions are emphasis, de-emphasis and contrast.

M. Karali

This work is particularly focused on the epigraphical corpus of Delphi from the fifth century BCE to the second century CE.[87] M. Karali studies orders of main constituents (subject, verb and object) in main and subordinate clauses in different periods of time; Karali concludes that a verb usually precedes its subject in all types of clauses and in all periods of time, and direct object and indirect object tend to occur after subject and verb. Karali further proposes several factors which affect word orders: lexical factor (pronoun tends to be initial in a clause), morphological factor (long elements tend to move towards the end of a clause) and pragmatic

typological studies (though these two approaches have been strongly criticized by him): 'The crux of the issue has to do with the Greek VP: is it VO or OV? The previous statistical studies support both, with some authors (e.g. Herodotus) exhibiting a near 1–1 ratio of VO to OV; other authors (e.g. Plato) exhibiting a predominant order of OV; and still other authors (e.g. Luke) exhibiting a predominant VO order. Arguments from typology likewise support both possibilities' (p. 142).

87. Karali, 'Aspects of Delphi Word Order'. Karali studies the topic extensively by categorizing her studies periodically and syntactically. Periodically, she studies the dialect century by century, from fifth century BCE down to second century CE (and thus lengthy spaces and repeated message are being brought out throughout her work); syntactically, she studies the word order of the dialect in main clauses and many different types of subordinate clauses: conditional, temporal, temporal-conditional introduced by ἐπεί, causal clauses, consecutive and final clauses, relative clauses, ὅτι and διότι complement clauses, indirect questions and infinitival clauses; besides studying the word orders, Karali also studies positions of subordinate clauses (for positions of subordinate clauses, cf. G.C. Wakker, 'Purpose Clauses in Ancient Greek', in Nuyts and de Schutter [eds.], *Getting One's Words into Line*, pp. 89–101: Wakker takes 1 philosophical, 5 historical and 8 drama texts as her data, and finds 427 out of 495 [86 per cent] purpose expressions are in final position ['Purpose Clauses in Ancient Greek', pp. 91–92]; cf. her other work indicates Homeric purpose clauses also favour for a final position in a sentence: 'Purpose Expressions in Homeric Greek', in A. Rijksbaron, H.A. Mulder and G. Wakker [eds.], *In the Footsteps of Raphael Kühner. Proceedings of the International Colloquium in Commemoration of the 150th Anniversary of the Publication of Raphael Kühner's Ausführliche Grammatik der griechischen Sprache. II. Theil: Syntaxe. Amsterdam, 1986* [Amsterdam: J.C. Gieben, 1988], pp. 327–44 (338–40); see also Wakker's other work regarding position of Greek conditionals: *Conditions and Conditionals: An Investigation of Ancient Greek* [ASCP, 3; Amsterdam: Gieben, 1994], pp. 57–60 [also cf. related works in New Testament Greek, e.g. J.K. Elliott, 'The Position of Causal ὅτι Clauses in the New Testament', *FN* 3 (1990), pp. 155–57; S.E. Porter, 'Word Order and Clause Structure in New Testament Greek: An Unexplored Area of Greek Linguistics Using Philippians as a Test Case', *FN* 6 (1993), pp. 177–205, esp. pp. 197–98; *idem*, *Idioms of the Greek New Testament*, p. 292]).

factor (when a subject is a newly introduced element, or when it carries an essential information,[88] it precedes its verb; otherwise a verb precedes its subject as mentioned above). Karali's work not only studies the word order of a Greek dialect, but also tries to determine factors behind the order patterns in different aspects: lexical, morphological and pragmatic.

H. Dik

H. Dik tries to take a functional/pragmatic approach to the matter,[89] and to study the Greek word order of Herodotus' work from a point of view of Topic and Focus, which is derived from S. Dik's *Functional Grammar*.[90] After an introduction and a brief description of S. Dik's *Functional Grammar*, Dik then focuses her work on different levels of Topic and Focus on a variety of topics in four chapters: Greek particles which includes postpositives, ἄρχω and βασιλεύω, four forms of the verb λέγω: λέγει, ἔλεγε, εἶπε, and ἔλεξε. The method and approach of Dik's work is strange and largely disappointing. Dik has not shown clear criteria of choosing the above mentioned topics.[91] In fact, it is difficult to see why Dik has particularly chosen these four topics to be the centre of her studies, and it is difficult to see any interrelationships between these topics, and how the results of these particular chapters contribute to the title of the work: a pragmatic account of word order variation in Herodotus. Working on the above four areas definitely does not give a representative figure of Herodotus' writing.[92] Dik's attempt to study the area pragmatically on the theory of Topic and Focus is a good try, but she fails to have a reasonable methodology and thus her work cannot give a satisfactory figure on Herodotus' pragmatic word order.

B.D. Frischer et al.

B.D. Frischer and a number of scholars work on selected texts of Latin and Classical Greek.[93] They particularly study the orders of accusative direct objects and their governing verbs. Their results indicate the frequency of a direct accusative object being located before its governing verb in Greek is similar to the frequency of being located after it.

---

88.   Actually it is not easy to judge what is 'essential' and Karali fails to give sufficient explanations or criteria on how to define an element carries 'essential' information.

89.   Dik, *Word Order in Ancient Greek*.

90.   Cf. S.C. Dik, *Functional Grammar* (Dordrecht: Foris, 1978); *idem*, *The Theory of Functional Grammar*. I. *The Structure of the Clause* (Dordrecht: Foris, 1989).

91.   For example, why particularly the four forms of λέγω are chosen to be studied? Why is a verbal word chosen for the study? And why are the other verbal words not included (for example, λαλέω)?

92.   Although Dik has firstly mentioned that she is not going to represent an account of all aspects of Greek word order, the relative position of subject and predicate and others are at issue (p. 1), but the furthering content of the work does not seem to be matching with this statement.

93.   B.D. Frischer *et al.*, 'Word-Order Transference between Latin and Greek: The Relative Position of the Accusative Direct Object and the Governing Verb in Cassius Dio and Other Greek and Roman Prose Authors', *HSCP* 99 (1999), pp. 357–90. The number of people involved in

Summary
A substantial number of scholars have already tackled the area of Classical Greek word order.[94] A majority of them approach the topic grammatically/syntactically.[95] Although Giseke's studies are only based on some Homeric samples in one aspect (subordinate clause), his study of the orders of Homeric verbal structure seems to be a good starting point in the field. Short tries to work on the topic with more extensive sources but lacks concrete numeric evidence. Ebeling's work puts the result of the field's study a step forward as he works on the topic based on much more solid statistical data.

this work is numerous: B. Frischer; R. Anderson; S. Burstein; J. Crawford; R. Gallucci; A. Gowing; D. Guthrie; M. Haslam; D. Holmes; V. Rudich; R.K. Sherk; A. Taylor; F. Tweedie and B. Vine. The size of the work's selected samples is quite extensive: 60 passages written by 15 Latin and 10 Greek prose authors (authors of the selected Greek texts include Augustus, Cassius Dio, Dionysius of Halicarnassus, Herodotus, Marcus Aurelius, Musonius Rufus, Plutarch, Polybius, Thucydides and Xenophon). See Frischer and F.J. Tweedie's later work which states it can further confirm the result of this work: 'Analysis of Classical Greek and Latin Compositional Word-Order Data', *JQL* 6 (1999), pp. 85–97.

94.   Besides the works mentioned above, there are several other related works (they are not works on orders of the three main clause constituents [S, V, O]). For example, works on positions of attributive adjective relative to its noun (i.e. precedes it or follows it) such as: L. Bergson, *Zur Stellung des Adjektivs in der älteren griechischen Prosa* (Acta Universitatis Stockholmiensis, SGS, I; Stockholm: Almqvist & Wiksell, 1960); order of words within a phrase structure, and placement of some particles: K.S. Morrell, 'Studies on the Phrase Structure of Early Attic Prose' (PhD thesis, Harvard University, 1990); positions of conjunctions: S. Kuno, 'The Position of Relative Clauses and Conjunctions', *Ling Inq* 5 (1974), pp. 117–36; positions of interrogative elements: Thompson, 'The postponement of interrogatives in Attic drama', pp. 147–52; positions of clitics: G. Dunn, 'Enclitic Pronoun Movement and the Ancient Greek Sentence Accent', *Glotta* 67 (1989), pp. 1–19; M. Janse, 'Convergence and Divergence in the Development of the Greek and Latin Clitic Pronouns', in R. Sornicola *et al.* (eds.), *Stability, Variation and Change of Word-Order Patterns over Time* (Amsterdam: John Benjamins, 2000), pp. 231–58 (232–44) covering topics related to Ancient and NT Greek; Taylor, 'Clitics and Configurationality in Ancient Greek', which covers positions of clitics from Homer, Plato, Herodotus and New Testament; and *idem*, 'A Prosodic Account of Clitic Position in Ancient Greek', in A.L. Halpern and A.M. Zwicky (eds.), *Approaching Second: Second Position Clitics and Related Phenomena* (Stanford: Centre for the Study of Language and Information, 1996), pp. 477–503 (cf. R.S. Cervin, 'On the Notion of "Second Position" in Greek', *SLSc* 18 [1988], pp. 23–39; and A.L. Halpern, 'Topics in the Placement and Morphology of Clitics [Slavic, Greek, Sanskrit]' [PhD thesis, Stanford University, 1992]); orders of particles: J. Wills, 'Homeric Particle Order', *HS* 106 (1993), pp. 61–81 (cf. Monro, *A Grammar of the Homeric Dialect*, pp. 335–38); positions of negatives: Moorhouse, *Studies in the Greek Negatives*, pp. 69–156.

For works relating Greek word order and translation, see G. Marquis, 'Word Order as a Criterion for the Evaluation of Translation Technique in the LXX and the Evaluation of Word-Order Variants as Exemplified in LXX-Ezekiel', *Textus* 13 (1986), pp. 59–84; B.G. Wright, *No Small Difference: Sirach's Relationship to its Hebrew Parent Text* (SBLSCS, 26; Atlanta: Scholars Press, 1989), pp. 35–54; S. Olofsson, 'Studying the Word Order of the Septuagint: Questions and Possibilities', *SJOT* 10 (1996), pp. 217–37; M.Y. Gabr, 'Philological Studies on the Coptic Versions of the Gospel of John' (PhD thesis, University of Liverpool, 1990).

95.   Scholars who classify clause constituents grammatically or syntactically include Giseke, Short, Goodell, Ebeling, Thompson, Frisk, Dover, Friedrich, Cervin, Karali and Frischer *et al.*

Loepfe and Dik study the order of Greek constituents pragmatically; their works offer an alternative model of study to the traditional grammatical/syntactical approach.[96] Besides the many studies on word order patterns, several scholars try to examine the determinants which affect the Greek word orders. Cervin suggests pragmatic factors behind Greek order patterns; the rest of them propose factors in more than one aspect (Goodell: syntactic and euphonic; Dover: lexical/semantic, syntactic and logical; Karali: lexical, morphological and pragmatic).

Recent Studies on Word Order of New Testament Greek

The matter of word order in the New Testament has long been noticed and mentioned.[97] A number of significant works have been devoted to the topic and are being introduced as follows:

D.J. Wieand

D.J. Wieand studies the orders of three main elements in a clause (subject, verb and object) from selected materials of the four Gospels and Acts,[98] and then compares the results of investigations from passages from the Pauline writings, Genesis and Philostratus. Wieand tries to find patterns of word order in five main categories: (1) all main clauses except the clauses with implied verbs; (2) all declarative clauses; (3) all declarative clauses which do not contain verbs of 'saying'; (4) imperative word order; (5) all independent clauses which contain verbs of 'saying'. Wieand's work concludes that the most frequent word orders in the Gospels and Acts are VO, SVO, SV and VS.[99] Wieand's work takes a syntactic approach (classifying constituent elements by their syntactic structure: subject, verb and object), and it is the first lengthy work devoted to the topic of study.

96.   See also Dunn's works on word order of Herodotus and other ancient Greek writers; his Head/Modifier approach is actually much related to a functional approach.

97.   For example, this topic has been frequently mentioned in NT Greek grammars. Many NT Greek grammarians have observed some usual patterns of word order and positions of words in the Greek NT: G.B. Winer, *A Treatise on the Grammar of New Testament Greek* (trans. W.F. Moulton; Edinburgh: T&T Clark, 9th English edn 1882), pp. 684–702; E.D. Burton, *Syntax of the Moods and Tenses in New Testament Greek* (Edinburgh: T&T Clark, 3rd edn 1900), pp. 166–67, 175, 177; A.T. Robertson, *A Grammar of the Greek New Testament in the Light of Historical Research* (Nashville: Broadman Press, 1934), pp. 417–25; C.F.D. Moule, *An Idiom Book of New Testament Greek* (Cambridge: Cambridge University Press, 2nd edn 1959), pp. 166–70; F. Blass and A. Debrunner, *A Greek Grammar of the New Testament and Other Early Christian Literature* (trans. and rev. R.W. Funk; Chicago: University of Chicago Press, 1961), pp. 248–53; N. Turner, *Syntax* in J.H. Moulton, *A Grammar of New Testament Greek*, III; Edinburgh: T&T Clark, 1963, pp. 347–50; R.A. Young, *Intermediate New Testament Greek: A Linguistic and Exegetical Approach* (Nashville: Broadman & Holman, 1994), pp. 214–18.

98.   D.J. Wieand, 'Subject Verb Object Relationship in Independent Clauses in the Gospels and Acts' (PhD thesis, University of Chicago, 1946).

99.   Wieand, 'Subject Verb Object Relationship', p. 123.

T. Friberg

T. Friberg's doctoral thesis is on the topic of New Testament word order.[100] Friberg tries to study many different types of word order, which results in 28 different order categories to be studied, from main constituent orders and particle orders in clauses to element orders in noun phrases. These include very detailed patterns such as order of head noun and genitive noun, order of noun and modifying adjective and order of adverb with respect to modified adjective. Two categories even have sub-categories; for example, the category of 'The Order of Noun and Modifying Adjective' has been classified into four sub-categories: interrogative adjectives, relative adjectives, indefinite adjectives, participles and descriptive adjectives.

Friberg's classification of his 28 categories is largely morphologically based. This is not surprising since this work has benefited much from the computer programme which has also much assisted one of his previous works and his two later works,[101] which are all solely morphologically oriented. The data of these 28 categories are first presented, and then determinations of markedness and various explanations for the marked status such as syntactic, stylistic, semantic and pragmatic factors are proposed. The last section of the work is to compare the findings to the theories stated by Greenberg, Lehmann and Vennemann, where Friberg finds his findings largely agree with these three linguists' findings. This work is a good attempt to study the Greek order in very

100. T. Friberg, 'New Testament Greek Word Order in Light of Discourse Considerations' (PhD thesis, University of Minnesota, 1982). This title is a little misleading; firstly, although the title of this work is 'New Testament Greek Word Order', the actual texts examined are mainly from the Gospel of Luke (as also noticed by C.S. Cervin: 'his [Friberg] database, Luke's Gospel, is not necessarily representative of Koiné Greek generally and is far too narrow to support his claims' ['A critique of Timothy Friberg's dissertation: New Testament Greek word-order in light of discourse consideration', *JOTT* 6 (1993), pp. 56–85 (56)]: for a detailed review and summary of Friberg's work, see J. Callow, 'Word Order in New Testament Greek, Part I', *START* 7 [1983], pp. 3–50; for an application to Friberg's studies and proposal, see H. Harm's work on the orders of verb/object and verb/indirect object in the Letter of Jude: 'Word Order in Jude', *START* 8 [1983], pp. 32–39), Friberg chooses a narrative genre because he thinks this genre is more 'varied' and 'an analysis of one of them (narrative genre) will insure a sample that is reasonably representative of the language as a whole', and chooses Luke based on the belief that he is a native speaker of the language (Friberg, 'New Testament Greek Word Order', pp. 3–4); secondly, the area covered by this work is a little beyond 'word order', in fact, clause order (or clause structure) is also included in Friberg's 28 categories, where order of main clause and subordinate clause is studied (pp. 163–66, 278–81).

101. Friberg, 'New Testament Greek Word Order', pp. 1–2. The related works are: B. Friberg and T. Friberg (eds.), *Analytical Greek New Testament* (Grand Rapids: Baker Book House, 1981); P.S. Clapp, B. Friberg and T. Friberg (eds.), *Analytical Concordance to the Greek New Testament* (2 vols.; Grand Rapids: Baker Book House, 1991); B. Friberg, T. Friberg and N.F. Miller (eds.), *Analytical Lexicon of the Greek New Testament* (Grand Rapids: Baker Book House, 2000).

detailed patterns. It tries to compare the results with works on this topic from linguists, but some of the classifications seem to be too specific,[102] and fail to show the values in certain detailed analyses.[103]

Works by translators and translation consultants of the Summer Institute of Linguistics
A number of works in the area have been done by translators and translation consultants of the Summer Institute of Linguistics (SIL),[104] whose works can be summarized as follows:

J.R. Radney. J.R. Radney's published MA thesis is focused on orders of subject, verb and object in the Letter to the Hebrews.[105] Radney argues the usual word order of Koine Greek is VSO;[106] his proposal of six factors which influence elements being located in front of the verb form the main part of his thesis.[107]

---

102. For example, in the category of finding the order between subject and object, where the verb is a third person indicative, the subject is classified as S (single noun subject), Sp (subject in a form of pronoun), [S] (a subject contains a verbal form). The same thing happens to object and indirect object, and it is surprising and unreasonable that the combination of agent is also included in this category, thus making the total number of combinations of S, V, O, IO and agent to be up to 150 types (pp. 24–38).

103. Friberg studies the topic according to his 28 classified categories. However, his classification of the categories seems to be too specific and may not be necessarily fruitful. For example, the order between subject, object and their governing verb is one of these 28 categories; this category is then further classified into 9 sub-categories according to different moods and different possible structures. One of these 9 sub-categories is structures with governing verb in optative mood. The classification of this sub-category seems to be unnecessary since there are only a total of 11 instances of optative mood in Lukan verbs (Friberg's study is mainly based on Luke, and these 11 instances can hardly demonstrate the usual NT word order patterns formed by verbs in optative mood [see Friberg, 'New Testament Greek Word Order', pp. 44–45]).

104. For the school of the thought of SIL and its contributions to NT studies, see S.E. Porter, 'Discourse Analysis and New Testament Studies: An Introductory Survey', in S.E. Porter and D.A. Carson (eds.), *Discourse Analysis and Other Topics in Biblical Greek* (JSNTSup, 113; Sheffield: Sheffield Academic Press, 1995), pp. 14–35 (24–27).

105. J.R. Radney, 'Some Factors That Influence Fronting in Koine Clauses', *OPTAT* 2 (1988), pp. 1–79.

106. Radney, 'Some Factors That Influence Fronting in Koine Clauses', pp. 1, 8–10 (particularly for event-clauses: clauses with transitive and intransitive verbs). Radney believes that verb preceding object is the usual order in NT Greek; this coheres with many authors' view; e.g. J.R. Roberts, 'The Syntax of Discourse Structure', *NOT* 11 (1997), pp. 15–34, in which Robert suggests NT Greek is a VO language (and also a P[NP] language [prepositional: placing the adposition before their object]).

107. The proposed six factors are interrogative and relative pronouns (interrogative elements and relative pronouns [in relative clauses] tend to be placed at initial location), pronoun location (e.g. a subject is fronted when it appears in a form of pronoun and functions as an actor), correlative constructions (elements are usually fronted for comparison and contrast, e.g. comparisons and contrasts expressed in constructions such as 'on one hand...and on the other hand...'), negative construction (e.g. a negation is located immediately before the verb of a clause when it is negating the entire clause), subject introduction (newly introduced subject is located before the

R.E. Smith. R.E. Smith has made a short study on the orders of verb, object and indirect object when both the object and indirect object are in a form of pronoun.[108] Smith has considered 15 instances of such occurrences and concludes the unmarked order is verb, object and indirect object.

J.C. Callow. After publishing two lengthy works on the topic of New Testament word order,[109] J.C. Callow studies copula clauses in 1 Corinthians and Romans,[110] and presents his arguments in three main divisions: subject-initial copula clauses, complement-initial copula clauses and verb-initial copula clauses.[111] Rather than giving normal patterns of word order of these clauses in 1 Corinthians, Callow suggests factors which affect the word order in these three types of clauses: contrast, emphasis, focus, information interrogative and thematic significance.[112]

verb in its clause) and motif marking (the concept of emphasis: focusing the reader's attention from a larger setting to some detail). For a detailed review and summary of Radney's work, see J. Callow, 'Word Order in New Testament Greek, Part II, III', *START* 8 (1983), pp. 3–32, esp. pp. 3–19.

108. R.E. Smith, 'The Unmarked Order of Pronominal Objects and Indirect Objects', *START* 12 (1984), pp. 24–26.

109. Callow, 'Word Order in New Testament Greek, Part I', 'Word Order in New Testament Greek, Part II, III'; Part I and II are respectively two detailed reviews and summaries of Friberg ('New Testament Greek Word Order') and Radney's theses ('Some Factors That Influence Fronting in Koine Clauses'), Part III is a summary of the two authors' works.

110. J. Callow, 'Constituent Order in Copula Clauses: A Partial Study', in D.A. Black and D.S. Dockery (eds.), *Linguistics and New Testament Interpretation* (Grand Rapids: Zondervan, 1991), pp. 68–89.

111. Callow further divides each of these three sections into two groups, which results in a total of six groups of copula clauses (SCV and SVC in the first section, CVS and CSV in the second, VSC and VCS in the third).

112. Callow's paper may offer certain insights to the factors behind the six different word order patterns of copula clauses, though some of his proposals may be confusing and lack sufficient evidence (especially the proposals of emphasis and focus). Callow defines 'emphasis' and 'focus' mainly based on what K. Callow defines (*Discourse Considerations in Translating the Word of God* [Grand Rapids: Zondervan, 1974]): 'Kathleen Callow defines "emphasis" as follows: "normally involves the speaker-hearer relationship in some way." She also states that emphasis highlights information that is "of particular interest or significance" or "which will be surprising to the hearer"' (p. 71) and 'Focus is defined by K. Callow as "spotlighting items of particular interest." In this paper, a focused concept, either the complement or part of it, is a significant concept for the following material' (p. 73), and proposes emphasis and focus as one of the factors of fronting complement before the verb in SCV copula clauses. Unfortunately, the examples which are cited following the definition of 'emphasis' can hardly distinguish the 'emphasis' which Callow wants to argue (p. 72). For example, in the case of the cited example of 1 Cor. 5.2 (καὶ ὑμεῖς πεφυσιωμένοι ἐστέ: "and yet you are full of yourselves!"), is the fronted complement emphasized as Callow states, or can it be actually a focus as Callow proposes later in the paper: 'a significant concept for the following material' (p. 73)? The same confusion also occurs in his other cited examples: in 1 Cor. 4.8 (ἤδη κεκορεσμένοι ἐστέ: "already you have eaten your fill!" [p. 72]), is the fronted complement really emphasized, or can it actually be a significant concept for its following material (4.8b: Already you have become rich! Without us you have become kings! And would that you did reign, so that we might share the rule with you! [RSV])? Also 1 Cor. 4.9 (ὅτι

S.H. Levinsohn. S.H. Levinsohn approaches the matter pragmatically.[113] In an article regarding constituent order of Philippians, Levinsohn argues for the pragmatic considerations of topicality and focality.[114] His study provides understandings of constituent order changes in Philippians and Koine Greek, for example, topicalization and marking salience cause fronting of element in a clause.

θέατρον ἐγενήθημεν τῷ κόσμῳ καὶ ἀγγέλοις καὶ ἀνθρώποις: "because we have become a public spectacle to the world and to angels and to mankind" [p. 72]), is the fronted complement really emphasized, or can it actually be a significant concept for its following material (4.10 'We are fools for Christ's sake, but you are wise in Christ. We are weak, but you are strong. You are held in honor, but we in disrepute.' [RSV])?

113. Levinsohn has devoted four entire chapters to constituent order in his *Discourse Features of New Testament Greek: A Coursebook on the Information Structure of New Testament Greek* (Dallas: SIL International, 2nd edn 2000), where he considers the matter of constituent order pragmatically (in the form of Topic–Comment), and suggests factors which affect fronting in a clause such as focus and emphasis for emphatic prominence (pp. 2–67) (For Levinsohn's pragmatic considerations about fronting of constituent element, cf. his other works such as his published doctoral thesis: *Textual Connections in Acts* [SBLMS, 31; Atlanta: Scholars Press, 1987], pp. 6–60; where he considers the forefronting of subject [theme] [this forefronting means locating before the verb, and is not necessarily at the front of a clause], temporal and spatial expression as thematic prominence in Acts. Levinsohn proposes the forefronting of thematic, temporal and spatial elements is to contrast or replace a corresponding aspect of the last described events, and thus an absence of such a forefronting element is an indication of a continuity of situation with context. The subject of a clause preceding its verb gives a switch of attention to a different subject [this is described as a temporary focus: attention is immediately switched to a second participant (pp. 17–19, 23–37). This (the subject [theme] is placed before its verb) would appear in situations when a sentence or a clause is 'not in sequence' (two events occur at the same time, and the second is not a response to the first, or the situation of the second is not related in time or space to the first) with its preceding sentence or clause; this is to switch attention from one subject to another (pp. 10–15)], or to represent the emphasis of its size and extent [pp. 6–9]. The majority of forefronted temporal and spatial elements emphasize the size, extent and duration of their referents, and replace the setting of the previous events, and establish the spatial-temporal setting for the next events to be described [pp. 44–60]. Levinsohn works on the order of subject and verb pragmatically, where he takes the theme of a clause as subject, and provides several reasons for placing a subject before its verb [such as temporary focus and emphatic prominence]. This work is a good attempt in a pragmatic approach, but the criteria of determining subject [syntactic] and theme [pragmatic] are not clearly defined, which may cause the mixing of defining the subject syntactically/grammatically and pragmatically) (cf. Levinsohn's other works on the similar topic: 'Initial Elements in a Clause or Sentence in the Narrative of Acts', *START* 4 [1981], pp. 2–23; 'Phrase Order and the Article in Galatians: A Functional Sentence Perspective Approach' *OPTAT* 3 [1989], pp. 65–82).

114. S.H. Levinsohn, 'A Discourse Study of Constituent Order and the Article in Philippians', in Porter and Carson (eds.), *Discourse Analysis and Other Topics in Biblical Greek*, pp. 60–74 (cf. the abstract of this article in *idem*, 'A Discourse Study of Constituent Order and the Article in Philippians', *NOT* 8 [1994], pp. 25–26). Levinsohn's consideration of 'topicality' and 'focality' is based on S.C. Dik's theories on functional grammar (*The Theory of Functional Grammar*).

M.E. Davison. M.E. Davison mainly studies text samples from Romans, the Gospel of Luke and Epictetus Book I,[115] and studies the following six categories of structures: (1) noun and demonstrative adjective; (2) noun and descriptive adjective; (3) noun and modifying genitive; (4) noun and relative clause; (5) subject, verb and object (VSO, SVO, SOV, VOS, OVS, OSV); (6) noun phrase and adposition. Davison's studies of his samples indicate the relative basic orders of Romans and Luke are NDem, NAdj, NGen, VSO/SVO, preposition-noun phrase; while in Epictetus Book I they are: DemN, AdjN, NGen, NRel, SVO, preposition-noun phrase. Davison concludes that his findings fulfill most of Greenberg and Hawkins' proposed word order universals.[116]

S.E. Porter

S.E. Porter mainly studies the constituent order at the clause level in Philippians.[117] In his work Porter studies the topic in four categories: independent clauses, dependent clauses, participial clauses and infinitival clauses.[118] Porter's work concludes that an explicit subject preceding predicate and other constituent elements serves as a topic marker and/or shifter, which occurs primarily in independent clauses.[119]

---

115. M.E. Davison, 'A Computer-Assisted Analysis of Word Order in the Greek New Testament' (MA thesis, The Queen's University of Belfast, 1987) (Davison's work is later summarized and published as 'New Testament Greek Word Order', *LLC* 4 [1989], pp. 19–28). Davison's study on the Gospel of Luke and Romans is mainly based on a computer readable text prepared by Baraba and Timothy Friberg and their team (the text which is fundamental to their later work: *Analytical Greek New Testament*), while his work on Epictetus Book I is mainly done manually.

116. Davison, 'A Computer-Assisted Analysis of Word Order', pp. 105–06. Cf. Greenberg, 'Some Universals of Grammar', and Hawkins, *Word Order Universals*; also cf. Davison, 'New Testament Greek Word Order', pp. 25–26.

117. Porter, 'Word Order and Clause Structure'; this paper not only studies the constituent orders in Philippians at clause level, but clause orders at the clause complex level are also studied (the ordering of main and subordinate clauses); cf. *idem, Idioms of the Greek New Testament*, pp. 286–97.

118. Porter studies the topic in terms of constituent elements (subject, predicate and complement, instead of subject, verb and object). In the category of independent clauses, the most frequent structure is found to be predicate-complement, the second most frequent one is complement-predicate, and then simply predicate structure; in the category of dependent clauses, the simply predicate structure is predominant, followed by complement-predicate, predicate-complement and subject-predicate; in the category of participial clauses, almost all of the occurrences are equally distributed by three structures: predicate, predicate-complement and complement-predicate; in the category of infinitival clauses, the occurrences are composed by similar numbers of predicate and complement-predicate structures (Porter, 'Word Order and Clause Structure', pp. 192–93).

119. Porter, 'Word Order and Clause Structure', pp. 194, 200–01; these topic markers signal shifting of a new topic, and many times a new event or a new person becomes a new centre of focus (topic), which gives new or emphatic information, and is elucidated in predicate (comment); Porter suggests some of the fronted explicitly expressed subjects in dependent clauses may also serve as topic shifter or marker (part of these serve as a topic marker/shifter of an entire clause

Summary
Quite a number of scholars have tried to tackle the matter of New Testament Greek word order.[120] The majority of the works approach the matter syntactically,[121]

complex as the ones in independent clauses do, while some others may only serve temporarily or as a temporary focus of attention) (p. 195) (cf. *idem, Idioms of the Greek New Testament*, pp. 295–97).

120. Besides the works mentioned above, there are a number of works related to the topic of New Testament Greek word order that have not been mentioned above because they are not mainly dealing with the three main clause elements (subject, verb, object; or subject, predicate and complement). These works are numerous, for example, for the order of noun and adjective: G.D. Kilpatrick, 'The Order of Some Noun and Adjective Phrases in the New Testament', *NovT* 5 (1962), pp. 111–14; cf. Wallace, 'The Relation of Adjective to Noun', p. 130 n. 4 is related to the topic in various NT Greek grammars); personal pronoun and possessive: W.G. Pierpont, 'Studies in Word Order: Personal Pronoun Possessives in Nominal Phrases in the New Testament', *START* 15 (1986), pp. 3–25; cf. H.H. Hess, 'Dynamics of the Greek Noun Phrase in Mark', *OPTAT* 4 (1990), pp. 353–69 for element orders within noun phrases; article and conjunction: D.A. Black, 'The Article, Conjunctions and Greek Word Order', *BR* 9 no. 5 (1993), pp. 23, 61 (cf. S.L. Black, *Sentence Conjunction in the Gospel of Matthew: καί, δέ, τότε, γάρ, οὖν and Asyndeton in Narrative Discourse* [JSNTSup, 216; SNTG, 9; Sheffield: Sheffield Academic Press, 2002], who has taken the constituent order of subject and verb [S-V or V-S] into consideration when studying sentence conjunctions of the Gospel of Matthew); position of a vocative: J. Banker, 'The Position of the Vocative *adelphoi* in the Clause', *START* 11 (1984), pp. 29–36.

There are other works related to applications of word order and prominence in New Testament. They include I. Larsen, 'Word Order and Relative Prominence in New Testament Greek', *NOT* 5 (1991), pp. 29–34; J.T. Reed, 'Identifying Theme in the New Testament: Insights from Discourse Analysis', in Porter and Carson (eds.), *Discourse Analysis and Other Topics in Biblical Greek*, pp. 75–101 (87–89, 95–96); cf. *idem, A Discourse Analysis of Philippians: Method and Rhetoric in the Debate over Literary Integrity* (JSNTSup, 136; Sheffield: Sheffield Academic Press, 1997), pp. 116–18, 387–90; G. Martín-Asensio, 'Participant Reference and Foregrounded Syntax in the Stephen Episode', in S.E. Porter and J.T. Reed (eds.), *Discourse Analysis and the New Testament: Approaches and Results* (JSNTSup, 170; SNTG, 4; Sheffield: Sheffield Academic Press, 1999), pp. 235–57 (253–54) (which later appeared in his published doctoral thesis: *Transitivity-based Foregrounding in the Acts of the Apostles: A Functional-Grammatical Approach to the Lukan Perspective* [JSNTSup, 202; SNTG, 8; Sheffield: Sheffield Academic Press, 2000], pp. 87–111).

For the works related to the topic because of translation and textual criticism, see G.J.C. Jordaan, 'The Word-Order Differences between the Greek and the Latin Text in Codex Bezae', in J.H. Petzer and P.J. Hartin (eds.), *A South African Perspective on the New Testament: Essays by South African New Testament Scholars Presented to Bruce Manning Metzger during his Visit to South Africa in 1985* (Leiden: E.J. Brill, 1986), pp. 99–111; and J. Heimerdinger, 'Word Order in Koine Greek: Using a Text-Critical Approach to Study Word Order Patterns in the Greek Text of Acts', *FN* 9 (1996), pp. 139–80, in which Heimerdinger studies some of Acts' variant readings of three codices by comparing word orders within noun phrases; cf. *idem, The Bezan Text of Acts: A Contribution of Discourse Analysis to Textual Criticism* (JSNTSup, 236; London: Sheffield Academic Press, 2002), pp. 62–115.

121. These works classify clause elements syntactically: subject, verb and object (authors working on this approach are Wieand, Friberg, Radney, Smith and Davison). Callow and Porter's classification is more functional. Callow classifies the constituent elements as subject, verb and complement (instead of object); where subject and complement may not be necessary a noun phrase, it can be in the form of a clause (Callow, 'Constituent Order in Copula Clauses', p. 81: 'Here, the subject is in form of a clause') (cf. Reed's similar approach to the topic: *A Discourse*

while there is work studying the topic pragmatically.[122] Wieand's work sets to be the first attempt to study the topic thoroughly; Friberg, Davison and Porter's works provide an interaction with the results of modern linguistics on word order universals such as Greenberg's work. Besides the contributions on the word order patterns through different books, many works try to propose explanations on the matter of forefronting in clauses.[123]

Analysis of Philippians, p. 117 n. 184: 'The letter O [=complements] here signifies various types of sentence completive, including dative and genitive direct objects, rank-shifted infinitive and participle clauses, and indirect objects'). Porter also classifies the constituent elements as subject, predicate and complement, but his classification is determined within an even larger and broader context: a noun phrase or an entire clause can function as a subject in a clause, similarly a noun phrase, a clause or even an entire paragraph can function as a complement in a larger framework (e.g. an entire paragraph such as the content of a direct speech functioning as the complement of the predicate with verbal process) (cf. Martín-Asensio's similar approach on the topic adopted from Porter's work: *Transitivity-based Foregrounding in the Acts of the Apostles*, pp. 64–69, 108 n. 85). Porter's approach is thus different from the majority of his predecessors' approaches. This approach is more functional and gives analyses from a much wider and larger linguistic framework. The present study in this work is based on the same approach.

122. For example, Levinsohn's works.

123. These authors include Friberg, Radney, Callow, Levinsohn and Porter.

Chapter 2

STUDYING THE WORD ORDER OF THE GOSPEL OF LUKE:
A METHODOLOGICAL CONSIDERATION

Introduction

Although scholars have long been paying attention to the language of the Gospel of Luke,[1] few have focused their work on the word order of the Gospel.[2] The scope of this work is to investigate the constituent order of the Gospel, and to study some marked word orders and their related prominent messages.[3] The different patterns of constituent orders of the Gospel will firstly be classified, some marked word order patterns will then be particularly studied regarding their relationship with prominence and foregrounded messages as expressed in their related passages of the Gospel. This chapter indicates the process of the study and provides the criteria of the study.

1.   Works focusing onto the language of the Gospel are numerous; for example, W.K. Hobart, *The Medical Language of St. Luke: A Proof from Internal Evidence That "The Gospel According to St. Luke" and "The Acts of the Apostles" Were Written by the Same Person, and That the Writer was a Medical Man* (Dublin University Press Series; London: Longmans, Green, 1882); H.J. Cadbury, 'Four Features of Lukan Style', in L.E. Keck and J.L. Martyn (eds.), *Studies in Luke-Acts* (Nashville: Abingdon Press, 1966), pp. 87–102; *idem*, 'Some Lukan Expressions of Time (Lexical Notes on Luke-Acts VII)', *JBL* 82 (1963), pp. 272–78; *idem*, *The Style and Literary Method of Luke* (HTS, 6; Cambridge: Harvard University Press, 1920); A.W. Argyle, 'The Greek of Luke and Acts', *NTS* 20 (1973–74), pp. 441–45; D. Davies, 'The Position of Adverbs in Luke', in J.K. Elliot (ed.), *Studies in New Testament Language and Text: Essays in Honour of George D. Kilpatrick on the Occasion of his Sixty-fifth Birthday* (NovTSup, 44; Leiden: E.J. Brill, 1976), pp. 106–22; N. Turner, 'The Quality of the Greek of Luke-Acts', in Elliot (ed.), *Studies in New Testament Language and Text*, pp. 387–400; F.J.G. Collison, 'Linguistic Usages in the Gospel of Luke' (PhD thesis, Southern Methodist University, 1977); J.A. Fitzmyer, *The Gospel According to Luke* (AB, 28; New York: Doubleday, 2nd edn 1981), pp. 107–27; L. Alexander, *The Preface to Luke's Gospel: Literary Convention and Social Context in Luke 1.1-4 and Acts 1.1* (SNTSMS, 78; Cambridge: Cambridge University Press, 1993), pp. 91–101, 104–42; K. Paffenroth, *The Story of Jesus According to L* (JSNTSup, 147; Sheffield: Sheffield Academic Press, 1997), pp. 66–95; J.M. Watt, *Code-Switching in Luke and Acts* (BILS, 31; New York: Peter Lang, 1997).

2.   The only work focusing on the word order of the third Gospel is Friberg's work ('New Testament Greek Word Order'); although the work is titled as 'New Testament Greek Word Order', the work is actually much focused on the third Gospel (see Chapter 1 of this work regarding Friberg's work).

3.   Here the term 'marked' may simply be understood as 'seldom occurring' or 'unusual'. Many times the concept of 'emphasis' is explained to be very much related to 'unusual' or

Process of Study

Four main constituents are mainly taken into consideration in this study: subject, predicate, complement and circumstantial adjunct. The investigation of the orders of these four constituents in the entire Gospel will be conducted in six categories: independent clauses, dependent clauses, participial clauses, infinitival clauses, embedded clauses and their dependent clauses; while studying the constituent order of the clauses, the tense form of each predicate will also be classified.[4] Special attention will be particularly paid to some marked word orders. Passages containing these marked word orders will be studied in the aspect of foregrounding messages and prominence;[5] the marked word orders of these passages are mainly

---

'changing of word positions' in NT Greek by many writers. For example, Winer, *A Treatise on the Grammar of New Testament Greek*, pp. 684, 686; Robertson, *A Grammar of the Greek New Testament*, pp. 417–18 ('The emphasis consists in moving a word from its usual position to an unusual one' [p. 417]); Davison, 'A Computer-Assisted Analysis of Word Order', pp. 38, 41, 58–59, 63–64; Callow, 'Constituent Order in Copula Clauses', pp. 71–75, 83–84 (e.g. 'that the complements precede the verb because they are emphasized or focused' [p. 83] and so on). Some would even regularly relate 'fronting' of an element to 'emphasis'; for example, F.P. Cotterell, 'The Nicodemus Conversation: A Fresh Appraisal', *ExpTim* 96 (1985), pp. 237–42; in which Cotterell regularly believes a fronted element is thematic in a clause (e.g. 'Of course *nuktos* is not marked, it is not brought into emphatic position by fronting... John could have marked *nuktos* in our passage by fronting it' [pp. 238–39], '...allows John to bring into marked position as the "left hand element" in the sentence the word "Rabbi"' [p. 239], 'The qualifying *apo theou* is marked by being fronted' [p. 239]).

The same situation (changing of word position is regularly explained to be related to 'emphasis') happens in the area of Classical Greek. For example, see Denniston, *The Greek Particles*, pp. iviii–lx; *idem*, *Greek Prose Style*, pp. 44–48; H. Thesleff, *Studies on Intensification in Early and Classical Greek* (CHL, 21.1; Helsingfors: Centraltryckeriet, 1954), pp. 18–19; Moorhouse, *Studies in the Greek Negatives*, pp. 74–75, 148–51.

Frequently the concept of 'emphasis' is related to changing of word order. Scholars have already noticed too many times the factor of 'emphasis' is explained when order of elements is different. For example, cf. Radney's similar viewpoint: 'The study of Koine word order, which is the subject of this thesis, stems from my dissatisfaction with the current Greek scholarship, specifically with the paradoxical claims that (1) no rules of clause order can be formulated accurately; and (2) clause elements out of their proper place are there for emphasis' ('Some Factors that influence fronting in Koine Clauses', p. 3). The main scope of this work is not only studying the constituent order of the Gospel, but also studying *how* the marked orders are incorporated with other linguistic phenomena to express a foregrounded message (this part is mainly done in Part III of this work).

4. Every clause of the Gospel will be analyzed and the results will be presented in Part II and the Appendix at the end of this work.

5. This will be presented in Part III of the work. A major concern of the current study is to study how the marked orders are being incorporated with other linguistic phenomena to represent a foregrounded message. For the concept of foregrounding, Martín-Asensio has rightly pointed out the function of foregrounding in a discourse: 'Through linguistic means such as lexico-grammatical structures, tense-aspect morphology, or choices from the transitivity network the writer attempts to guide his readers through the text, highlighting various levels of meaning or drawing attention to the episodes or themes that matter in light of his overall rhetorical strategy' (*Transitivity-based Foregrounding in the Acts of the Apostles*, p. 51); cf. J.P. Hopper and S.A. Thompson's words: 'Users of a language are constantly required to design their utterances in

studied in a question of how they are incorporated with other linguistic phenomena such as verbal aspect to express foregrounded messages and prominence.[6]

A Consideration of the Concept of Markedness

A major consideration of the study is the markedness of the word order patterns. It is necessary to define the concept of markedness here. The concept of markedness was originally developed by the Prague School.[7] J. Lyons has classified

accord with their own communicative goals and with their perception of their listeners' needs. Yet, in any speaking situation, some parts of what is said are more relevant than others. That part of a discourse which does not immediately and crucially contribute to the speaker's goal, but which merely assists, amplifies, or comments on it, is referred to as background. By contrast, the material which supplies the main points of the discourse is known as foreground' ('Transitivity in Grammar and Discourse', *Lang* 56 [1980], pp. 251–99 [280]); and see J.-M. Heimerdinger, *Topic, Focus and Foreground in Ancient Hebrew Narratives* (JSOTSup, 295; Sheffield: Sheffield Academic Press, 1999), pp. 221–25; Black, *Sentence Conjunctions in the Gospel of Matthew*, pp. 65–71; for the function of backgrounding in a discourse, see J. Grimes, *The Thread of Discourse* (JLSMin, 207; The Hague: Mouton, 1975), pp. 55–60. For the history of studying the phenomenon of foregrounding, see Martín-Asensio, *Transitivity-based Foregrounding in the Acts of the Apostles*, pp. 51–57; and cf. W. van Peer, *Stylistics and Psychology: Investigation of Foregrounding* (London: Croom Helm, 1986), pp. 5–6.

A major concern of Part III of the work is foregrounding and prominence; for the concept of prominence, see J.T. Reed and R.A. Reese's comment on it: 'The concept PROMINENCE (also known as emphasis, grounding, relevance, salience) typically refers to the study of the linguistic means (spoken or written) by which a speaker/author draws the listener/reader's attention to important topics and motifs of the discourse and supports those topics with other less-prominent material... Prominence is defined here as those semantic and grammatical elements of discourse that serve to set aside certain subjects, ideas, or motifs of the text as more or less semantically and pragmatically significant than others' ('Verbal Aspect, Discourse Prominence, and the Letter of Jude', *FN* 9 [1996], pp. 181–99 [185–86]).

6.   The position of the present work about verbal aspect is very much similar to S.E. Porter's (*Verbal Aspect in the Greek of the New Testament, with Reference to Tense and Mood* [SBG, 1; New York: Peter Lang, 1989]) (Verbal aspect of NT Greek has been a major issue in recent studies of the NT Greek tense system. Besides Porter's monograph, another major monograph of the area is B.M. Fanning's: *Verbal Aspect in New Testament Greek* [Oxford: Clarendon Press, 1990]; other works include: K.L. McKay, *A New Syntax of the Verb in New Testament Greek: An Aspectual Approach* [SBG, 5; New York: Peter Lang, 1994]; T.R. Hatina, 'The Perfect Tense-Form in Recent Debate: Galatians as a Case Study', *FN* 8 [1995], pp. 3–22; *idem*, 'The Perfect Tense-Form in Colossians: Verbal Aspect, Temporality and the Challenge of Translation', in S.E. Porter and R.S. Hess [eds.], *Translating the Bible: Problems and Prospects* [JSNTSup, 173; Sheffield: Sheffield Academic Press, 1999], pp. 224–52 [cf. *idem*, *In Search of a Context: The Function of Scripture in Mark's Narrative* (JSNTSup, 232; SSEJC, 8; Sheffield: Sheffield Academic Press, 2002), pp. 101–02]; R.J. Decker, *Temporal Deixis of the Greek Verb in the Gospel of Mark with Reference to Verbal Aspect* [SBG, 10; New York: Peter Lang, 2001]; for discussions of these recent approaches of verbal aspect to NT Greek, see S.E. Porter and D.A. Carson (eds.), *Biblical Greek Language and Linguistics: Open Questions in Current Research* [JSNTSup, 80; Sheffield: Sheffield Academic Press, 1993], pp. 18–82; Reed and Reese, 'Verbal Aspect, Discourse Prominence', pp. 181–85; Decker, *Temporal Deixis of the Greek Verb*, pp. 11–28).

7.   The concept of markedness is firstly raised by the Prague School (for the history of studying the topic, see H. Andersen, 'Markedness Theory – the First 150 Years', in O.M. Tomíc

three types of markedness: formal marking, semantic markedness and distributional markedness.[8] Distributional markedness is directly related to the frequency of occurrence of a lexeme, and this is much related to the one which is incorporated in this work: the frequency of occurrences of different word order types. Basically having a similar view on the above three types of markedness,

[ed.], *Markedness in Synchrony and Diachrony* [TILSM, 39; Berlin: Mouton de Gruyter, 1989], pp. 11–46). The concept of 'marked' and 'unmarked' is then applied to opposing structural entities by J.H. Greenberg ('Language Universals', in C.A. Ferguson *et al*. [eds.], *Theoretical Foundations* [CTIL, 3; The Hague: Mouton, 1966], pp. 61–112; and its slightly expanded version: *idem, Language Universals: With Special Reference to Feature Hierarchies* [JLSMN, 59; The Hague: Mouton, 1966]) ('Marked' and 'Unmarked' are highly related, and thus it is not surprising that Yishai Tobin states: 'The unmarked form may appear in an idiom or expression where the marked form sounds a bit strange. The "strangeness" of the marked form stems from the fact that these expressions imply a perception of entities in discontinuous space for which the meaning of the unmarked form is more appropriate.' [Y. Tobin, *Invariance, Markedness and Distinctive Feature Analysis: A Contrastive Study of Sign Systems in English and Hebrew* (CILT, 111; Amsterdam: John Benjamins, 1994), p. 80]; for the idea of 'Unmarked', see German natural morphologist Willi Mayerthaler's definition on unmarkedness: 'in agreement with the typical attributes of the speaker', people generally agree unmarked properties are those that are typical in communication and writing [as cited in E.L. Battistella, *The Logic of Markedness* (Oxford: Oxford University Press, 1996), p. 11; cf. J. Gvozdanović, 'Defining markedness', in Tomić (ed.), *Markedness in Synchrony and Diachrony*, pp. 47–66]); also cf. E. Moravcsik and J. Wirth, 'Markedness: An Overview', in F.R. Eckman, E.A. Moravcsik and J.R. Wirth (eds.), *Markedness* (New York: Plenum Press, 1986), p. 3.

8. J. Lyons, *Semantics* (2 vols.; Cambridge: Cambridge University Press, 1977), vol. 1, pp. 305–11. Though Lyons has classified markedness into three types, the first two types (formal marking and semantic marking) are actually much related to the third type (distributional marking). Basically the formal marking is directly related to morphological changes in lexemes, and thus the term may also be referred to as morphological markedness (H.J. Schriefers, *On Semantic Markedness in Language Production and Verification* [Druck: Stichting Studentenpers Nijmegen, 1985], p. 5); for example, in the pair of oppositions 'suitable' and 'unsuitable', 'unsuitable' is formally marked with a prefix; the pair of opposition 'lion' and 'lioness', 'lioness' is formally marked with a suffix. This type of marking is actually much related to distribution, for example, the pair of opposition 'good' and 'bad', 'good' is the unmarked or 'neutralized' part, and 'bad' is much restricted in use, this can be illustrated in these examples: "How good is your school life?", "Have a good evening!", but usually not "How bad is your school life? " and "Have a bad evening!". A formally marked lexeme is also usually more restricted in distribution than the formally unmarked one, for example, 'lion' has a wider distribution than 'lioness', since 'male lion' and 'female lion' are acceptable collocations, but not 'male lioness' and 'female lioness'. For semantic marking, a semantically marked lexeme is semantically more specific than the corresponding unmarked one, and usually a semantically marked lexeme is more restricted in its distribution, for example, 'salmon' is semantically more specific than 'fish', 'dictionary' is semantically more specific than 'book', both the unmarked ones 'fish' and 'book' are more widely distributed. In summary, formal marking is considered morphologically, and semantic markedness is considered semantically, both are less distributed than their corresponding unmarked ones. The third type is distributional markedness, this is mainly based on the frequency of occurrence of an item in natural language use. The study of markedness on the matter of word order of this work is very much related to distributional markedness, it is mainly based on the consideration of frequency and distribution of various word order patterns.

S. Greenbaum simply modifies this view into two types of language use: 'normal' and 'non-normal' forms; based on these two different forms, Greenbaum considers the importance of prominence: the non-normal form implies a prominence. This applies to the positions of elements in a sentence, or word order in a clause: 'One form is said to be the norm from which others diverge… informational prominence can be given to an element by placing it in a non-normal position'.[9] The normal form of language is thus to be said to be in 'dominance' in a distributional sense,[10] and the non-normal form can be regarded as representing 'prominence'.[11]

Criteria of the Study

The study is being conducted according to different types of clauses in the Gospel. It is necessary to define different categories of clauses and clause constituents here.

Independent Clauses
An independent clause is a clause which does not have dependency of other clauses and thus it can stand alone (e.g. 2.9 καὶ δόξα κυρίου περιέλαμψεν αὐτούς).[12]

---

9.   S. Greenbaum, 'Syntactic Frequency and Acceptability', in T.A. Perry, (ed.), *Evidence and Argumentation in Linguistics* (Berlin: Walter de Gruyter, 1980), pp. 301–14 (303); cf. W. Croft, *Typology and Universals* (CTL; Cambridge: Cambridge University Press, 1990), pp. 64–94; and L.J. Whaley, *Introduction to Typology: The Unity and Diversity of Language* (Thousand Oaks: Sage, 1997), pp. 102–04.

10.   Cf. L.J. Schwartz, 'Syntactic Markedness and Frequency of Occurrence', in Perry (ed.), *Evidence and Argumentation in Linguistics*, pp. 315–33 (315–16).

11.   PART III of this work will try to demonstrate the relationship between the markedness of several word order patterns and related messages with prominence.

12.   An independent clause does not have dependency of other clauses, but it does not mean that it does not have relationships with other clauses (for definition of a clause, cf. V.S. Poythress' definition of a Koine Greek clause: 'A clause in turn can be roughly defined as either [a] a verbless equative or attributive clause with an implicit verb einai, or [b] a grammatical unit with a single central verb, together with other material grouped around it by various types of modification' ['The Use of the Intersentence Conjunctions DE, OUN, KAI, and Asyndeton in the Gospel of John', *NovT* 26 (1984), pp. 312–40 (314)]). In fact, an independent clause always has interrelationships with other independent or dependent clauses and forms a clause complex; and clause complexes further form a meaningful text. M.A.K. Halliday has introduced two types of interdependency in a clause complex: parataxis and hypotaxis (*An Introduction to Functional Grammar* (London: Edward Arnold, 2nd edn 1994), pp. 217–19; cf. C. Nesbitt and G. Plum, 'Probabilities in a Systemic-functional Grammar: The Clause Complex in English', in R.P. Fawcett and D. Young [eds.], *New Developments in Systemic Linguistics*. II. *Theory and Application* [London: Pinter, 1988], pp. 13–15). Parataxis occurs between two elements with equal status (one is initiating and the other is continuing), this can often be represented in a form of two independent clauses with a conjunction 'and'. For example, 1.80 τὸ δὲ παιδίον ηὔξανεν καὶ ἐκραταιοῦτο πνεύματι. Although the primary (τὸ δὲ παιδίον ηὔξανεν) and the secondary (ἐκραταιοῦτο πνεύματι) clauses are both independent and can individually stand alone, they form a paratactic relationship with the conjunction καί. The primary clause initiates and the secondary continues; this clause complex gives an 'extending' meaning (Halliday has also classified another

Dependent Clauses
A dependent clause is a clause which cannot exist all by itself; its existence has to depend on another clause.[13] It expresses a hypotactic relationship with the main clause of the clause complex to which it belongs. Dependent clauses consist of many different types of clause as follows:[14]

Purpose Clauses. A purpose dependent clause indicates a result which the process or action described in a main clause intends to get. It is usually expressed in a subjunctive mood (e.g. 21.34 προσέχετε δὲ ἑαυτοῖς μήποτε βαρηθῶσιν ὑμῶν αἱ καρδίαι ἐν κραιπάλῃ καὶ μέθῃ καὶ μερίμναις βιωτικαῖς) (the subjunctive mood in a purpose clause is also always accompanied with a ἵνα; e.g. 14.23 ἔξελθε εἰς τὰς ὁδοὺς καὶ φραγμοὺς καὶ ἀνάγκασον εἰσελθεῖν, ἵνα γεμισθῇ μου ὁ οἶκος), or in an infinitival mood (e.g. 4.29 καὶ ἀναστάντες ἐξέβαλον αὐτὸν ἔξω τῆς πόλεως καὶ ἤγαγον αὐτὸν ἕως ὀφρύος τοῦ ὄρους ἐφ' οὗ ἡ πόλις ᾠκοδόμητο αὐτῶν ὥστε κατακρημνίσαι αὐτόν).

Temporal Clauses. A temporal dependent clause expresses its dependency to a main clause in the sense of temporal meaning.[15] It may be expressed in an indicative mood (e.g. 24.21 τρίτην ταύτην ἡμέραν ἄγει ἀφ' οὗ ταῦτα ἐγένετο), in a subjunctive (e.g. 1.20 καὶ ἰδοὺ ἔσῃ σιωπῶν καὶ μὴ δυνάμενος λαλῆσαι ἄχρι ἧς ἡμέρας γένηται ταῦτα; and in many cases it comes with a ὅταν; e.g. 23.42 μνήσθητί μου ὅταν ἔλθῃς εἰς τὴν βασιλείαν σου), in an infinitival mood (e.g. 8.42 ἐν δὲ τῷ ὑπάγειν αὐτὸν οἱ ὄχλοι συνέπνιγον αὐτόν), or in a participial mood (usually in a form of genitive absolute, e.g. 8.23 πλεόντων δὲ αὐτῶν ἀφύπνωσεν).

aspect of interrelationships between clauses: expansion and projection. Expansion consists of three: elaborating [one clause expands another by elaborating it], extending [one clause expands another by extending it] and enhancing [one clause expands another by embellishing around it]; where projection consists of two: locution and idea) (*An Introduction to Functional Grammar*, p. 220). Hypotaxis is a relationship between two elements with unequal status (one is a dominant element and one is a dependent element), which is best represented by the dependency between an independent clause and its dependent clause.

13. As Porter has defined: 'A dependent clause is a clause with a finite verb which cannot stand alone... but it enters into a definable grammatical and semantic relationship (one of dependency) with another clause' (*Idioms of the Greek New Testament*, p. 230).

14. For classifications of dependent clauses, see Porter, *Idioms of the Greek New Testament*, pp. 230–43.

15. The temporal meaning can be further classified into different categories. Halliday has classified temporal hypotactic enhancing clauses into two categories: same time and different time. The first (same time) is in three aspects: extent (usually expressed in English 'as' and 'while'), point (usually expressed in English 'when', 'as soon as' and 'the moment') and spread ('whenever' and 'everytime'); the second (different time) is in two aspects: later ('after' and 'since') and earlier ('before' and 'until') (*An Introduction to Functional Grammar*, pp. 234–37). Cf. Porter's classification of 'Time at Which' and 'Time up to Which' (*Idioms of the Greek New Testament*, pp. 240–42).

Locative Clauses. A locative clause expresses a meaning of location relative to a main clause,[16] which is usually expressed by adverbs ὅπου (e.g. 12.33 ποιήσατε ἑαυτοῖς βαλλάντια μὴ παλαιούμενα, θησαυρὸν ἀνέκλειπτον ἐν τοῖς οὐρανοῖς, ὅπου κλέπτης οὐκ ἐγγίζει οὐδὲ σὴς διαφθείρει) and πόθεν (e.g. 13.25 οὐκ οἶδα ὑμᾶς πόθεν ἐστέ), and a neuter relative pronoun's singular genitive form (οὗ) (e.g. 4.17 εὗρεν τὸν τόπον οὗ ἦν γεγραμμένον).

Conditional Clauses. This type of clause consists of two categories: positive condition and negative condition. The positive condition is usually introduced by subordinating conjunction ἐάν or εἰ, and negative is by ἐάν or εἰ with a negative particle (e.g. positive condition: 4.3 εἰ υἱὸς εἶ τοῦ θεοῦ, εἰπὲ τῷ λίθῳ τούτῳ ἵνα γένηται ἄρτος; and negative condition: 9.13 οὐκ εἰσὶν ἡμῖν πλεῖον ἢ ἄρτοι πέντε καὶ ἰχθύες δύο, εἰ μήτι πορευθέντες ἡμεῖς ἀγοράσωμεν εἰς πάντα τὸν λαὸν τοῦτον βρώματα).

Causal Clauses. A causal clause provides the cause of the process described in the clause on which the causal clause is dependent. Various conjunctions (e.g. καθότι, διότι, εἵνεκεν, and ὅτι) are used with the indicative mood in this type of clause (e.g. 1.7 καὶ οὐκ ἦν αὐτοῖς τέκνον, *καθότι ἦν ἡ Ἐλισάβετ στεῖρα*, 2.7 ἀνέκλινεν αὐτὸν ἐν φάτνῃ, *διότι οὐκ ἦν αὐτοῖς τόπος ἐν τῷ καταλύματι*; 4.18 πνεῦμα κυρίου ἐπ᾽ ἐμὲ οὗ *εἵνεκεν* ἔχρισέν με εὐαγγελίσασθαι πτωχοῖς; 4.32 ἐξεπλήσσοντο ἐπὶ τῇ διδαχῇ αὐτοῦ, *ὅτι ἐν ἐξουσίᾳ ἦν ὁ λόγος αὐτοῦ*).[17]

Result Clauses. A result clause provides the result of the process described in the clause on which the result clause is dependent.[18] This is usually expressed by a subordinating conjunction ἵνα with a subjunctive mood or ὥστε with an infinitive mood (5.7 ἔπλησαν ἀμφότερα τὰ πλοῖα *ὥστε βυθίζεσθαι αὐτά*).

Comparative Clauses. A comparative clause provides a comparison which is often expressed by conjunctions καθώς and ὡς (e.g. 11.1 δίδαξον ἡμᾶς προσεύχεσθαι, *καθὼς καὶ Ἰωάννης ἐδίδαξεν τοὺς μαθητὰς αὐτοῦ*).

Indirect Content Clauses. An indirect content clause represents contents of the indirect discourse of a verbal or a mental process. It is usually expressed in forms

---

16. Cf. the further possible classifications of location (or spatial) dependent clauses: extent (usually with conjunction 'as far as' in English), point (with conjunction 'where') and spread (with conjunction 'wherever') (Halliday, *An Introduction to Functional Grammar*, p. 237).

17. ὅτι is the conjunction most frequently employed in dependent causal clauses, this type of clauses is usually located after their main clauses (cf. Elliott, 'The Position of Causal ὅτι Clauses in the New Testament', pp. 155–57).

18. At certain events it may not be easy to distinguish between a result clause and a purpose clause. Porter's definition on this type of clause provides a helpful guideline on this matter: 'In contexts where the main clause does not have a verb of intention, direction or purpose, or the action would normally come about without some motivating force, a result clause is a distinct possibility' (*Idioms of the Greek New Testament*, p. 234).

of an indicative mood or a ἵνα with a subjunctive mood (1.22 ἐπέγνωσαν ὅτι ὀπτασίαν ἑώρακεν ἐν τῷ ναῷ; 8.31 παρεκάλουν αὐτὸν ἵνα μὴ ἐπιτάξῃ αὐτοῖς εἰς τὴν ἄβυσσον ἀπελθεῖν).

Infinitival and Participial Clauses. Infinitival and participial clauses occur frequently in the Gospel. In many cases they function within a clause: acting as one of the constituents of the clause (this is common in both infinitival and participial clauses); and in many other cases they function within a group: acting as modifiers of different constituents of an outer clause (this typically occurs in some participial clauses). These kind of clauses are not members of the above two types of clauses (independent and dependent). Because they occur very frequently throughout the Gospel, these clauses are thus studied in the heading of a new category.[19] They are classified into two groups according to their formal grammatical structures: infinitival and participial.

1. *Infinitival Clauses*: An infinitival clause may function as a substantive (subject, complement and circumstantial adjunct) in a clause (subject: e.g. 15.32 εὐφρανθῆναι δὲ καὶ χαρῆναι ἔδει; complement: e.g. 14.9 ἄρξῃ μετὰ αἰσχύνης τὸν ἔσχατον τόπον κατέχειν, here the infinitival clause complements the finite verb ἄρξῃ; circumstantial adjunct: e.g. 12.58 ἐν τῇ ὁδῷ δὸς ἐργασίαν ἀπηλλάχθαι ἀπ' αὐτοῦ, here the infinitival clause functions as a circumstantial element to the process of the main clause, it provides the intention or purpose of the action described in the main clause).

2. *Participial Clauses*: A participial clause may function as a substantive (subject, object, indirect object or other nominal group, and circumstantial adjunct) or a modifier (modifier of substantives) in a clause (e.g. subject: e.g. 2.18 πάντες οἱ ἀκούσαντες ἐθαύμασαν περὶ τῶν λαληθέντων ὑπὸ τῶν ποιμένων πρὸς αὐτούς; object: e.g. 6.32 καὶ εἰ ἀγαπᾶτε τοὺς ἀγαπῶντας ὑμᾶς; circumstantial adjunct: e.g. 23.20 πάλιν δὲ ὁ Πιλᾶτος προσεφώνησεν αὐτοῖς θέλων ἀπολῦσαι τὸν Ἰησοῦν; where the participial clause functions as a causal adjunct, which provides the reason of the action in the main clause; modifier of substantives: e.g. 4.23 ὅσα ἠκούσαμεν γενόμενα εἰς τὴν Καφαρναοὺμ ποίησον καὶ ὧδε ἐν τῇ πατρίδι σου, here the participial clause [γενόμενα εἰς τὴν Καφαρναοὺμ] functions as a modifier of the object [ὅδα] of the verb ἠκούσαμεν).

Other Clauses
The rest of the clauses which do not belong to the above three categories are mainly instances of some relative clauses. They are usually rank-shifted and function as a qualifier of a noun in a clause (e.g. 2.4 ἀνέβη δὲ καὶ Ἰωσὴφ ἀπὸ τῆς Γαλιλαίας ἐκ πόλεως Ναζαρὲθ εἰς τὴν Ἰουδαίαν εἰς πόλιν Δαυὶδ ἥτις καλεῖται Βηθλέεμ).[20]

19. Not all infinitival and participial clauses belong to this category; a few of them may belong to the categories of independent and dependent clauses, e.g., some occurrences of genitive absolute constructions.
20. These clauses are rank-shifted and can be regarded as embedded clauses. Many times they function as a qualifier of a noun and thus function within a nominal group. A qualifier is considered as rank-shifted because it is supposed to be ranked higher than the unit which it

Main Clausal Constituents

A clause may consist of different types of constituents. Four main types of constituents are considered in the present study: subject, predicate, complement and circumstantial adjunct.[21]

Subject. An element functioning as a subject in a clause may include various forms. It may be an article with pronominal force (e.g. 22.71 οἱ δὲ εἶπαν), a noun (e.g. 22.48 Ἰησοῦς δὲ εἶπεν αὐτῷ), or a nominal clause (e.g. 14.33 πᾶς ἐξ ὑμῶν ὅς οὐκ ἀποτάσσεται πᾶσιν τοῖς ἑαυτοῦ ὑπάρχουσιν οὐ δύναται εἶναί μου μαθητής,

qualifies (the qualifier of a noun is a clause unit, and the noun which it qualifies is a word or phrase unit). This rank-shifted unit (or embedded clause) does not function directly in the structure of the outer clause, it only functions directly within the structure of the group, and thus it does not have direct relationship with the other constituents of the outer clause (Halliday, *An Introduction to Functional Grammar*, pp. 187–88, 242–43; cf. G.R. Kress [ed.], *Halliday: System and Function in Language* [Oxford: Oxford University Press, 1976], pp. 57–59; and W. McGregor, 'The Concept of Rank in Systemic Linguistics', in E. Ventola [ed.], *Functional and Systemic Linguistics: Approaches and Uses* [TILSM, 55; Berlin: Mouton de Gruyter, 1991], pp. 121–38 (122–24); C.M.I.M. Matthiessen and J.A. Bateman, *Text Generation and Systemic-Functional Linguistics. Experience from English and Japanese* [London: Pinter, 1991], pp. 78–79). For more about relative clauses, see Givón, *Syntax*, pp. 645–50.

   21.   These four types of constituents are particularly chosen for this study based on the following reasons: (i) subject, predicate and complement are widely accepted as main constituents in a clause, and these three elements are the main topics in the previous studies in word orders (or in many studies the interest of studies is purely grammatical/syntactical: subject, verb and object); (ii) as stated above, many of the previous studies on Greek word order are based on the orders of the three main elements only, and most of them work on the topic based on a grammatical/syntactical analysis; while the present study takes the approach of syntactical and functional (e.g. an entire clause can be considered as a 'subject' or 'complement', and an entire clause or an entire paragraph can be considered as one single 'complement'; this functional classi-fication is much broader than many pure grammatical/syntactical analyses [e.g. under such analyses only a noun phrase can be considered to be the case of 'subject' and 'object']); besides these three elements being taken into consideration in this study, the circumstantial adjunct is the fourth element to be taken into consideration (adjuncts may be composed of three types: modal, conjunctive and circumstantial, but it is not the scope of this study to include all types of adjunct in this work) (seldom have works tried to tackle the matter related to circumstantial adjuncts; cf. P.L. Danove, 'Verbs of Experience: Toward a Lexicon Detailing the Argument Structures Assigned by Verbs', in S.E. Porter and D.A. Carson [eds.], *Linguistics and the New Testament: Critical Junctures* [JSNTSup, 168; SNTG, 5; Sheffield: Sheffield Academic Press, 1999], pp. 144–205, where Danove has taken several circumstantial elements into consideration while proposing a new lexicon: cause, instrument, temporal, locative, purpose, manner, source [etc.] under the classification of 'Semantic Functions' [where these semantic functions are divided into two types: required and optional (though the criteria of this division is not clear in his work)]; and also *idem, Linguistics and Exegesis in the Gospel of Mark: Applications of a Case Frame Analysis* [JSNTSup, 218; SNTG, 10; Sheffield: Sheffield Academic Press, 2001] [cf. *idem, The End of Mark's Story: A Methodological Study* (BIS, 3; Leiden: E.J. Brill, 1993), pp. 239–42]; and Levinsohn, *Textual Connections in Acts*, pp. 44–60, for his proposal of emphatic prominence for forefronting the temporal and spatial expressions in Acts based on a pragmatic approach; also cf. a grammatical approach related to the matter: Davies, 'The Position of Adverbs in Luke', pp. 106–22).

here the noun phrase with an embedded clause functions as the subject of the outer clause; 19.5 σήμερον γὰρ ἐν τῷ οἴκῳ σου δεῖ με μεῖναι, here the infinitival clause σήμερον γὰρ ἐν τῷ οἴκῳ σου and με μεῖναι forms the subject in this δεῖ clause;[22] 2.23 καθὼς γέγραπται ἐν νόμῳ κυρίου ὅτι πᾶν ἄρσεν διανοῖγον μήτραν ἅγιον τῷ κυρίῳ κληθήσεται, the entire content introduced by the subordinate conjunction ὅτι [that] functions as the subject of the predicate γέγραπται).[23]

Predicate. The predicate of a clause is normally the verbal group of the clause.[24] This is the same in different types of clause: independent (e.g. 4.13 ὁ διάβολος ἀπέστη ἀπ᾿ αὐτοῦ ἄχρι καιροῦ), dependent (e.g. 10.6 ἐὰν ἐκεῖ ᾖ υἱὸς εἰρήνης), embedded relative (e.g. 16.1 ὃς εἶχεν οἰκονόμον), infinitival (e.g. 5.18 αὐτὸν εἰσενεγκεῖν καὶ θεῖναι [αὐτὸν] ἐνώπιον αὐτοῦ), participial (e.g. 5.20 ἰδὼν τὴν πίστιν αὐτῶν).

Complement. Complement normally completes a predicate.[25] This can be a nominal group, a clause, or an entire paragraph (e.g. the entire content of a direct speech, which is many times introduced by a complementizer ὅτι).[26] Several

22. Here the infinitival clause is classified as the subject of the main clause (subject of the main clause: 'for me to stay [I stay] in your house today'; predicate of the main clause: 'is necessary' [δεῖ]). The verb δεῖ has always been classified as an impersonal verb and thus the sentence may be translated as something like 'it is necessary for me to stay in your house today'. However, there may be another way to look at this sentence by considering the entire infinitival clause (for me to stay in your house today) to be equivalent to the word 'it'. This makes the sentence to be 'for me to stay (I stay) in your house today' (subject) is necessary (predicate).

23. It is also common to have a clause beginning with 'that' in English to function as subject in a clause, e.g., 'It surprised me that you showed up last night' (here the that clause 'that you showed up last night' is equivalent to 'It' and is functioning as the subject of the main clause; see P.S. Rosenbaum, *The Grammar of English Predicate Complement Construction* [Cambridge: MIT. Press, 1967], pp. 71–80) (in many cases Greek nominal clauses are similar to English nominal clauses [for English nominal clauses, see R. Quirk, S. Greenbaum and G. Leech (eds.), *A Grammar of Contemporary English* (London: Longman, 1972), pp. 348, 734–42]).

24. See Lyons, *Semantics*, pp. 430–38.

25. Complement completes or complements a predicate (see T. Givón, 'The Binding Hierarchy and the Typology of Complements', *SL* 4 [1980], pp. 333–77; *idem, Syntax*, pp. 515–36; and Porter, *Idioms of the Greek New Testament*, pp. 294, 310; cf. P. Danove's studies of complements to NT Greek verbs [though his definition of complement is slightly different, which considers a complement includes subject, object, indirect object and others such as circumstantial elements]: P. Danove, 'The Theory of Construction Grammar and its Application to New Testament Greek', in Porter and Carson (eds.), *Biblical Greek Language and Linguistics*, pp. 119–51; *idem*, 'Verbs of Experience', pp. 144–205; and cf. *idem, Linguistics and Exegesis in the Gospel of Mark*).

26. ὅτι is the most common complementizer throughout Classical and Koine Greek (see S. Cristofaro, 'Grammaticalization and Clause Linkage Strategies: A Typological Approach with Reference to Ancient Greek', in A.C. Ramat and P.J. Hopper [eds.], *The Limits of Grammaticalization* [TSL, 37; Amsterdam: John Benjamins, 1998], pp. 59–88). The use of the complementizer ὅτι is quite similar to the 'that' complementizer in English (see Rosenbaum, *The Grammar of English Predicate Complement Construction*, pp. 31–51), except Greek may also have the ὅτι as its complementizer in direct speech, which is not the case in English.

syntactic elements can function as a complement in a clause: it can be a direct object of a predicate (e.g. 16.3 τί ποιήσω), an indirect object of a ditransitive predicate (e.g. 24.27 διερμήνευσεν αὐτοῖς ἐν πάσαις ταῖς γραφαῖς τὰ περὶ ἑαυτοῦ), an infinitival clause which is required to complete certain verbs (e.g. 5.12 δύνασαί με καθαρίσαι; 10.1 ἤμελλεν αὐτὸς ἔρχεσθαι),[27] a noun or an adjective completing a copula verb like εἰμί and γίνομαι (4.3 εἰ υἱὸς εἶ τοῦ θεοῦ), direct content of a verbal process (e.g. 16.7 ἔπειτα ἑτέρῳ εἶπεν, Σὺ δὲ πόσον ὀφείλεις;), indirect content of a verbal process (e.g. 8.56 ὁ δὲ παρήγγειλεν αὐτοῖς μηδενὶ εἰπεῖν τὸ γεγονός), direct and indirect content of a mental process (e.g. 12.51 δοκεῖτε ὅτι εἰρήνην παρεγενόμην δοῦναι ἐν τῇ γῇ).[28]

Circumstantial Adjunct. Circumstantial adjunct in a clause is mostly expressed by adverbial groups and prepositional constructions;[29] it gives circumstantial information at the level of experiential metafunction. Circumstantial adjuncts in the Gospel are being classified as follows:[30]

27. Certain verbs cannot stand by themselves and must be completed by an infinitival clause (e.g. verbs like δύναμαι, θέλω, μέλλω).

28. Some linguists classify the projecting verbs as assertive predicates, which can be divided into strong (verbs such as say and speak) and weak (verbs such as think, know and believe) (see E.N. Ransom, *Complementation: Its Meanings and Forms* [TSL, 10; Amsterdam: John Benjamins, 1986], p. 9). Ransom even further classifies these assertive predicates into two points of view: (i) information modalities: truth, future truth, occurrence and action; and (ii) evaluation modalities: predetermined (verbs such as predict, believe and manage), determined (verbs such as decide, promise, command and intend), undetermined (verbs such as hope) and indeterminate (verbs such as wonder, ask) (Ransom, *Complementation*, pp. 6–15). The combination of these two modalities would incorporate different lexical choices which are described as higher predicates (pp. 86, 176–82) and form different speech acts (p. 149).

29. Basically there can be three types of adjuncts in a clause: circumstantial, modal and conjunctive. Modal adjunct plays an important role in interpersonal metafunction in a clause, and gives meaning for modality. It is usually used to express degrees of certainty, probability and usuality, obligation and inclination (for NT words typically used for these categories, see Reed, *A Discourse Analysis of Philippians*, p. 83) in a clause. This is to express the speaker's judgment on the message in the clause (see S. Eggins, *An Introduction to Systemic Functional Linguistics* [London: Pinter, 1994], pp. 167–71; for words typically used for modal adjuncts in English clauses, see Halliday, *An Introduction to Functional Grammar*, p. 49). A conjunctive adjunct provides textual meaning to a clause and is usually carried out by conjunctives (e.g. καί, ἀλλά, γάρ), it makes up structural links between parts to create cohesions and thus plays an important role at the three levels in clause complex: elaboration, extension and enhancement (see Halliday, *An Introduction to Functional Grammar*, pp. 83–85, 323–30; for classifications of conjunctive adjuncts, see *idem, An Introduction to Functional Grammar*, p. 49; for clause complex, see *idem, An Introduction to Functional Grammar*, pp. 215–73). A circumstantial adjunct is usually expressed by adverbial groups and prepositional phrases; it mainly gives meaning at the level of experiential metafunction. Besides the process (verbal group) and different participating roles (subject and object, actor and goal etc.) in a clause, a circumstantial adjunct gives extra information of the message: time (when?), place (where?), cause (why?), means (by what?), quality (how?), accompaniment (with whom?), matter (about what?) etc. (for examples of these circumstantial elements in the NT, see Reed, *A Discourse Analysis of Philippians*, pp. 70–75).

30. Halliday has classified circumstantial elements into nine groups: Extent (distance, duration), Location (place, time), Manner (means, quality, comparison), Cause (reason, purpose,

1. *Spatial*: The meaning of a spatial adjunct can be near or remote (e.g. here and there), location or extent (e.g. at my house and all through the country). This is always expressed by a prepositional phrase.

2. *Temporal (1)*: This includes location and extent. This type of circumstantial adjunct is always expressed by a prepositional phrase. For example, 'I have been to London (spatial: location) for five days (temporal: extent)' (e.g. 2.41 καὶ ἐπορεύοντο οἱ γονεῖς αὐτοῦ κατ' ἔτος εἰς Ἰερουσαλήμ [spatial: location] τῇ ἑορτῇ τοῦ πάσχα [temporal: location]).

3. *Temporal (2)*: This type of adjunct is typically expressed by Greek participles with reference to the temporal relationship with its related predicate, and is being classified into three types: earlier, contemporary and later. Earlier temporal (occurs before the action of the finite verb) adjuncts tend to locate before the predicate (e.g. 8.34 ἰδόντες [temporal: earlier] δὲ οἱ βόσκοντες τὸ γεγονὸς ἔφυγον καὶ ἀπήγγειλαν εἰς τὴν πόλιν καὶ εἰς τοὺς ἀγρούς);[31] the contemporary and later ones tend to locate after the predicate.[32]

4. *Manner*: Manner consists of three types: means, quality and comparison. They represent different aspects of the manner of how a process is being carried out.

a. Means. Means is an adjunct referring to the means or instrument by which a process takes place, i.e. it refers to a process being carried out with 'what?' or 'how?' It is usually expressed by a prepositional phrase with ἐν, or simply a dative case (e.g. 3.16 ἐγὼ μὲν ὕδατι [means] βαπτίζω ὑμᾶς).

b. Quality. Quality expresses how a process happens, or how (or in what manner) a process is carried out. It answers a question 'in what kind of a manner does a process take place?' This is typically expressed by an adverbial group (e.g. 22.62 καὶ ἐξελθὼν ἔξω ἔκλαυσεν πικρῶς).[33]

c. Comparison. Comparison shows the manner of a process taking place. It answers a question of the process being carried out 'like what?',[34] or provides a degree of comparison in terms of similarity or difference (e.g. 24.11 καὶ ἐφάνησαν ἐνώπιον αὐτῶν ὡσεὶ λῆρος τὰ ῥήματα ταῦτα).

5. *Cause*: Cause can be classified in four groups: reason, purpose, behalf and result. This refers to the process being carried out for what reason, for what purpose, for whom and to what result.

behalf, result), Contingency (condition, concession, default), Accompaniment (comitation, addition), Role (guise, product), Matter and Angle (*An Introduction to Functional Grammar*, pp. 151–58; cf. W. McGregor, 'The Place of Circumstantials in Systemic-functional Grammar', in M. Davies and L. Ravelli [eds.], *Advances in Systemic Linguistics: Recent Theory and Practice* [London: Pinter, 1992], pp. 136–49; J.R. Martin, *English Text: System and Structure* [Amsterdam: John Benjamins, 1992], pp. 153–55; Givón, *Syntax*, pp. 128–33; Lyons, *Semantics*, pp. 690–703; and cf. Reed's adaptation of this model about circumstantial elements to NT Greek: *A Discourse Analysis of Philippians*, pp. 70–75). My classification on Lukan circumstances mainly follows Halliday's with little alteration.

31. See Porter, *Idioms of the Greek New Testament*, pp. 188–89.

32. The one exception is ἀποκρίνομαι, e.g. 4.8 καὶ ἀποκριθεὶς ὁ Ἰησοῦς εἶπεν αὐτῷ, here the adjunct is a temporal contemporary one.

33. See D. Young, *The Structure of English Clauses* (London: Hutchinson, 1980), pp. 113–15; Quirk, Greenbaum and Leech (eds.), *A Grammar of Contemporary English*, pp. 460–61.

34. Many times it is expressed with the particle ὡς; cf. T. Muraoka, 'The Use of ὡς in the Greek Bible', *NovT* 7 (1964–65), pp. 51–72 (53–60); and cf. G. Tucker, 'An Initial Approach to Comparatives in a Systemic Functional Grammar', in Davies and Ravelli (eds.), *Advances in Systemic Linguistics*, pp. 150–65.

a. Reason. This kind of adjunct shows the reason for a process to take place, or the cause behind the process. This is always expressed with a prepositional phrase beginning with διά (e.g. 8.19 οὐκ ἠδύναντο συντυχεῖν αὐτῷ διὰ τὸν ὄχλον).

b. Purpose. Purpose adjunct expresses the purpose of a process to take place, or the intention behind the process. It answers a question of 'for what ?' This is typically expressed by an infinitival clause (e.g. 5.1 ἐγένετο δὲ ἐν τῷ τὸν ὄχλον ἐπικεῖσθαι αὐτῷ καὶ ἀκούειν τὸν λόγον τοῦ θεοῦ; 9.16 καὶ ἐδίδου τοῖς μαθηταῖς παραθεῖναι τῷ ὄχλῳ).

c. Behalf. This adjunct represents an action taking place on behalf of a person. It answers a question of 'who is the action for?' It is always expressed by a dative case (e.g. 12.33 ποιήσατε ἑαυτοῖς βαλλάντια μὴ παλαιούμενα).

6. Result. Result adjunct represents the result of an action, typically in the form of an infinitival clause (e.g. 6.42 καὶ τότε διαβλέψεις τὸ κάρφος τὸ ἐν τῷ ὀφθαλμῷ τοῦ ἀδελφοῦ σου ἐκβαλεῖν).

7. *Contingency*: Contingency consists of two types: condition and concession.

a. Condition. This expresses a condition under which a process would take place. This is always expressed in the form of a participial clause (e.g. 11.17 πᾶσα βασιλεία ἐφ᾽ ἑαυτὴν διαμερισθεῖσα ἐρημοῦται).

b. Concession. This occurs only a few times in Luke. It represents a process being carried out in spite of some condition (e.g. 5.5 δι᾽ ὅλης νυκτὸς κοπιάσαντες οὐδὲν ἐλάβομεν).

8. *Accompaniment*: Accompaniment consists of two types: comitative and additive.

a. Comitative. Comitative adjunct consists of comitative positive and comitative negative. This kind of adjunct represents a single instance of process which is carried out by its relative actor with or without an accompaniment (with whom/what and without whom/what), and it is typically expressed by a prepositional phrase beginning with σύν or μετά (e.g. 15.31 τέκνον, σὺ πάντοτε μετ᾽ ἐμοῦ [comitative positive] εἶ;).

b. Additive. Additive adjunct consists of additive positive and negative. This represents a process as two or more instances, and the relative actors share (or do not share) the same particular function (and who/what, and not who/what) (e.g. 11.11 καὶ ἀντὶ ἰχθύος [additive negative] ὄφιν αὐτῷ ἐπιδώσει).

9. *Role*: Role adjunct consists of two parts: guise and product. The guise adjunct answers the question of a process being carried out 'as what?', and product adjunct answers the question of a process being carried out 'into/become what?' (e.g. 13.19 καὶ ἐγένετο εἰς δένδρον [product]).

10. *Matter*: This adjunct co-relates strongly with mental and verbal processes. It answers a question of a process being carried out 'about what?', 'on the matter of what?' or 'with respect to what?' It is always expressed by a prepositional phrase beginning with περί (e.g. 2.17 ἰδόντες δὲ ἐγνώρισαν περὶ τοῦ ῥήματος; 4.38 καὶ ἠρώτησαν αὐτὸν περὶ αὐτῆς).

11. *Angle*: Angle answers the question of a process being carried out 'in what angle?', 'according to what?', 'from the standpoint of what?' It is frequently expressed by a prepositional phrase beginning with κατά (e.g. 23.56 καὶ τὸ μὲν σάββατον ἡσύχασαν κατὰ τὴν ἐντολήν).

11. *Agent*: This type of adjunct answers the question of a process being carried out 'by whom?' This element is conflated with the actor in a clause with a passive verb at the experiential level. It is usually expressed by a prepositional phrase beginning with ὑπό (e.g. 8.29 ἠλαύνετο ὑπὸ τοῦ δαιμονίου [agent] εἰς τὰς ἐρήμους).

PART II

UNMARKED WORD ORDERS OF THE GOSPEL OF LUKE

Chapter 3

Relative Positions of Main Constituents in Lukan Clauses

Main constituents of a Greek clause include subject, predicate and complement. This chapter presents a study of the relative positions between these three main constituents (subject and predicate, predicate and complement, subject and complement) of the entire Gospel. The study is done according to different types of clauses: independent clauses, dependent clauses, infinitival clauses, participial clauses, embedded clauses and dependent clauses of embedded clauses. The statistical result of the study contributes to the figure of relative positions between the three main constituents in two aspects: unmarked word order patterns and tendencies of certain word order patterns—a very high percentage of occurrence of a certain word order pattern indicates an unmarked order (a very regular/typical order pattern, e.g., subject precedes the complement in a clause [as stated below]); a relatively high percentage of occurrence of a certain word order pattern indicates a certain degree of tendency of having such a word order (the percentage of a certain pattern is not as high as the unmarked ones, but it is still relatively high to demonstrate a certain degree of tendency of having such a word order pattern, e.g., subject tends to precede its predicate in independent clauses [as stated below]). The relative positions of the three main constituents and their associated grammatical features are presented as follows:[1]

Independent Clauses
Predicate
A large number of independent clauses in Luke are only composed of a predicate as a main constituent; these types of clause may only consist of a predicate (172x), or a predicate with adjunct(s) (273x).

---

1. The distribution of all types of Lukan clauses according to their different word orders is presented in the Appendix at the end of the work, which includes the distribution of the predicates of the clauses according to their different tense forms. Certain items may affect the figure of the distribution, e.g., the verb εἰμί and οἶδα (many traditional grammars believe that the verb εἰμί does not have the aorist tense but has the imperfect instead [though this is believed by many traditional grammars, Porter believes that εἰμί is 'aspectually vague' and does not have tense form (*Verbal Aspect in the Greek of the New Testament*, pp. 443–44)] and the verb οἶδα only has perfect and pluperfect tense form), the perfect passive form of γράφω (it is often to have the perfect passive form of the word in the Gospel) and the citations of LXX; thus the data in the Appendix are presented in two formats for reference: one includes all types of clauses, and one excludes all incidents of the above mentioned items.

Commands and prohibitions are frequently expressed in this category, and they are mainly expressed in imperative forms. This can be shown in the following table:

Table 3.1 *Occurrences of Imperatives in Independent Clauses with only Predicate as Main Constituent*

	P[2]	PA[3]	AP[4]	APA[5]
Total number	172	157	67	49
Pres. imp.	33	14	4	2
Aor. imp.	16	16	5	1
Total imp.	49	30	9	3

The above table indicates a large number of imperative forms are employed to function as commands and prohibitions in the category of clauses which only consist of predicate (**P**) (49 out of 172x), and the number of present imperatives is much higher than the aorist ones (33x vs. 16x).[6] This feature of preferring

2.   In the rest of the work, bolded form of clause components means a combination of similar constructions. For example, **P** means all clauses with only one main clause constituent: predicate; **PA** means all clauses with only predicate as main constituent and with one or more adjunct(s) located after it; this includes all instances of PA, PAA and PAAA. **AP** means all clauses with only predicate as main constituent and with one or more adjunct(s) located before it; this includes instances of AP and AAP. **APA** means all clauses with only predicate as main constituent and with one or more adjunct(s) located before and after it; this includes all instances of APA, APAA, APAAA, AAPA, AAPAA and AAAPA.

3.   30x out of 157 **PA** are imperatives; 14x are present imperatives: PA (3.14; 6.28, 35; 7.50; 8.39, 48; 12.15; 13.31; 19.30; 20.42 [this one is a LXX citation (other instances of LXX citations in the rest of the work will be indicated by the symbol 'LXX')]; 22.51; 23.28); PAA (10.7; 21.36) (in which two instances are used as prohibitions [10.7; 23.28]; the other two prohibitions in **PA** are in aorist subjunctive [12.4; 14.8]). 16x are in aorist imperative: PA (4.35; 5.4, 8; 6.8, 23; 13.25, 27 [LXX]; 14.10, 23; 17.6; 19.13; 21.8; 23.30 [LXX]; 24.29); PAA (5.14; 14.21).

4.   9x out of 67 **AP** are imperatives; 4x are in present imperative: PA (9.4, 4; 22.46; 23.28); and 5x are in aorist imperative: AP (8.50; 17.7, 19; 19.5; 22.12).

5.   2x are in present imperative: APA (5.24) and APAA (10.7); 1x is in aorist imperative: APA (14.10).

6.   There are 33x of present imperative forms (1.13, 28, 30; 2.10; 5.10, 23, 23, 24; 6.8, 35, 37, 37, 37, 38; 7.6, 8, 13; 8.50, 52, 54; 9.50; 10.3, 37; 11.9, 9, 9; 12.7, 15, 19, 19, 29, 32; 14.17), in which 13x are used with negative particles as prohibitions (1.13, 30; 2.10; 5.10; 6.37, 37; 7.6; 8.50, 52; 9.50; 12.7, 29, 32). This number is much greater than the frequency of prohibitions with aorist subjunctives, which is only four times (3.14; 17.23, 23; 18.20, 20; 21.9) (two occurrences [18.20, 20] are citations from LXX; this gives the total number four rather than six). 16x are aorist imperatives (4.35; 5.13; 6.23; 7.8, 14, 40; 12.19, 19; 13.31; 15.23; 17.6; 18.42; 21.28; 22.64, 67; 24.39). When a clause is composed of a predicate only, the number of present imperatives is much greater than the one of aorist imperatives.

This is much different from the clauses which have predicate with adjunct(s), of which the frequency of present and aorist imperatives is evenly distributed: **PA** (14x and 16x), **AP** (4x and 5x) and **APA** (2x and 1x). In the category of **P**, the figure of total present and aorist predicate is 54x and 93x, the number of aorist predicate is much higher than the present; the figure is conversed when it is considered on the imperative forms (33x and 16x, the number of present imperative is much higher than the aorist imperative).

present imperative rather than aorist imperative is only found in the clauses with predicate as the only main clause constituent. For example, in the other clause types such as clauses without subject and with predicate followed by complement,[7] aorist imperatives are more frequent than present ones. This is illustrated as follows:

Table 3.2 *Distribution of Imperatives in PC Structures of Independent Clauses*

	PC[8]	PCA[9]	APC[10]	APCA[11]
Total number	476	119	123	27
Pres. imp.	32	3	4	1
Aor. imp.	75	16	10	2
Total imp.	107	19	14	3

As is shown above, the aorist is dominant in the imperatives of PC clause types (PC and other PC with adjunct[s]); this is also true in the figure of all imperatives in the Gospel.[12]

7.   Imperatives occur much more frequently in the clauses without subject; for example, in the clause type of PS (with or without adjunct[s]), there are only three occurrences of having an imperative (PS 7.7; 11.2, 2; which are all in aorist).

8.   This includes instances of PC, PCC, PCCC. 32 out of 476x are present imperatives: PC (5.27; 6.27, 28, 35, 36; 8.18, 39, 49; 9.23, 59; 10.4 , 8, 9, 20; 11. 35; 13.24; 14.12, 13, 18; 15.23; 17.3, 32; 18.16, 20 [LXX]; 20.46; 21.34; 22.40; 23.18, 21) (four are used for prohibitions [8.49; 10.4; 14.12 and 18.16] [while there are only two aorist subjunctives used for prohibitions: PC (3.8; 12.11)]); and 75 out of 476x are aorist imperatives: PC (3.4 [LXX], 8; 4.23; 6.10, 42; 7.7, 8; 9.12, 23; 10.2, 35; 11.41; 12.5, 27, 33, 33; 13.7; 14.23; 15.6, 9, 22; 16.2, 6, 7, 7, 24, 24, 25, 29; 17.3, 3, 8, 13; 18.6, 13, 22, 22, 38, 39; 19.24, 39; 20.3; 21.20, 28; 22.17, 17, 32, 36, 67; 23.30 [LXX], 34, 35, 37, 39, 42; 24.6, 39); PCC (4.3; 9.59, 60; 10.40; 11.1, 4; 12.13, 24, 27; 14.9; 15.12; 17.5; 18.16; 20.2, 24, 25; 23.18; 24.39) (one syntactic figure is worthy to be mentioned here: many aorist imperatives follow a vocative in the clause [15 out of 75x-PC: 4.23; 6.42; 16.24, 25; 17.13; 18.13, 38, 39; 19.39; 23.34, 42; and PCC: 9.59; 11.1; 12.13; 15.12; while there is none in the instances of present imperative]). Here the number of aorist imperatives is much more than the one of present imperatives (75x vs. 32x).

9.   This includes instances of PCA, PCCA, PCAC, PCAA, PCCAA, PCAAA, PCAAAA and PCCACAAAA, PAC and PACA. 3 out of 119x are in present imperatives: PCA (6.31; 12.1), PAC (12.22, which is used as prohibition); and 16 out of 119x are in aorist imperative: PCA (5.4; 9.14, 23; 13.8; 15.19, 22; 18.3; 19.27; 22.10, 42), PCAA (4.9) and PAC (6.42; 9.41; 12.33; 19.24; 21.14) (13.8 is the only instance with an aorist imperative following a vocative in the category of PCA). Again here the number of aorist imperatives is more than the one of present imperatives (16x vs. 3x).

10.   This includes instances of APC, APCC, APCCC, AAPC and AAPCC. 4 out of 123x are in present imperative: APC (3.4 [LXX]; 6.27; 10.5, 20 [used as prohibition]); and 10 out of 123x are in aorist imperative: APC (10.10; 15.22; 16.6; 21.19), APCC (5.14; 9.61; 13.32; 17.14; 22.8), APCCC (7.22). Number of aorist imperatives is more than the one of present imperatives (10x vs. 4x).

11.   This includes instances of APCA, APCCA, APCAA, APACA, APACAA, AAPCA and AAAPCAA.
The present imperative is APCA (2.29); the aorist imperatives are APCA (12.58; 16.9).

12.   Aorist is dominant in all of the imperatives in Luke (213x are aorist, while only 134x are present) (though the figure of imperative in the clause types with complement located before the

It is concluded that the imperatives tend to be in aorist in the Gospel. However, in the category of **P** (only with one main constituent: predicate, and without adjunct) in independent clauses, when the predicate is an imperative, it tends to be present.

Relative Positions of Subject and Predicate
Subject and predicate are main constituents of a clause. This section presents the figure of frequency of these two elements' relative positions. Overall, the subject tends to precede the predicate in independent clauses (612x vs. 323x).

Table 3.3 *Frequencies of Relative Positions of Predicate and Subject in Independent Clauses*

	PS	SP
Only predicate and subject	71	64
With adjunct(s) only	104	169
With complement(s) or complement(s) and adjunct(s)	148	379
Total	323	612

For clauses which only consist of predicate and subject, the relative positions of the two elements are evenly distributed (71x vs. 64x). In the clauses which consist of predicate, subject and adjunct(s), subject tends to precede the predicate (104x vs. 169x); the tendency is much further apparent in the clauses including complement(s) (148x vs. 379x).

When an infinitival clause functions as a subject in a clause, this subject is predominantly an aorist infinitival clause and located at the end of the main clause as a **PS** clause type,[13] and the predicate of this type of **PS** clause (with an infinitival clause as subject) tends to be present.[14]

---

predicate is different; for example, in the total occurrence of 101 instances of **CP** [instances of having one or more complements located before the predicate], the number of present imperatives is 7x [CP: 3.18; 6.30; 9.35; 10.28; CCP: 11.7 (prohibition); CPC: 6.29; 10.11], while there are only two instances of aorist imperative [CP: 12.5; 18.22]; in the events compiled with adjunct[s] [49x], 5x are in present imperative [CPA: 9.3; 22.19; CPCA: 11.3; ACP: 6.29 (prohibition); ACAPA: 9.5], and 4x are in aorist imperative [CPA: 14.21; 19.27; CPAA: 4.23; ACP: 19.30]).

13.   There is a total of 23 incidents of having an infinitival clause functioning as a subject in an independent clause, 21x out of them are located at the end of the clause (**PS** clause types) (the number of these infinitival clauses is actually greater than 23, because a number of these subjects are composed of more than one infinitival clause, e.g. 9.22 is composed of four; this gives a total of 34 infinitival clauses [31x belong to **PS** clause type, and 3x belong to **SP** clause type]).

In the **PS** clause type, 28 out of the 31 infinitival clauses are in aorist (PS [9.22(4x); 11.42(2x); 13.16; 14.3; 16.22(2x); 19.5; 20.22; 21.9; 22.37; 24.7(3x), 26(2x), 46(3x)], CPS [8.10; 16.17; 17.1; 18.25], PCS [1.3], PCAS [2.26]); while there are only 2x of present infinitival clauses as subject in PS clause types (PS [13.33; 22.24]) and 1x of perfect infinitive as subject (PCS [10.36]). There are only two incidents of an infinitival clause functioning as a subject located before the predicate in a main clause (**SP** clause type), and they are all aorist infinitival clauses (4.43; 15.32[2x]).

14.   Present predicate is dominant here: present is 13x, while aorist is only 2x (present: 13x [9.22; 10.36; 13.33; 14.3; 16.17; 17.1; 18.25; 19.5; 20.22; 21.9; 22.24, 37; 24.7], imperfect: 4x

It can be concluded that subject tends to precede its predicate in independent clauses (tendency: **S + P**). When the subject is an infinitival clause, it is an unmarked pattern to have an aorist infinitival clause located after the present predicate of the main clause (unmarked: P[pres.] + S[aor. inf. clause]).

Relative Positions of Predicate and Complement
This section presents the figure of preferred relative position of predicate and complement in independent clauses. Overall, it is apparent that the complement is predominantly located after the predicate.

Table 3.4 *Frequencies of Relative Positions of Predicate and Complement in Independent Clauses*

	PC	CP	CPC
Only predicate and complement(s)	476	82	19
With adjunct(s) only	175	41	8
With subject or subject and adjunct(s)	462	96	14
Total	1113	219	41

From the above table, it is clear that the complement is predominantly located after the predicate (476x vs. 82x in clauses with only predicate and complement[s]; 175x vs. 41x in clauses with predicate, complement[s] and adjunct[s]; 462x vs. 96x in other clauses; 1113x vs. 219x in overall figure).

It is common to have two complements in a clause. For non-verbal processes having two complements (usually direct object and indirect object), there is not much difference between the frequencies of having direct object placed before indirect object,[15] and indirect object before direct object.[16]

[2.26; 11.42; 13.16; 24.26], aorist: 2x [1.3; 16.22], perfect: 2x [8.10; 24.46 (both are perfect passive form of γράφω)]) (this figure of distribution of predicates would not be changed too much even though the incidents of verb εἰμί are not counted [3x and are all in CPS: 16.17; 17.1 and 18.25]). In the events of infinitival clause as subject in **SP** clause types, only one is with present predicate (4.43) of the main clause and one with imperfect (15.32).

As is shown above, the predicate of a main clause tends to be present when an infinitival clause functions as the subject in a main clause (this figure is different from the whole figure such as PS and SP clauses [PS (present predicate: 15x; aorist predicate: 25x); SP (present predicate: 31x; aorist predicate: 8x)], where aorist predicate is dominant in PS clauses; the distribution of PS and SP is similar [71x vs. 64x], and **PS** is predominant when the subject is an infinitival clause [21x vs. 2x]).

15. There are 33 instances having direct object placed before indirect object: PCC (4.40; 5.6; 7.15; 9.42; 17.9; 20.9, 16, 25), PCCA (5.29), PCCACAAA (1.69-70), APCC (5.14; 14.14; 24.9), AAPCC (10.35), SPCC (1.12), SAPCC (18.43), ASPCC (11.13), SCPC (23.9), SCCP (2.23 [LXX]), CPC (7.41; 10.11; 16.5; 23.25), CCP (7.45; 19.8), CPCA (11.3), CCAP (7.44), ACCP (11.11), CPCS (20:15), CSPC (7.5; 10.35), CSCP (16.11, 12).

Aorist predicate is dominant in these instances (17 out of 32x) (aorist: 17x [1.69-70; 4.40; 5.14, 29; 7.5, 15, 44, 45; 9.42; 10.35; 14.14; 18.43; 20.9, 25; 23.9, 25; 24.9]; imperfect: 2x [5.36; 7.41]; present: 5x [10.11; 11.3; 16.5; 17.9; 19.8]; future: 8x [1.12; 2.23 (LXX); 10.35; 11.11, 13; 16.11, 12; 20.15, 16]).

16. There are 39 instances having indirect object placed before direct object: PCC (2.10; 11.4,

For verbal processes, definitely it is an unmarked pattern to have the indirect object located before the content of the verbal process,[17] and the predicate is an aorist.[18]

In many instances a predicate is completed with an infinitival clause. This mainly happens in **PC** clause types, and the tendencies of having present and aorist infinitival clauses are similar.[19]

5, 12; 14.9; 15.3, 12; 17.5; 18.15; 20.24; 23.18; 24.10), PCCA (10.19), APCC (4.23; 9.1, 61; 19.13; 20.10; 22.8; 24.40), APCCA (4.5; 7.3), AAPCC (11.8), PCSC (1.32), SCPC (22.12), SPCC (15.12; 21.15; 24.42), ASPCC (9.10; 14.21), CPC (4.6, 6; 6.29; 7.31; 15.29; 20.18), CCP (11.7; 12.41), CPAC (9.36).

Aorist predicate is predominant in these instances (21x aorist predicates compared with only 4x of present predicates) (aorist: 21x [4.5; 7.3; 9.1, 10, 61; 11.4; 14.9, 21; 15.3, 12, 12, 29; 17.5; 19.13; 20.10, 18, 24; 22.8; 23.18; 24.40, 42]; present: 4x [2.10; 4.6; 6.29; 11.5]; imperfect: 2x [18.15; 24.10]; future: 8x [1.32; 4.6; 4.23; 7.31; 11.8, 12; 21.15; 22.12]; perfect: 1x [10.19]).

A large proportion of the predicates in these instances are in imperative form (10 out of 39x are in imperative form; these imperatives are mainly in aorist [8x] and in **PCC** clause type: PCC [11.4; 14.9; 15.12; 17.5; 20.24; 23.18; APCC 9.61; 22.8]; there are only 2x in present imperative form: CCP [11.7] and CPC [6.29]). This is much greater than the number of imperative as predicates in the clause types with direct object located before indirect object (only 4x out of 33x are in imperative form, three in aorist: PCC [20.25], APCC [5.14; 14.14] and one in present: CPCA [11.3]). It may thus indicate here that when an imperative is employed as the predicate in a non-verbal process clause with two complements, it is more likely to have indirect object located before the direct object.

17.   A total of 140 out of 142 instances have the indirect object located before the direct object (or receiver located before the content of a verbal process): PCCC (18.9), PCCAA (14.7), APCC (3.11; 4.25; 4.41; 5.3; 6.10; 7.22; 8.41; 13.2, 25, 32; 14.25-26; 16.2, 5; 17.14, 37; 18.31; 20.3, 23-24; 22.4, 40), APCCC (7.22), PCSC (1.13; 2.10, 48; 4.3, 4, 6; 5.10; 8.9, 30, 37, 38; 9.50, 58, 62; 10.37; 11.37; 12.20; 16.3; 18.19; 19.9; 20.34; 22.11), PCSCC (20.3), PACSC (3.16), APCSC (4.12; 10.41), PSCC (1.18, 30, 34. 6.9; 7.36; 9.57; 11.1, 39; 12.13; 13.23; 14.23; 15.12, 21, 22; 16.8; 17.5; 19.33; 20.42 [LXX]; 22.52), PSCCA (9.33), SPCC (2.15; 3.7, 13; 4.43; 5.14, 33, 34; 7.43; 8.48, 56; 10.26; 12.14; 13.23; 14.16, 18; 15.27, 31; 16.6; 17.7, 37; 18.39, 42; 19.39; 20.8, 8, 25; 22.9, 10, 25, 33, 38, 48; 23.4; 24.19, 25), SCPC (11.9), SAPCC (8.21, 50; 10.29; 11.17; 13.8; 15.29; 23.13-14, 22), ASPCC (1.19, 35; 4.8; 5.31; 7.40; 9.12; 11.27, 45; 14.9, 15, 21; 18.22; 19.5, 8; 24.18), ASAPCC (5.22; 13.14), SCPC (16.9; 70), ACPC (23.3), SACPC (18.11), CPC (5.24; 14.5; 16.7; 19.24; 23.43), CPCC (6.27), ACPC (7.9, 44), and ACPSC (6.3). There are only two instances of verbal process having the direct object placed before the indirect object: PCCA (12.6) and PCCAA (18.1) (besides these two instances, there are two miscellaneous instances: PCCC [6.39 and 21.29], both of these events have direct object firstly appeared before predicate [verbal process], then the direct object (content of the verbal process) reappears after the predicate as the content of the verbal process).

18.   114 out of 142x are in the aorist tense (1.13, 18, 19, 30, 34, 35; 2.10, 48; 3.7, 13, 16; 4.3, 4, 6, 8, 12, 43; 5.3, 10, 14, 22, 31, 33, 34; 6:3, 9, 10; 7.9, 22 [2x], 40, 43, 44; 8.21, 30, 37, 48, 50, 56; 9.12, 33, 50, 57, 58, 62; 10.26, 29, 37, 41; 11.1, 17, 27, 39; 12.13, 14, 20; 13.2, 23, 23, 32; 14.5, 15, 16, 18, 21, 23, 25-26; 15.12, 21, 22, 27, 29, 31; 16.2, 3, 6, 7, 8; 17.5, 14, 37; 18.9, 19, 22, 31, 42; 19.5, 8, 9, 24, 33, 39; 20.3, 8, 23-24, 25, 34, 42 [LXX]; 22.4, 9, 10, 25, 33, 38, 40, 48, 52, 70; 23.3, 4, 13-14, 22; 24.18, 19, 25); where present, imperfect and future predicates are 12x (4.25; 5.24; 6.27; 11.9, 37, 45; 13.8; 16.9; 17.37; 20.8; 22.11; 23.43), 12x (2.15; 3.11; 4.41; 7.36; 8.9, 38, 41; 13.14; 14.7; 16.5; 18.11, 39) and 4x (13.25; 14.9; 17.7; 20.3) respectively.

19.   In **PC** clause types, there is a total of 80x of having an infinitival clause as a complement,

Overall, the number of aorist predicates is much more than the number of present predicates, and imperfect is more than future. This is also true in the case of **PC**,[20] but the situation is different in the case of **CP**, where the number of aorist

37x of which are present infinitival clauses (PC [4.21; 7.15, 24; 11.29; 12.1, 56; 13.26; 15.24; 16.2, 13; 20.9; 11.40; 23.2, 30], PAC [14.9, 18; 21.14], APC [12.56], APCA [6.42; 19.45-46], PCSA [5.21], PCS [6.39; 7.49; 12.45], PSCA [11.35 (2x)], PSCCA [19.37], SPC [6.19; 7.2; 9.12, 44; 14.27, 30, 33; 15.14; 16.13; 22.33], SAAAAPC [7.37-38]; the order of distributions of the predicates according to their frequencies in these **PC** clause types are aorist [21x], present [8x], imperfect [3x], future [3x] and perfect [2x]: aorist [4.21; 5.21; 7.15, 24, 37-38, 49; 9.12; 11.29, 35, 35; 12.1; 14.18, 30; 15.14, 24; 19.37, 45-46; 20.9; 21.14; 22.33; 23.2]; present [6.39, 42; 9.44; 12.45; 14.27, 33; 16.2, 13]; imperfect [6.19; 7.2; 11.40]; future [13.26; 14.9; 23.30]; perfect [12.56, 56 (both of these two instances are the verb οἶδα)]); 42x of which are aorist infinitival clause (PC [3.16; 5.12, 18, 32, 34; 7.25, 26; 9.9, 45; 12.39, 50; 13.24; 13.34; 14.23, 30; 15.16, 28; 19.3, 11, 12; 22:5; 23:8], PCA [1.20 ; 6.48; 8.19; 14.6; 20.26], PAC [7.24; 11.7], PACA [23.8], APC [1.22; 14.20; 22.15], PCS [3.8], PSCA [20.19], SPC [18.26; 19.47], SPCC [10.24 (2x)], SPCA [5.21], SAPC [12.25; 13.18]; the order of distributions of the predicates of these **PC** clause types is aorist [18x], present [12x], imperfect [10x], future [1x] and perfect [1x]: aorist [1.22; 6.48; 7.24, 25, 26; 8.19; 10.24, 24; 12.39; 13.34; 14.6, 23, 30; 19.11, 12; 20.26; 22.5, 15]; present [3.8, 16; 5.12, 21, 34; 11.7; 12.25, 50; 13.24; 14.20; 18.26; 20.19]; imperfect [5.18; 9.9, 45; 13.18; 15.16, 28; 19.3, 47; 23.8, 8]; future [1.20]; perfect [5.32]; this order is not much different from the order of **PC** clause types with present infinitival clause as complement, except the number of imperfect predicate is significantly increased [from 3x to 10x; this is not due to the occurrences of verb εἰμί, since there is only one in the imperfect group (23.8), the only other is in the present group (3.16)]); there is only one instance of having a perfect infinitival clause as complement in **PC** clause types (13.25, which has an aorist subjunctive as predicate).

For **CP** clause types, it is very rare to have an infinitival clause as complement (there are only three occurrences, two are present infinitival clause [16.3, 3], and one is aorist infinitival clause [20.36]; all these three instances are with present predicate).

20.   In the case of all **PC** clause types in independent clauses, the aorist predicate is predominant among all different tense forms: aorist (665x), present (261x), imperfect (140x), future (115x), perfect (17x) and pluperfect (3x) (PC [p: 87x, imf: 35x, f: 33x, a: 140x, pf: 9x, ppf: 2x], PCC [p: 51x, imf: 16x, f: 11x, a: 89x], PCCC [a: 3x], PCA [p: 9x, imf: 17x, f: 7x, a: 46x], PCCA [a: 2x, pf: 1x], PCAC [imf: 1x], PCAA [p: 1x, a: 7x], PCCAA [imf: 2x], PCAAA [a: 2x, pf: 1x], PCAAAA [f: 1x], PCCACAAA [a: 1x], PAC [p: 2x, imf: 1x, f: 5x, a: 12x], PACA [imf: 1x], APC [p: 19x, imf: 10x, f: 13x, a: 37x, pf: 1x, ppf: 1x], APCC [p: 2x, imf: 4x, f: 2x, a: 22x], APCCC [a: 1x], APCA [p: 6x, imf: 1x, a: 15x], APCCA [a: 2x], APCAA [a: 1x], APACA [a: 1x], APACAA [a: 1x], AAPC [p: 1x, imf: 3x, a: 5x], AAPCC [f: 1x, a: 1x], AAPCA [f: 1x, a: 1x], AAAPCAA [a: 1x], PCS [p: 4x, imf: 6x, f: 1x, a: 13x], PCSC [p: 3x, imf: 3x, f: 1x, a: 18x], PCSCC [f: 1x], PCSA [p: 1x, imf: 2x, f: 2x, a: 9x], PCSAA [a: 1x], PACSC [a: 1x], APCS [imf: 2x, f: 1x], APCSC [a: 2x], AAPCSAA [f: 1x], PSC [p: 8x, imf: 3x, f: 6x, a: 32x], PSCC [imf: 1x, a: 18x], PSCA [f: 2x, a: 1x], PSCCA [a: 1x], PSAC [a: 2x], PASC [a: 1x], SPC [p: 47x, imf: 25x, f: 14x, a: 55x, pf: 5x, ppf: 1x], SPCC [p: 1x, imf: 2x, f: 3x, a: 36x], SCPC [p: 1x], SPCA [p: 5x, imf: 4x, f: 3x, a: 8x], SPCAC [f: 1x], SPCAA [a: 1x], SPAC [p: 1x], SAPC [p: 7x, imf: 7x, f: 2x, a: 15x], SAPCC [p: 2x, a: 8x], SAPCA [p: 1x, f: 1x, a: 3x], SAPAC [a: 1x], SAAPC [a: 2x], SAAPCA [a: 1x], SAAAAPC [a: 1x], ASPC [p: 1x, imf: 1x, a: 21x], ASPCC [p: 1x, f: 2x, a: 16x], ASPCA [imf: 2x, a: 4x], ASAPC [a: 2x], ASAPCC [imf: 1x, a: 1x], ASAAPCA [a: 1x]). The order of predicates according to the frequencies of different tense forms (aorist [665x], present [261x], imperfect [140x], future [115x], perfect [17x] and pluperfect [3x]) is parallel to the entire figure of all independent clauses (aorist [1118x], present [590x], imperfect [303x], future [267x], perfect [42x]

predicates is less than the number of present predicates, and future is more than imperfect.[21]

and pluperfect [5x]). This indicates aorist predicate is predominant over other tense forms, both in the **PC** clause types and in the overall picture.

The order is the same when instances of verb εἰμί, οἶδα, γράφω (passive perfect) and direct citations of LXX are not counted: aorist (656x), present (222x), imperfect (130x), future (100x), perfect (6x) and pluperfect (1x), which indicates aorist predicate is predominant over other tense forms in **PC** clause types (PC [p: 80x, imf: 30x, f: 30x, a: 138x, pf: 1x], PCC [p: 51x, imf: 16x, f: 11x, a: 89x], PCCC [a: 3x], PCA [p: 8x, imf: 14x, f: 6x, a: 45x], PCCA [a: 2x, pf: 1x], PCAC [imf: 1x], PCAA [p: 1x, a: 7x], PCCAA [imf: 2x], PCAAA [a: 2x], PCAAAA [f: 1x], PCCACAAAA [a: 1x], PAC [p: 2x, imf: 1x, f: 5x, a: 12x], APC [p: 17, imf: 10x, f: 12x, a: 36x, ppf: 1x], APCC [p: 2x, imf: 4x, f: 2x, a: 22x], APCCC [a: 1x], APCA [p: 6x, imf: 1x, a: 15x], APCCA [a: 2x], APCAA [a: 1x], APAC [a: 1x], APACAA [a: 1x], AAPC [p: 1x, imf: 3x, a: 5x], AAPCC [f: 1x, a: 1x], AAPCA [f: 1x, a: 1x], AAAPCAA [a: 1x], PCS [p: 3x, imf: 5x, a: 13x], PCSC [p: 2x, imf: 3x, f: 1x, a: 18x], PCSCC [f: 1x], PCSA [p: 1x, imf: 2x, f: 1x, a: 9x], PCSAA [a: 1x], PACSC [a: 1x], APCS [imf: 2x, f: 1x], APCSC [a: 2x], AAPCSAA [f: 1x], PSC [p: 8x, imf: 1x, f: 1x, a: 31x], PSCC [imf: 1x, a: 17x], PSCA [f: 2x, a: 1x], PSCCA [a: 1x], PSAC [a: 2x], PASC [a: 1x], SPC [p: 19x, imf: 17x, f: 11x, a: 54x, pf: 4x], SPCC [p: 1x, imf: 2x, f: 3x, a: 36x], SPCA [p: 5x, imf: 4x, f: 3x, a: 8x], SPCAC (f: 1x), SPCAA (imf: 1x, a: 1x), SPAC [p: 1x], SAPC [p: 7x, imf: 7x, f: 2x, a: 15x], SAPCC [p: 2x, a: 8x], SAPCA [p: 3x, f: 1x, a: 1x], SAPAC [a: 1x], SAAPC [a: 2x], SAAPCA [a: 1x], SAAAAPC [a: 1x], ASPC [p: 1x, imf: 1x, a: 21x], ASPCC [p: 1x, f: 2x, a: 16x], ASPCA [imf: 2x, a: 4x], ASAPC [a: 2x], ASAPCC [a: 1x], ASAAPCA [a: 1x]).

21. The order of predicates according to their frequencies is different in the **CP** clause types: present (111x), aorist (55x), future (34x), imperfect (14x) and perfect (2x) (SCP [p: 23x, imf: 4x, f: 1x, a: 9x], SCCP [p: 1x, f: 1x], SCPA [p: 3x, f: 1x, a: 3x], SCAP [p: 1x], SACP [p: 2x, f: 1x, a: 2x], SACPA [imf: 1x], CP [p: 39x, imf: 3x, f: 18x, a: 17x, pf: 1x], CCP [p: 3x, a: 1x], CPA [p: 4x, imf: 2x, f: 3x, a: 7x], CPAA [a: 1x], CAP [f: 1x, a: 1x], CCAP [a: 1x], CAPA [imf: 1x], ACP [p: 8x, imf: 1x, f: 2x, a: 5x], ACCP [f: 1x], ACPA [p: 1x, f: 1x], ACAPA [p :1x], CPS [p: 18x, imf: 2x, f: 2x, a: 4x, pf: 1x], CPSA [a: 1x], CPSAA [p: 1x], ACPSAA [a: 1x], CSP [p: 7x, f: 2x, a: 1x], CSPA [a: 1x]).

The order of predicates according to their frequencies is similar when instances of the verbs εἰμί, οἶδα, γράφω (passive perfect) and direct citations of LXX are not counted: present (56x), aorist (54x), future (28x), imperfect (6x) and perfect (2x) (SCP [p: 15x, imf: 1x, a: 9x], SCCP [p: 1x], SCPA [f: 1x, a: 3x], SACP [a: 2x], SACPA [imf: 1x], SACCPC [imf: 1x], CP [p: 22x, imf: 1x, f: 15x, a: 16x, pf: 1x], CCP [p: 3x, a: 1x], CPA [p: 3x, f: 3x, a: 7x], CPAA [a: 1x], CAP [f: 1x, a: 1x], CCAP [a: 1x], CAPA [imf: 1x], ACP [p: 7x, f: 2x, a: 5x], ACCP [f: 1x], ACPA [p: 1x], ACAPA [p: 1x], CPS [p: 1x, imf: 1x, f: 2x, a: 4x, pf: 1x], CPSA [a: 1x], CPSAA [p: 1x], ACPSAA [a: 1x], CSP [p: 1x, f: 1x, a: 1x], CSPA [a: 1x], CSCP [f: 2x]). This indicates the situation of **CP** clause types is different from the one of **PC** clause types. In **PC** clause types, aorist predicate is predominant, which is then followed by the order of present, imperfect, future and perfect; while in **CP** clause types, the percentage of present predicate is much increased and thus both the present and aorist predicates are predominant, and the percentage of future predicates being employed is also significantly increased. (Cf. the situation of **CPC** clause types; it is similar to the one in **CP** types. The order of predicates according to their frequencies is aorist [17x], present [15x], future [5x], imperfect [2x] and perfect [1x]: SCPC [p: 3x, f: 1x, a: 4x], SACPC [a: 1x], SACCPC [imf: 1x], CPC [p: 8x, imf: 1x, f: 2x, a: 6x, pf: 1x], CPCC [p: 1x], CPCA [p: 1x], CPAC [f: 1x, a: 1x], ACPC [p: 2x, a: 2x], ACPAC [a: 1x], ACPSC [a: 1x], CSPC [f: 1x, a: 1x]; the order of predicates according to their frequencies is similar when instances of verb εἰμί, οἶδα, γράφω (passive perfect) and direct citations of LXX are not counted: aorist [17x], present [12x], future [6x], imperfect [1x]: SCPC [p: 1x, f: 1x, a: 4x], SACPC [a: 1x], SACCPC [imf: 1x], CPC [p: 8x, f: 2x, a: 6x], CPCA [p: 1x], CPAC [f: 1x, a: 1], ACPC [p: 2x, a: 2x], ACPAC [a: 1x], CPCS [f: 1x], ACPSC [a: 1x], CSPC [f: 1x, a: 1x])

It is concluded that it is an unmarked order to have an aorist predicate located before its complement in an independent clause (unmarked: P[aor.] + C). In a verbal process, it is an unmarked order to have an aorist predicate located before two complements, where the indirect object located before the content of the verbal process (unmarked: P[aor.][verbal] + C[indirect object] + C[content]).

Relative Positions of Subject and Complement
In the relative positions of subject and complement(s), it is an unmarked order to have subject located before the complement (502x vs. 108x) (unmarked: S + C). This can be shown in the following table:

Table 3.5 *Frequencies of Relative Positions of Subject and Complement in Independent Clauses*

	SC	CS	CSC
Only subject and complement(s)	42	27	0
With adjunct(s) only	6	2	0
With predicate or predicate and adjunct(s)	454	79	33
Total	502	108	33

Dependent Clauses
Relative Positions of Subject and Predicate
The preference of relative positions of subject and predicate in dependent clauses is slightly different from the one in independent clauses. For the dependent clauses which are only composed with predicate and subject, or with adjunct(s), the predicate tends to precede the subject (51x vs. 26x and 43x vs. 26x respectively) (tendency: P + S [on the contrary, subject tends to precede the predicate in independent clauses]). The situation slightly changes in the clauses which consist of complement(s) (53x vs. 63x).

Table 3.6 *Frequencies of Relative Positions of Predicate and Subject in Dependent Clauses*

	PS	SP
Only predicate and subject	51	26
With adjunct(s) only	43	26
With complement(s) or complement(s) and adjunct(s)	53	63
Total	147	115

Genitive absolutes are commonly used in dependent clauses. They more likely occur in PS order, rather in SP order, and more likely appear in the present tense, rather than in the aorist (tendency [genitive absolute]: P[pres.] + S).[22]

22. 35 out of 51x of genitive absolutes in dependent clauses are in PS order. 24 of the PS orders are in present predicate: PS (2.2; 3.1, 1, 15; 4.40; 8.4, 23, 45; 9.42; 13.17; 19.36; 20.45; 22.60), PSA (7.42; 9.57; 17.12; 24.41), PSAA (19.37), APSAA (22.53), PSC (19.11, 33; 21.28), PSCA (20.1), PSAAC (3.15); and 11x are in aorist predicate: PS (4.2, 42; 7.24; 12.1; 18.40), PSA (9.37; 22.10), APS (11.53), PCS (15.14), PSC (14.29), CPS (24.5).

Another grammatical structure that commonly occurs in dependent clauses is the articular infinitive. Articular infinitives in a form of ἐν τῷ plus an infinitive are commonly used in dependent clauses to express temporal meaning. They all occur in **PS** order, and are dominant with the present predicate (unmarked: ἐν τῷ + **P** [pres. inf.] + **S**).[23]

Relative Positions of Predicate and Complement

The preference of relative positions of predicate and complement in dependent clauses is the same as the situation in independent clauses, predicate is predominantly located before the complement.

Table 3.7 *Frequencies of Relative Positions of Predicate and Complement in Dependent Clauses*

	PC	CP	CPC
Only predicate and complement(s)	95	40	4
With adjunct(s) only	36	13	1
With subject or subject and adjunct(s)	67	27	3
Total	198	80	8

In the dependent clauses with complement located after the predicate, the predicate tends to be aorist; while in the case of the dependent clauses having complement located before the predicate, the tendency of having a present predicate increases.[24]

---

16 out of the 51x of genitive absolutes are in **SP** order. 12 of the **SP** orders are in present predicate: SP (3.1, 1; 8.49; 11.29; 22.47), SPA (9.43), SAP (14.32; 15.20), SAPA (7.6; 8.4), SPAC (21.5), CSP (9.34; 24.36); and 4 of the **SP** orders are in aorist predicate: SP (3.21; 6.48; 11.14; 23.45).

This indicates the genitive absolutes tend to have **PS** orders rather than **SP** orders (35x vs. 16x), and in both cases the predicate tends to be in the present (**PS**: 24x vs. 11x; **SP**: 12x vs. 4x; this gives a total of 36x vs. 15x).

Genitive absolutes in dependent clauses tend to appear in two elements only (subject and predicate) (27x), rather than with other elements (with adjunct only: 14x; with others such as complement: 11x). This figure is different from the one on the whole, where the three categories are quite evenly distributed in all **PS** dependent clause types (51x vs. 43x vs. 53x), and the third category in all **SP** dependent clause types is predominant (26x vs. 26x vs. 63x).

23.   All these instances are in **PS** order (22x out of 22x). A majority of them (17x out of 22x) are in present predicate: PS (8.40, 42; 9.29, 51; 10.35, 38; 17.14; 24.15), PSA (9.18, 33; 18.35; 24.4), PSAA (1.8-9; 11.1), PAS (1.21), PSC (11.27; 24.51); 5 are in aorist predicate: PS (9.36), PSA (9.34; 19.15; 24.30), PSAA (14.1).

This type of articular infinitive more likely occurs with subject and predicate only (9x), or in subject, predicate and adjunct (11x), but seldom with a complement (2x). Again it is different from the figure of all the **PS** dependent clause types, where more than a third of them come with the complement (53 out of 147x).

24.   Dependent clauses which have complement located after the predicate tend to have aorist predicate (107 out of 181x) (PC [p: 22x; imf: 2x; a: 51x], PCC [p: 1x; imf: 1x; a: 8x], PCA [p: 7x; imf: 1x; a: 13x], PCAA [a: 2x], PAC [a: 3x], APC [p: 2x; a: 5x], PCS [p: 2x; a: 4x], PCCS [a: 1x], PCSA [imf: 1x], PCASA [a: 1x], PSC [p: 9x; imf: 2x; a: 4x], PSCC [a: 2x], PSCA [p: 1x; a: 1x], PSAC [a: 1x], PSAAC [p: 1x], APSC [p: 1x], SPC [p: 12x; a: 7x], SPCA [p: 2x; a: 2x], SPCAA

There are instances of an infinitival clause functioning as a complement, and all these complements are located after the predicate.[25]

Aorist subjunctives are frequently used as predicates in the dependent clauses which do not contain a subject (both in the clauses with predicate preceding the complement and located after the complement).[26]

[p: 1x], SPAC [p: 1x], SAPC [p: 4x; a: 1x], ASPC [p: 1x], ASPAC [a: 1x]; this gives a figure of present: 67x, imperfect: 7x and aorist: 107x [cf. the entire figure of all dependent clauses: 218 x present and 273 x aorist]).

The picture in the dependent clauses which have complement located before the predicate is a little different, where the tendency of these instances to have present predicate increases (50 out of 85x) (SCP [p: 11x; imf: 2x], SCPA [p: 1x; a: 1x], SCPAA [p: 1x], SCAP [p: 1x; a: 1x], CP [p: 19x; imf: 1x; a: 17x], CPA [a: 3x], CAP [a: 2x], ACP [p: 2x; a: 4x], ACAP [a: 1x], CPS [p: 7x; a: 2x], CAPS [a: 1x], CSP [p: 7x], CSPA [p: 1x]; this gives a figure of present: 50x, imperfect: 3x and aorist: 32x) (cf. the figure of **CPC** clause types in dependent clauses: SCPC [p: 1x], CPC [p: 2x; a: 2x], ACPC [a: 1x]; which gives a total of 3x present and 3x aorist predicate).

The number of present predicate is decreased when the occurrences of the verb εἰμί and LXX citations are not counted (For predicate preceding the complement: PC [p: 20x; imf: 2x; a: 49x], PCC [imf: 1x; a: 7x], PCA [p: 7x; imf: 1x; a: 12x], PCAA [a: 2x], PAC [a: 2x], APC [p: 2x; a: 5x], PCS [p: 2x; a: 4x], PCSC [a: 1x], PCCS [a: 1x], PCASA [a: 1x], PSC [p: 6x; imf: 1x; a: 4x], PSCC [a: 2x], PSCA [p: 1x; a: 1x], PSAC [a: 1x], PSAAC [p: 1x], APSC [p: 1x], SPC [p: 4x; a: 7x], SPCA [p: 2x; a: 2x], SPCAA [p: 1x], SPAC [p: 1x], SAPC [p: 4x; a: 1x], ASPC [p: 1x], ASPAC [a: 1x]; this gives a picture of present: 53x, imperfect: 5x and aorist: 105x, and it shows aorist predicate is dominant in dependent clauses with predicate preceding the complement. For dependent clauses with complement following the predicate: SCP [p: 2x], SCPA [a: 1x], SCPAA [p: 1x], SCAP [a: 1x], CP [p: 11x; a: 17x], CPA [a: 3x], CAP [a: 2x], ACP [p: 2x; a: 4x], ACAP [a: 1x], CPS [p: 3x; a: 2x], CAPS [a: 1x], CSP [p: 4x]; this gives a picture of present: 23x and aorist: 32x). Although the number of present predicates is decreased when the occurrences of the verb εἰμί, and LXX citations are not counted, it still shows that the tendency of having a present predicate increases when the complement precedes the predicate in dependent clauses.

25. A total of 20 instances having an infinitival clause functioning as complement in dependent clauses, they are all located after the predicate. The tense of the predicates of these dependent clauses are mainly present and aorist (present [10x]: PC [1.62; 6.7; 12.5; 19.4], PSC [10.1; 21.7, 21.28], SPC [9.23; 10.40; 14.29-30]; aorist [9x]: PC [14.14, 29; 17.22], PCC [21.36], PAC [11.31], PSC [12.32], SPC [1.1; 13.24, 31]; perfect [1x]: PC [22.34 (οἶδα)]) (number of subjunctive mood employed as predicate is frequent [6x: 6.7; 12.45; 14.29-30; 21.7, 36; 22.34], all are in aorist subjunctive except 21.7 is in present subjunctive). These infinitival clauses functioning as complement tend to have aorist predicate (present [7x: 1.62; 9.23; 13.31; 14.14, 29; 21.7, 28]; imperfect [2x: 10.1; 19.4]; future [1x: 17.22]; aorist [13x: 1.1; 6.7; 10.40; 11.31; 12.32, 45 (4x); 14.29-30; 21.36 (2x)]).

26. In the clauses with predicate preceding the complement (not containing a subject), a large number of predicates are in subjunctive form (52 out of 131x are in subjunctive form: 39.7%), and they are mainly in the aorist (42 out of 52x) (present [9x]: PC [6.33; 10.8, 10; 14.12; 16.28], PCA [12.11, 58], APC [7.3; 22.2]; aorist [42x]: PC [1.4, 26; 4.3; 6.7, 22, 34, 42; 9.12, 40, 45, 54; 12.45, 54; 13.8, 25, 35; 15.4; 16.24; 17.2, 10; 19.4, 15; 20.5, 6, 20; 21.9, 20, 31; 22.34], PCC [8.31, 32; 20.43 (LXX); 21.36], PCA [13.9; 16.4, 9, 24, 27], PCAA [6.22], PAC [4.11 (LXX)], APC [18:5]; perfect [1x]: PC [5.24 (οἶδα)]). For clauses with predicate located after the complement (not containing a subject), subjunctives are also frequently employed as predicates in these clauses (19 out of 53x: 35.9%), and they are also mainly in aorist (17 out of 19x) (present [2x]: CP [14.13; 18.15]; aorist [17x]: CP [10.40; 12.5, 11, 11, 22, 22, 29, 29, 59; 17.8; 19.48;

Ditransitive verbs occur in dependent clauses, and the relative positions of these direct objects and indirect objects are quite evenly distributed.[27] There are several incidents of verbal process in dependent clauses, and all have indirect object (receiver) placed before direct object (content of the verbal process).[28]

It is concluded that it is an unmarked order that the predicate precedes its complement in dependent clauses (unmarked: P + C).

Relative Positions of Subject and Complement
As in independent clauses, the dominant tendency is to have the subject located before the complement in dependent clauses (unmarked: S + C).

Table 3.8 *Frequencies of Relative Positions of Subject and Complement in Dependent Clauses*

	SC	CS	CSC
Only subject and complement(s)	1	1	0
With adjunct(s) only	3	0	0
With predicate or predicate and adjunct(s)	78	19	2
Total	82	20	2

22.67], CPA [10.2], CAP [18.41], ACP [9.58], ACPC [22.4], ACAP [22.11]) (The situation is similar in the dependent clauses which only consist of predicate [or with adjunct], where subjunctive is frequently employed as predicate [46 out of 114x: 40.4%], and is mainly in aorist [36 out of 46x] [present (10x): P (5.12; 11.2; 13.3, 5), PAA (22.30), AP (8.10, 10; 9.57; 10.8), AAP (16.26); aorist (36x): P (6.22, 34; 12.50; 14.10; 15.8; 16.9; 17.3, 8, 8; 18.39, 41; 21.8, 30; 22.8, 68), PA (9.26; 11.37; 13.8; 16.4; 22.16, 46; 23.42; 24.49), PAA (14.8), AP (7.6; 8.12; 9.4, 12; 10.5, 10; 12.38; 15.29; 22.9), APA (12.36; 17.4), APAA (17.4)]]).

The situation is different in the clauses consisting of a subject. When the subject is present, the percentage of using a subjunctive as predicate is much smaller (39 out of 256x: 15.2%), these subjunctive predicates are also mainly in aorist (30 out of 39x) (present [9x]: APS [10.6], PSC [21.7], SP [16.26], SPC [8.16; 9.5], SCP [11.33, 34, 34; 20.28 (LXX)]; aorist [30x]: PS [2.35; 13.25; 14.10, 23; 17.3; 21.24; 22.32], PSA [1.43; 11.50; 21.34], PAS [5.35; 21.34], PSC [14.12], PSAC [12.45], CPS [6.26], SP [14.34; 21.32; 22.18], SPA [4.7; 11.24; 16.28, 30; 20.28 (LXX)], SAP [16.31], SPC [14.12; 15], SPCA [12.8; 14.29-30], SAPC [11.22], ASPAC [9.13]) (several occurrences of the present subjunctives here are the verb εἰμί: 10.6; 11.34, 34; 20.28).

27. 6 out of 14 incidents are events having the direct object located before the indirect object (PCC [1.68; 10.21], PSCC [1.58], SCPC [12.58], CPC [6.11], CPC [11.13]), and the rest (8x) are events having the direct object located after indirect object (PCC [24.32], PCSC [22.29], PCCS [1.49], PSCC [11.30], CPC [8.56; 9.21], ACPC [22.4], CPSC [11.11]). For the tense of the predicate, the aorist is preferred among all these occurrences (present [2x: 9.21; 11.13]; imperfect [1x: 24.32]; future [2x: 11.11; 12.58]; aorist [9x: 1.49, 58, 68; 6.11; 8.56; 10.21; 11.30; 22.4, 29]).

28. There are five occurrences of verbal process: PCC (8.31, 32; 14.10; 22.61) and SCPC (19.31), and they all have receiver located before the content of the verbal process.

Infinitival Clauses

Relative Positions of Subject and Predicate

The frequencies of **PS** and **SP** clause types in infinitival clauses are evenly distributed,[29] and both of these two clause types tend to have an aorist predicate (tendency: **P** [aor.] + **S**; **S** + **P** [aor.]).[30]

Table 3.9 *Frequencies of Relative Positions of Predicate and Subject in Infinitival Clauses*

	PS	SP
Only subject and predicate	10	8
With adjunct(s) only	6	10
With complement(s) or complement(s) and adjunct(s)	6	5
Total	22	23

Relative Positions of Predicate and Complement

In infinitival clauses, the predicate tends to precede its complement (unmarked: **P** [aor.] + **C**). It is infrequent to have a subject in the **PC** and **CP** infinitival clause types (only 5 out of 113x of **PC** have a subject, and 5 out of 51x of **CP** have a subject; a majority of **PC** and **CP** only consist of predicate and complement[s] [86 out of 113x and 38 out of 51x respectively]). This is very different from the situation of independent clauses.

Table 3.10 *Frequencies of Relative Positions of Predicate and Complement in Infinitival Clauses*

	PC	CP	CPC
Only predicate and complement(s)	86	38	2
With adjunct(s) only	22	8	0
With subject or subject and adjunct(s)	5	5	1
Total	113	51	3

Both **PC** and **CP** infinitival clause types tend to have an aorist predicate.[31] In

---

29. This order of Lukan clauses is contrary to C.W. Votaw's comment on the usual position of the subjects in biblical infinitival clauses: 'The position of the subject in the clause regularly is immediately before, or less frequently after, the infinitive' (*The Use of the Infinitive in Biblical Greek* [Chicago: Published by the Author, 1896], p. 58).

30. Both clause types favor an aorist predicate (a total of 6x present, 17x aorist and 1x perfect) (for **PS** clause types: PS [p: 4x; a: 6x], PSA [a: 1x], PSAA [a: 1x], PAS [p: 1x], PASAA [a: 1x], APS [p: 1x; a: 1x], PCCS [p: 1x], PSC [p: 1x], PSAC [a: 1x], CPS [p: 1x; a: 1x], CPSC [a: 1x], this gives 9x present and 13x aorist; for **SP** clause types: SP [a: 8x], SPA [a: 3x], SPAS [a: 1x], SPAA [p: 1x], SAP [p: 2x; a: 2x], ASP [p: 1x], AASP [a: 1x], SPC [p: 2x], SCP [a: 1x; pf: 1x], SCCP [a: 1x], this gives a picture of 6x present, 17x aorist and 1x perfect).

31. There is a tendency to have an aorist predicate in **PC** infinitival clause types (72 out of 116x: PC [p: 27x; a: 45x], PCC [p: 7x; a: 7x], PCA [p: 2x; a: 9x], PCCA [a: 2x], PCAC [p: 2x; a: 1x], PCAAA [p: 1x], PAC [a: 3x], APC [a: 3x], APCC [a: 1x], APCAAA [p: 1x], PCCS [p: 1x], PSC [p: 1x], PSAC [a: 1x], SPC [p: 2x]; this gives a picture of 44x present and 72x aorist).

processes with ditransitive verbs as predicate, it is more likely to have the indirect object preceding direct object with an aorist predicate.[32] For verbal processes, it is normal to have the receiver (indirect object) placed before the content of the verbal process, and the predicate tends to be present (unmarked: **P** [pres.][verbal] + **C** [indirect object] + **C** [content]).[33]

Relative Positions of Subject and Complement

It is more likely to have subject preceding the complement in infinitival clauses.

Table 3.11 *Frequencies of Relative Positions of Subject and Complement in Infinitival Clauses*

	SC	CS	CSC
Only subject and complement(s)	0	0	0
With adjunct(s) only	0	0	0
With predicate or predicate and adjunct(s)	7	3	1
Total	7	3	1

There is also a tendency to have an aorist predicate in **CP** infinitival clause types (34 out of 49x: SCP [a: 1x], SCCP [a: 1x], CP [p: 12x; a: 24x], CCP [p: 1x; a: 1x], CPA [p: 1x; a: 4x], CPAA [a: 1x], ACP [a: 1x], CPS [p: 1x; a: 1x]; this gives a picture of 15x present and 34x aorist). Both **PC** and **CP** infinitival clause types tend to have an aorist predicate (there are only three incidents of **CPC** infinitival clause types: CPC [p: 1x], CPCC [p: 1x], CPSC [a: 1x]).

The figure is similar when instances of the verb εἰμί are excluded: 68 out of 106x are in aorist in **PC** infinitival clause types (PC [p: 23x; a: 43x], PCC [p: 6x; a: 7x], PCA [p: 2x; a: 7x], PCCA [a: 2x], PCAC [p: 2x; a: 1x], PCAAA [p: 1x], PAC [a: 3x], APC [a: 3x], APCC [a: 1x], APCAAA [p: 1x], PCCS [p: 1x], PSC [p: 1x], PSAC [a: 1x], SPC [p: 1x]; this gives 38x present and 68x aorist) and 34 out of 48x are in aorist in **CP** infinitival clause types (SCP [a: 1x], SCCP [a: 1x], CP [p: 12x; a: 24x], CCP [p: 1x; a: 1x], CPA [p: 1x; a: 4x], CPAA [a: 1x], ACP [a: 1x], CPS [a: 1x]; this gives a picture of 14x present and 34x aorist).

32. 10 out of 16 instances have the indirect object preceding the direct object in processes with ditransitive verbs (PCC [1.17, 19, 73-74; 12.32; 20.40], PCCS [18.5], SCCP [20.22], CPCC [20.9], CCP [22.5], CPSC [4.43]; with 3x present [18.5; 20.9, 40] and 7x aorist [1.17, 19, 73-74; 12.32; 20.22; 22.5]). 6 instances have indirect object following direct object (PCC [17.18], PCCA [1.54-55, 77], PCAC [22.6], APCC [3.8], CCP [23.2]; with 1x present [23.2] and 5x aorist [1.54-55, 77; 3.8; 17.18; 22.6]) (with a total of 12 out of 16 incidents have an aorist predicate).

33. All verbal processes have their receiver preceded the content of the verbal process (8x) (PCC [3.8; 4.21; 6.42; 7.49; 14.17; 22.23; 23.30 (LXX)], PCAC [12.1]), and the majority of the predicates are in present (7 out of 8x are in present: 3.8; 4.21; 6.42; 7.49; 12.1; 22.23; 23.30; only one is in aorist: 14.17).

Participial Clauses
Relative Positions of Predicate and Complement

Table 3.12 *Frequencies of Relative Positions of Predicate and Complement in Participial Clauses*

	PC	CP	CPC
Only predicate and complement(s)	325	39	1
With adjunct(s) only	43	4	0
With subject or subject and adjunct(s)	0	0	0
Total	368	43	1

Participial clauses are mainly composed of predicate and complement only,[34] they do not frequently come with adjuncts. The predicate is predominantly located before the complement as other clause types do (368x vs. 43x), and the predicate tends to be present (unmarked: P [pres.] + C).[35] In verbal processes, it is also a norm to have the receiver preceding the content of the verbal process (unmarked: P [pres.][verbal] + C [indirect object] + C [content]).[36] There are certain instances of participial clauses having an infinitival clause functioning as a complement, and these participial clauses tend to have a present predicate.[37]

34. Participial clauses rarely come with a subject, there are only three such instances (PS [20.17], PSAA [23.7], PAS [2.24]).

35. In the **PC** participial clause types, the dominant pattern is to have the present predicate (233x present and 121x aorist: PC [p: 203x; a: 101x], PCC [p: 8x; a: 2x], PCA [p:13x; a: 12x], PCAA [p: 1x; a: 1x], PAC [p: 3x; a: 3x], APC [p: 4x; a: 2x], APCA [p: 1x]); there is also a tendency to have the present predicate in **CP** participial clause types (25x present and 18x aorist: CP [p: 21x; a: 18x], CPA [p: 2x], CAP [p: 1x], ACP [p: 1x]) (there is only one occurrence of **CPC** participial clause type, which is also in present predicate: CPC [23.36]). (This present predicate oriented feature mainly occurs in the clauses composed of predicate and complement, e.g. PC [203x present and 101x aorist]; the situation is different in the clauses composed of predicate only, e.g. P [89x present and 151x aorist]. On the whole figure of all participial clauses, present predicate is still dominant [433x present and 372x aorist])

The figure is similar when the occurrences of the verb εἰμί are excluded. The present predicate is dominant in both **PC** and **CP** participial clause types (229x present and 122x aorist in **PC** clause types: PC [p: 199x; a: 101x], PCC [p: 8x; a: 2x], PCA [p: 13x; a: 12x], PCAA [p: 1x; a: 1x], PAC [p: 3x; a: 3x], APC [p: 4; a: 2x], APCA [p: 1x]; and 24x present and 18x aorist in **CP** participial clause types: CP [p: 20x; a: 18x], CPA [p: 2x], CAP [p: 1x], ACP [p: 1x]).

36. This type of process is strictly in PCC order with a present predicate (8 out of 8x: PCC [7.3, 6; 8.25; 13.31; 14.7; 15.6; 19.46; 20.2]) (there are only three incidents of processes with a ditransitive verb as predicate; two with the direct object located before the indirect object [PCC: 10.37 and CPC: 23.36] and one with the direct object located after the indirect object [PCC: 20.20]).

37. They are almost strictly in PC order (12 times; only one in CP order [8.20]); 12 out of these 13 participial clauses have present predicate (3.7; 8.20; 13.11; 14.28, 31; 16.21; 20.35, 46; 21.36; 22.23; 23.2, 20; 24.21), only one is in aorist (20.35). The complements are 5x in present infinitival clause (20.46; 21.36; 22.23; 23.2; 24.21) and 8x in aorist infinitival clause (3.7; 8.20; 13.11; 14.28, 31; 16.21; 20.35; 23.20).

Embedded Clauses

Relative Positions of Subject and Predicate

In embedded clauses, the subject is dominantly located before the predicate (unmarked: **S + P**).[38]

Table 3.13 *Frequencies of Relative Positions of Predicate and Subject in Embedded Clauses*

	PS	SP
Only predicate and subject	0	12
With adjunct(s) only	10	24
With complement(s) or complement(s) and adjunct(s)	13	52
Total	23	88

Relative Positions of Predicate and Complement

Table 3.14 *Frequencies of Relative Positions of Predicate and Complement in Embedded Clauses*

	PC	CP	CPC
Only predicate and complement(s)	5	34	5
With adjunct(s) only	4	5	1
With subject or subject and adjunct(s)	44	19	2
Total	53	58	8

A large number of complements preceding the predicate in **CP** clause types is because many of these complements are relative pronouns in embedded clauses.[39]

The number of present and aorist predicates is evenly distributed in embedded **PC** clause types; while the predicate tends to be an aorist in **CP** clause types.[40]

---

38.   A total of 88x vs. 23x. This is mainly due to the instances where the subject is in the form of a relative pronoun, since a relative pronoun predominantly favors the initial position in an embedded clause (70 out of the total 88x **PS** clauses are under this reason: 1.20; 2.4, 10, 11, 37; 4.40; 5.10, 17, 18, 21, 29; 6.2, 16, 18, 48; 7.1, 2, 32, 38, 39, 49; 8.2, 3, 13, 13, 15, 17, 17, 18, 18, 27 [LXX], 43; 9.24, 24, 26, 27, 30, 31, 48, 48, 50; 10.30, 42; 12.1, 2, 2, 33; 13.30, 30; 14.15, 27, 33; 15.7; 16.1; 17.12, 31, 33, 33; 18.17, 29, 30; 20.47; 21.6; 23.19, 29, 29, 51, 55; 24.19, 23).

39.   51 out of 58x **CP** embedded clause types are such cases (2.20, 31; 3.19; 4.6, 23; 5.9; 6.13, 14, 46; 7.22, 47; 8.39; 9.10, 36, 43; 10.23, 24, 24, 35; 11.27; 12.3, 3, 20, 24, 37, 42, 43, 48; 48; 13.16; 14.22; 15.9, 16; 18.12, 22; 19.20, 21, 21, 22, 22, 26, 37; 20.17 [LXX]; 21.4, 6; 23.14, 25, 41; 24.1, 17, 25); all **CPC** embedded clause types are such cases (8 out of 8x: 1.73; 2.15, 50; 7.4; 8.39; 11.6; 19.15; 24.44).

40.   The number of present and aorist predicates in embedded **PC** clause types are similar (17x present, 14x imperfect, 7x future and 14x aorist: PC [p: 2x; imf: 2x; a:1x], PCA [a: 1x], APC [p: 2x], AAPC [f: 1x], PCS [f: 1x], PSC [p: 1x], SPC [p: 11x; imf: 6x; f: 3x; a: 6x], SPCA [p: 1x; imf: 4x; f: 2x; a: 5x], SPAC [imf: 2x], SAPC [a: 1x]).

The embedded **CP** clause type favors an aorist predicate (16x present, 5x imperfect, 4x future, 32x aorist and 1x perfect: SCP [p: 2x; f: 1x; a: 1x], CP [p: 9x; imf: 4x; a: 18x; pf: 1x], CCP [a: 2x], CPA [p: 1x; a: 1x], CCPA [a: 1x], CPAA [p: 1x], CAP [a: 1x], CPS [p: 1x; imf: 1x; a: 5x], CCPS [a: 1x], CPSA [a: 1x], CPSAA [f: 1x], CSP [p: 2x], CSPA [a: 1x], CASP [f: 2x]) (cf. the figure

Dependent Clauses of Embedded Clauses
Relative Positions of Subject and Predicate
PS and SP clause types are evenly distributed.

Table 3.15 *Frequencies of Relative Positions of Subject and Predicate in Dependent Clauses of Embedded Clauses*

	PS	SP
Only predicate and subject	3	2
With adjunct(s) only	2	2
With complement(s) or complement(s) and adjunct(s)	2	4
Total	7	8

Relative Positions of Predicate and Complement
PC and CP clause types are evenly distributed.

Table 3.16 *Frequencies of Relative Positions of Predicate and Complement in Dependent Clauses of Embedded Clauses*

	PC	CP
Only predicate and complement	3	2
With adjunct(s) only	1	1
With subject or subject and adjunct(s)	3	3
Total	7	6

Conclusion
This chapter provides a framework of the distributions of the relative orders of the three main constituents of Lukan clauses in association with the classifications of the correlated predicates' different tense forms. This framework represents some unmarked relative orders between these three elements with numeric data, and illustrates some usual syntactic and grammatical features associated with these unmarked orders. Some typical unmarked word order patterns can be concluded here:

in CPC clause type [2x future, 5x aorist and 1x pluperfect: CPC (f: 2x; a: 2x; ppf: 1x), CPCAC (a: 1x), CPCS (a: 1x), CSPC (a: 1x)]).

The figure is similar when occurrences of the verb εἰμί and LXX citations are excluded. Embedded PC clause types are similar in number of present and aorist predicates (14x present, 8x imperfect, 3x future and 14x aorist: PC [p: 1x; imf: 2x; a: 1x], PCA [a: 1x], APC [p: 2x], PSC [p: 1x], SPC [p: 9x; imf: 3x; f: 2x; a: 6x], SPCA [imf: 3x; f: 1x; a: 5x], SAPC [p: 1x; a: 1x]).

Aorist predicate is dominant in embedded CP clause types (15x present, 5x imperfect, 3x future, 31x aorist and 1x perfect: SCP [p: 2x; f: 1x; a: 1x], CP [p: 9x; imf: 4x; a: 18x; pf: 1x], CCP [a: 2x], CPA [p: 1x; a: 1x], CCPA [a: 1x], CPAA [p: 1x], CAP [a: 1x], CPS [imf: 1x; a: 4x], CCPS [a: 1x], CPSA [a: 1x], CSP [p: 2x], CSPA [a: 1x], CASP [f: 2x]) (cf. the CPC clause types [2x future, 5x aorist and 1x pluperfect: CPC (f: 2x; a: 2x; ppf: 1x), CPCAC (a: 1x), CPCS (a: 1x), CSPC (a: 1x)]).

(i) **P** (pres.) + **S** (aor. inf. clause)

This is particularly applied in independent clauses. When the subject is an infinitival clause in an independent clause, it is an unmarked order to have the subject (an aorist infinitival clause) located after its predicate (in present).

(ii) **P + C**

It is an unmarked order to have the complement located after its predicate. This is almost true in all categories of clauses (except in embedded clauses, this is due to the usual pattern of locating a relative pronoun at the front of an embedded clause). Independent clauses predominantly have an aorist predicate (**P** [aor.] + **C**); while participial clauses predominantly have a present predicate (**P** [pres.] + **C**).

(iii) **P** (verbal) + **C** (indirect object) + **C** (content)

For verbal processes, it is an unmarked order to have the predicate followed by the indirect object, and then the indirect object followed by the content of the verbal process. This is true in many categories of clauses. Independent clauses predominantly have an aorist predicate (**P** [aor.] + **C** [indirect object] + **C** [content]); while infinitival clauses and participial clauses predominantly have a present predicate (**P** [pres.] + **C** [indirect object] + **C** [content]).

(iv) **S + C**

It is an unmarked order to have the subject located before the complement. This is true in almost all categories of clauses (except in participial clauses, since they rarely come with subject).

(v) ἐν τῷ + **P** (pres. inf.) + **S**

This is only true in dependent clauses. When an infinitive is employed with the phrase ἐν τῷ to express a temporal meaning, it is an unmarked order to have its subject located after it, and the infinitive is in present.

Besides the typically occurring patterns summarized above, there are a number of patterns indicating that they have tendencies to have such patterns. This can be concluded as follows:

(i) tendency: **S + P**

This is only true in independent clauses. Subject tends to precede the predicate.

(ii) tendency (genitive absolute): **P** (pres.) + **S**

This is only true in dependent clauses. When a genitive absolute is employed to function as a dependent clause, the predicate tends to be in present and precedes its subject.

(iii) tendency: **P** (aor.) + **S**; **S + P** (aor.)

This is only true in infinitival clauses. When the predicate comes with its subject in an infinitival clause, the predicate tends to be in aorist.

This chapter provides some typical order patterns, and some order patterns indicating their tendencies of having such order patterns. This provides the bases for studying the marked order patterns in Part III of the work.[41]

---

41. This is particularly helpful in the studies in Chapter 5 and 6, where marked orders such as CP, CCP and CPS are discussed. These order patterns can be classified as 'marked' based on the result of this chapter: subject typically precedes the complement; predicate also typically precedes the complement.

Chapter 4

THE POSITIONS OF CIRCUMSTANTIAL ADJUNCTS IN LUKAN CLAUSES

This chapter studies the relative positions of different kinds of circumstantial adjuncts with respect to their associated predicates in different tense forms. The study is carried out according to the different clause groups in the Gospel: independent clauses, dependent clauses, infinitival clauses, participial clauses, embedded clauses and embedded dependent clauses. The result of the study gives a figure of frequencies of these relative positions, and the result indicates certain word order patterns in two aspects: (i) typical occurrence (unmarked order), and (ii) some order patterns with tendencies-certain patterns tend to have such order patterns. These are presented as follows:

Independent Clauses

All circumstantial adjuncts placed before their associated predicates in Luke's independent clauses are summarized in the following table. The numbers of their occurrences are classified according to the tense forms of their associated predicates.

Table 4.1 *Distributions of Circumstantial Adjuncts Located before Predicate in Independent Clauses*

	Pres.	Imf.	Fut.	Aor.	Pf.	Ppf.	Total
Spatial	25	4	14	18	2		63
Temporal (1): Location	8	2	10	21	2		43
Temporal (1): Extent	2	2		2		1	7
Temporal (2): Earlier	16	25	10	180			231
Temporal (2): Contemporary	5	8	1	38			52
Manner: Means	10	4	10	10			34
Manner: Quality	14	3	3	10			30
Manner: Comparison		2	8	2			12
Cause: Reason	19	5	4	9	1		38
Cause: Purpose				1			1
Cause: Behalf	1			1			2
Result		2					2
Contingency: Condition	1						1
Contingency: Concession				1			1
Accompaniment: Comitative (Positive)	2		1	1			4
Accompaniment:			1				1

	Pres.	Imf.	Fut.	Aor.	Pf.	Ppf.	Total
Comitative (Negative) Accompaniment:			1				1
Additive (Negative) Matter	3						3
Angle	1		2	1			4
Total	107	57	64	296	5	1	530

The frequencies of all circumstantial adjuncts placed after their associated predicates in independent clauses are summarized as follows:

Table 4.2 *Distributions of Circumstantial Adjuncts Located after Predicate in Independent Clauses*

	Pres.	Imf.	Fut.	Aor.	Pf.	Ppf.	Total
Spatial	41	55	44	199	4	2	345
Temporal (1): Location		9	12	20			41
Temporal (1): Extent	4	7	4	11	1		27
Temporal (2): Earlier		1		5	1		7
Temporal (2): Contemporary	17	48	5	53	4	3	130
Temporal (2): Later	1	5		11			17
Manner: Means	6	8	10	19			43
Manner: Quality	2	2	1	6			11
Manner: Comparison	7		1	9			17
Cause: Reason	5	5	2	16			28
Cause: Purpose	6	10	5	40	3	1	65
Cause: Behalf	2		1	5			8
Result	1	1	2	5	1		10
Contingency: Condition	2						2
Accompaniment: Comitative (Positive)	3	4	5	13			25
Accompaniment: Comitative (Negative)				2			2
Accompaniment: Additive (Negative)	2			4			6
Role: Product	1		2	4			7
Matter	2	11	1	5			19
Angle	2	1		4			7
Agent	1	3	3	2			9
Total	105	170	98	432	14	6	825

There are a number of direct citations from LXX, which may slightly affect the actual figure of the results; the study consists of distributions of associated predicates' tense forms. The verb εἰμί may also affect the figure (which does not have an aorist tense form). The following figures are results of all such occurrences being excluded.

Table 4.3 *Distributions of Circumstantial Adjuncts Placed before Predicate in Independent Clauses*

	Pres.	Imf.	Fut.	Aor.	Pf.	Ppf.	Total
Spatial	16	3	9	18	2		48

Temporal (1): Location	8		5	21	2		36
Temporal (1): Extent	2	2		2		1	7
Temporal (2): Earlier	16	25	10	180			231
Temporal (2): Contemporary	5	8	1	38			52
Manner: Means	10	4	7	10			31
Manner: Quality	13	3	3	10			29
Manner: Comparison		2	8	2			12
Cause: Reason	17	5	4	9	1		36
Cause: Purpose	1			1			2
Result		2					2
Contingency: Condition	1						1
Contingency: Concession				1			1
Accompaniment: Comitative (Positive)	1			1			2
Accompaniment: Comitative (Negative)				1			1
Accompaniment: Additive (Negative)			1				1
Matter	1						1
Angle				1			1
Total	91	54	48	295	5	1	494

Table 4.4 *Distributions of Circumstantial Adjuncts Placed after Predicate in Independent Clauses*

	Pres.	Imf.	Fut.	Aor.	Pf.	Ppf.	Total
Spatial	33	26	36	196	4	2	297
Temporal (1): Location		3	9	20			32
Temporal (1): Extent	4	3	3	11	1		22
Temporal (2): Earlier		1		5	1		7
Temporal (2): Contemporary	13	39	4	50	4	3	113
Temporal (2): Later	1	4		11			16
Manner: Means	6	5	6	19			36
Manner: Quality	2		1	6			9
Manner: Comparison	6			9			15
Cause: Reason	4	3		16			23
Cause: Purpose	6	8	5	40		1	60
Cause: Behalf	2		1	4			7
Result	1	1	2	5	1		10
Contingency: Condition	2						2
Accompaniment: Comitative (Positive)	3	1	4	13			21
Accompaniment: Comitative (Negative)				2			2
Accompaniment: Additive (Negative)	2			4			6
Role: Product	1		1	4			6
Matter	2	10		5			17
Angle	2	1		4			7
Agent		2	1	2			5
Total	91	108	73	428	11	6	717

On the whole, circumstantial adjuncts tend to occur after the predicate. The overall figure is 530x (before predicate) and 825x (after predicate), in which there are certainly a number of circumstantial adjuncts that tend to occur after the predicate, but there are also a certain number of adjuncts that tend to occur before the predicate.[1] The distribution of these adjuncts is discussed below.

Spatial

Spatial adjunct is typically expressed by a prepositional phrase beginning with ἐν. This adjunct tends to occur after the predicate.[2] In the clauses where spatial adjuncts are placed after the predicate, the predicates are predominantly in the aorist tense,[3] which is very different from the figures of the clauses with spatial adjuncts placed before the predicate;[4] thus it is an unmarked order to have a spatial adjunct located after its associated predicate. When the adjunct is located after its predicate, the predicate tends to be an aorist (unmarked: **P** [aor.] + **A** [spatial]). On the contrary, when a spatial adjunct is located before its related predicate, the tendency of having a present predicate is much increased.[5]

---

1.   An abbreviated form will be used to stand for different circumstantial adjuncts located before and after the predicate. For example, A(spatial)P means spatial adjunct located before the predicate, PA(comp) means comparative adjunct located after the predicate.

2.   There are 345 spatial adjuncts placed after the predicate, and in contrast only 63 spatial adjuncts located before the predicate: AP (3.9; 6.39; 8.16, 27; 9.4, 4; 10.6, 15, 15; 10.30; 13.25, 26, 27; 22.12), APAA (10.7), AAP (16.25; 24.43), AAAPA (24.1), APS (1.65; 6.45; 11.21; 13.28; 22.11), APSA (4.26, 33), APC (6.44; 12.44; 14.35; 23.33, 46 [LXX]), APCA (12.58; 15.13), AAPC (5:3), AAAPCAA (5.19), SAPA (14.5; 21.4; 22.27), SAPAA (15.7), SAAP (11.7, 33; 15.17), ASP (10.26; 12.34; 16.26; 17.37; 19.26; 21.11, 11), ASAP (3.9; 18.24; 19.9), SAPC (6.45, 45), SAAPC (11.7), SACP (21.4), CAP (10.4; 12.46), CCAP (7.44), ACP (6.29, 30, 44; 7.9), ACAPA (9.5). Although the number is 63x, in fact, the actual figure is even smaller, since there are two occurrences where the spatial adjuncts are used as interrogative elements, and it is a norm to have an interrogative element placed at the front of a clause, these two occurrences are 13.25 (an interrogative particle πόθεν is used as a spatial adjunct, which is usually placed at front) and 22.11 (ποῦ is used here, which is also usually placed at front).

3.   A better figure can be obtained by excluding occurrences of LXX citations and the verb εἰμί (there are 43 incidents of verb εἰμί, 29 of them are in imperfect instead of aorist; this significantly affects the actual figure), 196 out of the 297 occurrences are placed after an aorist predicate, where only 33x are after a present, and 26x after an imperfect. The overall figure of all adjuncts placed after a present predicate is 91x, after an imperfect is 108x, and after an aorist is 428x, where the number of adjuncts after present and imperfect have a higher percentage than the ones in the category of spatial adjunct.

4.   The number of spatial adjuncts placed before an aorist predicate is much decreased. The number of spatial adjuncts located before a present predicate is 16x, before an aorist is 18x (after exclusions of LXX citations and the verb εἰμί), which gives a much increased ratio of having a spatial adjunct located before present predicate. This is contrary to the overall figure: 91x before present predicate and 295x before aorist predicate.

5.   From Table 4.1, the numbers of spatial adjuncts located before present, imperfect and aorist predicate are 25, 4, 18; or the figure is 16, 3, 18 in Table 4.3, which shows the percentage of spatial adjunct located before present predicate is much higher than the figures in Table 4.2 and Table 4.4 (the numbers of this adjunct located after present, imperfect and aorist predicate in Table 4.2 are 41x, 55x, 199x and 33x, 26x, 196x in Table 4.4).

Temporal (1)
Location. The number of location temporal adjuncts placed before the predicate[6] is similar to the number placed after the predicate.[7] There is no present predicate in all the PA(loc tem), which is different from the figure of A(loc tem)P.[8] When a locative temporal adjunct is placed after the predicate, the predicate tends not to be in present tense form.

Extent. It is a trend to have an extent temporal adjunct placed after the predicate. In fact, the number of A(ext tem)P is only 7x,[9] while PA(ext tem) is 27x (unmarked: **P + A** [ext tem]).[10]

Temporal (2)
All the adjuncts in the category temporal (2) are in participial form. These participial clauses all carry their own processes; these processes either happen at the same time of the predicate of the main clause, or at a different time.

Different Time: Earlier than the Predicate of the Main Clause. For the adjuncts with a temporal meaning prior to the main predicate, the position of the adjunct is predominantly before the predicate, and the tense form of the main predicate is mainly aorist.[11] It is an unmarked order to have an aorist participle as an adjunct

---

6.   A total of 43x in Table 4.1: AP (6.49; 13.32; 18.33), APA (9.41; 10.21; 19.42; 23.56), AAP (16.25), AAPA (23.42), AAAPA (24.1[2x]), APSA (3.1-2; 4.21; 6.1, 6; 13.31; 17.29, 34; 22.69), APSAAA (1.26-27), APC (2.46), APCC (20.10), APCA (2.29; 7.21), AAPCC (10.35), AAPCA (22.61[2x]), APCS (1.48), SAPA (24.13), ASP (11.7; 21.7; 22.36; 23.31), ASPA (5.13; 17.31), ASAP (3.9; 19.9), SAPCC (23.22), SAPCA (13.15), SAPC (20.33), SACP (10.12), ACP (5.10), ACPA (12.20). There are only 2 incidents where the adjunct is placed in front because of functioning as an interrogative element (9.41 [πότε]; 21.7 [πότε]).

7.   The total number of temporal (location) adjuncts placed after the predicate is 41x: PA (1.59; 5.17; 6.23; 8.22; 9.28, 37; 11.50; 17.27; 19.13; 20.1), PAA (1.80; 11.5; 13.10; 22.18), PAAA (4.16), APA (1.15; 17.30), PSA (1.64; 12.46[2x]; 17.24), PSAA (3.23; 13.1), PSAAA (2.41), PAS (12.52; 22.34), PCA (1.20; 13.8; 14.14), PCAA (14.17), APCAA (4.13), PCSA (23.12), PSCA (20.19), PASC (19.42), SAPA (14.5), SPAA (1.10; 4.25, 27; 23.44), SPCA (1.36), SPCAC (12.12), CPA (18.21).

8.   In PA(loc tem), the numbers of the categories of present, imperfect and aorist are 0x, 9x, 20x in Table 4.2, and 0x, 3x, 20x in Table 4.4 respectively; while the numbers of A(loc tem)P are 8x, 2x, 21x in Table 4.1, and 8x, 0x, 21x in Table 4.3.

9.   APA (13.7), AAP (21.37), APSA (2.1), APSAA (6.12), APC (8.29; 15.29), AASPA (15.13).

10.   PA (5.35; 17.26, 28; 18.4, 12; 20.9), PAA (1.24, 33; 19.47; 21.36), PAAA (21.37, 24.53), APA (2.44), PSAA (4.56), PSAAA (2.41), PAS (1.5), PCA (4.2; 9.23), PCAA (19.14), PACA (23.8), APCCA (4.5), AAPCA (22.61), SPAA (2.36), CPA (13.32), CPCA (11.3), CPAC (9.36), ACPSAA (1.25).

11.   There are 231x of temporal (earlier) adjunct placed before the predicate, with 180x before the aorist predicate (the numbers before present, imperfect and future are only 16, 25 and 10). There are only 7x of temporal (earlier) adjunct placed after the predicate, they are either present participle: PSAA (4.28), PCCAA (14.7); aorist participle: PSA (1.12), SPAA (2.36), ASPAA (4.35), SPCA (20.10); or perfect participle: PSAAA (18.14).

with a temporal meaning prior to its predicate.[12] In fact, when a temporal (2) adjunct is located before the predicate, there are only three times where a present participle is used to act as an adjunct with a temporal meaning prior to its predicate.[13] Thus it is an unmarked order to have an aorist participle as a temporal earlier adjunct located before the predicate (unmarked: **A** [tem ear][aor. part.] + **P**). The distribution of temporal (earlier) adjuncts can be summarized as follows:

	A(tem ear)P	PA(tem ear)	Total
Present participial clause	3	2	5
Aorist participial clause	228	4	232
Perfect participial clause	0	1	1
Total	231	7	238

Same Time: Contemporary to the Predicate of the Main Clause. For an adjunct with a temporal meaning contemporary to the predicate of the main clause, the position is more likely after the predicate.[14] It is a very common pattern to have an aorist participle of the verb ἀποκρίνομαι placed before a verbal process of a clause functioning as a circumstantial adjunct to express a contemporary temporal meaning.[15] On the other hand, it is a norm to have a present participle of the verb

---

12.   A total of 228 times located before the predicate: AP (2.48; 6.4, 8; 7.36; 8.8; 10.31, 33; 11.37; 13.15; 17.7, 19; 20.15; 22.46, 54; 23.16, 22, 46; 24.30), APA (1.63; 2.17, 44; 4.38, 42; 5.24; 6.17; 8.6; 11.26; 14.10; 15.18, 20, 20; 19.4; 22.41, 62, 64; 24.23, 33), APAA (8.29; 9.10, 28, 52; 15.5; 19.28, 41; 22.39), AAP (4.20[2x]; 22.19[2x]; 24.43), AAPA (8.28[2x]), AAPAA (5.25[2x]), APS (8.34), APSA (8.33), APC (1.22, 28; 2.38; 4.17, 39, 39; 5.6, 20; 7.14; 8.51; 9.32, 55; 10.10, 40; 11.25; 12.37; 14.4; 15.15, 17, 26; 16.6; 17.8, 20; 18.33, 36; 19.35; 20.16, 20; 21.1; 22.13, 51; 23.56; 24.3, 12, 30, 50), APCC (5.3, 14; 6.10; 8.41; 9.1; 13.32; 14.25-26; 16.2, 5; 17.14, 14; 18.31; 19.13; 22.4, 8, 40; 24.9, 40), APCCC (7.22), APCA (4.29; 5.13; 8.24; 9.11; 10.34, 34; 15.6, 9; 19.45-46; 23.7, 53), APCCA (4.5; 7.3), APCAA (4.13), APACA (23.26), AAPC (5.3, 11[2x], 28[2x]; 9.16[2x]; 10.23; 16.23; 22.17[2x], 45[2x]), AAPCC (10.35; 11.8), AAAPCAA (5.19[2x]), SAP (8.37; 20.12, 29), SAPA (5.36; 8.54; 12.48; 17.15; 23.8; 24.12), SAPAA (24.52), SAAP (11.33; 23.48), SAAAP (10.32[3x]), ASP (13.12), ASPA (7.13; 19.7), ASPAA (4.35; 5.8; 7.18-9), ASPAAA (1.39), ASAP (8.47), AASPA (15.13), SAPC (5.2, 39; 6.20; 8.24, 43-44; 9.11, 60; 14.31; 15.28; 18.28; 20.17; 22.58; 23.6, 52; 24.15), SAPCC (8.50; 12.28; 18.43; 23.13-14), SAPCA (7.29; 8.16; 18.8), SAPAC (23.14), SAAPC (20.11[2x]), SAAPCA (9.47), SAAAAPC (7.37-38[3x]), ASPC (7.9, 10, 20; 8.7; 9.54; 18.15, 24; 19.32; 22.49, 61; 23.28), ASPCC (9.10, 12; 14.9, 15, 21, 21; 18.22; 19.5; 23.55), ASPCA (7.39; 20.14, 27; 23.1, 47), ASAPC (22.56), ASAPCC (5.22[2x]), ASAAPCA (23.11[3x]), SACP (16.23), ACP (19.30), ACPC (7.9, 44), ACCP (6.13), ACPAC (8.47).

13.   APAAA (9.6), APC (8.8), SAPC (16.21).

14.   There are 130x of temporal (contemporary) adjunct placed after the predicate, with a significant number of them placed after an imperfect predicate (48x, the number after aorist predicate is 53x in Table 4.2) (or the numbers after imperfect and aorist are 39x and 50x in Table 4.4; while there is a big difference between the overall numbers in the categories of imperfect and aorist in Table 4.4 [108x and 428x]); while there are only 52x of temporal (contemporary) adjunct placed before the predicate.

15.   There are 35x of such occurrences: APC (19.40), APCC (3.11; 7.22; 13.2, 25; 17.37; 20.3), APCSC (4.12; 10.41), SAPC (9.19, 20; 10.27), SAPCC (8.21; 13.8; 15.29), SAAPC (11.7), ASPC (1.60; 5.5; 7.43; 9.41, 49; 10.30 [this time ὑπολαβών is used instead of the

λέγω placed after a verbal process of a clause as an adjunct with a contemporary temporal meaning.[16] The other A(tem con)P adjuncts are in either present participial form or aorist participial form.[17]

It is also a trend to have a contemporary temporal adjunct placed after an earlier temporal adjunct. This is not only the case when a contemporary temporal adjunct is placed after the predicate, but also when both the temporal adjuncts are located before the predicate. PA(tem con) adjuncts are all mainly present participles,[18] with only a few instances of perfect participles.[19] The distribution of temporal (contemporary) adjuncts can be summarized as follows:

	A(tem con)P	PA(tem con)	Total
Present participial clause	8	125	133
Aorist participial clause	43	2	45
Perfect participial clause	1	3	4
Total	52	130	182

The result is summarized as follows when the occurrences of the formulaic uses of ἀποκρίνομαι and λέγω as temporal (contemporary) adjuncts are excluded:

	A(tem con)P	PA(tem con)	Total
Present participial clause	8	60	68
Aorist participial clause	8	0	8
Perfect participial clause	1	3	4
Total	17	63	80

formulaic wording ἀποκριθείς]; 17.17; 20.39; 22.51), ASPCC (1.19, 35; 4.8; 5.31; 7.40; 11.45; 24.18), ASAPC (23.40), ASAPCC (13.14), SACPC (23.3).

16. There are 67x of such instances: PA (1.67; 18.38; 20.2), PAA (1.24; 5.26; 23.18), APA (1.63; 8.25; 22.41, 64), APAA (19.28), PSA (15.2; 23.35), PSAA (1.66; 4.41; 5.30; 10.17), PCA (4.36; 7.16; 8.38; 9.18; 12.17; 13.25; 18.13; 19.29; 20.21; 21.7; 22.8 [an aorist participle εἰπών is used here instead of the formulaic wording λέγων; the other similar use is 9.22]; 22.19; 24.29), PCCA (12.16), PCCAA (19.14), PCCAA (14.7; 18. 1), PAC (13.27), APCA (15.6, 9; 19.45-6), PCSA (3.10, 14; 4.35; 5.21; 7.6; 18.18), PCSAA (23.36-37), PACSC (3.16), SPA (9.38; 22.57, 59; 23.5, 21), SPAA (9.35; 20.5; 21.8), SAPA (8.54), ASPA (19.7), ASPAA (5.8), SPCA (17.13; 23.3, 39), SPCAA (7.20), ASPCA (7.39; 14.3; 20.14, 27; 23.47).

17. Present participle (8x) as A(tem con)P: APCC (4.41), SAPA (10.33), SAAP (23.48), SAAAAP (7.37-38), ASAPC (13.14), ASAAPCA (23.11), CAPA (22.65), ACAPA (9.5); aorist participle (8x) as A(tem con)P: APA (8.25), APC (10.39; 19.1), APCA (24.27), SAPC (16.24), ASPC (18.40), ASPCC (19.8), SACCPC (18.11); perfect participle (1x) as A(tem con)P: SAPC (18.13).

18. Present participle (60x) as PA(tem con): PA (1.64; 2.40; 6.35; 23.12), PAA (5.26; 8.29; 21.36; 22.30; 24.12), PAAA (12.22[2x]; 17.16; 21.37; 24.53), APAA (9.39; 10.7[2x]; 15.5; 19.28), APAAA (9.6[2x]), AAPAA (5.25), AAAPA (24.1), PSA (2.20; 6.43; 17.35; 23.10, 35), PSAA (3.23; 7.33[2x], 34[2x]), PASA (8.32), APSA (4.33), PCA (16.19; 18.43), PCAA (22.66; 23.5[2x]), APCA (6.42) APACAA (2.13[2x]), PCSA (22.10), PSCA (11.53), PSAC (19.37), SPA (13.11), SAPA (17.15), SPAA (2.8[2x]; 4.15; 18.35), SPAAA (8.1[2x]; 16.20; 18.2[2x]), APCA (2.19; 22.63), SCPA (7.8).

19. These include PSA (9.27), PCSA (1.11) and PSCCA (9.33). The use of perfect tense form at these three incidents is understandable. Luke has used the perfect participle for verbs with meaning of 'standing' several times (1.11; 5.1, 2; 9.27; 18.13); and 9.33 is the verb οἶδα.

The above table shows it is an unmarked order to have a temporal (contemporary) adjunct located after the predicate, and the adjunct is in a form of present participial clauses (unmarked: **P** + **A** [tem con][pres. part.]).

Different Time: Later. All the adjuncts with a temporal meaning after its predicate are positioned after the predicate, and all are in the present participle.[20] It is an unmarked order to have a temporal (later) adjunct located after the predicate, and the adjunct is in the form of a present participle (unmarked: **P** + **A** [tem lat][pres. part.]).

Summary. The above studies show that when the temporal meaning of a temporal adjunct is prior to its predicate, the adjunct tends to be placed before the predicate, and the tense of the adjunct tends to be aorist. When the temporal meaning of an adjunct is contemporary or after the predicate, the adjunct tends to be placed after the adjunct, and the tense of the adjunct tends to be present.[21] The distribution of all the temporal (2) adjuncts can be summarized as follows:

	A(temporal [2])P	PA(temporal [2])	Total
Present participial clause	8	145	153
Aorist participial clause	274	5	279
Perfect participial clause	1	4	5
Total	283	154	437

The above two tables show the overall number of A(temporal [2])P is almost two times that of PA(temporal [2]). In the A(temporal [2])P category, it is certainly an unmarked pattern to have an aorist participial clause to be the adjunct; it is also certainly an unmarked pattern to have a present participial clause in the category of PA(temporal [2]).

Manner

Manner adjunct has three categories: means, quality and comparison.

Means. There is not much difference between the numbers of means adjuncts placed before the predicate and those placed after the predicate.[22] The adjunct is mostly expressed by prepositional phrases and dative nouns,[23] and in either

---

20.   A total of 17x: PA (8.39), PAA (18.3), PAAA (4.1), APA (24.23), PSA (19.16, 18), PSAA (8.49; 13.1), PASA (22.43), APSA (13.31), PCA (11.24), APCA (5.13; 8.24), SPAA (5.16; 10.25; 19.20), SPCA (18.16).

21.   The main exceptional case to this unmarked pattern is the formulaic use of the contemporary temporal adjunct expressed by the verb ἀποκρίνομαι, which is always placed before its predicate, and is expressed in the aorist tense.

22.   A(means)P is 36x, and PA(means) is 43x.

23.   A total of 21x (without counting the ones in participial forms): A(means)P: AP (7.38, 44; 14.34), APA 1.15), APS (1.34; 4.4 [LXX]), APC (1.18; 4.11 [LXX], 36; 6.38; 8.28; 11.15; 19.22; 21.19), SAPC (3.16; 7.44, 46), ACP (7.46; 20.2, 21; 22.48). There are four occasions where the means adjunct is used as an interrogative element to express a question, and thus the adjunct is

present or aorist participial forms.[24] The distribution of this adjunct can be summarized as follows:

	A(means)P	PA(means)	Total
Present participial clause	6	6	12
Aorist participial clause	7	1	8
Others	21	36	57
Total	34	43	77

Although there is not much difference between the total figures of A(means)P and PA(means) (34x vs. 43x), the means adjunct has a tendency to appear after predicate (tendency: **P + A** [means]).[25] In the category of participial clause as means adjunct, the tense of the participial form tends to be present when it is placed after predicate (6 out of 7x). When the participial adjunct is placed before its predicate, the tense of the participle is either present or aorist (6x vs. 7x).

Quality. Almost all quality adjuncts are expressed by adverbs or adverbial particles,[26] only a few of them are expressed by participles.[27] It can be seen that the quality adjunct tends to appear before the predicate (tendency: **A** [quality] + **P**).[28] The distribution is summarized as follows:

placed at the front of a clause (1.18 [κατὰ τί], 34 [πῶς]; 14.34 [ἐν τίνι]; 20.2 [ἐν ποίᾳ ἐξουσίᾳ]). This gives a figure of 15x when these four instances (1.18, 34; 14.34 and 20.2) and the two LXX citations (4.4 and 4.11) are not counted. For PA(means), there is 36x (without counting the ones in participial forms): PA (2.9, 42; 3.14; 7.38; 22.49), PAS (1.41), PAA (5.26; 8.29), PSAA (4.28), PSAAA (3.22), PCA (1.51; 4.31; 9.14, 39; 23.9), PCAAAA (10.27[4x] [LXX]), PAC (4.33; 8.4), APCA (16.9; 23.53), SPA (1.67; 4.38; 6.11; 9.32; 11.39; 12.6, 47), SAPA (12.48), SPAA (21.8; 23.23), SAPCA (8.16), SCPA (3.16), CPA (1.53; 3.17). It gives a figure of 32x when the four instances of LXX citations (10.27) are not counted. This figure (32x) is more than double the ones before the predicate (15x). This shows the means adjunct still tends to appear after the predicate.

24. A(means)P in present participial form (6x): AP (13.14), AAP (21.37), APC (3.18; 21.30), SAPC (4.40; 12.25); A(means)P in aorist participial form (7x): AP (15.23), APA (19.11), APCA (14.32), ASPC (23.46), ASPCC (11.27), ACP (10.25; 18.18) (the means adjunct of 18.18 is used as an interrogative element [τί ποιήσας] and is thus normally placed in front). For PA(means) in present participial form (6x): PA (21.12), PCA (6.1), APCA (10.34; 15.13), PCSAA (23.36-37[2x]); there is only one PA(means) in aorist participial form: PAC (11.7).

25. See note 23.

26. There is a total of 28x of A(quality)P: AP (7.43, 47; 8.50; 9.39; 10.26, 28; 12.50; 20.21, 39), APAA (9.39), AAP (22.44), APS (11.18; 17.25), APC (3.4 [LXX]; 6.27; 10.5; 12.49; 14.5; 15.22; 18.39; 22.15), APCC (4.23, 25; 9.61), APCA (6.42), APACAA (2.13), ASAP (18.24), ASPC (12.24). Three of these having the adjunct placed at front due to the adjuncts functioning as interrogative elements (6.42 [πῶς]; 10.26 [πῶς]; 11.18 [πῶς]). For PA(quality), there is a total of 9x: PA (8.55; 15.8), APA (22.62), PAS (5.15), PAA (14.21), PCA (18.8), PAC (6.42), SAPA (23.8), SPCAA (7.4).

27. A(quality)P in present participial form: SAPC (2.48), in aorist participial form: AP (19.5, 6); PA(quality) in present participial form: PCA (19.6), in aorist participial form: PA (2.16).

28. The overall figure of locating before and after the predicate is 30x vs. 11x, or 26x vs. 11x when the three instances (6.42; 10.26; 11.18) which function as interrogative elements and the LXX citation (3.4) are excluded.

29. There is a total of 12x of A(comp)P: AP (13.3, 5), APA (21.35; 22.52), APC (12.48; 13.18,

	A(quality)P	PA(quality)	Total
Present participial clause	1	1	2
Aorist participial clause	1	1	2
Others	28	9	37
Total	30	11	41

Comparison. Comparison adjunct is more likely to be placed after the predicate (tendency: **P + A** [comp]).[29]

Summary. The distributions of the above three categories in the category of manner adjunct give a summary as follows:

	A(manner)P	PA(manner)	Total
Present participial clause	7	7	14
Aorist participial clause	8	2	10
Others	61	62	123
Total	76	71	147

This shows the overall number of A(manner)P and PA(manner) is very similarly distributed. When a manner adjunct is in a participial form, it is more likely to be in the present tense form when it is placed after the predicate (7x in present and 2x in aorist tense form); when it is placed before the predicate, the number in present and in aorist is similar (7x vs. 8x); this is different from the figure of temporal (2) adjuncts, where the participial adjunct has a very clear tendency to be in the aorist tense form when it is located before the predicate (8x in present and 274x in aorist of A[temporal (2)]P).

Cause
Cause adjunct includes reason, purpose and behalf.

Reason. Reason adjuncts are mainly expressed by prepositional phrases and the interrogative particle τί, in questions. Participial and infinitival forms are also employed to function as reason adjunct. There is a difference between the number of reason adjuncts placed before and after the predicate. The number of A(reason)P is originally more than the number of PA(reason), but the actual figure is vice versa, since over half of the A(reason)P are placed at the front of a clause because of their role of being an interrogative element in questions.[30] The distribution of reason adjuncts is summarized as follows:

20), APCS (6.23, 26), ASPCC (11.13), SAPC (7.42), ACPSAA (1.25); in which 13.18 (τίνι) and 13.20 (τίνι) are placed at front because the two comparison adjuncts function as interrogative element. For PA(comp), there is a total of 17x: PA (9.15; 12.38, 54), PSA (22.44), PAAS (24.11), PSAAA (3.22), PCA (6.31; 10.3; 15.19), APCA (2.48), PCSA (17.2), SPA (10.37; 12.27; 22.26), SAPA (22.27), SAPAA (15.7). Thus the distribution of comparison adjunct before and after the predicate is about 10x vs. 17x (excluding 13.18 and 13.20 from A[comp]P).

30. For A(reason)P, there are instances of the adjunct in present participial form: SAPCC (10.29), SACPA (11.16), ACP (11.45); aorist participial form: APAA (2.45), AAP (22.44), APCC (20.23-24); and perfect participial form: SAPCC (11.27), SAAPCA (9.47) (these two

	A(reason)P	PA(reason)	Total
Present participial clause	3	6	9
Aorist participial clause	3	3	6
Perfect participial clause	2	0	2
Present infinitival clause	1	3	4
Aorist infinitival clause	0	1	1
Others	29	15	44
Total	38	28	66

The number excluding the occurrences of A(reason)P as interrogative is as follows:

	A(reason)P	PA(reason)	Total
Present participial clause	3	6	9
Aorist participial clause	3	3	6
Perfect participial clause	2	0	2
Present infinitival clause	1	3	4
Aorist infinitival clause	0	1	1
Others	9	15	24
Total	18	28	46

Purpose. Almost all of the purpose adjuncts are positioned after the predicate (65 out of 66x) (unmarked: **P + A** [purpose]). They are mainly composed of infinitival and participial clauses. An infinitival clause is the most frequently employed form to function as a purpose adjunct;[31] almost all participial purpose adjuncts are in present tense form (9 out of 10x). The distribution of this adjunct is summarized as follows:

participles are in perfect tense due to the verb οἶδα). There are also instances of the adjunct in present infinitival form: APC (18.5). The other forms of the reason adjunct are: AP (3.22; 19.31; 22.46; 24.38), APA (5.22), AAP (5.30; 12.26), APC (2.49; 5.5; 6.2, 41; 10.20; 12.56; 14.20; 19.33; 20.5), APCA (2.48; 19.23; 24.5), AAPCC (11.8), AAPCSAA (1.78-79 [2x]), SAAP (15.17), ASPA (10.31; 24.38), ACP (13.7; 20.44), ACPC (6.46; 18.19); all these give A(reason)P a total of 38x. In fact, most of these occurrences of A(reason)P are due to the reason adjuncts functioning as interrogative elements in questions (2.48, 49; 5.22, 30; 6.2, 41, 46; 12.26, 56; 13.7; 18.19; 19.23, 31, 33; 20.5, 44; 22.46; 24.5, 38, 38) (20x). Interrogative particle τί is frequently used in these instances: 2.48, 49; 5.22; 6.2, 41, 46; 12.26; 18.19; 19.33; 22.46; 24.5, 38; interrogative phrase διὰ τί is also employed: 5.30; 19.23, 31; 20.5; 24.38; and interrogative particle πῶς: 12.56; 20.44; and also the interrogative particle ἱνατί: 13.7. This gives the actual number of A(reason)P is 18x after excluding the number of occurrences due to interrogative elements. For PA(reason), there are instances of present infinitival form as adjunct: PA (9.7), APA (19.11), PACA (23.8); aorist infinitival form as adjunct: PCA (6.48); present participial form as adjunct: PA (12.4[2x]), PCA (1.6), SPAA (8.20), SPCA (23.20), CPA (20.36); aorist participial form as adjunct: PCA (8.53), SAPCA (7.29), SCPA (7.30). The other PA(reason) adjuncts in other forms: PA (15.4; 19.3), PAA (2.27; 5.14; 21.17), APA (8.6; 10.21), APAA (19.41), PSA (1.47; 21.26), PSAA (15.10), PCA (8.19), SAPAA (15.7), SPCA (5.9; 10.17); these gives PA(reason) a total of 28x. These results show that reason adjunct tends to be placed after the predicate (number of A[reason]P and PA[reason] is 18x vs. 28x with excluding all reason adjuncts functioning as interrogative elements).

31. The only one instance of A(purpose)P is APC (23.34), which is a LXX citation. For PA(purpose), present infinitival form as purpose adjunct (15x): PSA (2.3), PSAA (5.15[2x]), PASA

	PA*(purpose)*
Present participial clause	9
Aorist participial clause	1
Present infinitival clause	15
Aorist infinitival clause	35
Others	5
Total	65

Behalf. There are only ten occurrences of behalf adjunct. It can be noted that this adjunct tends to occur after the predicate (8 out of 10x) (tendency: **P + A** [behalf]).[32] Over half of the associated predicates of these ten instances are in imperatival form (6 out of 10x).[33]

Summary. The overall figure of the distribution of the cause adjunct is summarized as follows:

	A*(cause)*P	PA*(cause)*	*Total*
Present participial clause	3	15	18
Aorist participial clause	3	4	7
Perfect participial clause	2	0	2
Present infinitival clause	1	18	19
Aorist infinitival clause	0	36	36
Others	31	28	59
Total	40	101	141

The above figure shows the majority of cause adjuncts tend to be located after the predicate (40x vs. 101x). The difference between the two numbers is much wider after the 20 instances of reason adjuncts functioning as interrogative elements are excluded, which gives a figure of 20x vs. 101x in the number of cause adjuncts placed before and after the predicate. This figure (20x vs. 101x) shows it is an unmarked pattern to have a cause adjunct placed after the predicate (unmarked: **P + A** [cause]).

(15.1), PCA (4.42; 24.45), PCAA (9.2[2x]; 15.15), PCCAA (18.1) APCA (12.58), APACA (23.26), SPAAA (21.38), SCPA (9.51), CPA (5.17); aorist infinitival form as the purpose adjunct (35x): PA (1.59; 4.16, 32; 8.35; 12.49; 14.9; 19.7; 24.29), PAA (1.19[2x]), PAAA (1.76-77[2x]), APA (1.9), APAA (9.28, 52), PSA (19.10[2x]), PSAAA (2.4), APSAA (6.12), PCA (1.54-55; 9.16; 22.47), PCAA (14.17), PCAAA (2.22-24[2x]; 4.18-19[3x] [LXX]), PCCACAAAA (1.69-75), AAPCSAA (1.78-79), ASPA (17.31), SPAA (18.10), SPAAA (19.12 [2x]), SPAAAA (1.17[2x]); present participial form as purpose adjunct: PA (13.6), APA (13.7), PAA (3.3), APAA (2.45), APCCA (7.3), SPA (19.48), SPAAA (16.20), ASPAA (7.18-19), SPCAA (7.20); and only once of the aorist participial form as purpose adjunct: PCA (5.7); other forms as purpose adjunct: PAA (5.14), APCA (14.32), PCSA (24.20); SPAA (2.34), SCPA (22.19); this gives PA(purpose) a total of 65x, which includes three occurrences of LXX citation at 4.18-19.

32. For A(behalf)P, there are only two instances: AP (23.28) and APCA (16.9); for PA(behalf), there are 8x: PA (6.28; 13.25; 23.28), PCA (20.28 [LXX]), PAC (12.33; 15.30), PSCA (19.43), SPA (22.32).

33. For A(behalf)P, 23.28 comes with a present imperative and 16.9 comes with an aorist imperative. For PA(behalf), 6.28 and 23.28 come with a present imperative (23.28 is a prohibition); 12.33 and 13.25 come with an aorist imperative.

Result

There are only two result adjuncts placed before the predicate;[34] while there are ten occurrences of this kind of adjunct placed after the predicate. All these PA(result) are in infinitival forms and have a tendency to be in the aorist tense (tendency: **P** + **A** [result][aor. inf.]).[35] The distribution is summarized as follows:

	A(result)P	PA(result)	Total
Aorist participial clause	2	0	2
Present infinitival clause	0	3	3
Aorist infinitival clause	0	7	7
Total	2	10	12

Contingency

Contingency adjunct has three categories: condition, concession and default. There are only four instances of condition and concession that occur in the Gospel.

Condition. There are only three instances of this adjunct. They are all in aorist participial forms. One is situated before the predicate; two are situated after the predicate.[36]

Concession. There is only one instance of this adjunct. It is located before the predicate in an aorist participial form.[37]

Summary. The distribution of the contingency adjuncts is summarized as follows:

	A(contingency)P	PA(contingency)	Total
Aorist participial clause	2	2	4
Total	2	2	4

All four contingency adjuncts are in aorist participial forms. Two are located before the predicate; two are after the predicate.

Accompaniment

Accompaniment adjunct includes comitative and additive; they both include positive and negative.

Comitative. Comitative adjuncts are mostly expressed by prepositional phrases beginning with μετά or σύν. They consist of two categories: positive and negative.
   1. *Positive Comitative.* Almost all positive comitative adjuncts are located after

---

34. These two result adjuncts are both in aorist participial form: AAPC (24.37[2x]).

35. PA(result), present infinitival clause as adjunct: PSA (6.2), PCCA (10.19), CPA (7.21); aorist infinitival clause as adjunct: PA (6.42), PCCACAAAA (1.69-75), PCSA (9.13), AAPCSAA (1.78-79), SPA (24.16), CPSA (1.57), ACPSAA (1.25).

36. A(cond)P: SAPCA (15.4); PA(cond): CPSAA (9.25[2x]).

37. ACP (5.5)

the predicate (unmarked: **P + A** [com +]).[38] There are only four placed before the predicate.[39]

2. *Negative Comitative*. There are only three occurrences of negative comitative adjuncts in the Gospel. One is placed before the predicate;[40] two are after the predicate.[41]

Additive. Additive adjunct can be positive or negative. All seven occurrences of this kind of adjunct in the Gospel are negative. The majority of them are located after the predicate;[42] while only one is located before the predicate (tendency: **P + A** [add]).[43]

Summary. The following table represents the summary of distribution of accompaniment adjuncts, which also shows it is an unmarked pattern to have this adjunct located after the predicate (unmarked: **P + A** [accom]).

	A(accompaniment)P	PA(accompaniment)
Total	6	33

Role

Role adjunct can be in category of guise or product. All seven occurrences of the role adjunct are in the category of product, they are all located after the predicate. This pattern is an unmarked order (unmarked: **P + A** [role]).[44]

Matter

Matter adjunct placed after the predicate is an unmarked order. In fact, 19 out of 22 matter adjuncts are located after the predicate;[45] only three are before the predicate (unmarked: **P + A** [matter]).[46]

38.   There is a total of 25x: PA (2.51; 7.50; 8.48; 24.29), PAA (23.18), APA (9.41; 22.52), PSA (17.20; 20.1), PSAA (4.14, 56; 10.17), PAS (1.44), PAC (14.9), APACAA (2.13), SPA (1.66; 7.6, 12), SPAA (11.31, 32; 24.4), SPAAAA (1.17), SAPAA (24.52), ASPAAA (1.39), CPA (7.12).

39.   AP (22.37 [LXX]), AAP (5.30), AAPA (23.42), SAAP (11.7).

40.   AAPC (10.23)

41.   APAA (9.10), PSA (9.36).

42.   APSA (4.26), PCA (17.18), SPA (4.27), SPCA (5.21; 10.22; 11.29).

43.   ACCP (11.11)

44.   PA (13.19), PSA (3.5), PCA (21.13), PCAAA (10.1), SAPA (21.4), CPA (1.53), ACAPA (9.5); 3.5 is a citation of LXX.

45.   PA (matter): PA (4.22, 32; 10.41), APA (2.17), PSA (2.33, 47; 9.43), PCA (4.38; 14.6), PAC (2.38; 12.22), APCA (9.11), PCSA (7.18), SPA (2.18; 10.40; 13.17), SPAA (24.14), CAPA (22.65), CPAC (4.10 [LXX]). In these 19 instances, a majority of them (11 out of 19x) is accompanied with an imperfect predicate (2.33, 38, 47; 4.22, 32; 9.11, 43; 10.40; 13.17; 22.65; 24.14) (2.33 is in a periphrastic construction, which carries an imperfect instead of aorist because of the verb ἐστίν), only 2x are with a present (10.41; 12.22 [present imperative]), 5x with an aorist (2.17, 18; 4.38; 7.18; 14.6). This is not a normal figure, this can be seen by comparing the figures of total adjuncts located after present, imperfect and aorist predicate are 105x, 170x and 432x in Table 4.2 (or 91x, 108x and 428x in Table 4.4), where the percentage of adjuncts located after imperfect predicate is much lower than the ones after aorist predicate.

46.   A(matter)P: AAP (12.26), SACP (16.10, 10).

Angle
Angle adjunct is commonly expressed by a prepositional phrase beginning with κατά.[47] This adjunct is more likely to be placed after the predicate,[48] rather than before the predicate (tendency: **P + A** [angle]).[49]

Agent
All the agent adjuncts are placed after its predicate in passive voice (unmarked: **P + A** [agent]).[50] Most of them are expressed by a prepositional phrase beginning with ὑπό.[51]

Dependent Clauses
This section will focus the study on the relative positions of different circumstantial adjuncts and their associated predicates in dependent clauses. The distributions of all the circumstantial adjuncts placed before and after their associated predicates in dependent clauses are listed out as follows:

Table 4.5 *Distribution of Circumstantial Adjuncts Located before Predicate in Dependent Clauses*

	Pres.	Imf.	Fut.	Aor.	Pf.	Total
Spatial	14	2	2	16		34
Temporal (1): Location	6			3		9
Temporal (1): Extent	1			2		3
Temporal (2): Earlier	1			5		6
Temporal (2): Contemporary				1		1
Manner: Means	7	1		2	1	11
Manner: Quality	3			5		8
Manner: Comparison				3		3
Cause: Reason				3		3
Cause: Behalf				1		1
Contingency: Concession	3					3
Accompaniment: Comitative (Positive)	1	1		2		4
Matter				2		2
Total	36	4	2	45	1	88

47. 1.9, 38; 2.29; 42; 4.16; 17.30; 22.39; 23.56. The other incidents are in a dative form (10.14; 11.41) and a prepositional phrase beginning with ἐπί.

48. 7x: PAA (1.38), APA (23.56), APAA (22.39), PAAA (4.16), PSA (2.42), PCAC (1.59) and APCA (2.29).

49. 4x: APA (1.9; 17.30), SCAP (11.41), ACPA (10.14). 1.9 is the only incident where the an angle adjunct is placed before a material process (ἔλαχε), the other three incidents (10.14; 11.41 and 17.30) are all in a relational process.

50. 9x: PA (21.16), PAA (21.17), APAA (8.29), PAAA (4.1), PCAS (2.26), SPA (21.24; 23.15), SCPA (10.22); about half of them are in a passive periphrastic construction (2.26; 21.17; 24; 23.15).

51. 2.26; 8.29; 10.22; 21.16, 17, 24. The other two are 4.1 (expressed by a prepositional phrase beginning with ἐν [ἤγετο ἐν τῷ πνεύματι]) and 23.15 (expressed by a dative case [ἐστὶν πεπραγμένον αὐτῷ]).

Table 4.6 *Distribution of Circumstantial Adjuncts Located after Predicate in Dependent Clauses*

	Pres.	Imf.	Fut.	Aor.	Pf.	Total
Spatial	31	4	1	56	4	96
Temporal (1): Location	1			7		8
Temporal (1): Extent				3		3
Temporal (2): Earlier			1	1		2
Temporal (2): Contemporary	1			5		6
Manner: Means	1			3		4
Manner: Quality				2		2
Manner: Comparison	2			3		5
Cause: Reason	2		1	1		4
Cause: Purpose	2			5		7
Cause: Behalf				2		2
Result	3			1		4
Contingency: Concession	1					1
Accompaniment: Comitative (Positive)	4			5		9
Accompaniment: Comitative (Negative)	1					1
Matter	4		1			5
Angle	1			2		3
Agent	1			1		2
Total	55	4	4	97	4	164

Spatial

In dependent clauses, spatial adjunct apparently tends to appear after the predicate[52] rather than before the predicate.[53] Given a figure of 96x vs. 34x on the number of PA(spatial) and A(spatial)P, or even a figure of 96x vs. 26x,[54] it can be seen that it is an unmarked order to have a spatial adjunct located after the predicate, and they are all mainly in the form of prepositional phrase (unmarked: P + A [spatial]).

---

52.   PA(spat): PA (3.7; 7.12; 8.29, 37, 41; 11.32; 13.8; 16.4, 24; 17.11; 18.16; 19.5; 22.16, 40, 46; 23.33, 42), PAA (12.58; 14.8; 19.29[2x]; 22.30[2x]), APA (15.25; 17.4), PSA (1.43, 44; 2.4; 8.30; 9.33, 34, 37, 57; 17.12; 18.35; 22.10), APAA (17.4), PSAA (1.8-9; 19.37), PSAAA (14.1), PAS (1.21; 2.23; 3.4; 5.35; 19.15; 21.34), PAAS (2.15[2x]), APSAA (22.53), PCA (3.20; 4.25; 10.21; 11.43[2x]; 12.11, 58; 16.4, 9, 27; 20.20; 22.55; 24.5, 32), PAC (4.11; 11.31), PCSA (2.7), PCASA (2.11), PSCA (20.1), PSAC (12.45), PSAAC (3.15), SPA (4.7; 8.42; 9.53, 54; 10.20; 11.24; 12.15; 13.28; 14.26; 16.28, 30; 17.2; 18.40; 19.14), SPAA (11.6[2x]), SAPA (7.6; 8.4), ASPA (10.21), SPCA (12.8; 16.3), SPCAA (5.24), SCPA (12.58), SCPAA (5.24), CPA (1.22; 10.2); gives a total of 96x (in which there are two occasions of LXX citations: 4.11and 9.54).

53.   AP (7.6; 8.31, 32; 9.4, 57; 10.5, 8, 10; 22.9; 23.40; 24.28), AAP (9.12[2x]; 16.26[2x]), APS (10.6, 13; 11.53; 12.34; 23.53), APC (5.3; 12.17; 20.10), SAP (6.19; 7.7; 11.18; 14.32; 15.20; 16.31), SAPA (8.4), ASP (12.33), ACP (9.58; 19.17), ACAP (22.11); gives a total of 34x. The actual figure is much less than this, since it is a norm to have the adverb οὖ, ποῦ or ὅπου to begin a dependent clause; a number of the above occurrences belong to this category, where one of the above three adverbs functions as a spatial adjunct and is thus placed before the predicate (οὖ: 23.53; ποῦ: 9.58; 12.17; ὅπου: 12.33; 22.11). There are three other instances which are in similar circumstance, but are using a relative pronoun instead of an adverb (10.5, 8, 10). This gives the figure of A(spatial)P is 26x when these eight occurrences are reduced.

54.   See note 53.

Temporal (1)
The temporal (1) adjuncts are mainly expressed by prepositional phrases, both in location and extent.

Location. The occurrences of this adjunct are similarly distributed before and after the predicate.[55]

Extent. There are not too many occurrences of this adjunct, and they are also similarly distributed before and after the predicate.[56]

Summary. The distributions of temporal (1) adjuncts are summarized as follows:

	A(temporal [1])P	PA(temporal [1])
Total	12	11

Temporal (2)
The temporal (2) adjuncts are all in participial form. These include adjuncts with temporal meaning contemporary to the predicate of the main clause, and adjuncts with temporal meaning different from the predicate of the main clause.

Same Time. There are only a few occurrences of this adjunct, and they are all in the form of present participial clause. Only one of them is placed before the predicate;[57] all the rest are placed after the predicate (tendency: **P + A** [tem con][pres. part.]).[58] The distribution is summarized as follows:

	A(tem con)P	PA(tem con)	Total
Present participial form	1	6	7
Total	1	6	7

Different time: Earlier. There are eight instances of this adjunct. Most are in aorist participial form and are located before the predicate (tendency: **A** [tem ear][aor. part.] **+ P**),[59] which are summarized as follows:

---

55. There are 9x of A(loc tem)P: AP (6.7; 10.13; 12.38; 24:.8), APS (13.14), ASP (12.39, 40), SCAP (16.8), ACP (23.31); and there are 8x of PA(loc tem): PAA (1.70), APA (11.38), PSA (11.50), PSAAA (14.1), PAS (6.9), PCA (13.9; 24.35), PCASA (2.11).

56. There are three instances that are located before the predicate: APA (17.4), APAA (17.4), APSAA (22.53); and also three instances after the predicate: PA (17.26), PSA (4.25), PCA (13.9).

57. APA (15.25)

58. There are six instances of PA(tem con): APAA (17.4), PSAA (11.1), PCAA (24.6-7[2x]), SPA (20.28), SPCA (14.29-30). One of these is a LXX citation (20.28); two of them (14.29-30 and 24.6-7) are associated with a predicate of verbal process, and have a present participle of λέγω as a contemporary temporal adjunct located after it (which has become a norm in independent clauses) (17.4 also has a present participle of λέγω, but does not belong to this category since its predicate is not a verbal process).

59. There are a total of six instances of A(tem ear)P, they are mainly in aorist participial form: AP (9.12), APC (7.3; 9.59), SAPC (11.22), ASPAC (9.13); there is only once in perfect participial

	A(tem ear)P	PA(tem ear)	Total
Aorist participial form	5	2	7
Perfect participial form	1	0	1
Total	6	2	8

Summary. The distributions of these temporal (2) adjuncts are summarized as follows:

	A(temporal [2])P	PA(temporal [2])	Total
Present participial form	1	6	7
Aorist participial form	5	2	7
Perfect participial form	1	0	1
Total	7	8	15

Manner

Means adjunct is more likely to be located before the predicate rather than after the predicate (11x vs. 4x) (tendency: **A** [manner] + **P**).[60] This tendency is slightly different from the one in independent clauses.

Quality. It is an unmarked order to have a quality adjunct located before the predicate (8 out of 9x) (unmarked: **A** [quality] + **P**), rather than after the predicate.[61]

Comparison. Comparison adjunct is more likely to be placed after the predicate, rather than before it.[62]

Summary. The results of the manner adjuncts are summarized as follows:

A(manner)P	PA(manner)	Total
22	10	32

form: SAPC (11.21). There are two instances of PA(tem ear) and both are in aorist participial form: PSA (19.15), PCAA (11.8).

60. There is a total of 11x of A(means)P. One of them is in present participial form: APC (18.5); the rest of them are: AP (8.37; 21.5), APC (11.46; 22.2), APSC (11.18), SAPC (11.19, 36), ASPC (11.20), ACP (20.8), ACPC (22.4). 22.2 and 22.4 have an interrogative particle πῶς acting as a means adjunct, and thus it is placed before the predicate (an interrogative particle always occupies the first slot of a clause; this is also true in independent clauses). There are only 4x of PA(means): PAA (1.70), PSA (21.34), PCA (11.46; 16.24).

61. There are 8x of A(quality)P: AP (8.18; 16.8), APA (11.38; 12.36), APS (8.47), SAP (12.27), SAPA (7.6) and CAPS (6.26). 12.27 has an interrogative particle πῶς as quality adjunct, and is thus placed at the front of the clause. The use of the particle πῶς here is different from the two in 22.2 and 22.4, the one in 12.27 functions as a quality adjunct and shows its related process to be undertaken 'in what manner'; while the other two (22.2 and 22.4) show their associated processes to be proceeded 'by what means'. The only occurrence of PA(quality) is PA (7.47). This gives the figure of the two categories to be 8x vs. 1x, or 7x vs. 1x when 12.27 is excluded.

62. A(comp)P: ASPA (10.21), SCAP (13.2), CAP (7.43). For PA(comp): PA (18.11), PCA (17.6), PCAA (6.22), SCPA (13.4), CPA (22.31). This gives a figure of 3x vs. 5x.

This shows the manner adjuncts tend to appear before the predicate in dependent clauses (tendency: **A** [manner] + **P**).

Cause
Cause adjuncts in dependent clauses include reason, purpose and behalf.

Reason. There are not too many reason adjuncts, and they are similarly distributed before and after the predicate.[63] The result is summed up as follows:

	A(reason)P	PA(reason)	Total
Present participial form	0	2	2
Aorist participial form	1	0	1
Others	2	2	4
Total	3	4	7

Purpose. All seven purpose adjuncts are in infinitival form, and are located after the predicate. The majority is in aorist form (unmarked: P + A [purpose][aor. inf.]),[64] which is shown as follows:

	PA(purpose)
Present infinitival form	1
Aorist infinitival form	6
Total	7

Behalf. There are only three instances of this adjunct; one is before and two are after the predicate.[65]

Summary. A summary of distributions of cause adjuncts is shown below and it illustrates that a cause adjunct tends to occur after the predicate (tendency: **P** + **A** [cause]).

	A(cause)P	PA(cause)	Total
Present participial form	0	2	2
Aorist participial form	1	0	1
Present infinitival form	0	1	1
Aorist infinitival form	0	6	6
Others	3	5	8
Total	4	14	18

63. A(reason)P: AP (4.43; 8.12), APC (8.47), in which 8.12 is in an aorist participial form. For PA(reason): PCAA (6.22; 11.8), SCPA (19.22[2x]), where the two instances in 19.22 are both in present participial form. This gives an overall figure of 3x vs. 4x.

64. Present infinitival clause as purpose adjunct: SPCA (5.1); aorist infinitival clause as purpose adjunct: PA (12.51), PCA (4.18, this is a citation of LXX), PSCA (2.27), CPA (8.55), CSPA (21.22), PSAAA (14.1). This shows the majority of the purpose adjuncts are in aorist infinitival form.

65. A(behalf)P: CAP (18.41); PA(behalf): APA (12.36), ASPAC (9.13).

Result

There are only four instances of result adjunct. They are all positioned after the predicate and are summed up as follows:[66]

	PA(result)
Present infinitival form	1
Aorist infinitival form	1
Others	1
Total	3

Contingency

The category of contingency has only got four instances of concession in dependent clauses, where three occasions are put before the predicate, and one is put after the predicate:[67]

	A(contingency)P	PA(contingency)	Total
Present participial form	2	0	2
Others	0	1	1
Total	2	1	3

Accompaniment

There are only comitative adjuncts in dependent clauses. They are mainly positive ones (13 out of 14x). In the cases of positive comitative ones, it is more likely to have the adjunct situated after the predicate than before it.[68] The only occurrence of a negative one is located after the predicate (tendency: **P + A** [accom]):[69]

	A(accompaniment)P	PA(accompaniment)	Total
Total	4	10	14

Matter

It is more likely to have a matter adjunct situated after the predicate, rather than before it.[70]

Angle

There are only three instances of this adjunct and all are situated after the predicate.[71]

---

66. Present infinitival clause as adjunct: SCPAA (5.24); aorist infinitival as adjunct: PSA (2.21[an articular infinitival form is used at here as the adjunct]; 7.42); prepositional phrase as adjunct: PA (14.28 εἰς ἀπαρτισμόν).

67. The two instances of locating before the predicate are in present participial form: AP (8.10, 10) and SAPC (11.13). The one after the predicate is in the form of a prepositional phrase (ἀπὸ τῆς χαρᾶς): PSA (24.41).

68. A(com+)P: AP (15.29), APS (4.32), SAP (5.34), ACAP (22.11). For PA(com+): PA (8.38, 9.26, 49; 11.37), PSA (8.51; 24.30), PAC (12.13), PAA (12.58), APSAA (22.35).

69. PSA (9.18)

70. There are only two instances of A(matter)P: ACP (16.11, 12). For PA(matter), there are five instances: PSA (24.4), PSAAC (3.15), SPA (9.43), SPCA (12.10), SPAC (21.5).

71. PSA (2.22), PSAA (1.8-9), PCA (2.39).

Agent
There are only two instances of this adjunct and both are situated after the predicate.[72]

Infinitival Clauses
The allocations of different circumstantial adjuncts with respect to their different associated predicates are listed as follows:

Table 4.7 *Distribution of Circumstantial Adjuncts Located before Predicate in Infinitival Clauses*

	Pres.	Aor.	Pf.	Total
Spatial	4	7	1	12
Temporal (1): Location		4		4
Temporal (1): Extent	1		1	2
Manner: Means		2		2
Manner: Quality	2	2		4
Cause: Reason		1		1
Accompaniment: Comitative (Positive)	1	2		3
Accompaniment: Comitative (Negative)	1			1
Total	9	18	2	29

Table 4.8 *Distribution of Circumstantial Adjuncts Located after Predicate in Infinitival Clauses*

	Pres.	Aor.	Total
Spatial	11	25	36
Temporal (1): Location	1	2	3
Temporal (1): Extent	1	2	3
Temporal (2): Contemporary	2	1	3
Manner: Means	2	5	7
Manner: Quality	1	2	3
Cause: Behalf		2	2
Contingency: Default		1	1
Accompaniment: Comitative (Positive)	1	3	4
Matter	5	2	7
Angle		2	2
Agent	1	4	5
Total	25	51	76

Spatial
Spatial adjunct tends to be put after the predicate (36 out of 48x) (tendency: **P** + **A** [spatial]).[73]

72. PAA (14.8), SPA (14.8).
73. 12x in A(spatial)P: AP (7.7; 8.43; 9.23; 13.25), AAP (22.33); APS (2.49), APC (12.25), APCC (3.8), SAP (9.33; 18.25, 25), AASP (19.5); and 36x (or 34x with the two LXX citations [3.18, 18] excluded) in PA(spatial): PA (4.42; 5.15; 6.18; 9.44, 51; 12.5, 58; 13.24; 21.36; 23.26;

Temporal (1)
The occurrences of this type of adjunct in infinitival clauses are evenly distributed before and after the predicate.

Location. The seven instances of this adjunct are evenly distributed before and after the predicate (4x vs. 3x).[74]

Extent. There are five instances of this adjunct. Two are before the predicate;[75] three are after it.[76]

Summary. Results of this temporal (1) adjunct are summed up as follows:

	A(temporal [1])P	PA(temporal [1])
Total	6	6

Temporal (2)
There are three occasions of this adjunct; they all belong to same time: the process occurs contemporary to that of the predicate, and they are all put after the predicate (tendency: **P + A** [tem con]):[77]

	PA(temporal [2])
Present participial form	2
Aorist participial form	1
Total	3

Manner
Manner adjunct consist of means and quality in infinitival clauses.

Means. This adjunct is mainly expressed in a form of prepositional phrase, and is put after the predicate.[78]

24.26), PAA (10.19[2x]; 16.26[2x]; 24.46), PSA (2.21), PSAA (16.22), PCA (1.17, 79; 3.17, 18, 18; 5.18), PASAA (24.47), PAC (20.18), APCAAA (1.74-75), SPA (13.33; 24.7), SPAS (22.37), CPA (9.31; 12.49, 51; 14.31; 18.13) and SPAA (13.16).

74. Four instances in A(loc tem)P: AP (9.22; 14.3; 24.7), AASP (19.5); and three instances in PA(loc tem): PAA (24.46), SPAA (13.16), CPAA (22.15).

75. SAP (13.33), ACP (22.34).

76. PCCA (1.54-55), PAC (12.42), APCAAA (1.74-75).

77. Two are in a form of present participial clause: PCA (23.2 [in present participial form of λέγω: λέγοντες]), PCAAA (19.37); one is in aorist participial form: PASAA (24.47).

78. For A(means)P, there are only two instances: APC (14.18, which is in aorist participial form) and APC (14.31, which is in prepositional phrase). For PA(means), there are seven instances: PA (1.9, which is in aorist participial form) and the rest are in the form of a prepositional phrase (PA [15.16; 16.21], PCCA [1.77], APCAAA [1.74-75], PASAA [24.47]) and nominal group in dative case (PCAAA [19.37]).

Quality. There are seven occasions of quality adjunct. They are evenly distributed before and after the predicate.[79]

Summary. Results of manner adjunct are listed as follows (tendency: **P + A** [manner]):

	A(manner)P	PA(manner)	Total
Aorist participial form	1	1	2
Others	5	9	14
Total	6	10	16

Cause
Cause adjunct only occurs a few times in infinitival clauses. This includes reason and behalf.

Reason. There is only one instance of this adjunct; it is before the predicate and is in the form of an aorist participial clause.[80]

Behalf. The only two occasions of behalf adjunct are both put after the predicate and are in the form of a dative nominal group.[81]

Summary. The number of cause adjuncts is as follows:

	A(cause)P	PA(cause)	Total
Aorist participial form	1	0	1
Others	0	2	2
Total	1	2	3

Contingency
There is only one contingency adjunct (default) in infinitival clauses, which is in a form of prepositional phrase and is put after the predicate.[82]

Accompaniment
There are only eight comitative adjuncts (seven positive and one negative) in the category of accompaniment, which are mainly positive ones.[83] Four of the accompaniment adjuncts are located before the predicate; the other four are after the predicate.

---

79.   Four instances in A(quality): PAP (11.53), APS (6.48), APCAAA (1.74-75) and ACP (1.3). Three instances in PA(quality): PA (13.11), PCAC (12.1), SPA (21.9).
  80.   AP (20.26)
  81.   PA (9.52) and PAC (19.12).
  82.   PCAC (22.6)
  83.   For positive comitative, the ones situated before the predicate: AP (19.7; 23.32) and AAP (22.33); the ones situated after the predicate: PA (2.5; 20.46; 24.29) and CPAA (22.15). For negative comitative, there is only once, which is placed before the predicate: ASP (10.40).

Matter
All seven matter adjuncts are put after the predicate (tendency: **P** + **A** [matter]).[84]

Angle
There are only two occurrences of angle adjunct. They are both put after the predicate.[85]

Agent
There are five agent adjuncts. They are all put after the predicate (tendency: **P** + **A** [agent]).[86]

Participial Clauses

This section presents the distributions of circumstantial adjuncts located before and after their associated predicates in participial clauses. The distributions are as follows:

Table 4.9 *Distribution of Circumstantial Adjuncts Located before Predicate in Participial Clauses*

	Pres.	Aor.	Pf.	Total
Spatial	11	7	2	20
Temporal (1): Location	1	2		3
Temporal (1): Extent	2	1		3
Temporal (2): Earlier	1			1
Manner: Means	3		1	4
Manner: Quality	4	4		8
Manner: Comparison		1		1
Cause: Reason			1	1
Cause: Behalf	2			2
Accompaniment: Comitative (Positive)	2			2
Matter		1		1
Agent	2			2
Total	28	16	4	48

Table 4.10 *Distribution of Circumstantial Adjuncts Located after Predicate in Participial Clauses*

	Pres.	Aor.	Pf.	Total
Spatial	50	61	14	125
Temporal (1): Location	4	6	4	14
Temporal (1): Extent	10	2		12
Manner: Means	6	4	1	11
Manner: Quality	3	3	1	7
Manner: Comparison	1			1

84. PA (23.8; 24.25), PCA (1.1; 9.45; 11.53), PCAAA (19.37) and PCAC (7.24).
85. PCA (2.24) and PSAC (2.27).
86. PA (3.7; 9.22; 17.25), PSAA (16.22) and PAS (9.7).

Cause: Reason	2	1		3
Cause: Purpose	1	2		3
Cause: Behalf	1			1
Result	4			4
Contingency: Default		1		1
Accompaniment: Comitative (Positive)	5	4	2	11
Matter	5	3	2	10
Angle	1	1		2
Agent	6	2	1	9
Total	99	91	24	214

Spatial

It is an unmarked order to have a spatial adjunct located after the predicate in participial clauses (unmarked: **P + A** [spatial]).[87]

Temporal (1)

It is an unmarked pattern to have a location (temporal) adjunct placed after the predicate.[88] This is also true in the case of extent (temporal) adjunct.[89] The distribution of A(temporal [1])P and PA(temporal [1]) is 6x vs. 26x (unmarked: **P + A** [temp (1)]).

Temporal (2)

There is only one instance of the adjunct, which belongs to different time (earlier). It is put before the predicate and is in a form of an aorist infinitival clause.[90]

Manner

The means adjunct tends to appear after predicate, rather than before it.[91] The occurrences of quality adjuncts are evenly allocated before and after the predicate.[92]

---

87. There is a total of 20x in A(spatial)P: AP (1.74, 79; 5.2; 7.8, 32; 8.14; 9.27; 10.13; 11.17; 12.21; 15.17; 18.13; 23.12; 23.14), APA (16.23), AAP (12.28), APC (8.39, 43), CAP (9.48) and ACP (4.40). For PA(spatial), there is a total of 125x: PA (1.1, 6, 9, 11, 19, 28; 2.12, 16, 19, 46; 3.4; 4.22, 23, 30, 38, 39; 5.2, 3, 12, 19, 27; 6.47; 7.4, 10, 20, 36, 44; 8.27, 32, 33, 35, 37, 41, 44, 46, 47, 51; 9.5, 12, 16, 62; 10.8, 10, 11, 13, 23, 32, 36, 39; 11.44; 12.54; 13.4, 6, 34; 15.6; 16.18; 17.7; 19.4, 20, 28, 45; 20.18; 21.12, 26, 35, 37; 22.3, 40, 44, 45, 45, 52, 56, 62; 23.5, 19, 26, 28, 52; 24.2, 6, 9, 27, 47), PAA (7.38[2x]; 8.43; 17.24[2x]; 21.12, 27; 22.28; 23.5[2x]; 24.13[2x], 18, 22, 44), APA (5.25; 14.31; 23.25), PSAA (23.7), PAS (2.24), PCA (4.35; 5.11; 6.20, 29; 9.62; 10.34; 12.9; 13.6, 7; 16.15; 19.35; 20.15; 23.49), PCAA (2.8; 6.49), PAC (6.13; 7.8; 18.9; 21.1, 2) and CPA (13.22).

88. There are only three instances of A(loc tem)P: AP (2.38), APA (5.25) and AAP (12.28). For PA(loc tem), there is a total of 14x: PA (1.7, 18, 39; 6.21, 21, 25, 25; 11.50, 50; 12.28; 24.33), PAA (2.21; 24.22) and PAAA (2.36).

89. There are only three instances of A(ext tem)P: AP (5.5; 13.14) and APA (4.2). For PA(ext tem), there is a total of 12x: PA (12.19; 21.23), PAA (8.43; 16.19; 24.18), PAAA (2.36), APA (2.37), PSAA (23.7), PCA (8.27; 18.7), PCAA (2.8) and CPA (13.11).

90. APCA (12.5)

91. There are four instances of A(means)P: AP (7.25), APA (2.37) and APC (9.49; 17.15). For PA(means), there is a total of 11x (in which one is a citation of LXX [13:35]): PA (2.40; 6.1; 7.29, 38; 13.35; 19.38; 21.30; 23.46), PAA (2.21; 18.31) and PAC (2.17).

92. There are 8x in A(quality)P: AP (4.9; 5.31;7.2; 14.28; 17.7; 18.5) and APC (4.35;

There are only two instances on the comparison adjunct. One is before the predicate;[93] and one is after it.[94] All these give the distribution of manner adjunct as follows:

	A(manner)P	PA(manner)
Total	13	19

Cause

There are four instances of reason adjunct, where one is before the predicate,[95] and three are after it;[96] three times in purpose adjunct, where all are put after the predicate;[97] and three times in behalf, where two are before the predicate,[98] and one is after it.[99] The overall figure is shown below (tendency: **P + A** [cause]):

	A(cause)P	PA(cause)
Aorist infinitival form	0	2
Others	3	5
Total	3	7

Result

All four result adjuncts are put after the predicate. Two of them are in present infinitival form; the other two are in the form of an aorist infinitival clause.[100]

Contingency

The only occurrence of this adjunct is default, which is in the form of a prepositional phrase and is put after its associated predicate.[101]

Accompaniment

All the accompaniment adjuncts belong to positive comitative. The norm is to have them put after the predicate (11 out of 13x) (unmarked: **P + A** [accom.]).[102]

23.10). For PA(quality), there are 7x: PA (9.59; 14.31; 15.13; 16.6), PAA (16.19), APA (16.23) and PCA (1.3).

93. AP (10.18)

94. PA (12.43)

95. APA (23.25)

96. PA (22.45), PAA (21.12) and PCA (5.19).

97. PA (5.7; 11.54), both of these two are in the form of an aorist infinitival clause; the other occurrence: PA (23.48), which is in the form of a prepositional phrase.

98. AP (22.19, 20), both are in the form of a prepositional phrase.

99. PA (12.21), this one is in the form of a dative nominal group.

100. PCA (8.8; 14.35), which are in the form of a present infinitival clause; PCA (12.4) and APCA (12.5), these two are in the form of an aorist infinitival clause.

101. PCAA (6.49)

102. There are two instances of A(com+)P: AP (6.3) and APA (14.31). For PA(com+), there is a total of 11x: PA (6.17; 9.31; 11.23, 23; 17.35; 24.44), PAA (21.27; 22.28), PAAA (2.36), PCA (15.30; 23.11).

Matter
The norm is to have this adjunct put after the predicate (unmarked: **P** + **A** [matter]).[103]

Angle
There are two times of this adjunct and they are both put after the predicate.[104]

Agent
This adjunct tends to appear after the predicate (tendency: **P** + **A** [agent]).[105]

Other Embedded Clauses
The distribution of circumstantial adjuncts located before and after their different associated predicates is listed below:

Table 4.11 *Distribution of Circumstantial Adjuncts Located before Predicate in Other Embedded Clauses*

	Pres.	Imf.	Fut.	Aor.	Pf.	Ppf.	Total
Spatial	3	1	1	5		4	14
Temporal (1): Location	5	1		4			10
Temporal (1): Extent	3		2	1			6
Temporal (2): Earlier	2		3	5			10
Temporal (2): Contemporary	1						1
Manner: Means	2			1			3
Accompaniment: Comitative (Positive)	1						1
Role: Product				1			1
Matter	1				1		2
Agent	2						2
Total	19	2	6	17	1	4	49

Table 4.12 *Distribution of Circumstantial Adjuncts Located after Predicate in Other Embedded Clauses*

	Pres.	Imf.	Fut.	Aor.	Total
Spatial	4	6	6	10	26
Temporal (1): Location			1	1	2
Temporal (1): Extent	1			1	2
Temporal (2): Earlier				1	1
Temporal (2): Contemporary	1	1		1	3
Manner: Means	1	1			2
Manner: Quality	1				1

103. There is only one instance of A(matter)P: AP (12.10). For PA(matter), there is a total of 10x: PA (2.33, 33; 7.3; 20.26), PAA (3.19; 18.31; 24.44) and PCA (2.17, 20; 13.1).
104. PA (12.47; 21.4)
105. There are only two instances of A(agent)P: AP (7.4; 23.8). For PA(agent), there is a total of 9x: PA (4.15; 6.18; 7.30; 13.17; 21.20), PAA (3.19), APA (4.2), PCA (1.45) and PAC (17.20).

Manner: Comparison				1	1
Cause: Reason		1		4	5
Cause: Purpose			1		1
Accompaniment: Comitative (Positive)		2			2
Accompaniment: Additive (Negative) 1					1
Matter	2				2
Angle	1				1
Total	12	11	8	19	50

A majority of this category are instances of relative clauses. The relative pronoun of a relative clause is usually located at the front of the clause. This relative pronoun may be the subject, complement or a circumstantial adjunct of the clause. This grammatical feature causes many instances of circumstantial adjuncts located at the front of an embedded clause when they are relative pronouns.

Spatial

It is a trend to locate a spatial adjunct after the predicate. There are 26x of such case; while there are only four instances of this adjunct situated before the predicate (tendency: **P + A** [spatial]).[106]

Temporal (1)

There are only three instances of location adjunct when all the related cases of relative pronouns are excluded.[107] There are seven extent adjuncts. Five of them are located before the predicate (in which two are relative pronouns); and there are two located after the predicate.[108]

Temporal (2)

The different time (earlier) adjunct tends to occur before the predicate and is in aorist participial form (unmarked: **A** [tem ear][aor. part.] + **P**).[109] The same time

---

106. There are originally 14x of A(spatial)P: AP (5.25; 11.22; 20.28; 22.10), APS (8.38). APSA (13.4); APC (6.34), AAPC (19.30), SAAP (8.15), ASP (4.29; 8.2, 35; 19.30), CAP (12.3); all but four (6.34; 8.15; 12.3; 13.4) are relative pronouns and are thus placed at the front of a clause. On the contrary, there are 26x of PA(spatial): PA (8.26; 14.27), APSA (13.4; 17.27, 29; 21.6), PCA (6.48), SPA (5.17; 8.2 ; 9.50; 10.42; 17.12, 31), SPAA (23.19), ASPA (13.19, 21), SPCA (7.27; 8.3; 14.15), SPAC (7.38; 23.55), CPA (2.31), CCPA (12.3), CPAA (24.17), CSPA (13.1), CPSAA (12.42), in which 7.27 is a LXX citation.

107. Many instances of circumstantial adjunct are located at the front of an embedded clause because the circumstantial adjunct is a relative pronoun; to obtain a more accurate figure of the distribution of the adjunct is to exclude these instances. For A(loc tem)P, there are 10x originally: AP (8.13; 12.46, 46; 19.13), APS (1.20; 22.7), APSA (17.27, 29) and ASP (17.30; 24.12); all the adjuncts are relative pronouns except 8.13. For PA(loc temp), there are only two: SPA (1.20) and SPCA (18.30).

108. A(ext tem)P: AP (1.25; 23.29), APS (13.14), APSA (21.6) and SAP (8.13); in which 1.25 and 23.29 are relative pronouns. The two PA(ext tem) are SPA (6.2) and CPSA (13.16).

109. For A(tem ear)P, there are 9x in the form of an aorist participial clause: SAAP (8.15), SAAPA (10.30[2x]), SAAAP (8.14), ASPA (13.19, 21), SAPC (8.43) and CASP (12.37, 43); there is only one instance of present participial clause as adjunct: AAPC (19.30). For PA(tem ear), there is only one instance and it is in the form of an aorist participial clause: SAAPA (10.30).

(contemporary) adjunct has a total of four instances. They are all in present participial form and three of them are put after the predicate.[110] The distribution of the temporal (2) adjunct is listed as below:

	A(temporal [2])P	PA(temporal [2])	Total
Present participial form	2	3	5
Aorist participial form	9	1	10
Total	11	4	15

Manner
There are only seven cases of manner adjunct: five of them are means, one is quality and one is comparison.[111] They make a total number of A(manner)P to be 3x, and PA(manner) to be 5x.

Cause
There is a total of six times of cause adjunct, five of them are reason adjuncts, which are all put after the predicate;[112] one is purpose adjunct, which is also put after the predicate.[113]

Accompaniment
There are three positive comitative[114] and one negative additive.[115] Among these four there is only one located before the predicate.

Role
The only case of role adjunct is a product adjunct, which is located before the predicate.[116]

Matter
There is a total of four instances with two before and two after the predicate.[117]

Angle
There is only one instance of this adjunct and it appears after the predicate.[118]

---

110. A(tem con)P: SAAAP (8.14) and PA(tem con): SPCA (2.37), CPCAC (24.44), CPAA (24.17).

111. A(means)P: AP (1.4; 6.38; 17.1), in which only 17.1 is not a relative pronoun. There are two instances of PA(means): SPA (1.61) and SPCA (4.40). The quality adjunct is PA (8.15) and the comparison adjunct is SPCA (18.17).

112. SPA (7.23), SPAA (23.19) and SPCA (9.24, 48; 18.29).

113. CPSAA (12.42, which is in the form of an aorist infinitival clause).

114. One is before the predicate: SAPC (8.13); two are after it: SPA (5.29), SPCA (5.10).

115. This only negative additive is located after the predicate: PSA (6.4).

116. AP (8.17).

117. A(matter)P: APS (7.27), APC (9.9); both cases are relative pronouns. PA(matter): PA (16.2), CPA (23.14).

118. SPCA (7.1)

Agent
There are two instances of this adjunct and they appear before the predicate.[119]

Dependent Clauses of Other Embedded Clauses
There are only a few occurrences of such instances, which are summarized as follows:

Spatial
There are only four. One is located before the predicate;[120] and three are after it.[121]

Temporal (1)
There is only one, which is a location and is placed before the predicate.[122]

Manner
There are only three manner adjuncts. One is a means adjunct and is located before the predicate;[123] the other two are quality adjuncts and are also placed before the predicate.[124]

A Summing Analysis of the Positions of Circumstantial Adjuncts
Positions of All the Adjuncts
Positions of different kinds of circumstantial adjuncts in each of the six clause categories have been discussed in the above sections of this chapter. Some particular adjuncts tend to be before the predicate, while some other particular adjuncts tend to be after the predicate. A summing up picture can be obtained from a summarized table of the positions of all these different circumstantial adjuncts in the six clause categories:

---

119. AP (22.22), SAAAP (8.14)
120. AP (23.7)
121. PA (7.37), SPA (9.7; 19.27)
122. APS (17.20) (this one is in the form of an indirect question, where an interrogative particle πότε is used as a temporal adjunct and is thus placed at the front of the clause)
123. APC (5.19)
124. APS (8.36), ACP (14.7)

	Ind.		Dep.		Inf.		Part.		Emb.		Dpemb.		Total	
	AP	PA	AP	PA	AP	PA	AP	PA	AP	PA	AP	PA	AP	PA
Spatial	63	345	34	96	12	36	20	125	14	26	1	3	144	631
loc tem	43	41	9	8	4	3	3	14	10	2	1	0	70	68
ext tem	7	27	3	3	2	3	3	12	5	2			20	47
ear tem	231	7	6	2			1	0	10	1			248	10
con tem	52	130	1	6	0	3			1	3			54	142
lat tem	0	17											0	17
Means	34	43	11	4	2	7	4	11	3	2	1	0	55	67
Quality	30	11	8	2	4	3	8	7	0	1	2	0	52	24
Comp.	12	17	3	5			1	1	0	1			16	24
Reason	38	28	3	4	1	0	1	3	0	5			43	40
Purpose	1	65	0	7			0	3	0	1			1	76
Behalf	2	8	1	2	0	2	2	1					5	13
Result	2	10	0	4			0	4					2	18
Cond	1	2											1	2
Concess	1	0	3	1									4	1
Default					0	1	0	1					0	2
Com+	4	25	4	9	3	4	2	11	1	2			14	51
Com-	1	2	0	1	1	0							2	3
Add-	1	6							0	1			1	7
Product	0	7							1	0			1	7
Matter	3	19	2	5	0	7	1	10	2	2			8	43
Angle	4	7	0	3	0	2	0	2	0	1			4	15
Agent	0	9	0	2	0	5	2	9	2	0			4	25

Total	AP: 530		AP: 88		AP: 29		AP: 48		AP: 49		AP: 5		AP: 749	
	PA: 825		PA: 164		PA: 76		PA: 214		PA: 50		PA: 3		PA: 1332	

It can be seen from the above table that circumstantial adjuncts tend to be placed after the predicate. In the overall figure, predicate tends to precede the circumstantial adjunct (PA vs. AP is 1332x vs. 749x). The overall figure of each of the first four categories of clauses is similar: predicate tends to precede the circumstantial adjunct. This is shown from the table above (PA vs. AP of the first four categories of clauses are 852x vs. 530x, 164x vs. 88x, 76x vs. 29x, 214x vs. 28x respectively). The ratio of AP and PA is similar in the embedded clause category. This is mainly because many adjuncts of this type of clause appear in a form of relative pronoun and thus locate at the front of the clauses. On the individual types of adjuncts, their positioning tendency is almost the same in every clause category.[125] There are a certain number of adjuncts which have shown their tendency to be placed after the predicate: spatial, temporal (1) (extent), temporal

---

125. For example, the overall figure shows spatial adjunct tends to appear after the predicate (144x vs. 631x). This tendency is also true in all other clause categories: independent clauses (63x vs. 345x), dependent clauses (34x vs. 96x), infinitival clauses (12x vs. 36x), participial clauses (20x vs. 125x), embedded clauses (14x vs. 26x), embedded dependent clauses (1x vs. 3x). All these figures agree the overall figure: spatial adjunct tends to appear after the predicate. This situation (almost every individual figure agrees with the overall figure) is the same in most of the other adjuncts.

(2) (contemporary, later), purpose, result, positive comitative, negative additive, product, matter, angle and agent. The adjuncts which have shown their tendency to be before the predicate are: temporal (2) (earlier) and quality.

As shown before, some of these order patterns are unmarked (typical occurrence) (e.g. **P + A** [spatial], **A** [tem ear] + **P**, **P + A** [tem con], **P + A** [tem lat], **P + A** [matter], etc.); and some show their tendencies of having such patterns (e.g. **P + A** [com +], **P + A** [angle], etc.). The word order patterns obtained in this chapter are important in defining the marked order patterns regarding circumstantial adjuncts. This is particularly helpful in the studies in Chapter 5 and 6 of the work, where marked orders related to the positions of certain circumstantial adjuncts are studied (e.g. spatial).

Positions of Participial and Infinitival Adjuncts

Circumstantial adjuncts are very frequently employed in participial and infinitival forms. These adjuncts all carry their own tense form. This section will try to study the relationship of their tense forms and their positions with respect to their associated predicates.

Participial Adjuncts. Participial form frequently appears as a circumstantial adjunct in the Gospel. This is summarized according to the different clause types as follows:

1. *Independent Clauses*: Participial form is frequently employed as a circumstantial adjunct in independent clauses. They mainly occur in temporal (2), manner and cause adjuncts. Overall, when a participial adjunct appears before its related predicate, it tends to be in the aorist tense form; when it appears after its related predicate, it tends to be in the present tense form.[126] On individual categories, this is particularly true in temporal (2) adjuncts,[127] but it might not be the case in the categories of manner and cause adjuncts.[128] These figures can be observed from the summary of the distribution of participial adjuncts:

126. On the whole, there are 310 participial forms as adjuncts located before the predicate. 289x of them are in aorist tense; while only 18x of them are in present tense. There are 184 participial forms as adjuncts located after the predicate; 167x of them are in present tense, with only 13x of them in the aorist.

127. For adjuncts located before the predicate, 274 out of 282x are in the aorist; while for adjuncts located after the predicate, 145x out of 150x are in the present.

128. For participial manner adjuncts located before the predicates, there are seven instances in the present, and eight times in the aorist (which is different from the figure of temporal participial adjuncts, where the aorist is dominant when the adjuncts are located before the predicate); when participial manner adjuncts are located after the predicate, there are seven instances in the present, and two instances in the aorist (the situation of this category is similar to the one of temporal participial adjunct, where the present is dominant when the participial adjuncts are located after the predicate). For cause adjuncts, when they are located before the predicate, there are three instances in the present, and there are three instances in the aorist, where the aorist is not particularly dominant as in the cases of temporal participial adjuncts and the overall figure of participial adjuncts; when the cause adjuncts are located after the predicate, there are 15x of present, and 4x of aorist, where the present is dominant as in the cases of temporal participial adjuncts and the overall figure of participial adjuncts. The number of occurrences of

	Participial adjuncts located before predicate	*Participial adjuncts located after predicate*
Present participial adjunct	8 (temporal)	145 (temporal)
	7 (manner)	7 (manner)
	3 (cause)	15 (cause)
Aorist participial adjunct	274 (temporal)	5 (temporal)
	8 (manner)	2 (manner)
	3 (cause)	4 (cause)
	2 (result)	0 (result)
	2 (contingency)	2 (contingency)
Perfect participial adjunct	1 (temporal)	4 (temporal)
	2 (cause)	0 (cause)
Total	310	184

2. *Dependent Clauses*: The distributions of participial adjuncts in dependent clauses can be summarized as follows:

	Participial adjuncts located before predicate	*Participial adjuncts located after predicate*
Present participial adjunct	1 (temporal)	6 (temporal)
	1 (manner)	0 (manner)
	0 (cause)	2 (cause)
	2 (contingency)	0 (contingency)
Aorist participial adjunct	5 (temporal)	2 (temporal)
	1 (cause)	0 (cause)
Perfect participial adjunct	1 (temporal)	0 (temporal)
Total	11	10

For temporal participial adjuncts, the situation is similar to the one in independent clauses: it can be observed that the adjunct tends to be in the present tense form when it is located after the predicate (6x in present and 2x in aorist); when it is located before the predicate, the adjunct tends to be in the aorist tense form (5x in aorist and 1x in present). On the overall figure, the figure of participial adjuncts located after the predicate is the same: the adjunct tends to be in present (8x in present and only 2x in aorist), but the figure is not the same for the adjuncts located before the predicate: the number of present and aorist is quite evenly distributed.[129] It thus can be seen that it is an unmarked order to have a present participial adjunct located after the predicate, and an aorist participial adjunct located before the

these categories is not a great number (7x and 8x in present and aorist in manner adjuncts located before the predicate, 3x and 3x in present and aorist in cause adjuncts located before the predicate), but these figures may still represent a certain degree of difference in comparing to the overall figure of participial adjuncts.

129. There are 6x in aorist and 4x in present, this is mainly due to the cases of manner and contingency adjuncts, where the occurrences of manner (1x) and contingency (2x) are all in present when they are located before the predicate. The number is not large enough (only 1x and 2x) to make a conclusion here, but this figure still carries a certain degree of possibilities: it may not be a norm to have an aorist when these adjuncts (manner and contingency) are located before the predicate.

predicate in the case of temporal adjunct. It may also be a norm to have a present after the predicate in the other participial adjuncts,[130] but it may not be a norm to have an aorist when the other participial adjuncts are located before the predicate (manner and contingency).

3. *Infinitival Clauses*: The summary of participial adjuncts in infinitival clauses is as follows:

	Participial adjuncts located before predicate	Participial adjuncts located after predicate
Present participial adjunct	0 (temporal)	2 (temporal)
Aorist participial adjunct	0 (temporal)	1 (temporal)
	1 (manner)	1 (manner)
	1 (cause)	0 (cause)
Total	2	4

4. *Other Embedded Clauses*:

	Participial adjuncts located before predicate	Participial adjuncts located after predicate
Present participial adjunct	2 (temporal)	3 (temporal)
Aorist participial adjunct	9 (temporal)	1 (temporal)
Total	11	4

5. *Summary*: The overall figure of all the participial adjuncts in Luke can be obtained by summing up the above four tables, which is then summarized as follows:

	Overall participial adjuncts located before predicate	Overall participial adjuncts located after predicate
Present participial adjunct	11 (temporal)	156 (temporal)
	8 (manner)	7 (manner)
	3 (cause)	17 (cause)
	2 (contingency)	0 (contingency)
	Total: 24	Total: 180
Aorist participial adjunct	88 (temporal)	9 (temporal)
	9 (manner)	3 (manner)
	5 (cause)	4 (cause)
	2 (result)	0 (result)
	2 (contingency)	2 (contingency)
	Total: 306	Total: 18
Perfect participial adjunct	2 (temporal)	4 (temporal)
	2 (cause)	0 (cause)
	Total: 4	Total: 4
Total	334	202

130. For example, there are 2x in the present and 0x in the aorist in participial cause adjuncts. This may only represent a degree of possibilities since the number of occurrences is so small.

The above table shows it is a norm that the participial adjunct is in the present tense form when it is placed after the predicate and in the aorist tense form when it is placed before the predicate in the overall figures.[131] In fact, the number of occurrences of temporal participial adjunct is apparently dominant in the above figures, and the figure of this particular adjunct affects the overall figures. Once we look at the figures of this adjunct and the rest of the adjuncts separately, a clearer picture occurs. It is certainly an unmarked order that a temporal participial adjunct is in the aorist when it is located before the predicate, and in the present when it is located after the predicate.[132] This tendency is overall true in all the clauses of Luke as well as in different individual categories of clauses,[133] but it is not the case in manner and cause adjuncts when their location is before the predicate. When a manner or cause participial adjunct is located after the predicate, it follows the above discussed tendency: it tends to be in the present when it is located after the predicate,[134] but they do not follow the above discussed tendency when they are located before the predicate.[135] Thus it can be concluded that an aorist temporal participial adjunct in Luke located before the predicate is an unmarked pattern, and a present temporal participial adjunct located after the predicate is also an unmarked pattern. In the case of other kinds of participial adjuncts, they may also tend to be in the present when they are located after the predicate, but they do not tend to be in the aorist when they are located before the predicate.

131. When it is located before the predicate, 306x are in the aorist and 24x in the present; when it is located after the predicate, 180x are in the present and 18x in the aorist. Cf. Porter, *Idioms of the Greek New Testament*, pp. 188–89; *idem, Verbal Aspect in the Greek of the New Testament*, pp. 365–91 and *idem*, 'Word Order and Clause Structure in New Testament Greek', pp. 199–200.

132. When it is located before the predicate, 288x are in the aorist, only 11x are in the present; when it is located after the predicate, 156x are in the present, only 9x are in the aorist.

133. For independent clauses, the number of occurrences of present and aorist temporal participial adjunct when they are located before the predicate are 8x and 274x, and 145x and 5x when they are located after the predicate; for dependent clauses, the numbers are 1x and 5x when the location is before the predicate, and 6x and 2x after the predicate; for infinitival clauses, the numbers of present and aorist are 2x and 1x when the location is after the predicate (there is no occurrence of this kind of adjunct in this category); for other embedded clauses, the numbers are 2x and 9x when they are located before the predicate, and 3x and 1x when they are located after the predicate. All these show the tendency to have an aorist before the predicate, and a present after the predicate.

134. The overall figure of manner adjuncts located after the predicate is 7x in the present tense form and 3x in the aorist; the overall figure of cause adjuncts located after the predicate is 17x in the present and 4x in the aorist. This shows these two participial adjuncts tend to be in the present when they are placed after the predicate.

135. The overall figure of manner adjuncts located before the predicate is 8x in the present and 9x in the aorist; the overall figure of cause adjuncts located before the predicate is 3x in the present and 5x in the aorist (it is hard to conclude that the tendency is in the aorist here, since the numbers of occurrences here are small and their difference is small too [3x and 5x]). All these can not show these two participial adjuncts tend to be in the aorist when they are placed before the predicate.

Infinitival Adjuncts. Infinitival form also frequently appears as a circumstantial adjunct in the Gospel. This is summarized according to the different clause types.

1. *Independent Clauses*: Infinitival clause is another form frequently employed in adjuncts. The distribution of this adjunct in independent clauses can be summarized as follows:

	Infinitival adjunct located before predicate	Infinitival adjunct located after predicate
Present infinitival adjunct	1 (cause)	18 (cause)
	0 (result)	3 (result)
Aorist infinitival adjunct	0 (cause)	36 (cause)
	0 (result)	7 (result)
Total	1	64

Thus it can be seen that the unmarked order is to have an infinitival adjunct located after the predicate (mainly as cause adjunct), and it is more likely to have this adjunct in the aorist tense form than in the present (in the case of locating after the predicate, the number of present and aorist are 21x and 43x respectively).

2. *Dependent Clauses*: For the infinitival adjuncts, their distributions are as follows:

	Infinitival adjuncts located before predicate	Infinitival adjuncts located after predicate
Present infinitival adjunct	0 (cause)	1 (cause)
	0 (result)	1 (result)
Aorist infinitival adjunct	0 (cause)	6 (cause)
	0 (result)	1 (result)
Total	0	9

The above table shows that when an adjunct is in infinitival form, the unmarked order is to have it located after the predicate (9x vs. 0x), and the tense form tends to be the aorist (7x vs. 2x).

3. *Participial Clauses*: The summary of the distribution of infinitival adjuncts in participial clauses is as follows:

	Infinitival adjuncts located before predicate	Infinitival adjuncts located after predicate
Present infinitival adjunct	0 (result)	2 (result)
Aorist infinitival adjunct	1 (temporal)	0 (temporal)
	0 (cause)	2 (cause)
	0 (result)	2 (cause)
Total	1	6

4. *Other Embedded Clauses*:

	Infinitival adjunct located before predicate	Infinitival adjunct located after predicate
Aorist infinitival adjunct	0 (cause)	1 (cause)
Total	0	1

5. *Summary*: The overall figure of distributions of infinitival adjuncts in Luke can be obtained by summing up the above four tables:

	Overall infinitival adjuncts located before the predicate	Overall infinitival adjuncts located after the predicate
Present infinitival adjunct	1 (cause)	19 (cause)
	0 (result)	6 (result)
	Total: 1	Total: 25
Aorist infinitival adjunct	1 (temporal)	0 (temporal)
	0 (cause)	45 (cause)
	0 (result)	10 (result)
	Total: 1	Total: 55
Total	2	80

From the above table, it can be observed that the unmarked order is to have an infinitival adjunct located after the predicate (80x out of 82). It also shows that when an adjunct is in infinitival form, it tends to be in the aorist tense form.[136]

Summary
This chapter provides a framework of the distributions of the relative orders of different types of circumstantial adjuncts with their associated predicates. This study also illustrates the distributions of the circumstantial adjuncts related to the different tense forms of their associated predicates, and also the usual syntactic and grammatical features associated with the uses of the adjuncts. The study here represents the unmarked orders of these different types of circumstantial adjuncts with their predicates with substantial numeric data.

In general, there are a number of relative order patterns of predicate and circumstantial adjuncts which are predominant/or ones showing their tendencies of having such patterns:

(i) **P + A** (spatial)
This is almost true in all types of clauses. Predicate predominantly precedes the spatial adjunct.
(ii) **P + A** (ext tem)
This is mainly applied in independent clauses.
(iii) **A** (tem ear) + **P**; **P + A** (tem con); **P + A** (tem lat)
Temporal (earlier) adjunct predominantly precedes the predicate; temporal (contemporary) and temporal (later) adjuncts predominantly follow the predicate.
(iv) **P + A** (means)
This pattern tends to occur in independent clauses.
(v) **A** (quality) + **P**
This pattern tends to occur in independent and dependent clauses.
(vi) **P + A** (comp)
This pattern tends to occur in independent clauses.

136. In the case of this kind of adjunct located after the predicate, the number of the aorist is 55x; while the present is only 25x.

(vii) **P + A** (purpose)
This pattern predominantly occurs in independent and dependent clauses.
(viii) **P + A** (behalf)
This pattern tends to occur in independent clauses.
(ix) **P + A** (result)
This pattern tends to occur in independent clauses.
(x) **P + A** (com +)
This pattern predominantly occurs in independent clauses.
(xi) **P + A** (add)
This pattern tends to occur in independent clauses.
(xii) **P + A** (accom)
This pattern predominantly occurs in independent and participial clauses, and tends to occur in dependent clauses.
(xiii) **P + A** (role)
This pattern predominantly occurs in independent clauses.
(xiv) **P + A** (matter)
This pattern predominantly occurs in independent and participial clauses, and tends to occur in infinitival clauses.
(xv) **P + A** (angle)
This pattern tends to occur in independent clauses.
(xvi) **P + A** (agent)
This pattern predominantly occurs in independent and participial clauses, and tends to occur in infinitival clauses.

For participial adjuncts, generally they are predominantly in aorist tense form when they occur before the predicate; and they are in present tense form when they occur after the predicate. This is particularly true in temporal (2) adjuncts. For infinitival clauses, generally they occur predominantly after the predicate, and they tend to be in aorist tense form.

This chapter gives a general picture of the positions of circumstantial adjuncts. Chapter 3 of the work gives a general figure of the relative positions of the three main constituents (subject, predicate and complement). The figures of these two chapters provide unmarked word order patterns. They also form bases to define marked order patterns which are discussed in Part III of the work.

PART III

MARKED WORD ORDERS OF THE GOSPEL OF LUKE AND FOREGROUNDED MESSAGES

Chapter 5

Indirect Speeches in Luke and the Disciples' Understanding of Jesus

While commentating on a verse in ch. 8 of the Gospel of Luke, Plummer states in his commentary:

> To these two (calming the sea and healing of the demoniac)... and Lk. add the healing of the woman with the issue and the raising of the daughter of Jairus ... The full series gives us a group of representative miracles exhibiting Christ's power over the forces of nature and the powers of hell, over disease and over death.[1]

It has been a generally agreed view that Luke 8 is packed with Jesus' miracles, and these miracles are arranged in Luke 7–8 to show his deity and power. In this chapter, through a discussion of a series of uses of indirect speech I will show Luke 7–8 is not only packed with Jesus' miracles, but these miracles are narrated alongside with other nearby events recorded by Luke to show Jesus' disciples' lack of understanding of his mission and his role.

Discussions will firstly be focused on the passages related to the indirect speeches in Luke 7–8, which then subsequently introduce some other related surrounding passages to discussion. The surrounding passages in Luke 8–9 all share one or two of these key terms – fear and faithlessness. Together with the related marked word order patterns of these passages, the occurrences of this key term demonstrate a foregrounded message: Jesus' disciples' lack of understanding of his mission and his role.

Indirect Discourses Addressed to Jesus in the Gospel of Luke

Communications between characters in Luke occur very frequently in the entire Gospel. Almost all of these conversations are recorded in a form of direct speech. Indirect speeches (or so called reported projections) among characters are only occasionally used throughout the Gospel. In the events of indirect speeches being

---

1. A. Plummer, *A Critical and Exegetical Commentary on the Gospel According to S. Luke* (ICC; Edinburgh: T&T Clark, 5th edn 1922), p. 225; cf. C.H. Talbert and J.H. Hayesm, 'A Theology of Sea Storms in Luke-Acts', in D.P. Moessner (ed.), *Jesus and the Heritage of Israel: Luke's Narrative Claim upon Israel's Legacy* (LII, 1; Harrisburg: Trinity International, 1999), pp. 267–83 (277), who consider Jesus' power is demonstrated through a series of miracles in Luke 8 (8.22-25; 8.26-39; 8.43-48; 8.40-42, 49-56).

used, the verbal processes of these speeches are mostly in a form of imperfective aspect.[2] These imperfective indirect verbal processes are mainly in independent clauses. It is interesting and significant to notice that most of these events are describing a person (who is not one of Jesus' disciples) addressing an indirect speech to Jesus, and they are mainly located in Luke 7–8.[3] This chapter will concentrate on these incidents and study how these incidents subsequently introduce other related passages which contribute to a theme: Jesus' disciples' failure of understanding him.[4] These incidents are listed as follows:

7.3 ἀκούσας δὲ περὶ τοῦ Ἰησοῦ ἀπέστειλεν πρὸς αὐτὸν πρεσβυτέρους τῶν Ἰουδαίων ἐρωτῶν αὐτὸν ὅπως ἐλθὼν διασώσῃ τὸν δοῦλον αὐτοῦ
7.36 ἠρώτα δέ τις αὐτὸν τῶν Φαρισαίων ἵνα φάγῃ μετ' αὐτοῦ
8.9 ἐπηρώτων δὲ αὐτὸν οἱ μαθηταὶ αὐτοῦ τίς αὕτη εἴη ἡ παραβολή

2.   There are three verbal aspects in Greek. Perfective aspect includes aorist tense form, which is the least heavily weighted of the Greek verbal aspect; imperfective aspect includes present and imperfect tense forms, which is more heavily weighted; stative includes perfect and pluperfect, which is most heavily weighted (see Porter, *Idioms of the Greek New Testament*, pp. 21–23; idem, *Verbal Aspect in the Greek of the New Testament*, pp. 83–93).
   The indirect speeches with a perfective aspect in the Gospel are 8.37, 56; 9.21, 40; 22.4, 32. The indirect speeches with an imperfective aspect are: 4.41; 6.11; 7.3, 36; 8.9, 28, 31, 38, 41; 9.18, 20, 38; 11.18, 37; 12.13, 29; 15.26; 18.19, 36; 20.8, 41; 21.5; 22.23, 70; 23.23. Many of these indirect speeches are actually part of the content of a direct speech, which is introduced by the speaker of that direct speech rather than by the narrator (e.g. 9.18 καὶ ἐπηρώτησεν αὐτοὺς λέγων, *τίνα με λέγουσιν οἱ ὄχλοι εἶναι*; this indirect question is actually the content of Jesus' speaking, and is not the narrator's narrated event). When these incidents are excluded, indirect speeches with a perfective aspect narrated by the narrator of Luke are 8.37, 56; 9.21, 40 and 22.4; incidents with an imperfective aspect are 4.41; 6.11; 7.3, 36; 8.9, 31, 38, 41; 11.37; 15.26; 18.36; 21.5; 22.23; 23.23. Discussions of indirect speeches in this chapter are mainly based on these incidents which are actually narrated indirect speeches by the narrator of Luke.
   3.   Incidents of people speaking to Jesus in indirect speech with an imperfective aspect are 7.3, 36; 8.9, 31, 38, 41 and 11.37; most of these events describe a single person addressing an indirect speech to Jesus (except 8.9, where the speakers are a group of Jesus' disciples). Almost all of these incidents occur in independent clauses (six out of 7x) (these independent clauses are all in indicative mood: five in imperfect tense [7.36; 8.9, 31, 38, 41] and one in present tense form [11.37]); 7.3 is the only incident occurring in a present participial clause which functions as an adjunct of the main clause. The incident of Jesus addressing an indirect speech only occurs once (4.41, an independent clause in indicative mood and imperfect tense form) and the incidents of Jesus not being a participant of such a communication are 6.11; 15.26; 18.36; 21.5; 22.23; 23.23 (incidents of 6.11, 15.26, 18.36 occur in independent clauses [all are in indicative mood with imperfect tense form]; where incident of 21.5 occurs in an dependent clause [in a form of present participle], 22.23 is a present infinitival clause functioning as a complement of its main clause, and 23.23 is a present participial clause functioning as an adjunct of its main clause. The above analysis shows most of the imperfective indirect speeches are devoted to incidents narrating a single person speaking to Jesus, and they are mainly located in Luke 7–8 and in independent clauses with indicative mood and with an imperfect tense form.
   4.   Some scholars consider the disciples have been positively portrayed in Luke (e.g. K.J. Kim, *Stewardship and Almsgiving in Luke's Theology* [JSNTSup, 155; Sheffield: Sheffield Academic Press, 1998], pp. 89–94). However, this chapter of the work will concentrate on the topic of how Luke negatively portrays the disciples: their misunderstanding of Jesus.

8.31 καὶ παρεκάλουν αὐτὸν ἵνα μὴ ἐπιτάξῃ αὐτοῖς εἰς τὴν ἄβυσσον ἀπελθεῖν
8.38 ἐδεῖτο δὲ αὐτοῦ ὁ ἀνὴρ ἀφ' οὗ ἐξεληλύθει τὰ δαιμόνια εἶναι σὺν αὐτῷ
8.41 καὶ πεσὼν παρὰ τοὺς πόδας [τοῦ] Ἰησοῦ παρεκάλει αὐτὸν εἰσελθεῖν εἰς τὸν οἶκον αὐτοῦ
11.37 ἐν δὲ τῷ λαλῆσαι ἐρωτᾷ αὐτὸν Φαρισαῖος ὅπως ἀριστήσῃ παρ' αὐτῷ

All of these seven verses are indirect speeches addressed to Jesus. They all have verbs of 'asking' (etc.) that are imperfective. Except for 7.3, all of them are incidents in independent clause with an indicative mood.

Indirect Discourse in a Non-Independent Clause

Luke 7.1-10. Luke 7.3 is an indirect speech addressed to Jesus in a form of present participial clause (ἐρωτῶν αὐτὸν ὅπως ἐλθὼν διασώσῃ τὸν δοῦλον αὐτοῦ). This indirect speech is actually addressed to Jesus through the ones whom the centurion has sent.[5] Jesus' response in 7.9 (οὐδὲ ἐν τῷ Ἰσραὴλ τοσαύτην πίστιν εὗρον) comes with a marked ACP word order (as stated in Chapter 3 of the work, it is an unmarked order to have a complement following its predicate; and as stated in Chapter 4, it is an unmarked order to have a spatial adjunct located after its predicate), which shows the centurion's faith is the main cause of his servant's healing.[6]

Indirect Discourses in Independent Clauses

Luke 7.36-50. Luke 7.36 (ἠρώτα δέ τις αὐτὸν τῶν Φαρισαίων ἵνα φάγῃ μετ' αὐτοῦ) begins the episode of 7.36-50 and states Simon's invitation of Jesus to his home.[7] In this episode, it is highly acknowledged that the woman who anointed

---

5. The centurion has sent delegations twice (this is different from Matthew's reading in Mt. 8.5-13. See U. Wagner's thorough statistical analysis of the two synoptic passages: U. Wagner, *Der Hauptmann von Kafarnaum [Mt. 7.28a; 8.5-10, 13 par Lk. 7.1-10]: Ein Beitrag zur Q-Forschung* [WUNT, 2. 14; Tübingen: Mohr, 1985]; and cf. R.A.J. Gagnon's statistical studies on the topic and his criticism of Wagner's work [R.A.J. Gagnon, 'Statistical Analysis and the Case of the Double Delegation', *CBQ* 55 (1993), pp. 709–31]; and his later work discussing the functions of the two delegations relating to Lukan redaction: *idem*, 'Luke's Motives for Redaction in the Account of the Double Delegation in Luke 7.1-10', *NovT* 36 [1994], pp. 122–45).

6. D.R. Catchpole, 'The Centurion's Faith and its Function in Q', in F. Segbroeck, C.M. Tuckett, G. Belle and J. Verheyden (eds.), *The Four Gospels 1992* (BETL, 100; Leuven: Leuven University Press, 1992), I, pp. 517, 538.

7. I.H. Marshall has observed the order of words is unusual and suggests it relates to the nature of the invitation: 'The unusual order of words [τις αὐτὸν τῶν Φαρισαίων] stresses the unusual nature of the invitation' (*The Gospel of Luke: A Commentary on the Greek Text* [NIGTC; Exeter: The Paternoster Press, 1978], p. 308; cf. B.S. Easton, *The Gospel According to St. Luke: A Critical and Exegetical Commentary* [Edinburgh: T&T Clark, 1926], p. 105, who holds a similar position). Marshall does not give any explanation except only mentioning two other incidents for comparison (11.37 and 14.1). Probably Marshall finds the order unusual based on the pronoun αὐτόν being inserted between τις and τῶν Φαρισαίων. The nature of the invitation may not be as unusual as Marshall states, at least there are two more similar incidents in the Gospel (11.37 and 14.1) (as Marshall has already stated), also cf. Plummer, *Luke*, p. 210. In fact, the unusual order is not only this, but also a sequence of marked orders which will be discussed below.

Jesus with ointment is the centre of the story. The Pharisee Simon in the story is portrayed in sharp contrast to the woman: one has a good understanding of Jesus, and one has a misinterpretation of Jesus. The importance of Simon is first highlighted by his initiated interaction with Jesus, which is narrated in an indirect speech with an imperfective verbal process (7.36). His significance and contrast to the woman are then brought out by a sequence of marked word orders.

The woman's action is first enforced by two marked word orders in 7.38: καὶ στᾶσα ὀπίσω παρὰ τοὺς πόδας αὐτοῦ κλαίουσα τοῖς δάκρυσιν ἤρξατο βρέχειν τοὺς πόδας αὐτοῦ καὶ ταῖς θριξὶν τῆς κεφαλῆς αὐτῆς ἐξέμασσεν καὶ κατεφίλει τοὺς πόδας αὐτοῦ καὶ ἤλειφεν τῷ μύρῳ. The first one is in the participial clause παρὰ τοὺς πόδας αὐτοῦ κλαίουσα.[8] The second one is the infinitival clause τοῖς δάκρυσιν...βρέχειν τοὺς πόδας αὐτοῦ.[9] The woman's action is then further highlighted by a sequence of three clauses all with an imperfective (foreground) aspect: ἐξέμασσεν, κατεφίλει and ἤλειφεν. These three consequent imperfective aspects are used alongside the above two marked word orders to highlight what the woman has done to Jesus.

The woman's action is then compared to Simon's with a sequence of marked word orders.[10] This is contained in Jesus' statement to Simon in 7.44-46. This

8.   The order of the participial clause is marked by placing the circumstantial spatial adjunct παρὰ τοὺς πόδας αὐτοῦ before its predicate κλαίουσα. In participial clauses of Luke, the number of occurrence of this type of adjunct placed before and after its predicate is 20x and 125x respectively (as stated in Chapter 3 of the work, spatial adjunct predominantly occurs after the predicate).

9.   The predicate (ἤρξατο) of the main clause is followed by an infinitival clause as a complement. The infinitival clause has a marked APC order: the τοῖς δάκρυσιν is a circumstantial means adjunct; in infinitival clauses, means adjunct placed after its predicate is 7x, while before its predicate is only 3x. More strikingly, this means adjunct does not only precede its predicate and complement in its own clause, but also precedes the predicate ἤρξατο of the main clause, which makes this a highly marked pattern.

10.   Commentators and scholars have generally noticed the comparisons and contrasts between the deeds of Simon and the woman throughout the clauses starting from 7.44. E.g. J. Reiling and J.L. Swellengrebel state: 'The clause (7.44) introduces a series of contrasts between Simon and the woman in their behaviour concerning Jesus' (*A Translator's Handbook on the Gospel of Luke* [Leiden: E.J. Brill, 1977], p. 322); Marshall: 'the three aspects of the woman's deed are contrasted with three expressions of hospitality that Simon had not shown to Jesus' (*Gospel of Luke*, p. 311–12; and cf. E.E. Ellis, *The Gospel of Luke* [NCBC; Grand Rapids: Eerdmans, rev. edn 1974], p. 122; J.M. Creed, *The Gospel According to St. Luke: The Greek Text with Introduction, Notes, and Indices* [London: Macmillan, 1965], pp. 111–12; N. Geldenhuys, *Commentary on the Gospel of Luke* [London: Marshall, Morgan & Scott, 1950], p. 234; W. Manson, *The Gospel of Luke* [MNTC; London: Hodder & Stoughton, 1930], p. 85; L.T. Johnson, *The Gospel of Luke* [SPS, 3; Collegeville: The Liturgical Press, 1991], p. 129; D.A. Neale, *None but the Sinners: Religious Categories in the Gospel of Luke* [JSNTSup, 58; Sheffield: Sheffield Academic Press, 1991], p. 144; R.C. Tannehill, *The Narrative Unity of Luke-Acts: A Literary Interpretation*. I. *The Gospel According to Luke* [Philadelphia: Fortress Press, 1986], p. 106; J.O. York, *The Last Shall Be First: The Rhetoric of Reversal in Luke* [JSNTSup, 46; Sheffield: Sheffield Academic Press, 1991], p. 119). What I am trying to argue here is not only a series of comparisons and contrasts as commentators have already observed, but also how they are accompanied with a sequence of marked word order types, which will be discussed below.

statement is important, which can be foreseen in the highlighted preceded inter-action between the two participants in 7.40: καὶ ἀποκριθεὶς ὁ Ἰησοῦς εἶπεν πρὸς αὐτόν, Σίμων, ἔχω σοί τι εἰπεῖν. ὁ δέ, διδάσκαλε, εἰπέ, φησίν. Jesus' statement contains an infinitival clause functioning as the complement of the main verb ἔχω. This infinitival clause is in a highly marked order CCP: C(receiver: σοί) C(verbiage: τι) P(verbal process: εἰπεῖν).[11] Typically verbiages (content of verbal process) and receivers follow predicates in verbal processes (as stated in Chapter 3); here the receiver (σοί) and verbiage (τι) precede the verbal process (εἰπεῖν) and this forms a CCP pattern.[12] The clause of Simon's response is also highly marked (SCP) with the verbiage (διδάσκαλε, εἰπέ) preceding its verbal process (φησίν), which places the verbiage between the speaker and the verb.[13] This short interaction between Jesus and Simon with two similar marked patterns (verbiages placed before verbal processes) is to bring out the importance of the following statement of Jesus, especially 7.44-46, where Jesus is making a comparison between the woman and Simon. This comparison is first introduced by Jesus' action in 7.44: καὶ στραφεὶς πρὸς τὴν γυναῖκα τῷ Σίμωνι ἔφη.

Jesus turns to the woman and speaks to Simon.[14] This introduction is then followed by a sequence of marked orders to bring out the comparisons and contrasts in 7.44-46 (7.44 εἰσῆλθόν σου εἰς τὴν οἰκίαν, ὕδωρ μοι ἐπὶ πόδας οὐκ ἔδωκας· αὕτη δὲ τοῖς δάκρυσιν ἔβρεξέν μου τοὺς πόδας καὶ ταῖς θριξὶν αὐτῆς ἐξέμαξεν. 45 φίλημά μοι οὐκ ἔδωκας· αὕτη δὲ ἀφ᾽ ἧς εἰσῆλθον οὐ διέλιπεν καταφιλοῦσά μου τοὺς πόδας. 46 ἐλαίῳ τὴν κεφαλήν μου οὐκ ἤλειψας· αὕτη δὲ μύρῳ ἤλειψεν τοὺς πόδας μου). This statement first comes with a marked order in 7.44.[15] Jesus' following statement about Simon is even further marked: CCAP.

11.   σοί and τι appear before the verb which governs them (εἰπεῖν). This order is different from the usual practice and thus it indicates markedness (after studying some papyrus letters dating from the early-second to the late-fourth century CE, Horrock notices that clitic pronouns [cf. Dover, *Greek Word Order*, p. 13] tend to appear after their associated verb: 'clitic pronouns normally appear immediately after the verbs that govern them' [G. Horrocks, *Greek: A History of the Language and its Speakers* (London: Longman, 1997), p.115 (cf. p. 59)]) (σοί and τι only precede εἰπεῖν but not the main verb ἔχω; this is due to the feature of being postpositive words [Porter, *Idioms of the Greek New Testament*, p. 238; Dover, *Greek Word Order*, pp. 12–13]).

12.   The use of the verb ἔχω plus an infinitive is frequent in Luke and is widely agreed, as stated in Fitzmyer, *Luke*, p. 690; Marshall, *Gospel of Luke*, p. 310; J. Nolland, *Luke* (WBC, 35A, 35B and 35C; Dallas: Word Books, 1989–93), p. 355; cf. Paffenroth, *The Story of Jesus According to L*, p. 43 n. 98; but what is so significant here is the marked CCP order: the receiver and verbiage being placed before the verbal process (there is 3x of CCP order in Lukan infinitival clauses; while there are 14x in PCC).

13.   The unusualness of a verbal process being separated from its speaker is noticed by Marshall (*Gospel of Luke*, p. 310); also M.D. Goulder, *Luke: A New Paradigm* (JSNTSup, 20; Sheffield, Sheffield Academic Press, 1989), p. 406. In fact, this SCP order in 7.40 is marked because the numbers of SCP and SPC in independent clauses are 37x and 147x respectively (complement predominantly follows its predicate as stated in Chapter 3).

14.   Another marked type (CP): where the addressee 'Simon' is placed before the verbal process 'spoke' (it is a marked order of having a complement located before its predicate; e.g. there are 78x of CP in independent clauses, while there are 306x of PC).

15.   The modifier with possessive function (σου) in the nominal group precedes its head (τὴν

This CCAP is a marked order with a marked position of a purpose circumstantial adjunct.[16] The following statement about the woman (αὕτη δὲ τοῖς δάκρυσιν ἔβρεξέν μου τοὺς πόδας) is also marked: with the possessive modifier (μου) preceding its head (τοὺς πόδας). The comparison and contrast between the two persons is also brought out by the demonstrative pronoun αὕτη.[17] In 7.45, the statement about Simon is marked with C(φίλημα) C(μοι) P(οὐκ ἔδωκας), again with two complements preceding the predicate; the clause on the woman is marked with the dependent clause (ἀφ' ἧς εἰσῆλθον) placed between the components (αὕτη and οὐ διέλιπεν καταφιλοῦσά μου τοὺς πόδας) of the main clause. The demonstrative pronoun αὕτη is again used to state the contrast, and the complement (μου τοὺς πόδας) of the participial clause is again marked with the possessive modifier (μου) placed before its head (τοὺς πόδας) of the nominal group.[18] In 7.46, only a marked order is used to state the action of Simon: AC(τὴν κεφαλήν μου) P, again with complement placed before the predicate. The clause on the woman is again used with αὕτη to bring out the contrast between her and Simon.

The episode of 7.36-60 first uses marked orders to emphasize the actions of the woman. Some further marked patterns are used in Jesus and Simon's interaction (7.40) to highlight the content of Jesus' following statements (7.44-46) to Simon. 7.44-46 is used to bring out the comparisons and contrasts between Simon and the woman. The woman's genuine acceptance of Jesus is contrasted to Simon's invitation to Jesus, and the woman's approach to Jesus is a contrast to Simon's misunderstanding of Jesus.[19] This woman's genuine acceptance of Jesus leads her to be saved, which shows her faith in Jesus. As stated in 7.50, the woman's faith is the main cause of her salvation.

οἰκίαν), and even precedes εἰς. It is a common practice to have such a modifier placed after its head, instead of before it.

16. This pattern has two complements located before its predicate and is a marked order: C(ὕδωρ) C(μοι) A(ἐπὶ πόδας) P(οὐκ ἔδωκας) (there are only 4x of CCP in independent clauses, while there are 167x of PCC) (complement predominantly follows its predicate in independent clauses as stated in Chapter 3). The purpose circumstantial adjunct (ἐπὶ πόδας) precedes the predicate and is highly marked as well. In independent clauses, this is the only occurrence (7.44) of a purpose adjunct located before its predicate; while all the other purpose adjuncts (65x) are located after the predicate (purpose adjunct predominantly follows its predicate as stated in Chapter 4).

17. Cf. F.T. Gench, 'Luke 7.36-50', *Int* 46 (1992), p. 289; J.L. Resseguie, 'Automatization and Defamiliarization in Luke 7.36-50', *JLT* 5 (1991), pp. 137–50 (144).

18. Cf. Reiling and Swellengrebel, *Handbook*, p. 322.

19. Simon admits Jesus is a teacher (7.40) and wonders if Jesus is a prophet. In Simon's understanding, such a teacher (or even a prophet) should avoid the touch of a sinner (cf. J.F. Coakley, 'The Anointing at Bethany and the Priority of John', *JBL* 107 (1988), pp. 241–56 (250–51); Marshall, *Gospel of Luke*, pp. 304, 309 [where Marshall also states the use of λέγων in 7.39 as 'redundant'; in fact a present participle λέγων being placed after a verbal process which is in the form of an indicative verb is extremely common in Luke]). The woman's attitude to Jesus is just rightly contrasted to Simon's (cf. J.J. Kilgallen, 'John the Baptist, the Sinful Woman, and the Pharisee', *JBL* 104 [1985], pp. 675–79 (678–79); Gench, 'Luke 7.36-50', pp. 285–86; Resseguie, 'Automatization and Defamiliarization', pp. 144–46; D.A.S. Ravens, 'The Setting of Luke's Account of the Anointing: Luke 7.2-8.3', *NTS* 34 [1988], pp. 282–92 (282)).

Luke 8.9-10. Luke 8.9 (ἐπηρώτων δὲ αὐτὸν οἱ μαθηταὶ αὐτοῦ τίς αὕτη εἴη ἡ παραβολή) records the inquiry of Jesus' disciples about the meaning of the parable which Jesus has just told. Jesus and his disciples are the only participants in the incident of 8.9-10. The disciples' question is narrated in the form of an indirect discourse,[20] and Jesus' reply contains a marked order to show the emphasis of the disciples' privilege of knowing the mysteries of the kingdom of God.[21] The disciples do not understand the parable and thus they ask about its meaning; this event of the indirect question leads to Jesus' declaration of their privilege of knowing the secrets of God's kingdom.

Luke 8.26-39. In the episode of the demoniac in 8.26-39, the author has twice used a reported speech with an imperfective aspect to represent the demoniac's two requests to Jesus. The significance of their interaction is first highlighted by the marked orders in 8.27a (ἐξελθόντι δὲ αὐτῷ ἐπὶ τὴν γῆν, which describes the meeting of the two participants);[22] and the description of the man in 8.27b (καὶ

---

20. Although a few translations translate 8.9 as a direct question (e.g. KJV, NKJV; also cf. Reiling and Swellengrebel, *Handbook*, p. 332), the majority of different Bible translations translate this verse as an indirect question, e.g. ASV, RSV, NRSV, TEV, REB. Besides, commentators and scholars generally admit this is an indirect question. For example, Johnson, *Luke*, pp. 130, 132; Fitzmyer, *Luke*, pp. 108, 706 (although Fitzmyer translates 8.9 as a direct question in his own translation in his commentary, he admits it is an indirect question: 'Verse 9...revealed as such by the indirect question with the optative' [p. 706]; also 'in indirect questions:...8:9' [p. 108]); Creed (*Luke*, p. 115); Plummer: '... εἴη. It is only in Lk. in NT that we find the opt. in indirect questions' (*Luke*, p. 22; cf. p. 219); Nolland: 'a simple indirect question using the optative' (*Luke*, p. 379); cf. P.S. Minear, 'Luke's Use of the Birth Stories', in L.E. Keck and J.L. Martyn (eds.), *Studies in Luke-Acts. Essays Presented in Honor of Paul Schubert, Buckingham Professor of New Testament Criticism and Interpretation at Yale University* (Nashville: Abingdon Press, 1966), pp. 111–130 (114). The position of 8.9 functioning as an indirect question is also supported by some major NT grammars, e.g. N. Turner: 'optative in indirect speech ... (Lk.) 8:9' (*Style* [J.H. Moulton, *A Grammar of New Testament Greek*, IV; Edinburgh: T&T Clark, 1976], p. 62); Burton, *Syntax of the Moods and Tenses*, pp. 132–33; Blass and Debrunner, *A Greek Grammar*, p. 195; also cf. S.G. Green, *Handbook to the Grammar of the Greek Testament. Together with Complete Vocabulary and an Examination of the Chief New Testament Synonyms* (London: The Religious Tract Society, rev. edn 1912), pp. 315–17; Moule, *An Idiom Book of New Testament Greek*, pp. 23, 154.

21. Jesus' reply is in a marked order: CPAS, where the recipient (ὑμῖν) is placed before its predicate (δέδοται) (there are 27x of CPS in independent clauses; while there are 147x of SPC and 49x of PSC) (subject and predicate predominantly precede the complement as stated in Chapter 3). Besides the word order, the predicate is in static (frontground) aspect.

22. A number of commentators admit Luke has improved Mark's grammar by using the participial construction (ἐξελθόντι δὲ αὐτῷ [Lk. 8.27]) to replace Mark's use of a genitive absolute (ἐξελθόντος αὐτοῦ [Mk 5.2]) (e.g. Fitzmyer, *Luke*, p. 737; Marshall, *Gospel of Luke*, p. 337; Nolland, *Luke*, p. 407; Creed, *Luke*, p. 120). While they all rightly recognize Luke has improved Mark's grammar by using the participial construction in Lk. 8.27, Fitzmyer thinks this construction is not easily translatable, even though he also admits the use of the grammar by Luke through the participial phrase is better ('Lit. "him going out [of the boat] onto the land there met...". With this not-easily-translatable phrase, Luke has improved the questionable Greek of Mark' [*Luke*, p. 737]; also cf. Reiling and Swellengrebel, *Handbook*, p. 344, in which they may also imply the phrase is not easily translatable by particularly mentioning the syntax of the clause:

χρόνῳ ἱκανῷ οὐκ ἐνεδύσατο ἱμάτιον καὶ ἐν οἰκίᾳ οὐκ ἔμενεν ἀλλ' ἐν τοῖς μνήμασιν).²³ The first encounter of the demoniac and Jesus is marked in 8.28.²⁴ This is then followed by two reported speeches to Jesus by the demoniac, which are all with imperfective aspect:

> 8.31 καὶ παρεκάλουν αὐτὸν ἵνα μὴ ἐπιτάξῃ αὐτοῖς εἰς τὴν ἄβυσσον ἀπελθεῖν
> 8.38 ἐδεῖτο δὲ αὐτοῦ ὁ ἀνὴρ ἀφ' οὗ ἐξεληλύθει τὰ δαιμόνια εἶναι σὺν αὐτῷ

The content of the first reported speech comes with a marked order: the infinitival clause in 8.31 (εἰς τὴν ἄβυσσον ἀπελθεῖν). This infinitival clause has the spatial adjunct (εἰς τὴν ἄβυσσον) located before the predicate (ἀπελθεῖν).²⁵

8.38 comes alongside with 8.37 (καὶ ἠρώτησεν αὐτὸν ἅπαν τὸ πλῆθος τῆς περιχώρου τῶν Γερασηνῶν ἀπελθεῖν ἀπ' αὐτῶν) to make comparison and contrast to the reactions of the man and the people around the place after the

---

'participle in the dative, going with ὑπήντησεν' [p. 344]). In fact, what causes Fitzmyer to think this phrase is not easily translated is actually the unusual word order used by Luke in the clause: (i) the complement (αὐτῷ) of the main clause in 8.27 is placed before its predicate (ὑπήντησεν), where CP is a marked order in Luke (there is a total of 306x of PC in independent clause, while there are only 78x of CP); moreover, all the other occurrences of this verb in the NT have the complement (also in dative case) located after their predicates (Mt. 28.9: προσεκύνησαν αὐτῷ; Mk 5.2: ὑπήντησεν αὐτῷ; Jn 11.20: ὑπήντησεν αὐτῷ; 30: ὑπήντησεν αὐτῷ; 12.18: ὑπήντησεν αὐτῷ); (ii) the complement αὐτῷ is located within the participial group ἐξελθόντι ἐπὶ τὴν γῆν which is used to modify it.

23. This is a marked pattern: A(extent temporal χρόνῳ ἱκανῷ) PC and A(spatial ἐν οἰκίᾳ) P to describe the demoniac. In independent clauses, extent temporal adjunct preceding the predicate occurs 7x, and following the predicate occurs 27x; for spatial adjuncts, the ratio of locating before and after the predicate is 63x to 345x. Here the extent temporal adjunct and spatial adjunct are both located before their predicate.

24. The content of the demoniac's first request in 8.28 (μή με βασανίσῃς) is marked with a CP order. The number of occurrences of CP and PC in dependent clauses is 40x and 84x respectively. This demoniac's comment on Jesus' title is the most explicit and longest in Luke's account since Jesus has started his missionary work so far. When compared with the other instances of a demon's calling to Jesus, the one in 8.31 is the longest and the most explicit (cf. 4.7 'Son of God', 4.34 'Holy One of God' and 4.41'Son of God'; while 8.31 'Jesus, Son of the Most High God'); cf. P.J. Achtemeier, 'The Lukan Perspective on the Miracles of Jesus: A Preliminary Sketch', in C.H. Talbert (ed.), *Perspective on Luke-Acts* (Edinburgh: T&T Clark, 1978), p. 158.

25. Commentators have only noticed the redactional work of Luke by comparing to Mark's writing (Mk 5.10 ἔξω τῆς χώρας being changed to εἰς τὴν ἄβυσσον, Lk. 8.31) (e.g. Creed, *Luke*, p. 121; Fitzmyer, *Luke*, p. 739; Plummer, *Luke*, p. 231; and cf. Nolland, *Luke*, p. 410; and D.L. Bock, *Luke* [BECNT, 3A and 3B; Grand Rapids: Baker Books, 1994–96], p. 774). In fact, the prepositional phrase εἰς τὴν ἄβυσσον used by Luke is more than a redactional change. The location of the prepositional phrase (located before the predicate) is actually a quite unusual practice and thus it functions as a marked order (the number of spatial adjuncts preceding and following the predicate is 12x and 27x in infinitival clauses; and 63x and 345x in independent clauses) (spatial adjunct predominantly follows the predicate as stated in Chapter 4). In fact, all three other similar occurrences (the same verb plus a prepositional phrase beginning with εἰς as a spatial adjunct) have the spatial adjunct located after the predicate: Lk. 1.23 (ἀπῆλθεν εἰς τὸν οἶκον); 2.15 (ἀπῆλθον ἀπ' αὐτῶν εἰς τὸν οὐρανόν) and 5.25 (ἀπῆλθεν εἰς τὸν οἶκον).

healing of the man. 8.37 and 8.38 are both an indirect speech with the same pattern: P(reported verbal process) C(receiver) S(a nominal group as subject) C(an infinitival clause as the verbiage). The man is compared with the people around the area by the same order, with each constituent having similar function.[26] The contrast is carried out by the use of the tense forms. The request of the people in 8.37 has a perfective aspect in the predicate of the main clause and the infinitival clause (ἠρώτησεν and ἀπελθεῖν); while the request of the man in 8.38 has an imperfective aspect in both the main and infinitival clauses (ἐδεῖτο and εἶναι). 8.37 and 8.38 are drawn to make comparison by their similar word orders and structures, and they are brought into contrast to each other by the use of their verbal aspects (one in perfective and one in imperfective). This is to bring out the contrast between the two participants (the man and the people of the area): the man's acceptance of Jesus and the people's rejection of Jesus.[27] The man wants to stay with Jesus because of his realization of what Jesus has done to save him (8.39). Ironically, the people's rejection of Jesus is also based on the same reason: their realization of how the man is saved (8.36). This realization causes them to be scared (8.35, 37). A conjunction ὅτι in 8.37 shows the people's great fear is the main reason for them to ask Jesus to leave, the people's fear causes their rejection of Jesus.[28]

Luke 8.41-42a, 49-56. The episode of Jairus' seeking healing for his daughter is contained in 8.41-42a, 49-56, which contains another incident of an indirect discourse addressed to Jesus in an imperfective aspect: Lk. 8.41b (καὶ ἰδοὺ ἦλθεν ἀνὴρ ᾧ ὄνομα Ἰάϊρος καὶ οὗτος ἄρχων τῆς συναγωγῆς ὑπῆρχεν, καὶ πεσὼν παρὰ τοὺς πόδας [τοῦ] Ἰησοῦ παρεκάλει αὐτὸν εἰσελθεῖν εἰς τὸν οἶκον αὐτοῦ). The story begins with a marked order S(οὗτος) C(ἄρχων τῆς συναγωγῆς) P(ὑπῆρχεν) to introduce this ruler,[29] and is followed by the ruler's indirect request to Jesus with an imperfective aspect. The ruler's indirect discourse to Jesus is parallel to the people's reported statement in 8.53 (καὶ κατεγέλων αὐτοῦ εἰδότες ὅτι ἀπέθανεν), which is also in an imperfective aspect (κατεγέλων). The people laugh at Jesus;

---

26. Both 8.37 and 8.38 have the order PCSC, and both have reported verbal process as predicate, receiver as complement, a nominal group as subject and the verbiage in the form of an infinitival clause as the second complement. Here the order is marked with a complement located before the subject (subject predominantly precedes the complement as stated in Chapter 3).

27. Several commentators notice the contrast between the man and the crowd in v. 37 and v. 38 (e.g. Fitzmyer, *Luke*, p. 740; Plummer, *Luke*, p. 233). In fact, the contrast is brought out by Luke by using two different aspects (imperfective occurs twice in 8.38 as foreground plane; while perfective occurs twice in 8.37 as background plane); and the paralleled word order (PCSC, with the same relevant clause structure such as an infinitival clause as verbiage) as discussed above.

28. The repetition of the people's fear in Luke's narrative highlights the people's reaction to Jesus' healing in this episode and the reason for them to ask him to leave. Cf. Mk 5.15 (ἐφοβήθησαν) and Lk. 8.35 (ἐφοβήθησαν) and 8.37 (φόβῳ μεγάλῳ).

29. There are 147x of SPC in independent clauses; while there are only 37x of SCP.

30. The content of the people's laughing at Jesus is not recorded in this verse and thus this

apparently this includes verbal statements and is thus also an indirect speech.[30] These two indirect speeches with an imperfective aspect give parallelism and contrast between Jairus and the people. One admires and respects Jesus (falls at Jesus' feet and asks him) and one humiliates and mocks Jesus; Jairus shows his sincere needfulness of Jesus and this contrasts with the people's attitude to Jesus. When the ruler is told that his daughter has already died, Jesus asks him not to fear, but only to believe. The ruler's daughter is finally saved. The faith and fearlessness of the ruler plays as a key factor of the salvation: as it is stated in 8.50.

Luke 11.37-41. The last indirect speech addressed to Jesus in an imperfective aspect is 11.37 (ἐρωτᾷ αὐτὸν Φαρισαῖος ὅπως ἀριστήσῃ παρ' αὐτῷ). The order is marked with the subject located after the complement (subject predominantly precedes the complement as stated in Chapter 3). The Pharisee is astonished to see Jesus not washing his hands. Jesus' response to this Pharisee is basically a rebuke, which not only shows the Pharisees to be hypocrites, but also exposes their genuine foolishness (11.40a).

Related Incidents of Indirect Discourse
It can be observed that most of the above mentioned incidents involve healings and saving events (7.1-10; 7.36-50; 8.27-39; 8.41-42a, 49-56), and some of them have participants being contrasted with each other as discussed above.[31] These can be summarized in the following two tables:

Table 5.1 *Indirect Speeches in Non-Independent Clauses*

7.1-10	Participants to be contrasted: none
	Reason for the healing of the centurion's servant: faith

Table 5.2 *Indirect Speeches in Independent Clauses*

1. 7.36-50	Participants to be contrasted: Simon and the woman

event is not included in the early part of this chapter regarding the occurrences of indirect speeches. The people's response in 8.53 may also be counted as an indirect discourse, since the verb (κατεγέλων) here may include verbal communication (as J.P. Louw and E. Nida's comment on this verb: 'to make fun of or ridicule by laughing, but evidently also involving verbal communication' [*Greek-English Lexicon of the New Testament Based on Semantic Domains* [2 vols.; New York: United Bible Society, 2nd edn 1989], vol. 1, p. 435]; and thus this verb has been classified into the semantic domain of 'Communication' in the Lexicon). This time the verb used in 8.53 is in imperfect tense form, and thus it may also be classified as an indirect speech with an imperfective aspect.

31. Here Luke 7–8 presents a set of contrasts between characters. It is a normal pattern for Luke to make parallelisms and contrasts between people or events. For example, people addressed with blessings and woes (6.20-26); Martha and Mary (10.38-42); the Pharisee and the tax collector (18.9-14) (cf. J. Kodell, 'Luke and the Children: The Beginning and End of the Great Interpolation [Luke 9:45-56; 18:9-23]', *CBQ* 49 [1987], pp. 415–30 (417–18); though his main analysis of the 'similar contrasting pairs within each of the three periscopes: 9.46-48 disciples–child, 9.49-50 John–exorcist, 9.51-56 Samaritans–Jesus' [p. 422] is not convincing).

	Reason for the woman's saving: faith
2. 7.9-10	Participants to be contrasted: none
	Event not related to saving and healing
3. 8.27-39	Participants to be contrasted: the demoniac and the people of the area
	Reason for the people's rejection of Jesus: fear
4. 8.41-42a, 49-56	Participants to be contrasted: Jairus and the people around his house
	Reason for Jairus' daughter's healing: faith and fearlessness
5. 11.37-41	Participants to be contrasted: none
	Event not related to saving and healing

The above two tables have listed the incidents of indirect speeches addressed to Jesus. The majority of them occur in independent clauses, and the studies in this chapter will be concentrated on these events.

The second table shows that three incidents of indirect speech in independent clauses can be particularly grouped together: 7.36-50; 8.27-39; 8.41-42a, 49-56. These three incidents can be grouped together based on at least two common points which these three incidents all share (but do not occur among the two other incidents [7.9-10 and 11.37-41]). Firstly, these three incidents are all related to healing and saving. Each time Jesus is approached by someone else who needs him: the sinful woman (7.37-38), the demoniac (8.27-28), and Jairus (8.41). They all approach Jesus and every time someone is finally saved by Jesus, and the lexical item σώζω occurs in all three incidents (7.50 [σέσωκεν]; 8.36 [ἐσώθη] and 8.50 [σωθήσεται]). Secondly, they all have a pair of participants being placed in contrast relating to a certain aspect: (i) Simon is contrasted with the sinful woman; his invitation to Jesus is contrasted with the woman's genuine acceptance of Jesus, which leads to her salvation and thus her faith is singled out (7.50); (ii) the demoniac is contrasted with the people around the area; his acceptance of Jesus is contrasted with their rejection of Jesus, which singles out their fear (8.35, 37); (iii) Jairus is contrasted to the people around his house; his respect and reliance on Jesus are contrasted with their mockery and ridicule at Jesus; the healing of his daughter indicates his faith and fearlessness (8.50). These three incidents are related to each other based on the above two aspects. This leads to two key words being singled out: faith and fear. The people discussed in these three incidents represent their two different attitudes to Jesus: (i) genuine acceptance of Jesus, and (ii) non-genuine acceptance or even rejection of Jesus. The key factors behind their different attitudes are their faith and fear/fearlessness. This can be illustrated as follows:

Table 5.3 *Key Words of the Three Incidents*

Scripture	Key Word
7.36-50	Faith
8.27-39	Fear
8.41-42a, 49-56	Fearlessness, Faith

The topic 'faith' in the first passage (7.36-50) is reiterated in the third passage

(8.41-42a, 49-50) (πίστις in 7.50 and πίστευσον in 8.50), and the topic of 'fear' in the second passage (8.27-39) has an antonym in the third passage (ἐφοβήθησαν, φόβῳ μεγάλῳ in 8.35, 37 and μὴ φοβοῦ in 8.50). The key terms of 'faith/fearlessness' and 'fear' subsequently introduce other surrounding related passages as stated below.

Related Passages in Luke 8-9

The words 'faith' and 'fear/fearlessness' in the above mentioned passages (7.36-50; 8.27-39 and 8.41-42a, 49-50) represent people's two different responses and attitudes to Jesus. In fact, besides these three passages, words which are synonymous and antonymous to the words of 'faith' and 'fear' occur in surrounding passages of Luke 8-9. And most importantly, these surrounding related passages all contribute to a similar topic: the disciples' failure in understanding of Jesus.

Luke 8.22-25. In 8.22-25, the disciples rush to Jesus concerning the storm, and Jesus rebukes them by asking a question 'Where is your faith (πίστις)?' (8.25). Jesus' reply states that one with faith does not fear. The disciples' lack of faith causes them to fear (cf. Mt. 8.26 [δειλοί] and Mk 4.40 [δειλοί]) and thus they think they are losing their lives; moreover the disciples are described as being terrified (8.25 φοβηθέντες) even after Jesus has calmed the storm.[32]

Luke 8.42b-48. In this episode, the woman who has been having a bleeding problem for twelve years is healed by Jesus. Jesus' statement in 8.48 (ἡ πίστις σου σέσωκέν σε) clearly indicates her faith is the main cause of her healing.

Luke 9.28-35. 9.28-35 records Jesus' disciples are terrified (9.34 ἐφοβήθησαν) when they are entering the cloud in the episode of Jesus' transfiguration.[33] The three disciples are afraid when a cloud overshadows them; their fearfulness is highlighted by a marked clause structure (ἐφοβήθησαν δὲ ἐν τῷ εἰσελθεῖν αὐτοὺς εἰς τὴν νεφέλην).[34]

32. The disciples rush to Jesus with anxiety about the storm. Jesus' question 'Where is your faith?' implies the disciples ought not to have been frightened (cf. L. Morris, *The Gospel According to St. Luke: An Introduction and Commentary* [London: Inter-Varsity Press, 1974], p. 155) and they ought to have had faith (cf. Marshall, *Gospel of Luke*, p. 334). Ironically, when the disciples are challenged by Jesus about their faith, their faith is not roused even after encountering God's activity and power; instead they are frightened about what they have seen and experienced (Fitzmyer, *Luke*, p. 730; cf. Nolland, *Luke*, p. 400; and S. Brown, *Apostasy and Perseverance in the Theology of Luke* [Analecta Biblica, 36; Rome: Pontifical Biblical Institute Press, 1969], pp. 58–59).

33. Marshall suggests the disciples are frightened not only because of their entering into the cloud, but also the possibility of finding the others (especially Jesus) disappeared in the cloud (*Gospel of Luke*, p. 387; cf. C.F. Evans, *Saint Luke* [TPI New Testament Commentaries; London: SCM Press, 1990], p. 420).

34. 9.34b ἐφοβήθησαν δὲ ἐν τῷ εἰσελθεῖν αὐτοὺς εἰς τὴν νεφέλην. The main clause (ἐφοβήθησαν) and the dependent clause (ἐν τῷ εἰσελθεῖν αὐτοὺς εἰς τὴν νεφέλην) form a logical semantic relation: contemporary temporal. The infinitival clause with this hypotactic

Luke 9.37-45. A man asks help from Jesus for his son. This man has already tried to get help from Jesus' disciples, but they are not able to get his son healed. Jesus' immediate response to this is a heavy criticism to the generation: 'O faithless (ἄπιστος) and perverse generation' (9.41). This criticism indicates the main cause of the disciples' failure of their healing: lack of faith.[35]

Jesus predicts his death to his disciples in 9.44. The disciples not only fail to understand what Jesus says, they are also afraid (9.45 ἐφοβοῦντο) of asking about it. Their fear to ask may be due to their intellectual incomprehension.[36] They fear to hear more explicitly of what they do not want to hear,[37] which is contradictory to the glory which they have just seen in 9.22-36.[38]

As will be shown later, all these four passages with the key terms 'faith/fearlessness' and 'fear' contribute to the topic of the disciples' failure and their intellectual incomprehension. In fact, these passages are also very much related to the passages with the indirect speeches discussed above. This is illustrated below.

Incorporation of the Passages

The above four discussed passages (8.22-25; 8.42b-48; 9.28-36; 9.37-45) have a common point with the above mentioned three incidents of indirect speeches (for the sake of convenience. These two groups of passages will be abbreviated as Group A and Group B respectively). Each passage of both groups contains

(temporal) relation is predominantly located before the main clause (25x: 1.8; 2.6, 27, 43; 3.21; 5.1, 12; 8.5; 9.18, 29, 33, 36, 51; 10.35; 11.1, 27; 14.1; 17.11, 14; 18.35; 19.15; 24.4, 15, 30, 51); here the psychological effect of the disciples is highlighted by the reversed order: the infinitival clause with temporal (contemporary) semantics follows the main clause (9.34 is the only instance in the Gospel of having the hypotactic [temporal] infinitival clause located after the main clause; while all the rest of the clause type are located before the main clause [25x as stated above]).

35.   Commentators have different views on who is the addressee of 'O faithless and perverse generation' in 9.41. E.g. Tannehill (*Narrative Unity*, pp. 225–26) and Ellis (*Luke*, p. 144) think the criticism mainly refers to the disciples; some think the statement only refers to the father and the multitude, but not the disciples (e.g. Plummer, *Luke*, p. 255; Creed, *Luke*, p. 136). Most hold the position of Jesus' statement in 9.41: that is referring to both the disciples who have failed to heal the boy and all the people around the scene who have also failed to show their faith. E.g. Reiling and Swellengrebel: '"O faithless and perverse generation" best understood as being addressed to all people who are present and had failed to show faith enough for the healing of the boy' (*Handbook*, p. 387); also Fitzmyer, *Luke*, p. 809; Marshall, *Gospel of Luke*, p. 391; Evans, *Luke*, p. 423. The third position is most preferable and is best represented by Nolland: 'The criticism would seem to be addressed to the failed disciples as representatives of the generation' (*Luke*, p. 509). This criticism is issued because of the disciples' failure in healing due to their lack of faith, which is also a representation of the generation's failure in faith (cf. G.E. Sterling, 'Jesus as Exorcist: An Analysis of Matthew 17.14-20; Mark 9.14-29; Luke 9.37-43a', *CBQ* 55 [1993], pp. 467–93 (475), who strangely suggests the Lukan version of the hearing is to emphasize the compassion of Jesus when it is compared to the Matthean version).

36.   Evans, *Luke*, p. 426; cf. Morris, *Luke*, p. 175.

37.   Marshall, *Luke*, p. 394.

38.   The disciples have just experienced the glory of Jesus' transfiguration, which they want to retain. This will be discussed below.

synonymous or antonymous words of 'faith/fear'. The locations of these passages are strikingly interesting: each passage from Group B is located at every interval between passages of Group A. This is illustrated in Table 5.4 below:

Table 5.4 *Occurrences of Synonyms and Antonyms of 'Faith' and 'Fear'*

Group A: Passages of Indirect Discourse Group	Group B: Related Passages
Lk. 7.36-50	
πίστις (7.50)	
Corresponding participant: the woman	
	Lk. 8.22-25
	1. πίστις (8.25)
	2. φοβηθέντες (8.25)
	Corresponding participant: disciples
Lk. 8.27-39	
1. ἐφοβήθησαν (8.35)	
2. φόβῳ μεγάλῳ (8.37)	
Corresponding participant: people of the area	
	Lk. 8.42b-48
	πίστις (8.48)
	Corresponding participant: the woman
Lk. 8.41-42a, 49-56	
1. μὴ φοβοῦ (8.50) [39]	
2. πίστευσον (8.50)	
Corresponding participant: Jairus	
	Lk. 9.28-36
	ἐφοβήθησαν (9.34)
	Corresponding participant: disciples
	Lk. 9.37-45
	1. ἄπιστος (9.41)
	2. ἐφοβοῦντο (9.45)
	Corresponding participant: disciples

It is shown that each passage from Group B is located at every interval between passages of Group A. Much more interesting is that every passage in Group A does not contain the involvement of disciples, where each passage of Group B does contain the involvement of disciples. In Group A, in 7.36-50, the one who shows the synonymous word πίστις in 7.50 is the sinful woman. In 8.27-39, the people of the area is the participant corresponding to ἐφοβήθησαν in 7.35 and φόβῳ μεγάλῳ in 7.37. In 8.41-42a, 49-56, Jairus is the participant corresponding to μὴ φοβοῦ and πίστευσον in 8.50. The disciples are not participants in any of these three incidents, and they are not mentioned in these three passages at all. However, the situation in Group B is totally different. The disciples are participants in every passage in Group B; and more importantly, they are corresponding partic-

---

39. This passage is composed of 8.41-42a and 8.49-56. This passage is placed after 8.42b-48 rather than before it, because the synonymous words of 'faith' and 'fear' is mainly from Jesus' command: 'Do not fear, only believe' in 8.50, which belongs to the section of 8.49-56 and is located after 8.42b-48.

ipants of all the synonymous/antonymous words of 'faith/fear' in three passages of Group B. In 8.22-25, the disciples are corresponding to πίστις and φοβηθέντες in 8.25; they are also corresponding to ἐφοβήθησαν (9.34) in 9.28-36, and also ἄπιστος (9.41) and ἐφοβοῦντο (9.45) in 9.37-45. The only incident in Group B where the synonymous word is not related to the disciples is πίστις (8.48) in 8.42b-48.

The importance of the four passages of Group B is introduced by the synonyms and antonyms of 'faith' and 'fear' from passages of Group A. The significance of the four passages is enforced by their locations (located at every interval between passages of Group A). The fact of the disciples being participants in all four passages in Group B, and being the participants corresponding to the synonyms and antonyms of 'faith' and 'fear' (in 8.22-25; 9.28-36; 9.37-45) indicates the significance of the disciples' attitudes: they are fearful and they are faithless.

Lack of Understanding: A Semantic Chain
Semantic Chain on Passages of Group B. As stated above, the disciples are participants in all four passages in Group B, and they are directly related to the words 'faith' and 'fear' in three of them. In fact, there is another important concept occurring throughout the four passages in Group B: the concept of 'lack of understanding'. This concept occurs in all four passages of Group B and this forms a semantic chain;[40] and most importantly, this time the disciples are the corresponding participants of all the four occurrences of this semantic chain of 'lack of understanding'. This is illustrated below.

1. *Luke 8.22-25*: The disciples are frightened because of their lack of faith, their faithlessness causes their fear. They are still frightened even when Jesus has saved them from the danger of the storm. This time their fear is mainly because of their lack of understanding of Jesus. This can be shown from their question 'Who then is this?', which apparently shows the disciples' intellectual inability regarding Jesus' identity,[41] and this intellectual inability mainly causes them to have great fear.

2. *Luke 8.42b-48*: When Jesus asks a question after the woman has touched his garment, Peter and the people who come alongside give a reply with challenge (οἱ ὄχλοι συνέχουσίν σε καὶ ἀποθλίβουσιν). Jesus' answer shows a challenge to their

40. A semantic chain represents cohesion of information units (or information blocks), and these cohered information units present information of a larger unit ('cohesion in discourse appears to involve the further grouping of information blocks into larger units, rather like the way sentences are grouped into paragraphs in written discourse' [Grimes, *The Thread of Discourse*, p. 276]).

41. As Morris states: '*Who then is this?* This is the significant question which Luke does not want his readers to miss' (*Luke*, p. 155). This question is also the first incident which so apparently shows the disciples' confusion about Jesus' identity (cf. Marshall, *Gospel of Luke*, p. 334).

42. Peter and other people's reply comes with two foregrounded imperfective aspects (συνέχουσιν and ἀποθλίβουσιν [8.45]) to show the semantic weight of the challenge. Jesus' answer (8.46) is also with marked word order patterns. The first clause is with a marked PCS order (ἥψατό μού τις) (the number of occurrences of PCS in independent clauses is 24x; while SPC and PSC is 147x and 49x respectively) (subject predominantly precedes the predicate as stated before). The second clause (ἐγὼ γὰρ ἔγνων δύναμιν ἐξεληλυθυῖαν ἀπ' ἐμοῦ) comes with a

reply,[42] and it is actually a confrontation to what they have just said. Peter and other disciples' statement (8.45b) implies astonishment,[43] they think Jesus' question does not make sense at all.[44] Jesus knows (8.46 ἔγνων) power has gone out from him, this is what the disciples do not know. In fact, Peter and the other disciples' statement in 8.45b shows their lack of understanding of Jesus.[45] They do not understand Jesus' question in 8.45a and their challenge in 8.45b actually shows their ignorance about Jesus.

3. *Luke 9.28-36*: Seeing the glory of Jesus and the two prophets who are standing with him, Peter wants to retain this glory and experience by trying to ask them to stay,[46] but he actually does not know what he is speaking and it shows his lack of understanding of the situation.[47] The revelation of God (9.35 οὖτός ἐστιν ὁ υἱός μου ὁ ἐκλελεγμένος, αὐτοῦ ἀκούετε) from the cloud may imply the

personal pronoun (ἐγώ) as a repetition of the subject which can be derived from the predicate (ἔγνων) of the second clause. The participial clause in the content of his mental reported projection comes with a frontgrounded stative aspect (9.46: ἐξεληλυθυῖαν).

43. Reiling and Swellengrebel, *Handbook*, p. 356.

44. As Morris states: 'The implication is clear: so many had touched Jesus that the question became meaningless' (*Luke*, p. 159).

45. The disciples' failure in understanding here may be a contrast to Jesus' miraculous knowledge about his clothes being touched (cf. V.K. Robbins, 'The Woman Who Touched Jesus' Garment: Socio-Rhetorical Analysis of the Synoptic Accounts' *NTS* 33 [1987], pp. 502–15 (511); Jesus' miraculous knowledge here may also be echoed to his superior knowledge when he knows Simon's unspoken objection in 7.39-40 [J.T. Carroll, 'Luke's Portrayal of the Pharisees', *CBQ* 50 (1988), pp. 604–21 (610)]).

46. Morris, *Luke*, p. 172; Geldenhuys, *Luke*, p. 282; Creed, *Luke*, p. 135; Plummer, *Luke*, p. 252; S. Hall, 'Synoptic Transfigurations: Mark 9.2-10 and Partners', *KTR* 10 (1987), pp. 41–44 (42); S.H. Ringe, 'Luke 9:28-36: The Beginning of an Exodus', *Semeia* 28 (1983), pp. 81–99 (90); cf. A.A. Trites' suggestion of considering the glory of the transfiguration as a foreshadow of the glory of the future parousia ('The Transfiguration in the Theology of Luke: Some Redactional Links', in L.D. Hurst and N.T. Wright [eds.], *The Glory of Christ in the New Testament: Studies in Christology, in Memory of George Bradford Caird* [Oxford: Oxford University Press, 1987], pp. 71–81 [80–81]); also cf. J.J. Kilgallen, 'Jesus, Saviour, the Glory of Your People Israel', *Bib* 75 [1994], pp. 305–28 (323–25).

47. The narrator's comment (μὴ εἰδὼς ὃ λέγει) following Peter's suggestion in 9.33 clearly shows his ignorance of the vision and the situation. Cf. comments from Fitzmyer: 'it emphasizes Peter's lack of comprehension of the whole vision' (*Luke*, p. 801); Marshall: 'he (Peter) did not realize that the glorious scene has not come to stay' (*Gospel of Luke*, p. 387); Reiling and Swellengrebel: 'because he did not understand the situation...he didn't realize that his proposal was out of place' (*Handbook*, p. 383); also Tannehill: 'lack of understanding' (*Narrative Unity*, p. 224); and R.F. O'Toole, 'Luke's Message in Luke 9:1-50', *CBQ* 49 (1987), pp. 74–89 (82).

48. J.B. Tyson, 'Jews and Judaism in Luke-Acts: Reading as a Godfearer', *NTS* 41 (1995), pp. 19–38 (28); Ellis, *Luke*, p. 143; and as Fitzmyer states: 'They also put all three figures on the same level' (*Luke*, p. 801). αὐτοῦ ἀκούετε in 9.35 is a marked CP order, this word order is same as the one in Deut. 18.15 (αὐτοῦ ἀκούσεσθε [LXX]; cf. O'Toole, 'Luke's Message in Luke 9:1-50', pp. 78–79; B.P. Robinson, 'The Place of the Emmaus Story in Luke-Acts', *NTS* 30 [1984], pp. 481–97 (482); C.A. Evans, 'Luke's Use of the Elijah/Elisha Narratives and the Ethic of Election', *JBL* 106 [1987], pp. 75–83 (82)); when Moses mentions God will raise up another prophet like him (cf. D.P. Moessner, 'Luke 9:1-50: Luke's Preview of the Journey of the Prophet

disciples have wrongly equalized Jesus, Moses and Elijah,[48] and God's declaration is a correction to Peter's inappropriate proposal and a clarification of what the transfiguration reveals about Jesus' identity.[49] The incident of Jesus' transfiguration not only explicitly clarifies Jesus' identity, but also strongly reveals the disciples' ignorance.[50]

4. *Luke 9.37-45*: The extensive expansion in 9.45 (καὶ ἦν παρακεκαλυμμένον ἀπ' αὐτῶν ἵνα μὴ αἴσθωνται αὐτό and περὶ τοῦ ῥήματος τούτου) compared to Mark's writing (Mk 9.32) indicates Luke wants to emphasize the disciples' incomprehension of Jesus' prediction about his death.[51] The incident of Jesus' second prediction of his death reveals the disciples' incomprehension and ignorance, which are explicitly stated (9.45 ἠγνόουν τὸ ῥῆμα τοῦτο and μὴ αἴσθωνται αὐτό). This verse is so far the most explicit passage stating the disciples' ignorance and lack of understanding in the four passages of Group B.

5. *Summary*: The semantic chain is formed based on the existence of a semantic element of 'incomprehension, lack of understanding' in each passage of Group B. The disciples are the participants corresponding to every occurrence of this semantic element in the chain. This can be summarized together with passages of Group A in the following table:

like Moses of Deuteronomy', *JBL* 102 [1983], pp. 575–605; D.A.S. Ravens, 'Luke 9:7-62 and the Prophetic Role of Jesus', *NTS* 36 [1990], pp. 119–29 (125), who suggests the prophetic image of Jesus compared with readings from Exodus; and his suggestion of Jesus' prophetic role by the imitation of Elisha [2 Kings 5] in Lk. 7.36-50 ['Luke's Account of the Anointing: Luke 7.2-8.3', p. 287]). It may be right for Marshall to suggest that this order implies the emphasis of referring Jesus as the proper authority for the disciples to listen to (rather than other prophets such as Moses and Elijah) (Marshall, *Gospel of Luke*, p. 388); cf. Evans, *Luke*, p. 421; Morris, *Luke*, p. 173; Goulder, *Luke*, p. 441; Easton, *Luke*, p. 144; for a different point of view, cf. Nolland, *Luke*, p. 501: 'The point is not to hear Jesus rather than Moses and Elijah... The point is to hear what Jesus has been seeking to teach them.'

49.   E.E. Ellis, 'The Composition of Luke 9 and the Sources of its Christology', in G.F. Hawthorne (ed.), *Current Issues in Biblical and Patristic Interpretation: Studies in Honor of Merrill C. Tenny Presented by his Former Students* (Grand Rapids: Eerdmans, 1975), pp. 121–27 (121–22); Tannehill, *Narrative Unity*, p. 224; Ellis, *Luke*, p. 143; Fitzmyer, *Luke*, p. 802.

50.   After the transfiguration, the disciples keep silent and tell no one about the things they have seen (9.6b). This response of the disciples after the incident is reinforced by the two negative in 9.36b (οὐδενί and οὐδέν) (cf. Reiling and Swellengrebel, *Handbook*, p. 385), and also by the redundant personal pronoun (9.36b αὐτοί). Although Mk 9.9 indicates the silence of the disciples is due to the theory of Messianic Secret (cf. Mt. 17.9). It may be right for Tannehill to further suggest this is an indication of the disciples' continued fear and lack of understanding of what they have seen and experienced (*Narrative Unity*, p. 225; cf. O'Toole, 'Luke's Message in Luke 9:1-50', p. 75).

51.   Nolland, *Luke*, p. 514; Goulder, *Luke*, p. 449; cf. Evans, *Luke*, p. 426.

Table 5.5 *Formation of the Semantic Chain*

Group A	Group B
Group A	*Group B*
Lk. 36-50	
The woman	
Faithful	
	Lk. 8.22-25
	The disciples
	Lack of understanding
Lk. 8.27-39	
The people around	
Fearful	
	Lk. 8.42b-48
	The disciples
	Lack of understanding
Lk. 8.41-42a, 49-56	
Jairus	
Faithful and fearless	
	Lk. 9.28-36
	The disciples
	Lack of understanding
	Lk. 9.37-45
	The disciples
	Lack of understanding

The Semantic Chain and the Incidents of Indirect Speech

At the beginning of this chapter, seven incidents of indirect speeches addressed to Jesus with imperfective aspect are introduced. Six of them are incidents occurring in independent clauses. Four of these six incidents have already been studied together in three episodes (Group A: 7.36-50; 8.27-39 and 8.41-42a, 49-56) based on two common features they all have: (i) contrasting participants (7.36-50: Simon vs. the sinful woman; 8.27-39: the demoniac vs. the people of the area; 8.41-42a, 49-56: Jairus vs. the people around his house); (ii) synonyms and antonyms of 'faith/fear'. The other two incidents (8.9-10 and 11.37-41) do not have these two common features. They do not have contrasting participants, and they do not have synonyms and antonyms of 'faith/fear'. However, they are not unrelated to the studies discussed above; in fact, they play an important role regarding the studies and contribute to the theme of the disciples' lack of under-standing.

As stated above, a semantic chain of 'lack of understanding' is formed among the four passages in Group B. This semantic chain is based on the occurrences of the semantic element of 'incomprehension', this semantic element also occurs in the two incidents of imperfective indirect speech: Lk. 8.9-10 and Lk. 11.37-41.

Luke 8.9-10. The disciples *do not understand* the meaning of the parable which they have just heard, and thus they ask Jesus about it. Jesus' reply indicates the disciples are the chosen ones to know the mysteries of the kingdom of God, while the others would not understand no matter how they see or hear. However, the disciples ironically show their lack of understanding in the subsequent events, even though they are the chosen ones to be shown the mysteries of God's kingdom. *Luke 11.37-41.* In 11.40 Jesus rebukes the Pharisee who invites him by using the word ἄφρονες. This word strongly implies 'lack of understanding'.[52] Luke's use of this word ἄφρονες to refer to the Pharisees is unique among the Synoptic Gospels,[53] and is the first time in Luke that Jesus so explicitly rebukes the Pharisees.

Summary. The two incidents of imperfective indirect speech both contain semantic elements of 'lack of understanding', which allows them to be joined with the semantic chain formed from passages of Group B. This semantic chain coheres all incidents containing semantic element of incomprehension, and it contains four passages from Group B and two incidents of imperfective indirect speech. Five of these six passages contribute to a message: the disciples' incomprehension. This message (the incomprehension of the disciples) is then further foregrounded by other passages with marked word orders. This is stated below.

52. The word ἄφρων is generally given a meaning of 'foolish', 'ignorant', 'senseless' in Greek lexicons (e.g. W. Bauer, *A Greek-English Lexicon of the New Testament and other Early Christian Literature* [rev. and ed. F.W. Danker; Chicago: University of Chicago Press, 3rd edn 2000], p. 159; it is defined similarly for both Classical and Patristic periods, cf. H.G. Liddell and R. Scott, *A Greek-English Lexicon* [rev. H.S. Jones *et al.*; Oxford: Clarendon Press, 9th edn with a supplement 1968], p. 294, and G.W.H. Lampe [ed.], *A Patristic Greek Lexicon* [Oxford: Oxford University Press, 1961], p. 279; also cf. G. Bertram, 'ἄφρων', in *TDNT*, IX, p. 230). In Louw and Nida's Lexicon, ἄφρων is rightly classified into the semantic domain of 'Understand', and is further classified into the sub-domain of 'Lack of Capacity for Understanding' and is described as 'pertaining to not employing one's understanding' (*Greek-English Lexicon*, p. 387).

53. The other Lukan use of the word is Lk. 12.20; cf. other Gospel writers' narratives of the same incident: Mt. 23.25 (ὑποκριταί) and 23.26 (τυφλέ); Mk 7.6 (ὑποκριτῶν), the rebukes in other Gospels are 'hypocrites' and 'you blind Pharisees' rather than 'you foolish ones' in Lk. 11.40; cf. Fitzmyer, *Luke*, p. 947. Although the unique use (and the significance of the word, such as Plummer comments: 'a strong word' [*Luke*, p. 310]) of the word is generally recognized, commentators and scholars agree the word is only used to portray the intellectual inability (e.g. Evans: 'For their inability to see this the Pharisees are called fools' [*Luke*, p. 504]; Reiling and Swellengrebel: 'here used as a substantive indicating culpable not truly ignorance and carrying a strong note of reproach' [*Handbook*, p. 451]; Bertram: 'the Pharisees do know God as the Creator who makes both what is external and also what is internal' ['ἄφρων', pp. 230–31]) and moral ungodliness of the Pharisees (e.g. Marshall states the use of this word is to characterize 'the Pharisees as ungodly men in their false piety' [*Gospel of Luke*, p. 495]; Johnson: 'referring to those who resist the wisdom that comes from God' [*Luke*, p. 189]; Tannehill: 'The Pharisees are accused of hypocrisy' [*Narrative Unity*, p. 181]). Nolland proposes the uniqueness of Lk. 11.40 (compared with Matthew) to be 'a Lukan development, or perhaps it is more likely that we have here an independent fragment of tradition that Luke has fitted in here' (*Luke*, p. 664). What I argue is the unique use of the word 'fool' expresses Luke's view not only on the ungodliness of the Pharisees, but also mainly on their intellectual ignorance. I agree the use of the word 'fool' is a Lukan development, but it is developed to be related to the other incidents regarding the disciples' lack of understanding, which will be discussed below.

Failure of the Disciples: Lack of Understanding
Disciples and the Pharisees
The semantic chain stated above consists of two main sections: two incidents (Lk. 8.9-10 and 11.37-41) of imperfective indirect speech and four passages from Group B. In these six events, five of them are contributing to a theme that the disciples are the ones who lack understanding. The Pharisees mentioned in the last event of the chain are the ones who are rebuked by Jesus about their ignorance. The rebuke of the Pharisees raises an important question: How about the disciples? The Pharisees are rebuked heavily because of their ignorance, how about the disciples who are privileged to be shown the secret of God's kingdom (8.10)? Although the disciples have been told and shown the secret of God's kingdom in Luke 8–9, they are still consistently ignorant throughout the semantic chain. The event of Jesus' rebuke of the Pharisees' ignorance well causes the blindness of the disciples to stand out clearly. The semantic chain shows an important theme: the blindness of the disciples. This theme of the disciples' failure is further re-enforced by a sequence of Jesus' confrontation with them.

Jesus' Confrontations with the Disciples
Luke 9.46-62. The highlighted failure of the disciples' understanding in 9.45 provides a strong thread to the following paragraphs in the rest of Luke 9.[54] The explicit statement about the disciples' intellectual incomprehension in 9.45 is firstly followed by a dispute among the disciples, which shows their foolishness. It is then followed by a series of statements and confrontations between Jesus and his disciples packed in 9.46-62, which are also marked to highlight the disciples' failure in understanding.

9.49 records that John has given a statement regarding someone casting out demons by Jesus' name (εἴδομέν τινα ἐν τῷ ὀνόματί σου ἐκβάλλοντα δαιμόνια καὶ ἐκωλύομεν αὐτὸν, ὅτι οὐκ ἀκολουθεῖ μεθ' ἡμῶν).[55] This is then followed by two foregrounded aspects (ἐκωλύομεν and οὐκ ἀκολουθεῖ) to highlight the matter. The writing about Jesus' confrontation in 9.50 is also highlighted: εἶπεν δὲ πρὸς αὐτὸν ὁ 'Ιησοῦς (a marked order PC[πρὸς αὐτόν] SC[content of the projection]).[56] The content of the projection is then heavily weighted with a foregrounded aspect (μὴ κωλύετε) and a marked order S(ὃς γὰρ οὐκ ἔστιν καθ' ὑμῶν) CP.[57] The disciples' foolishness is further strengthened by their proposal in 9.54 and Jesus' rebuke in 9.55.[58] 9.58 records (εἶπεν αὐτῷ ὁ 'Ιησοῦς) Jesus'

---

54. Goulder, *Luke*, p. 449.

55. This is a marked SAPC order. The means adjunct (ἐν τῷ ὀνόματί σου) is placed before its predicate (the number of means adjunct placed before and after the predicate in participial clauses is 4x and 11x respectively).

56. The number of PCSC and SPCC is 25x and 42x in independent clauses respectively (subject typically precedes the complement).

57. The number of SCP and SPC is 37x and 147x in independent clauses respectively.

58. Fitzmyer, *Luke*, p. 830; Evans comments that the rebuke is emphatic, and the word ἐπετίμησεν used is 'a strong word, used in exorcisms of rebuking demons' (*Luke*, p. 438) (major NT lexicons generally agree the word carries strong degree of rebuke; e.g. Bauer: 'to express

another challenging response to a follower's offer, which is marked as PCSC(content of projection),[59] and the content of the projection is again prominent with two imperfective aspects (ἔχουσιν and ἔχει) and two marked orders: SCP (αἱ ἀλώπεκες φωλεοὺς ἔχουσιν) and CP (τὴν κεφαλὴν κλίνῃ).[60] Jesus' confrontation with the next one is also highlighted with the redundant use of a personal pronoun (σύ) with an imperfective verb (διάγγελλε) in 9.60.[61] Jesus' following confrontation with another one's offer in 9.62 is again marked: S(οὐδεὶς) A(ἐπιβαλὼν τὴν χεῖρα ἐπ' ἄροτρον καὶ βλέπων εἰς τὰ ὀπίσω) CP(ἐστιν),[62] with the complement (εὔθετος τῇ βασιλείᾳ τοῦ θεοῦ) being separated by the predicate ἐστίν.

The semantic chain mentioned before shows a major weakness of the disciples: their failure of understanding. This weakness is re-enforced by a series of Jesus' confrontation with his disciples as stated above.

Luke 12.49-56. Luke 12.49-56 consists of Jesus' two speeches being addressed to his disciples and a group of people respectively: 12.49-53 and 12.54-56.[63] The first speech (12.49-53) contains Jesus' further confrontation with his disciples about their lack of understanding (12.51), while the second one (12.54-56) contains a rebuke of Jesus to the people (12.56). Jesus' rebuke to the people in 12.54-56 is in fact much related to his confrontation to the disciples in 12.49-51. This is being shown below.

strong disapproval of someone' [*A Greek-English Lexicon*, p. 384]; Louw and Nida give exactly the same comment as Bauer's on the word : 'to express strong disapproval of someone' [*Greek-English Lexicon*, p. 436]; cf. G.T.D. Angel, 'ἐπιτιμάω', in *NIDNTT*, I, p. 572).

59. The number of PCSC and SPCC is 25x and 42x in independent clauses respectively.

60. The number of SCP and SPC is 37x and 147x in independent clauses respectively; CP and PC is 36x and 66x in infinitival clauses respectively.

61. Cf. Plummer, *Luke*, p. 267. The follower in 9.59 wants to delay his following; this reflects that he does not fully understand the importance and urgency of preaching the kingdom of God (9.60; cf. H. Conzelmann, *The Theology of St. Luke* [trans. G. Buswell; London: Faber & Faber, 1960], p. 105; and H.T. Fleddermann, 'Demands of Discipleship: Matt. 8.19-22 Par. Luke 9.57-62', in Segbroeck, Tuckett, Belle and Verheyden (eds.), *The Four Gospels 1992*. I, pp. 540–61 (551–52, 54), where he suggests the urgency of the preaching and the distinct demand of Jesus to his followers when it is compared with Elijah's permission of Elisha's delay in 1 Kgs 19.19-21), which is a central theme of Luke-Acts. The requirement of preaching the kingdom of God in fact looks ahead of the sending of the 70 in 10.1-12 and looks back to the sending of the 12 in 9.1-6 (M.G. Steinhauser, 'Putting One's Hand to the Plow: The Authenticity of Q 9.61-62', *Forum* 5 [1989], pp. 151–58 (153)).

62. The number of SCP and SPC is 37x and 147x in independent clauses respectively.

63. The audience of Lk. 12.49-53 is Jesus' disciples. This can be seen at 12.22: the audience is Jesus' disciples and is not changed until 12.54; the same incident occurring in Matthew is Mt. 10, where it shows the audience of the entire Mt. 10 is Jesus' 12 disciples (cf. Mt. 10.5 and Mt. 11.1). The topic of 'divided families' forms a connection between this passage (12.49-53) and the passage at the end of Lk. 9 (9.59-60), see A.D. Jacobson, 'Divided Families and Christian Origins', in R.A. Piper (ed.), *The Gospel behind the Gospels: Current Studies on Q* (NovTSup, 75; Leiden: E.J.Brill, 1995), pp. 306–80 (361–67); cf. M.L. Soards, 'Luke 2.22-40', *Int* 44 (1990), pp. 400–405 (403–04).

1. *Luke 12.49-53*: Lk. 12.51 (δοκεῖτε ὅτι εἰρήνην παρεγενόμην δοῦναι ἐν τῇ γῇ; οὐχί, λέγω ὑμῖν, ἀλλ᾽ ἢ διαμερισμόν) is a reported projection which comes with an imperfective aspect of a mental process (δοκεῖτε) indicating the disciples' misconception about the purpose of Jesus' coming. The infinitival clause in the projected clause carries a marked order: CPA.[64] This order is further marked by having the complement (εἰρήνην) of the infinitive (δοῦναι) placed before the predicate (παρεγενόμην) of the projected clause. The infinitive (δοῦναι) here functions as a purpose adjunct of the projected clause. Typically, the order of a clause with an infinitive functioning as a purpose adjunct in Luke is as follows:

(i) Predicate of the main clause + purpose adjunct (in infinitival form) + complement of the infinitival clause.[65]

(ii) Predicate of the main clause + purpose adjunct (in infinitival form) + adjunct of the infinitival clause.[66]

(iii) Predicate + purpose adjunct (in infinitival form).[67]

It is clear that the predicate of the main clause tends to be followed by an 'unbroken' infinitival clause (an infinitive followed immediately by its complement or adjunct). Luke 12.51 comes with a heavily marked order: complement of infinitive + predicate + purpose adjunct (in infinitival form). Here the infinitival clause is separated or 'broken' by the predicate (παρεγενόμην), and it is in a marked CP pattern as well.[68] The only other two occurrences of this pattern in independent clauses is 7.26 (ἀλλὰ τί ἐξήλθατε ἰδεῖν) and the divine judgment in 12.49 (πῦρ ἦλθον βαλεῖν ἐπὶ τὴν γῆν).[69] It is not difficult to see why 7.26 uses this pattern: it is a usual pattern to place the interrogative pronoun τί at the front of a clause. For 12.49, it is heavily marked by having this clause pattern: complement of the infinitival clause (πῦρ) + predicate of main clause (ἦλθον) + infinitival clause as purpose adjunct (βαλεῖν ἐπὶ τὴν γῆν); 12.50 has a similar heavily marked pattern: βάπτισμα (subject of the infinitival clause) δὲ ἔχω (predicate of the main clause) βαπτισθῆναι (predicate of the infinitival clause).[70] This time the infinitival clause

64. The total number of PC in infinitival clauses is 72x, where CP is 36x; and PCA is 11x, where CPA is 5x.

65. This occurs 32x in independent clauses, or 40x including participles functioning as a purpose adjunct.

66. This occurs 8x in independent clauses.

67. This occurs 7x in independent clauses.

68. The same incident occurring in Mt. 10.34 has an 'unbroken' infinitival clause located after the predicate. This order is repeated twice in the verse, and the infinitival clause is in a typical PC order: μὴ νομίσητε ὅτι ἦλθον *βαλεῖν εἰρήνην ἐπὶ τὴν γῆν* οὐκ ἦλθον *βαλεῖν εἰρήνην ἀλλὰ μάχαιραν* (Mt. 10.34); cf. Mt. 5.17 μὴ νομίσητε ὅτι ἦλθον *καταλῦσαι τὸν νόμον* ἢ τοὺς προφήτας.

69. M. Black, '"Not Peace but a Sword": Matt. 10.34ff; Luke 12.51ff', in E. Bammel and C.F.D. Moule (eds.), *Jesus and the Politics of His Day* (Cambridge: Cambridge University Press, 1984), p. 294.

70. Here the fire in 12.49 is followed by a baptism in 12.50. Though it is common for the Bible to mention fire and water together, it is not right of D.M. Derrett to suggest Lk. 12.49-50 is illuminated by other OT passages (Isa. 43.1-2; Ps. 66.10-12; Lam. 1.13) (D.M. Derrett, 'Three

functions as a complement of the main clause, and is again separated by the predicate (ἔχω) of the main clause; the subject (βάπτισμα) of the infinitival clause is separated from its predicate (βαπτισθῆναι) and is placed before the predicate (ἔχω) of the main clause.[71] Here it can be seen that 12.49, 50 and 51 all have a similar marked order: the predicate of the main clause + an infinitival clause as a complement or adjunct, and a constituent of the infinitival clause precedes the main clause of the predicate. The first two consecutive ones (12.49, 50) come together to highlight an important message: the work and mission of Jesus as described in 12.49, 50; then the third one comes with a foregrounded aspect (δοκεῖτε) to mark the misunderstanding of the disciples (12.51). The mission and work of Jesus is highlighted with the marked orders (12.49, 50); the similar marked order in 12.51 just shows how foolish are the disciples to misunderstand that, and how significant is Jesus' confrontation with his disciples about it.

2. *Luke 12.54-56*: Jesus switches his audience from the disciples to the people whom he describes as hypocrites in 12.49-56. A marked order similar to the one just discussed above occurs twice in Jesus' comments to the hypocrites in 12.56a: τὸ πρόσωπον τῆς γῆς καὶ τοῦ οὐρανοῦ (complement of the infinitival or dependent clause) οἴδατε (predicate of the main clause) δοκιμάζειν (predicate of the infinitival or dependent clause) and 12.56b: τὸν καιρὸν δὲ τοῦτον (complement of the infinitival clause) πῶς οὐκ οἴδατε (predicate of the main clause) δοκιμάζειν (predicate of the infinitival clause).

The order of a clause with an infinitival clause as a complement in Luke is usually as follows:

(i) Predicate of the main clause + predicate of the infinitival clause + complement of the infinitival clause.[72]

(ii) Predicate of the main clause + complement of the infinitival clause + predicate of the infinitival clause.[73]

(iii) Predicate of the main clause + complement (predicate of the infinitival clause).[74]

Here the order which occurs twice in 12.56 is a marked one. The predicate of the main clause has a 'broken' infinitival clause as its complement, where the complement of the infinitival clause is separated from its predicate and is located in front of the predicate of the main clause. The people in 12.54-56 are rebuked by Jesus in the title of 'hypocrites'; their ignorance is highlighted by the two marked orders and the foregrounded aspect (οἴδατε) in 12.56.

Shorter Contributions: Christ's Second Baptism [Lk. 12.50; Mk. 10.38-40]', *ExpTim* 100 [1988–89], pp. 294–95 [294]).

71. It is usual of Luke to have an infinitive following the verb ἔχω (cf. Fitzmyer, *Luke*, p. 690; S.J. Patterson, 'Fire and Dissension. Ipsissima Vox Jesu in Q 12.49, 51-53', *Forum* 5 [1989], pp. 121–39 (124)), but what is so significant and important here is the position of the complement of the infinitival clause.

72. This occurs 28x in independent clauses.

73. This occurs 15x in independent clauses.

74. This occurs 21x in independent clauses.

Similar to 12.49, 50 and 51, the two infinitival clauses in 12.56 are separated by the predicate οἴδατε (with the complement of the infinitive placed before οἴδατε). The author has used a foregrounded aspect to bring out a theme: the foolishness of the hypocrites.[75] This theme is further reinforced by using a marked pattern: the complement (the infinitival clause) is separated by the predicate, leaving the phrase τὸ πρόσωπον τῆς γῆς καὶ τοῦ οὐρανοῦ placed before οἴδατε in 12.56a, and τὸν καιρὸν δὲ τοῦτον before οἴδατε in 12.56b. This markedness is even further strengthened by having the phrase τὸν καιρὸν δὲ τοῦτον in 12.56b located before the adverb πῶς.[76] This marked order is used with the foregrounded aspect to highlight an important message: the foolishness of the hypocrites and their lack of understanding.

3. *Summary*: The marked pattern in 12.51 comes alongside with two other similar patterns at the beginning of the episode (12.49, 50) to emphasize the mission of Jesus: his baptism and casting fire on earth. His work (casting fire) is fully contradictory to what the disciples have thought: giving peace. This contradiction is well established with the marked order and the foregrounded aspect (δοκεῖτε) in 12.51 to bring out their lack of understanding of Jesus.[77] In the next closely related episode, a similarly marked pattern is used twice in 12.56: a mental process (οἴδατε) with a foregrounded aspect. The foregrounded mental process has a 'broken' projected infinitival clause, where the complement (τὸ πρόσωπον τῆς γῆς καὶ τοῦ οὐρανοῦ and τὸν καιρὸν δὲ τοῦτον) of the infinitive (δοκιμάζειν) is placed before the predicate of the main clause (οἴδατε). This is to bring out a similar theme: the foolishness and the misunderstanding of the hypocrites. At least three similarities occur between 12.51 and 12.56: (i) mental process in a reported projection; (ii) mental process in an imperfective aspect (δοκεῖτε and οἴδατε); (iii) similar marked patterns as discussed above. The similarities between 12.51 and 12.56 give a comparison between the disciples' foolishness and the hypocrites' lacking of understanding. The hypocrites fully lack understanding, and so do the disciples! The portrayal of the disciples' lack of understanding is compared and strengthened by Jesus' rebuke of the hypocrites' foolishness.

---

75. οἴδατε is in perfect tense, but it is being considered as imperfective aspect here, since this verb only occurs in perfect and pluperfect tense.

76. πῶς is typically located at the front of a clause. πῶς occurs 16x in Luke; 12.56b is the only occurrence that it is not located at the front of a clause (the situation is similar in the rest of the NT books: πῶς is typically located at the front of a clause).

77. The similarities of marked structures of 12.49, 50, 51 (and also 12.56) are not mentioned or recognized by all major commentators. Plummer has only noticed πῦρ is placed in the first position in 12.49 and thus he simply comments it is 'for emphasis' [*Luke*, p. 334]; Reiling and Swellengrebel agree with what Plummer says and thus they further comment the βάπτισμα in 12.50 is emphatic (*Handbook*, p. 492). However, the positions of πῦρ and βάπτισμα in 12.49 and 50 are not only used to represent emphasis. The actual significance here is how these strikingly similar unusual structures in 12.49 and 50 are being used with the one in 12.51, and to be compared with another similar one in 12.56 to bring out the disciples' failure in understanding. This is discussed below.

These passages of Jesus' rebuke of the Pharisees and his disciples come with marked word orders. This is to re-enforce the message represented by the preceding six passages regarding the disciples' failure. More importantly, this is to demonstrate a foregrounded message: the disciples' failure in understanding of Jesus and his role.

Conclusion

Incidents of indirect speech with imperfective aspect addressed to Jesus occur mainly in Luke 7–8. These instances subsequently introduce the semantic elements of 'faith/fear' in these incidents and other surrounding passages in Luke 8–9. These instances lead to the formation of a semantic chain of 'ignorance' throughout Luke 8–9, which includes two incidents of the indirect speeches. The semantic chain demonstrates an important message: the disciples' lack of understanding of Jesus. This message is then further re-enforced by a series of Jesus' confrontations and rebukes to the disciples by employing a number of marked word order patterns.

Chapter 6

HANDING OVER JESUS: A CONSIDERATION OF PILATE'S ACTION THROUGH THE CLAUSE STRUCTURES IN LUKE 23.1-25

The episode of Luke 23.1-25 narrates Jesus' trial before Pilate and Herod. It begins with people's accusations of Jesus and it ends with the final success of their request of crucifying Jesus. A significant clause type is employed at the beginning of the people's accusations and at the final success of their request in the episode: Jesus as complement located before the predicate – a marked order as stated before. The people's accusation of Jesus in 23.2 begins with a clause in a marked order with the complement located before its predicate (23.2 λέγοντες, τοῦτον εὕραμεν),[1] where Jesus (τοῦτον) is the complement of the clause; the episode ends in 23.25 with Pilate's final agreement of handing over Jesus to the people, at which the final clause of 23.25 is also a marked order with the complement located before its predicate (τὸν δὲ Ἰησοῦν παρέδωκεν τῷ θελήματι αὐτῶν),[2] where Jesus is also the complement of the clause. Between these two verses, there are another two instances where Jesus is also a complement located before the predicate (23.16 and 22 παιδεύσας οὖν αὐτὸν ἀπολύσω).[3]

---

1. G. Schneider states εὑρίσκω is in itself a favourite Lukan word (80x of its 176 occurrences in the New Testament are to be found in Luke's work); and the construction of εὑρίσκω + object + participle (sometimes in a different order) is also frequent in Luke (11x in Luke, compared with 5x in Matthew, 6x in Mark, 1x in John, 7x in Acts and 1x in Revelation) ('The Political Charge against Jesus [Luke 23.2]', in Bammel and Moule [eds.], *Jesus and the Politics of His Days*, pp. 403–14). However, what is significant here is not Luke's favourite word and structure, but the marked word order (a CP order: τοῦτον εὕραμεν; CP pattern is a marked order [the number of PC is 306x in independent clauses; while CP is only 78x]; though the instance of the one in 23.2 is always just simply classified as 'emphatic' [e.g. Marshall, *Gospel of Luke*, p. 852; Fitzmyer, *Luke*, p. 1474; Reiling and Swellengrebel, *Handbook*, p. 715]).

2. This is a marked CPA order (the number of PCA is 79x in independent clauses, and the number of CPA is only 16x) which has the complement located before its predicate. The clauses with Jesus as the complement located before its predicate are not only CP clauses; they may include other clause types such as CPA as the one in 23.25. All the clauses with Jesus as the complement located before its predicate in the Gospel will be abbreviated as **C(J)P** throughout the rest of the chapter.

3. There may be an ambiguity in this verse which causes an argument: the possibility of αὐτόν being the complement of παιδεύσας, or ἀπολύσω, or both. Fitzmyer's literal translation (Fitzmyer translates this clause following its literal word order: παιδεύσας comes first, αὐτόν follows it, and then finally ἀπολύσω) may imply his position of putting the pronoun αὐτόν as

The clause structure of Jesus as complement located before its predicate occurs a number of times in three different categories throughout the Gospel. This chapter is going to show the significance of these three different groups of instances, and how they are used with marked word order patterns to highlight a foregrounded message at the end of 23.1-25: the crime of Pilate's handing over an innocent man, Jesus, to death in his trial.

Three C(J)P Categories and their First Members
Three C(J)P Categories

Jesus being the complement in a CP pattern is not common in Luke when it is compared with the PC patterns with Jesus as complement.[4] There is a total of 24 instances in Luke of Jesus functioning as the direct object in a CP clause: C(J)P.[5] Almost all the instances with these C(J)P clauses are related to one particular theme: people's attitudes to Jesus; that is, how people react to Jesus' status of being the Son of God, or to his words and teachings. People with different attitudes to Jesus represented in these C(J)P instances may be classified into three categories: (i) the ones who wrongly support Jesus; (ii) the ones who reject Jesus; (iii) and the ones who rightly or genuinely support Jesus. These three categories are abbreviated as **WSC(J)P**, **REJC(J)P** and **RSC(J)P** respectively in this chapter.[6] All the instances

---

the complement of the participle παιδεύσας: 'Lit. "having disciplined him, I will release (him)"' (*Luke*, p. 1485); Reiling and Swellengrebel hold the similar position: 'so after disciplining him I shall release (him)' (*Handbook*, p. 723). My position is that αὐτόν belongs to the word ἀπολύσω, rather than παιδεύσας; thus αὐτόν is the complement of ἀπολύσω, and the clause is in the C(J)P pattern (αὐτὸν ἀπολύσω). Please see Appendix B at the end this chapter for my argument.

4.   PC pattern with Jesus as direct object occurs 133x in the Gospel (with excluding 4x of LXX citations where the complements are implied to be Jesus [4.10, 12, 18, 18]). The 133 instances are 1.31, 46, 69, 74; 2.7, 7, 7, 12, 16, 26, 27, 28, 46, 48, 48, 29; 4.5, 9, 22, 29, 29, 29, 34, 42, 42; 5.1, 11, 12, 28; 6.7, 7, 18, 19; 7.39; 8.3, 19, 19, 24, 25, 28, 40, 40, 42, 45, 45, 46, 47, 49, 53; 9.11, 18, 30, 35, 37, 48, 52, 53, 57, 61; 10.16, 25, 38; 11.27, 53, 54; 12.8, 9; 13.35; 14.25; 15.1; 17.16; 18.15, 22, 22, 33, 43; 19.3, 4, 6, 35; 20.20; 21.27, 38; 22.2, 4, 6, 21, 29, 39, 47, 57, 61, 63, 64, 64, 66, 67, 70; 23.1, 2, 3; 23.7, 8, 8, 10, 11, 11, 14, 15, 18, 20, 21, 26, 27, 27, 33, 35, 36, 37, 37, 39, 39, 39, 49; 24.16, 19, 20, 20, 21, 29, 31, 39, 52; and there are 47x of PC pattern with Jesus as indirect object: 1.32; 2.48; 4.3, 5, 6, 9, 17, 38; 5.12; 6.11; 7.3, 4, 6, 36; 8.9, 28, 31, 37, 38, 41; 9.10, 12, 33; 10.29; 11.1, 37; 12.13; 13.1, 23, 31; 14.15; 17.5; 18.18; 19.8, 39; 20.2, 3, 21, 24, 27, 40; 21.7; 22.9; 23.3, 9, 36. For CP pattern with Jesus as complement, there are 24x with excluding 2 LXX citations with implying Jesus as the object (4.8, 8). The 24 instances are 6.46; 9.48, 48; 10.16, 16, 16; 11.23; 12.14; 13.31; 18.19; 19.47, 48; 20.44; 22.34, 48, 54; 23.2, 2, 6, 16, 22, 25; 24.24, 39; and there are 3x of CP pattern with Jesus as indirect object: 4.6; 7.45 and 10.22.

5.   Lk. 6.46; 9.48, 48; 10.16, 16, 16; 11.23; 12.14; 13.31; 18.19; 19.47, 48; 20.44; 22.34, 48, 54, 64; 23.2, 2, 6, 16, 22, 25; 24.24, 39. There are two more instances in Lk. 4.8, which are citations from the LXX implying Jesus being equivalent to the complements of the two clauses in 4.8.

6.   The people represented by **WSC(J)P** are the ones who seem to admire Jesus' teachings or status; their attitudes to Jesus shown from their speaking or actions indicate that they seem

of each of these three categories (**WSC[J]P**, **REJC[J]P** and **RSC[J]P**) share similar clause structures and semantic features: (i) each with a marked order of having the complement located before the predicate; (ii) each with Jesus as the complement; (iii) each representing people's attitudes towards Jesus (wrongly supporting, rejecting or rightly supporting).

The First Members of the Three C(J)P Categories
C(J)P is a marked word order. Its significance is not only having Jesus as complement located before the predicate (complement preceding the predicate is a marked order as stated before), but also representing people's three different attitudes to him. The first instance of each type of **C(J)P** is significantly introduced—**WSC(J)P**, **RSC(J)P**, **REJC(J)P** (see below). These newly significantly introduced **C(J)P** instances are to illustrate the importance of the third type: **REJC(J)P**. This will be shown through an analysis of Given-New structures below.

*The First **WSC(J)P**.* Luke 6.46 is the first occurrence of the **C(J)P** pattern (τί δέ με καλεῖτε, κύριε κύριε), which has Jesus as the complement (με) preceding the predicate; it is also the first appeared element of **WSC(J)P**. Jesus asks a question to the ones who only call him Lord but do not follow his words; he gives a rebuke to these people who only apparently admire him, but do not truly accept him.[7] A related theme can also be seen from the surrounding passages. In 6.39-42, Jesus uses the term 'hypocrite' to condemn those who have their own 'specks'; and in 6.43-45, parallelism and contrast between a bad tree and a good tree are used to condemn fake discipleship; the paragraph which follows 6.46 also relates to the theme of condemnation with a parallelism between two opposites: a house with a good foundation and a house without a foundation (6.47-49). In fact, Luke artificially uses his language and wordings to portray the parallelisms in these two surrounding passages:

to be supporters of Jesus, but ironically they always receive rebukes from Jesus regarding their attitudes to him. These are the people who do not genuinely understand or support Jesus (for example, the followers mentioned in 6.46 who apparently do not follow what Jesus says and teaches). The people represented by **REJC(J)P** are apparently the enemies of Jesus, or the ones who are apparently not the supporters of Jesus. These people may show their rejections of Jesus, his status or his teachings through their actions or speaking (for example, Herod in 13.31 who wants to kill Jesus). The people represented by **RSC(J)P** are the genuine supporters of Jesus. They show their genuine faith to Jesus, they genuinely follow what Jesus says through their actions or speaking; for example, the one mentioned in 9.48 who demonstrates his receiving of Jesus by his deeds.

7.   As Fitzmyer interprets: 'Jesus rejects a discipleship which is content merely with an external acknowledgment of a relation to him' (*Luke*, p. 644). What Jesus rejects here is a fake discipleship which is actually not a genuine support to him; cf. Marshall, *Gospel of Luke*, p. 273.

Table 6.1 *Parallelisms and Contrasts in Luke 6.43, 45*

Luke 6.43, 45[8]
6.43 οὐ γάρ ἐστιν δένδρον καλὸν
ποιοῦν καρπὸν σαπρόν
6.45a ὁ ἀγαθὸς ἄνθρωπος ἐκ τοῦ
ἀγαθοῦ θησαυροῦ τῆς καρδίας
προφέρει τὸ ἀγαθόν

Luke 6.43, 45
6.43b οὐδὲ πάλιν δένδρον σαπρὸν ποιοῦν
καρπὸν καλόν
6.45b καὶ ὁ πονηρὸς ἐκ τοῦ πονηροῦ
προφέρει τὸ πονηρόν

Table 6.2 *Parallelisms and Contrasts in Luke 6.47-48 and Luke 6.49*

Luke 6.47-48
6.47 πᾶς ὁ ἐρχόμενος πρός με καὶ
ἀκούων μου τῶν λόγων καὶ ποιῶν αὐτούς
6.48a ὅμοιός ἐστιν ἀνθρώπῳ οἰκοδομοῦντι
οἰκίαν ὃς ἔσκαψεν καὶ ἐβάθυνεν καὶ
ἔθηκεν θεμέλιον ἐπὶ τὴν πέτραν
6.48b προσέρηξεν ὁ ποταμὸς τῇ οἰκίᾳ

Luke 6.49
6.49a ὁ δὲ ἀκούσας καὶ μὴ ποιήσας[9]

6.49b ὅμοιός ἐστιν ἀνθρώπῳ οἰκοδομήσαντι
οἰκίαν ἐπὶ τὴν γῆν χωρὶς θεμελίου

6.49c ᾗ προσέρηξεν ὁ ποταμός

The two parallelisms and contrasts in 6.43-45 and 6.47-49 obviously show a twofold theme which Luke wants to bring out: those who correctly accept or support Jesus and those who wrongly accept or support him. The ones who hear Jesus' words and follow them support him correctly; while the ones who hear his words but do not follow them do not genuinely accept him. These two types of people can be distinguished by their own fruit. Jesus' rebuke to the people who wrongly support him and the twofold theme from the parallelisms and contrasts in Lk. 6.39-49 can be summarized as follows:

1. Jesus' rebuke to the ones who do not genuinely support him (6.39-42).
    2. Twofold theme: those who genuinely support Jesus versus those who wrongly support Jesus, or positive versus negative (6.43-45).
3. Jesus' rebuke to the ones who do not genuinely support him (6.46).
    4. Twofold theme: those who genuinely support Jesus versus those who wrongly support Jesus, or positive versus negative (6.47-49).

Luke apparently emphasizes the rebuke which Jesus addresses to the ones who do not really accept him, or who only wrongly support him. This is repeated twice, and each time it is followed by a twofold theme (positive versus negative) to make contrasts; this is to make Jesus' rebukes stand out clearly. In 6.39-42, the entire paragraph is devoted to the rebuke of the ones who wrongly support Jesus, and the twofold theme in 6.43-45 functions as the reason for what the related person

8.   Words in italic forms are elements representing parallelisms and contrasts between the two columns.
9.   This parallelism is even more obvious than the one in Mt. 7.24 and 7.26. Although Mt. 7.24-27 also has a series of parallelisms in phrases and wordings, the grammatical forms used in the parallelisms are different (Mt. 7.24 uses two indicative forms [ἀλούει, ποιεῖ], but Mt. 7.26 uses two participial forms [ἀκούων, ποιῶν]); while both Lk. 6.47 and 49 have two participial forms (ἀκούων, ποιῶν and ἀκούσας, ποιήσας) to make an even much more perfect parallelism.

in 6.39-42 should do: take the log out of his own eye first. 6.47-49 also functions as a reason: the reason for Jesus' rebuke in 6.46—how wrong it is only to call Jesus as Lord, but not to follow his words.[10] This structure (rebuke of the ones who wrongly support Jesus followed by a twofold theme as reason of the rebuke) is repeated twice in order to emphasize the rebuke. The first one is by a parable (6.39-42); and the second is by a marked order: **C(J)P** pattern (6.46).

The First **RSC(J)P**. Luke 9.48 is the second occurrence containing the **C(J)P** pattern (ὃς ἐὰν δέξηται τοῦτο τὸ παιδίον ἐπὶ τῷ ὀνόματί μου, ἐμὲ δέχεται· καὶ ὃς ἂν ἐμὲ δέξηται, δέχεται τὸν ἀποστείλαντά με).[11] This **C(J)P** pattern is used to praise one who correctly accepts Jesus.[12] This time this second **C(J)P** pattern is the first instance of the **RSC(J)P**; similar to the situation in 6.46, this theme of 'rightly supporting Jesus' is highlighted by a series of contrasts and parallelisms from its surrounding passages: Luke 7-9.[13] As stated in Chapter 5 of this work, the faithful centurion (RS) is compared with the unfaithful Israelite (WS or REJ) (7.2-10); the woman who anoints Jesus (RS) is compared with the Pharisee Simon (WS), who invites Jesus into his home but obviously does not truly accept him (7.36-50); the man who has been possessed with demons (RS) is compared with the people of the surrounding area of the Gerasenes (REJ) (8.26-39); the

10.   Marshall rightly states that the contrast in 6.46 is slightly different from the parable which immediately follows it (6.47-49): 'This contrast between confession and obedience is slightly different from that between hearing and doing which dominates the following parable' (Marshall, *Gospel of Luke*, p. 274). This is because 6.46 only contains elements of Jesus' rebuke on the ones who wrongly support him; while the parable (6.47-49) contains both sides of the theme (positive and negative): a twofold theme. Evans also admits the connection between 6.46 and the parable (6.47-49): 'Luke's version with *and not do what I tell you* makes it an immediate introduction to the following parable' (*Luke*, p. 339); and similar is Geldenhuys' comment on these few verses (*Luke*, p. 215).

11.   Matthew and Mark have both got the same **C(J)P** pattern (Mt. 18.5 καὶ ὃς ἐὰν δέξηται ἓ παιδίον τοιοῦτο ἐπὶ τῷ ὀνόματί μου, ἐμὲ δέχεται and Mk 9.37 ὃς ἂν ἓ τῶν τοιούτων παιδίων δέξηται ἐπὶ τῷ ὀνόματί μου, ἐμὲ δέχεται· καὶ ὃς ἂν ἐμὲ δέχηται, οὐκ ἐμὲ δέχεται ἀλλὰ τὸν ἀποστείλαντά με).
The pronoun employed here is an emphatic form (ἐμέ), which appears before its associated predicate (ἐμὲ δέχεται and ἐμὲ δέξηται). Unemphatic pronoun usually follows its verb ('unemphatic pronouns tend to follow immediately on the verb' [Blass and Debrunner, *A Greek Grammar*, p. 248]). Here the pronoun is an emphatic form and thus it precedes its predicate and indicates emphatic meaning.

12.   Plummer recognizes the choice of the lexical term (ἐμέ) used for the pronoun and thus simply states: 'The pronoun is emphatic' (*Luke*, p. 258); similar is the statement by Reiling and Swellengrebel (*Handbook*, p. 392); Fitzmyer observes the position of the pronoun and comments: 'The prons. "me" are in an emphatic position before the verb' (*Luke*, p. 817). In fact, the significance of this verse is more than simply an 'emphatic' word; this will be discussed below.

13.   In the rest of the chapter, the kind of people who rightly support, wrongly support and reject Jesus are abbreviated as RS, WS and REJ respectively. These three kinds of people may not necessarily come with a **C(J)P** clause structure; the abbreviations representing them (RS, WS and REJ) are only to show their different attitudes to Jesus: rightly supporting, wrongly supporting or rejecting him.

faithful ruler Jairus (RS) is compared with the unfaithful people (WS or REJ) who only laugh at Jesus (8.41, 49-56). All of the above different events are used to portray the unfaithfulness of the disciples, their misinterpretation of Jesus (as it is discussed in Chapter 5). Although the disciples follow Jesus and listen to his words, they do not really accept him; they only incorrectly or wrongly support him (WS). The topic of correctly supporting Jesus (RS) (9.48) is brought out by the contrasts with the attitudes of the disciples (WS) before and after 9.48.

Ravens has rightly pointed out that Luke 9 is rich in the range of titles given to Jesus. Besides the infancy narratives, it is the first time that Jesus' Messianic role is revealed (9.20), and it is the first prediction of the suffering and future coming of the Son of Man (9.22, 26) and the status of God's chosen one (9.35).[14] Ironically, the disciples portrayed in Luke 9 are full of misunderstandings of Jesus' richly revealed mission and titles. They still have the misunderstanding while Jesus is being transfigured.[15] Indeed, a sequence of events in Luke 9 all reveal the

---

14. Ravens, 'Luke 9.7-62 and the Prophetic Role of Jesus', p.119; J.A. Fitzmyer has rightly pointed out that Herod's question ('Who is this?' [9.7-9]) is placed in Luke 9 to introduce Jesus' Messianic role being narrated in the following episodes (e.g. the mention of Elijah in 9.8 and 9.19 is echoed with the appearance of Elijah in 9.28-36, where it clearly shows Jesus is not Elijah, he is the one who is much more superior than him [9.35]) (see J.A. Fitzmyer, 'The Composition of Luke, Chapter 9', in Talbert [ed.], *Perspectives on Luke-Acts*, pp. 141–46; *idem*, *Luke*, pp. 756–58; cf. Achtemeier, 'The Lukan Perspective on the Miracles of Jesus: A Preliminary Sketch', p. 166; T.L. Brodie even suggests Jesus is imitated as Elijah from the episode of Simon and the sinful woman in 7.36-50 ['Luke 7.36-50 as an Internalization of 2 Kings 4.1-37: A Study in Luke's Use of Rhetorical Imitation', *Bib* 64 (1983), pp. 457–85; cf. *idem*, 'Animadversiones: The Departure for Jerusalem (Luke 9.51-56) as a Rhetorical Imitation of Elijah's Departure for the Jordan (2 Kgs 1.1-2.6)', *Bib* 70 (1989), pp. 96–109; also cf. Evans, 'Luke's Use of the Elijah/Elisha Narratives', pp. 671–83; and Fleddermann's suggestion of the comparison of Elijah/Elisha in 1 Kings 19.19-21 with Lk. 9.59-62 ('Demands of Discipleship', pp. 551–52)]; the Messianic role of Jesus in Luke 9 is not only echoed with his divine power in the feeding [9.12-17], Peter's confession in 9.18-20, his self description [9.22], his conversation with Moses and Elijah revealing his mission in Jerusalem [9.30-31] [S.R. Garrett, 'Exodus from Bondage: Luke 9.31 and Acts 12.1-24', *CBQ* 52 (1990), pp. 656–80 (656–57, 677)], God's own revelation [9.35], but also his firm determination of the journey to Jerusalem [9.51] [cf. F.J. Matera, 'Jesus' Journey to Jerusalem (Luke 9.51-19.46): A Conflict With Israel', *JSNT* 51 (1993), pp. 57–57 (57–58); also cf. Denaux's tripartite of the life of Jesus: mission in Galilee (4.14-9.50), going up to Jerusalem (9.51-19.27/28), ministry in Jerusalem (19.28/29-24.53): A. Denaux, 'The Delineation of the Lukan Travel Narrative within the Overall Structure of the Gospel of Luke', in C. Focant (ed.), *The Synoptic Gospels: Source Criticism and the New Literary Criticism* (BETL, 110; Leuven: Leuven University Press, 1993), pp. 357–92 (362)]).

15. The problem of the disciples (especially Peter), is that they think of Jesus on an equal level with Moses and Elijah. Indeed, Jesus is the one who is going to fulfill what has been described in Torah and Prophets, which are represented by Moses and Elijah respectively. God's words in 9.36 demonstrate Jesus is much superior to the two OT characters. Once the voice is stopped, Moses and Elijah retreat and Jesus is left alone; this is also true when the Torah and Prophets retreat after the coming of Christ: they let Jesus be the sole authority to fulfill what has been said in the Torah and Prophets: Jesus is God's son and the coming Saviour (Tyson, 'Jews and Judaism in Luke-Acts', pp. 28–29; cf. Marshall, *Gospel of Luke*, p. 388; Morris, *Luke*, p. 173; Goulder, *Luke*, p. 441; Easton, *Luke*, p. 144; Fitzmyer, *Luke*, p. 801; cf. Evans, *Luke*, p. 421; also Hall, 'Synoptic Transfigurations', p. 42).

disciples' misunderstanding, or wrong support of Jesus (the feeding, transfiguration and healing of the demon possessed boy).[16]

The foolishness of the disciples is then further and more explicitly indicated. It is the first time to have the disciples described with the words 'do not understand'. This has been stated twice (9.45); it is then followed by the dispute among the disciples (9.46), which leads to the first appearing of the **RSC(J)P** pattern in 9.48. The disciples' foolishness is then continuously portrayed after 9.48: the misunderstanding of the disciples illustrated by their stopping of the man who has cast out demons in Jesus' name (9.49-50); Jesus' condemnation of the disciples regarding their foolish suggestion of destroying the Samaritans (9.54-55); and the incorrect attitudes of three other followers in following Jesus (9.57-58, 59-60, 61-62).

In summary, the first **RSC(J)P** is located in 9.48. The significance of this first element of **RSC(J)P** is highlighted on one hand by contrasting a sequence of five of the disciples' WS events in Luke 9 (feeding [9.10-17], transfiguration [9.28-36], healing of the boy [9.37-42], not understanding Jesus' revealed mission [9.44-45], and the dispute among the disciples [9.46]) located before it, and on the other hand

---

16.   It may be the case that Luke 9 represents OT figures (the great omission of Mk 6.45-8.26 is to make a closer package of OT figures; packed events narrated in Luke 9 [the feeding in 9.12-17, the transfiguration in 9.28-36, the healing of the possessed boy after the disciples' lack of faith in 9.38-43] are to recall the historical events recorded in Exodus 16, 19, 24, 34, 32: the manna feeding in the wilds, Moses on Sinai and Israel's lack of faith in the event of the golden calf; see Ravens, 'Luke 9.7-62', p. 121; cf. D.P. Moessner, '"The Christ Must Suffer": New Light on the Jesus-Peter, Stephen, Paul Parallels in Luke-Acts', *NovT* 28 [1986], pp. 220–56 (235)). What is certain is that Luke 9 is packed with the disciples' lack of understanding about Jesus (for the incidents of the transfiguration and the healing of the demon-possessed son, see Chapter 5 of this work). The incident of feeding the five thousand represents the lack of understanding of the disciples. In the story of feeding the five thousand, marked orders are used in the interactions between Jesus and his disciples to highlight the confrontations with each other in their conversation. In 9.12, the disciples ask Jesus to send the people away. The second clause in their saying represents the reason of their request; and the order is marked: A(spatial)A(spatial)P (ὧδε ἐν ἐρήμῳ τόπῳ ἐσμέν). Spatial adjunct located before and after the predicate occurs 34x and 96x in dependent clauses respectively; and 62x and 345x in independent clauses (spatial adjunct predominantly follows the predicate as stated in Chapter 4). This time there is a sequence of two spatial adjuncts located before the predicate and thus this dependent clause is even more marked. Jesus' response is a refusal to the disciples' request; he gives a command to the disciples instead, which is also with marked order (9.13 δότε αὐτοῖς ὑμεῖς φαγεῖν) (this marked order is a PCSA order [the infinitive φαγεῖν functions as a circumstantial adjunct with result function], the number of occurrence of PCS, PSC and SPC in independent clauses is 24x, 49x and 147x respectively [the number of PCS is the least among the three]). The semantic significance of Jesus' command is even further increased by the redundant use of the personal pronoun ὑμεῖς as subject. The disciples' response represents the reason for their refusal to Jesus' command; it also gives the suggestion of an alternative practice. This confrontation is carried out in two clauses with marked order (9.13 οὐκ εἰσὶν ἡμῖν πλεῖον ἢ ἄρτοι πέντε καὶ ἰχθύες δύο, εἰ μήτι πορευθέντες ἡμεῖς ἀγοράσωμεν εἰς πάντα τὸν λαὸν τοῦτον βρώματα). The first clause is marked with PCS (see the word order types in 9.13 mentioned above); the semantic weight is further increased by the redundant use of the personal pronoun (ἡμεῖς) in the second clause. In summary, all these marked challenging statements and commands are used to highlight the disciples' misunder-

by contrasting with another sequence of the disciples' WS events (9.49-50, 54-55, 57-58, 59-60, 61-62) located after it.[17] This structure can be illustrated as follows:

5 WS vs. RSC(J)P vs. 5 WS

All ten instances of WS are related to Jesus' followers. They represent either the disciples' failure in understanding Jesus, or other followers' intellectual incomprehension about Jesus. The first five WS events lead to the first RSC(J)P. This RSC(J)P is then followed by another five WS events; all occur in Luke 9. This structure (5 WS + RSC[J]P + 5WS) makes the RSC(J)P stand out clearly: how wrong it is to support Jesus incorrectly; or in other words, how important it is to accept and support Jesus rightly and genuinely.[18]

The First REJC(J)P. 10.16 is the first instance of the REJC(J)P: it states people's rejection of Jesus. This time this REJC(J)P comes alongside with an instance of RSC(J)P in paralleled phrases and wordings:

10.16a ὁ ἀκούων ὑμῶν	ἐμοῦ ἀκούει (RSC[J]P)
10.16b καὶ ὁ ἀθετῶν ὑμᾶς	ἐμὲ ἀθετεῖ (REJC[J]P)
10.16c ὁ δὲ ἐμὲ ἀθετῶν (REJC[J]P)	ἀθετεῖ τὸν ἀποστείλαντά με[19]

In fact, 10.16b and 10.16c, which contain the structure of REJC(J)P, are unique

standing of Jesus.

17.   9.57-58 narrates a follower who may underestimate the difficulties in following Jesus. This is followed by scenes with similar topics (9.59-60 and 9.61-62): the men want to delay their following of Jesus; A. Droge may be right in classifying this sequence of events (Lk. 9.57-62) as 'Unsuccessful Call Stories' ('Call Stories in Greek Biographies and the Gospels', SBLSP [1983], pp. 245–57 (254); J.R. Butts has further modified these as 'Unsuccessful Call Stories' [Lk. 9.59-60] and 'Unsuccessful Discipleship Quests' [Lk. 9.61-62 and 9.57-58] ['The Voyage of Discipleship: Narrative, Chreia, and Call Story', in C.A. Evans and W.F. Stinespring (eds.), *Early Jewish and Christian Exegesis: Studies in Memory of William Hugh Brownlee* (Atlanta: Scholars Press, 1987), pp. 199–219 (213); cf. L.E. Vaage, 'Q1 and the Historical Jesus: Some Peculiar Sayings (7.33-34; 9.57-58, 59-60; 14.26-27)', *Forum* 5 (1989), pp. 159–76 (167); M.H. Smith, 'No Place for a Son of Man', *Forum* 4 (1988), pp. 83–107 (86); and Steinhauser, 'Putting One's Hand to the Plow', pp. 152–53]).

18.   Not only the structure of 5 WS + RSC(J)P + 5 WS is used to bring out the significance of the first appearance of RSC(J)P, but also its paralleled wordings and structure in 9.48 (ἐμὲ δέχεται and ἐμὲ δέξηται). This 'doubled' wordings and structure is also used to make comparison with the first appearance of REJC(J)P in 10.16 (ἐμὲ ἀθετεῖ and ἐμὲ ἀθετῶν) (with paralleled wordings and structure), which is being discussed below.

19.   The pattern of having a complement located before the predicate is a marked order (as mentioned before). 10.16 is even more significant for this structure, because there are three such structures (CP) in one verse. Although this unusualness of three CP structures packed in one single verse is apparent, surprisingly none of the major commentaries has raised any comment about this (e.g. see Plummer, *Luke*, p. 277; Marshall, *Gospel of Luke*, pp. 426–27; Reiling and Swellengrebel, *Handbook*, p. 410; Fitzmyer, *Luke*, pp. 856–58; Nolland, *Luke*, pp. 557–58; Ellis, *Luke*, p. 157; R.H. Stein, *Luke* [NAC, 24; Nashville: Broadman Press, 1992], p. 307; Easton, *Luke*, p. 158; Manson, *Luke*, pp. 124–25; W. Hendriksen, *Exposition of the Gospel According to Luke* [NTC; Grand Rapids: Baker Book House, 1978], pp. 577–80, 586; Morris, *Luke*, p. 184; Creed, *Luke*, p. 146; Geldenhuys, *Luke*, p. 301; A.A. Just, *Luke* [CC; 2 vols.; Saint Louis:

to Luke's Gospel;[20] and this structure appears twice (10.16b ἐμὲ ἀθετεῖ and 10.16c ἐμὲ ἀθετῶν).[21] This first instance of REJC(J)P is obviously highlighted. This can be observed from at least two points. The first is the parallelism with the wordings of its neighbour RSC(J)P (10.16a). As it is stated above, 10.16a (RSC[J]P) and 10.16b (REJC[J]P) are perfectly paralleled (both wordings and clause structures, and the number of words); on the contrary, in 10.16c the wordings are solely related to REJC(J)P. This leaves the instance of REJC(J)P in 10.16c to stand out significantly, and this makes the length of the wording of REJC(J)P much longer than the length of the wording of RSC(J)P in 10.16. The second is the co-text right (10.5-15) before 10.16. The passage of 10.5-15 presents an incident of the disciples being accepted (RS[disciples]) and an incident of the disciples being rejected (REJ[disciples]).[22] Comparisons are formed between these two types of figure (accepting and rejecting the disciples): the section of RS(disciples) begins with the wordings of εἰς ἣν ἂν πόλιν εἰσέρχησθε καὶ δέχωνται ὑμᾶς (10.8), and it ends with the content of a proclamation: ἤγγικεν ἐφ' ὑμᾶς ἡ βασιλεία τοῦ θεοῦ (10.9). These two features are paralleled with the wordings in the section of REJ(disciples): it begins with very similar wordings as the ones in 10.8: εἰς ἣν δ' ἂν πόλιν εἰσέλθητε καὶ μὴ δέχωνται ὑμᾶς (10.10),[23] it is also ended with very similar wordings as the ones in 10.9: ἤγγικεν ἡ βασιλεία τοῦ θεοῦ (10.11). Although the sections of RS(disciples) and REJ(disciples) are obviously compared with each other in 10.8-11 with similar beginning and closing wordings, the wordings (10.12-15) which follow 10.8-11 are solely related

Concordia, 1996–97], pp. 438–39; Evans, *Luke*, p. 452; Johnson, *Luke*, pp. 168–71; Goulder, *Luke*, p. 472, 476; Bock, *Luke*, p. 1005; F.L. Godet, *Commentary on Luke* [KRL; Grand Rapids: Kregel, 1981], p. 297; R.C. Tannehill, *Luke* [ANTC; Nashville: Abingdon Press, 1996], pp. 177–78).

20.   Matthew only contains wordings of RSC(J)P: Mt. 10.40 ὁ δεχόμενος ὑμᾶς ἐμὲ δέχεται, καὶ ὁ ἐμὲ δεχόμενος δέχεται τὸν ἀποστείλαντά με.

21.   This first incident of REJC(J)P comes with a double appearance, which is similar to the double appearance (ἐμὲ δέχεται and ἐμὲ δέξηται) of the first incident of RSC(J)P in 9.48. The similarities between the two (9.48 and 10.16) are actually not only this. In fact, the wording and clause structures are also similar in the following points: (i) 9.48a (ὃς ἐὰν δέξηται τοῦτο τὸ παιδίον ἐπὶ τῷ ὀνόματί μου, ἐμὲ δέχεται) is paralleled to 10.16b (ὁ ἀθετῶν ὑμᾶς ἐμὲ ἀθετεῖ): they are both in an order of SCP, and both subjects are in an embedded clause, and both complements are a personal pronoun referring to Jesus; (ii) 9.48b (ὃς ἂν ἐμὲ δέξηται, δέχεται τὸν ἀποστείλαντά με) is paralleled to 10.16b (ὁ δὲ ἐμὲ ἀθετῶν ἀθετεῖ τὸν ἀποστείλαντά με): besides the similarities in lexical items (e.g. τὸν ἀποστείλαντά με in both cases), they both have a SPC order, where both the subjects are in a clause itself with an order of SCP, and both the complements are in a participial clause with a PC order.

22.   Here the case of people accepting the disciples is abbreviated as RS(disciples), and the case of rejecting is abbreviated as REJ(disciples). Although 10.1-15 is related to the disciples rather than Jesus himself, this passage carries important relationship with 10.16. It is because as it is stated in 10.16, one who receives the disciples receives Jesus, and one who rejects the disciples rejects Jesus; thus the figures of RS(disciples) and REJ(disciples) contribute significant meanings to RSC(J)P and REJC(J)P in 10.16.

23.   In addition, these two comparing verses (10.8 and 10.10) are preceded with an introduction which begins with similar wordings (10.5: εἰς ἣν δ' ἂν εἰσέλθητε οἰκίαν); this makes the similarities between the opening wordings of 10.8 and 10.10 to be even more significant.

to REJ(disciples). This makes the total length of the wordings of REJ(disciples) much longer than the total length of the wordings of RS(disciples), and this causes the topic of REJ(disciples) to stand out significantly.

In summary, the above two discussed passages (10.5-15 and 10.16) all have the same pattern: RS + REJ + REJ.[24] Both of the two patterns have explicit parallelisms between their first two items (RS and REJ), which leads the third item (REJ) of both patterns to stand out significantly as a highlighted topic: the concept of rejecting the disciples and rejecting Jesus.[25] This is to highlight the first instance of REJC(J)P. Here in 10.16, the third item (REJ) of the pattern, which is also a **REJC(J)P**, stands out significantly; this is to state the fact of how wrong it is to reject Jesus, or how serious is the wrong action of rejecting Jesus: rejecting Jesus is rejecting the one who sends him (10.16c).

Focusing on the First REJC(J)P. As is shown above, the first instance of C(J)P is the first **WSC(J)P**; the second instance of C(J)P is the first **RSC(J)P**; and the fourth instance of **C(J)P** is the first **REJC(J)P**. Each of the above has comparisons and contrasts with other events in their surrounding texts: the **WSC(J)P** in 6.46 has comparisons and contrasts with several WS and RS before and after it; the **RSC(J)P** in 9.48 has comparisons and contrasts with events before and after it (with five of the disciples and followers' WS events before and after it: 5 WS + **RSC(J)P** + 5 WS); the **REJC(J)P** in 10.16 has comparisons and contrasts with RSC(J)P and similar descriptions of disciples (accepting and rejecting disciples) in its preceding texts (which leads to a sequence of two patterns of RS + REJ + REJ). All these different comparisons and contrasts are used to introduce every member of the three categories (the first **WSC[J]P**; the first **RSC[J]**; and the first **REJC[J]P**) and to make them stand out clearly with significant meanings. What is so significant is not only this; what is much more important is the occurrence of the third C(J)P (the first **REJC[J]P**), which is discussed below.

The comparisons in every first appearance of **WSC(J)P, RSC(J)P** and **REJ(C)P** can be summarized as follows:

---

24. The RS + REJ + REJ in 10.16 is related to people's different attitudes to Jesus (accepting and rejecting Jesus); while the RS + REJ + REJ in 10.5-15 is related to people's different attitudes to the disciples (accepting and rejecting the disciples). The occurrence of these two patterns of RS + REJ + REJ is to make one theme here stand out clearly: the significance of the first element of **REJC(J)P** in 10.16 (although the objects of the people's attitudes in these two passages are different [the one in 10.16 is Jesus; the one in 10.5-15 is the disciples], the pattern of RS + REJ + REJ is also contributed to the theme of rejecting Jesus, because accepting the disciples is equivalent to accepting Jesus, and rejecting the disciples is equivalent to rejecting Jesus [as 10.16 states]).

25. As has been stated before, rejecting the disciples is equivalent to rejecting Jesus; thus the concept of rejecting Jesus is the topic which is really being highlighted here. This is to highlight the first appearance of the **REJC(J)P**.

(i) 6.46 RS vs. **WSC(J)P**: highlighting **WSC(J)P** by the repeated rebukes (6.39-42 and 6.46) and the repeated twofold themes (6.42-45 and 6.47-49).

(ii) 9.48 WS vs. **RSC(J)P**: highlighting **RSC(J)P** by the ten WS in the same chapter, where five WS are located before 9.48, and the other five after it.

(iii) 10.16 **RSC(J)P** vs. **REJC(J)P**: highlighting **REJC(J)P** by a structure of **RSC(J)P** + **REJC(J)P** + **REJC(J)P**.[26]

The significance of the occurrences of the above structures in the above three verses (6.46; 9.48 and 10.16) can be seen by the concept of Information Unit: the theory of Given-New and Information Focus.[27] The verses (6.46; 9.48; 10.16) containing the first elements of each of the above three discussed categories (**WSC[J]P**, **RSC[J]P** and **REJC[J]P**) may form Given-New structures. This can be summarized as follows:

Table 6.3 *Given-New Structures in 6.46; 9.48 and 10.16*

	Parallelisms and contrast with co-texts	Given	New
6.46	RS vs. **WSC(J)P**		RS and **WSC(J)P**
9.48	WS vs. **RSC(J)P**	WS	**RSC(J)P**
10.16	RS vs. **REJC(J)P**	RS and **RSC(J)P**	**REJC(J)P**

6.46 contains the first instance of **WSC(J)P**; this first **WSC(J)P** is unknown to readers before and thus it functions as a New Information unit with the several events of RS from its co-texts. In 9.48, the first **RSC(J)P** is the New Information unit; it is highlighted by being contrasted with several incidents of WS. The concept of WS (wrongly supporting Jesus) has already been introduced in 6.46, it is 'known' to the reader and it thus functions as the Given (old) Information unit. In 10.16, the firstly appeared **REJC(J)P** is the New Information unit; it is highlighted by being contrasted with a **RSC(J)P** and an event of RS from its co-texts, which have already been introduced in 9.48 and in the co-texts of 6.46 and thus they are the Given in this verse. What is significant here is the first appeared **REJC(J)P** in 10.16. The above sequence of Given-New structures leads the first **REJC(J)P** to be the New Information unit within the three verses; this New Information is marked with prominence and it carries Information Focus. This first **REJC(J)P** carrying Information Focus represents the semantic weight and significance of the concept of rejecting Jesus (in **C[J]P** pattern), which leads to the significance of Pilate's action of handing over Jesus; this will be discussed below.

26.　The structure is **RSC(J)P** + **REJC(J)P** + **REJC(J)P** in 10.16; it can be simplified to be the pattern of RS + REJ + REJ as the pattern in its co-text 10.8-11[as has been discussed above].

27.　The theory of Given-New and Information Focus is one of the major theories discussed by Systemic Linguistics. In simplified terms, an information unit can be said to be usually composed of two main elements: an old (Given) and a new (New) information unit. 'Given' is known or predictable to readers; while 'New' is new or unpredictable, and it is usually marked by prominence and this prominence can be said to be carrying Information Focus (see Halliday, *An Introduction to Functional Grammar*, pp. 295–96) (for more detailed discussions of the theory of Given-New and its applications to Lukan passages, see Chapter 8 of the work).

Cohesion Chains and Prominence in 23.1-25
Cohesion Chain of C(J)P

As has been stated above, all the C(J)P incidents share similar clause structures and semantic features: (i) each with a marked order of having the complement located before the predicate; (ii) each with Jesus as the complement; (iii) each representing people's attitudes towards Jesus (wrongly supporting, rejecting or rightly supporting). Based on these similar features of all the instances of C(J)P, each instance is cohered with other instances to form cohesive ties. These cohesive ties are cohered with each other and thus subsequently a cohesion chain of C(J)P is formed.

The cohesion chain formed by the cohesive ties of C(J)P may be classified as a co-classificational chain under M.A.K. Halliday and R. Hasan's definitions of cohesive ties.[28] This is a co-classificational chain, because all of the cohesive ties of the chain belong to the classification of people's attitude to Jesus (wrongly supporting, rejecting or rightly supporting). This cohesion chain shares similar features and structures among its cohesive ties (as described above) and thus it is also a similarity chain.[29] This cohesion chain of C(J)P is composed of its cohesive ties which include members of RSC(J)P, WSC(J)P, and REJC(J)P. This can be summarized as follows, where the C(J)P structures are in italics:[30]

---

28. M.A.K. Halliday and R. Hasan have classified cohesive ties into three types: co-reference, co-classification and co-extension. Co-reference is typically expressed by personal pronouns, demonstrative pronouns and relative pronouns; it is used to express references to anaphoric or cataphoric elements. Co-classification is typically expressed by substitutions and ellipses; it is used to express the cohesive ties between elements which belong to the same class. Co-extension is used to express the cohesive ties within elements which are in the same general field of meaning, which can be further divided into five forms: reiteration, synonymy, antonymy, hyponymy and meronymy. For discussions of these classifications, see M.A.K. Halliday and R. Hasan, *Language, Context and Text: Aspects of Language in a Social-Semiotic Perspective* (Oxford: Oxford University Press, 2nd edn 1989), pp. 73–75; see also J.T. Reed, 'Cohesive Ties in 1 Timothy: In Defense of the Epistle's Unity', *Neot* 26 (1992), pp. 131–47 (134–38); *idem*, *A Discourse Analysis of Philippians*, pp. 93–98; *idem*, 'Discourse Analysis', in S.E. Porter (ed.), *Handbook to Exegesis of the New Testament* (NTTS, 25; Leiden: Brill, 1997), pp. 189–217 (208–11); C.S. Butler, *Systemic Linguistics: Theory and Application* (London: Batsford Academic and Educational, 1985), pp. 179–88; R. Hasan, 'Coherence and Cohesive Harmony', in J. Flood (ed.), *Understanding Reading Comprehension: Cognition, Language, and the Structure of Prose* (Newark: International Reading Association, 1984), pp. 181–219 (186–87, 205–06); and Martin, *English Text*, pp. 140–53.

29. A sequence of cohesive ties usually forms two kinds of chains: identity chains and similarity chains. Identity chains are expressed by co-referential ties, and similarity chains are expressed by co-classificational and co-extensional ties (Halliday and Hasan, *Language, Context and Text*, pp. 84, 93; Hasan, 'Coherence and cohesive harmony', pp. 211ff.; Reed, *A Discourse Analysis of Philippians*, p. 100).

30. C(J)P incidents of the chain are in italics in Table 6.4.

Table 6.4 *Members of the Cohesion Chain Formed by C(J)P Incidents*

Members of RSC(J)P	Members of WSC(J)P	Members of REJC(J)P	Others
	6.46 τί δέ με καλεῖτε, κύριε κύριε		
9.48 ὃς ἐὰν δέξηται τοῦτο τὸ παιδίον ἐπὶ τῷ ὀνόματί μου, ἐμὲ δέχεται· καὶ ὃς ἂν ἐμὲ δέξηται, δέχεται τὸν ἀποστείλαντά με·			
10.16 ὁ ἀκούων ὑμῶν ἐμοῦ ἀλούει		10.16(2x) καὶ ὁ ἀθετῶν ὑμᾶς ἐμὲ ἀθετεῖ ὁ δὲ ἐμὲ ἀθετῶν ἀθετει τὸν ἀποστείλαντά με	
		11.23 ὁ μὴ ὢν μετ' ἐμοῦ κατ' ἐμοῦ ἐστιν	
	12.14 τίς με κατέστησεν κριτήν		
		13.31 Ἡρῴδης θέλει σε ἀποκτεῖναι	
	18.19 τί με λέγεις ἀγαθόν		
19.48 ὁ λαὸς γὰρ ἅπας ἐξεκρέματο αὐτοῦ ἀκούων		19.47 οἱ δὲ ἀρχιερεῖς καὶ οἱ γραμματεῖς ἐζήτουν αὐτὸν ἀπολέσαι καὶ οἱ πρῶτοι τοῦ λαοῦ	
(20.44) Δαυὶδ οὖν κύριον αὐτὸν καλεῖ			(20.44) καὶ πῶς αὐτοῦ υἱός ἐστον
	(22.34) τρίς με ἀπαρνήσῃ εἰδέναι	22.34 τρίς με ἀπαρνήσῃ εἰδέναι	
		22.48 φιλήματι τὸν υἱὸν τοῦ ἀνθρώπου παραδίδως	
		22.54 συλλαβόντες δὲ αὐτὸν ἤγαγον	
		22.64 καὶ περικαλύψαντες αὐτὸν ἐπηρώτων λέγοντες	
		23.2 τοῦτον εὕραμεν	
			23.2 λέγοντα ἑαυτὸν Χριστὸν βασιλέα εἶναι
			23.6 Πιλᾶτος δὲ ἀλούσας ἐπηρώτησεν εἰ ὁ ἄνθρωπος Γαλιλαῖός ἐστιν
	23.16 παιδεύσας οὖν αὐτὸν ἀπολύσω		
	23.22 παιδεύσας οὖν		

αὐτὸν ἀπολύσω

23.25 τὸν δὲ Ἰησοῦν
παρέδωκεν τῷ
θελήματι αὐτῶν

24.24 αὐτὸν δὲ οὐκ
εἶδον
24.39 καθὼς ἐμὲ
θεωρεῖτε ἔχοντα

Chain Interactions in 23.1-25

There are four members of the C(J)P chain occurring in 23.1-25 with Jesus as complement located before the predicate. Jesus functions as the goal in all of these four C(J)P processes. In the first one, the actor is the crowd of people; while in the next three incidents, the actors are all the same person: Pilate.

Pilate is a major participant in the episode. All the references to Pilate in the episode form co-referential ties and eventually they compose another cohesive chain: an identity chain referring to Pilate. This identity chain is particularly mentioned here because it has consecutive interactions with the C(J)P chain in 23.1-25. In the two WSC(J)P events (23.16 and 23.22: παιδεύσας οὖν αὐτὸν ἀπολύσω),[31] Pilate functions as the actor of the two processes; in the REJC(J)P event (23.25: τὸν δὲ Ἰησοῦν παρέδωκεν τῷ θελήματι αὐτῶν), Pilate is also the actor of the process. Interactions of the two chains (C[J]P chain and the identity chain) occur at these three incidents (23.16, 22, 25) and thus a central token is formed showing the cohesiveness of the text.[32] The interactions of the two chains occur in close contexts (23.16, 22, 25; esp. 23.22 and 23.25) indicating the author is 'on about' a similar topic: Pilate's attitude to Jesus. What is significant here is Pilate's different attitudes to Jesus; at the central token of the two chains, Pilate switches his attitude to Jesus from WSC(J)P to REJC(J)P (the category of REJC[J]P has been much highlighted as the information focus in its first appearance in 10.16). After Jesus is sent from Herod back to Pilate,[33] Pilate

31. αὐτὸν ἀπολύσω in 23.16 and 22 is classified as WSC(J)P, because Pilate wants to chastise Jesus before releasing him despite knowing that Jesus is an innocent man. Although Pilate thinks Jesus is innocent, he still wants to chastise Jesus before releasing him. Pilate obviously does not understand or admit Jesus' status of being the Son of God; he wants to give him a scourging as an alternative to crucifixion instead of releasing him without any punishment (cf. Marshall, *Gospel of Luke*, p. 859). Pilate here at 23.16 and 23.22 clearly shows he does not genuinely support Jesus, instead he wrongly supports Jesus and belongs to the category of WSC(J)P.

32. Halliday and Hasan classify interactions between cohesion chains to be the central token. They suggest there should be two or more members of a chain standing in the same relation to the two members in another chain to form interaction (in 23.1-25 there are three members of the identity chain of Pilate standing in the same relation to three members in the classificational chain C[J]P; the central token is formed by these consecutive interactions); these interactions are central tokens and they represent textual cohesiveness in a text. Textual cohesiveness is significant in formation of a text, it represents potential coherence in a text and it shows that the author is 'on about' a similar topic (see Halliday and Hasan, *Language, Context and Text*, pp. 73ff.; Reed, *A Discourse Analysis of Philippians*, pp. 100–101).

33. Pilate sends Jesus to Herod because Jesus belongs to Herod's jurisdiction (23.7) (cf. E. Bammel, 'The Trial before Pilate', in Bammel and Moule [eds.], *Jesus and the Politics of His Days*,

becomes the actor of the two **WSC(J)P** in 23.16 and 22; his role is switched to be the actor of the **REJC(J)P** in 23.25. Pilate knows that Jesus is innocent and wants to release him (although he still wants to chastise him before releasing him). His final decision to hand over Jesus switches him from being the participant of the two **WSC(J)P** to the participant of the **REJC(J)P** in 23.25. **WSC(J)P** is ended when Pilate switches his attitude toward Jesus to **REJC(J)P** at the central token.[34] The interactions of the two chains showing Pilate's switching of his attitudes to Jesus in the central token are shown in Figure 6.1 below. After the role switching in the central token in 23.22-25, Pilate's role and action of handing over Jesus is much more highlighted by a very marked word order in 23.25,[35] which will be discussed below.

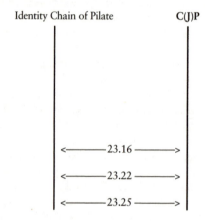

Identity Chain of Pilate   C(J)P

<------ 23.16 ------>

<------ 23.22 ------>

<------ 23.25 ------>

Figure 6.1 *Interactions of Chains*

pp. 415–51 [423]); H.W. Hoehner suggests Pilate's sending Jesus to Herod does not necessarily mean Pilate wants to help Jesus, it is probably only for his own sake ('Why Did Pilate Hand Over Jesus to Antipas?', in E. Bammel [ed.], *The Trial of Jesus: Cambridge Studies in Honour of C.F.D. Moule* [SBTSS, 13; London: SCM Press, 1970], pp. 84–90 [88–90]); for a similar view, see Marshall, *Gospel of Luke*, p. 855; Plummer, *Luke*, p. 522; Morris, *Luke*, p. 320.

34. **WSC(J)P** really stops at the central token of the two chains where Pilate is the actor of the last **WSC(J)P** in 23.22; Pilate switches to be the actor of the **REJC(J)P** in 23.25 and the incidents of **REJC(J)P** and **RS(J)P** continue throughout Luke's second volume: Acts. See Appendix 6A for discussions of the incidents of **REJC(J)P** and **RS(J)P** in Acts.

35. Pilate's participation in the trial of Jesus has been thought of being positively portrayed by Luke by a certain number of scholars (e.g. Goulder: 'Luke continues the steady process of establishing Jesus' innocence and exculpating Pilate' [*Luke*, p. 758] [for a view contrary to this, see R.E. Brown, *The Death of the Messiah: A Commentary on the Passion Narratives on the Four Gospels* (2 vols.; ABRL; London: Geoffrey Chapman, 1994), vol. 2, p. 859: 'The import of this stylization (Pilate's unease about Jesus) was not to exculpate Pilate']; Plummer thinks Pilate is portrayed to create contrast to the Jews' guilt of asking for Jesus' death: 'In the accounts of this Roman trial we have the attempts of the Jews to induce Pilate to condemn Jesus contrasted with Pilate's attempt to save him from execution' [*Luke*, p. 519]; also S. Cunningham: 'Emphatically stated in Luke's version, Pilate finds Jesus innocent and is thus not directly responsible for the

Marked Structure of the Passive Participial Clause in 23.25

23.25 closes the episode of Jesus' trial. It comes not only with a C(J)P pattern, but also with a highly marked order: ἀπέλυσεν δὲ τὸν διὰ στάσιν καὶ φόνον βεβλημένον εἰς φυλακὴν ὃν ᾐτοῦντο. The order of the participial clause is A(reason) PA(spatial). This is a very marked order in having a circumstantial adjunct located before its predicate, which is a passive perfect participle. In fact, it is very unusual to have a circumstantial adjunct placed before the predicate in a clause when the predicate is a passive perfect participle. In Luke, in the total of 21x of participial clause which have passive perfect participle as predicate with circumstantial adjunct(s), there are only two instances with a circumstantial adjunct preceding the passive perfect participle predicate; while all the rest in the Gospel have their circumstantial adjuncts placed after the predicate.[36] This is also true in Luke's second volume, Acts. In the total of 36 instances in Acts of participial clause with perfect participle as predicate with circumstantial adjunct(s), 22 of them are in passive voice; among these 22 incidents all but two have their circumstantial adjuncts placed after the predicate.[37] This highly marked pattern in 23.25

crucifixion... Thus the Romans are not portrayed as being the primary force behind Jesus' death' ['*Through Many Tribulations*': *The Theology of Persecution in Luke-Acts* (JSNTSup, 142; Sheffield: Sheffield Academic Press, 1997), p. 141]; and E.J. Via, 'According to Luke, Who Put Jesus to Death', in R.J. Cassidy and P.J. Scharper [eds.], *Political Issues in Luke-Acts* [Maryknoll: Orbis Books, 1983], pp. 122–45 [though Via thinks Luke has included Pilate with the ones who have put Jesus to death, she still considers 'Luke lays the responsibility for Jesus' death primarily on the Jerusalem rulers (leaders) of the Jewish people' (p. 131, 132, 140)]). Scholars and commentators have generally drawn attention to the explicit narrative of Pilate's declaration about Jesus' innocence [which is steadily repeated throughout the episode (Lk. 23.4, 14, 15, 22)], and his two attempts to release Jesus [Lk. 23.16, 22]; cf. Evans: 'Its dominant theme is Pilate's repeated declaration of Jesus' innocence, reinforced by that of Herod' [*Luke*, p. 843]; Marshall: 'The affirmation [his declaration of Jesus' innocence] is repeated in 23.14, 22 for emphasis' [*Gospel of Luke*, p. 853]; Fitzmyer: 'The Lukan form calls explicit attention to the *three* declarations of innocence' [*Luke*, p. 1488]; also cf. Morris, *Luke*, p. 322; Ellis, *Luke*, p. 264; Creed, *Luke*, pp. 279–80; Bock, *Luke*, p. 1831; Just, *Luke*, p. 911; Stein, *Luke*, p. 582. In fact, many have observed Pilate's three declarations of Jesus' innocence is a distinct feature of Luke, e.g., B.E. Beck, '"Imitatio Christi" and the Lukan Passion narrative', in W. Horbury and B. McNeil [eds.], *Suffering and Martyrdom in the New Testament: Studies presented to G.M. Styler by the Cambridge New Testament Seminar* [Cambridge: Cambridge University Press, 1981], pp. 28–47 [31]; Cunningham, '*Through Many Tribulations*', pp. 144–45; C.H. Talbert, *Literary Patterns, Theological Themes, and the Genre of Luke-Acts* [SBLMS, 20; Missoula, MT: Scholars Press, 1974], p. 22). However, Pilate's knowledge of Jesus' innocence reflects how wrong he is when he still sends Jesus to death in spite of knowing his innocence (cf. Acts 4.27; also F.J. Matera, *Passion Narratives and Gospel Theologies: Interpreting the Synoptics through their Passion Stories* [New York: Paulist Press, 1986], p. 178; E. Buck, 'The Function of the Pericope "Jesus before Herod" in the Passion Narrative of Luke', in W. Haubeck and M. Bachmann [eds.], *Wort in der Zeit* [Leiden: E.J. Brill, 1980], pp. 165–78 (166–70)).

36. In Luke, perfect passive participles with circumstantial adjuncts placed after them are 1.1, 45; 2.24, 26; 4.18; 6.25; 8.2; 9.45; 11.50; 12.6; 13.6, 34; 14.8; 16.18; 18.14, 31, 34; 23.15; 24.2; with circumstantial adjuncts placed before them are only 7.25 and 23.25.

37. In Acts, perfect passive participles with circumstantial adjuncts placed after them are. 2.16, 22; 3.20; 4.12; 5.23; 10.17, 33, 41, 42; 11.11; 12.6; 13.40; 16.4; 20.22; 22.3, 3, 3, 5; 24.8; 26.18; with circumstantial adjuncts placed before them are only 13.29 and 24.14.

is not only to highlight the reason for the imprisonment of Barabbas—his insurrection and murder, but it is also to highlight the degree of the seriousness of Barabbas' crime – insurrection and murder. This feature is highlighted to present a message: it is supposed to be indeed appropriate to have Barabbas imprisoned and punished according to the degree of his crime's seriousness; instead Pilate decides to crucify the innocent man Jesus but to release Barabbas who so deserves to get his punishment. Here Barabbas is a murderer; the seriousness of the crime he has committed is highlighted by the marked order (the circumstantial adjunct is located before the passive perfect participial predicate). In fact, this marked order foregrounds the seriousness of Pilate's crime of having the murderer Barabbas released and the innocent man Jesus crucified instead. Barabbas is a murderer; Pilate is in fact also a murderer in the episode. Pilate is not a person who has only made a mistake of handing over an innocent man; he is actually committing a crime of murder: the crime of putting a man to death whom he knows is actually innocent. The significance of **REJC(J)P** is particularly highlighted in its first instance (as discussed in the analysis of the Given-New structure stated above). Here Pilate's final decision in handing over Jesus is highlighted by the final instance of the particularly highlighted (as stated above) **REJC(J)P**,[38] and is re-enforced by the marked order of having the circumstantial adjunct located before its perfect passive participial predicate. This marked order is to illustrate a prominent message about the degree of the seriousness of Pilate's crime that he has committed, and how serious is Pilate's crime in having the murderer Barabbas released and having the innocent man Jesus murdered instead.

Conclusion

CP is a marked order in the Gospel of Luke. The marked **CP** order with Jesus as complement occurs throughout the Gospel and a cohesion chain of **C(J)P** is formed. This chain includes members of **WSC(J)P**, **RSC(J)P**, and **REJC(J)P**; the first member of each of these three categories (6.46; 9.48 and 10.16) is highlighted with contrasts and parallelisms with their surrounding passages. With a sequence of Given-New structures within the three verses (6.46; 9.48 and 10.16), the first **REJC(J)P** is particularly emphasized. This emphasized **REJC(J)P** incident is to highlight the significance and the semantic weight of the **REJC(J)P** type: it is a great mistake to have the attitude of rejecting Jesus. This **REJC(J)P** type is further highlighted in 23.1-25, where interactions occur between the **C(J)P** chain and the identity chain of Pilate. The central token of the two chains illustrates that Pilate's switching his attitude to Jesus is a main topic of the author in the episode. Pilate switches his attitude of **WSC(J)P** to **REJC(J)P** in 23.16-25, which carries with a

---

38. 23.25 (τὸν δὲ Ἰησοῦν παρέδωκεν τῷ θελήματι αὐτῶν) is the final instance of the **REJC(J)P**. This instance is well paralleled with the other incident of **REJC(J)P** in 22.48 (τὸν υἱὸν τοῦ ἀνθρώπου παραδίδως): both of the processes is used with the verb παραδίδωμι, and both of the complements are explicitly stated with Jesus' name or title ('Jesus' in 23.25 and 'Son of Man' in 22.48; while the majority of the other **C[J]P** members are in pronouns).

marked word order pattern in 23.25: a passive perfect participial clause with a circumstantial adjunct placed before the predicate. Barabbas' crime of murder is highlighted by this highly marked order; in fact this also reflects the seriousness of Pilate's crime of murder. Barabbas is a murderer; Pilate has also committed murder by sending a man to death whom he knows is innocent. The occurrence of the last instance of **REJC(J)P** in 23.25 and Pilate's role switching in 23.16-25 indicate an important message: it is very wrong for Pilate to have the attitude of rejecting Jesus; Pilate has actually committed a serious crime of murdering an innocent man by releasing a prisoner who has committed murder.

Appendix 6A

Incidents of **REJC(J)P** and **RSC(J)P** in Acts

Occurrence of the marked **C(J)P** order continues in Luke's second volume, Acts. The instances of this marked CP pattern with Jesus as complement occur throughout Acts and form a cohesion chain of **C(J)P**. This time the chain only consists of two types of members: **REJC(J)P** and **RSC(J)P** (the incident in Lk. 23.25 is the last instance of **WSC[J]P**). In Acts, God consistently functions as the actor in every instance of **RSC(J)P**. An identity chain of God can be formed in Acts and this chain consistently interacts with all the **RSC(J)P** members in the **C(J)P** chain (2.32, 36; 5.31; 10.38, 40) to form a central token (Jesus' exaltation and glory by God). The members of the **C(J)P** chain are summarized according to its two categories (**REJC[J]P** and **RSC[J]P**) as follows, where the **C(J)P** structures are in italics:

Table 6.5 *C(J)P Cohesion Chain in Acts*

Members of *REJC(J)P*	Members of *RSC(J)P*
2.22 Ἰησοῦν τὸν Ναζωραῖον, ἄνδρα ἀποδεδειγμένον ἀπὸ τοῦ θεοῦ εἰς ὑμᾶς 2.23 *τοῦτον* τῇ ὡρισμένῃ βουλῇ καὶ προγνώσει τοῦ θεοῦ ἔκδοτον διὰ χειρὸς ἀνόμων προσπήξαντες *ἀνείλατε*	
	2.32 *τοῦτον τὸν Ἰησοῦν ἀνέστησεν ὁ θεός*
2.36 *τοῦτον τὸν Ἰησοῦν* ὃν ὑμεῖς *ἐσταυρώσατε* 3.14 ὑμεῖς δὲ *τὸν ἅγιον καὶ δίκαιον ἠρνήσασθε* 3.15 *τὸν δὲ ἀρχηγὸν τῆς ζωῆς ἀπεκτείνατε*	2.36 *κύριον αὐτὸν καὶ Χριστὸν ἐποίησεν ὁ θεός*
	5.31 *τοῦτον ὁ θεὸς ἀρχηγὸν καὶ σωτῆρα ὕψωσεν τῇ δεξιᾷ αὐτοῦ* 10.38 Ἰησοῦν τὸν ἀπὸ Ναζαρέθ, ὡς ἔχρισεν αὐτὸν ὁ θεός 10.40 *τοῦτον ὁ θεὸς ἤγειρεν* [ἐν] τῇ τρίτῃ ἡμέρᾳ
13.27 οἱ ἄρχοντες αὐτῶν *τοῦτον ἀγνοήσαντες*	

Appendix 6B

THE CP ORDER IN LUKE 23.16, 22 AND 22.54

Both Lk. 23.16 and 23.22 contain a clause which may show ambiguity: παιδεύσας οὖν αὐτὸν ἀπολύσω. Grammatically and contextually, the accusative personal pronoun αὐτόν may function as a complement to the participle παιδεύσας or to the indicative ἀπολύσω, since both the participle and the indicative have the same direct object here. This appendix is an investigation showing the pronoun belongs to the indicative verb, and thus the word order in this clause is a **CP** pattern (αὐτὸν ἀπολύσω). A search of such similar structures is carried out throughout the third Gospel, and the search is done based on the following combinations:[1]

1)   a) participle + accusative personal pronoun + indicative
     b) participle + accusative noun + indicative
2)   a) indicative + accusative personal pronoun + participle
     b) indicative + accusative noun + participle
3)   a) participle + indicative + accusative personal pronoun
     b) participle + indicative + accusative noun

From the results of the above different constructions,[2] a pattern can be observed as follows:

  1.   The computer program being used is Bible Windows version 3.04, which carries a search function similar to GRAMCORD. The search is carried out with a maximum of one interval word between categories, for example, for 1a), it becomes participle + maximum of one interval word + accusative personal pronoun + maximum of one interval word + indicative. This means the search result may not be totally exhaustive, because this may miss out the combinations with more than one interval word; since such constructions with more than one interval word are not frequent, the result of the search with only maximum one interval word can still represent a very reliable figure of the distribution of such a construction.

  2.   The results of the above six categories are being classified according to the following categories: 1a, 1a(ambig.); 1b, 1b(ambig.); 2a, 2a(ambig.); 2b, 2b(ambig.); 3a, 3a(ambig.); 3b and 3b(ambig.). The categories with (ambig.) are those containing a complement which may be ambiguous, belonging to the participial clause or the indicative clause. For the sake of convenience, capital letters here represent constituents of an indicative clause, and small letters represent constituents of a participial clause, and capital letters with a bracket represent constituents which may belong to a participial or an indicative clause. E.g. pcP means a clause containing a participial clause with a complement (pc) as an adjunct and an indicative as the predicate (P) of the main clause; p(C)P means a clause having an element which may function as the complement of the participial clause or the complement of the main clause. The result of 1a is 2.48 pcP; 4.5 pcPCC; 6.3 pPC, 10 pcPCC; 7.9 pcPC; 9.10 pcPAA, 11 pcPCA; 10.31pcP, 34 pcaPCA; 11.45

The complement of each clause tends to be grouped with its own predicate and forms a single unit. That is, the complement of a participial clause tends to be placed next to its predicate and forms a single unit, and the same happens to an indicative clause. In fact, in the total of 91 occurrences in 1a, 1b, 2a, 2b, 3a, and 3b, all complements are clearly located next to their corresponding predicates (either before it or after it).[3]

There is a total of three instances in the category of 3a(ambig.); at each instance the object of the participial and the indicative clause are obviously the same and all three instances only have one complement placed behind the predicate of the indicative clause.[4] It is shown above that complements are typically grouped with their corresponding predicates to form single units; this significant feature indicates that the complements in these three instances belong to the indicative clauses rather than to the participial clauses.[5] The occurrence of these three instances indicates an important feature: when the complement of a participial and an indicative clause are the same, and if it is going to present one complement in the clause only, the complement of the indicative clause is preferred to be presented.[6]

A similar search of instances with a pattern of participle + dative case + indicative is carried out in the third Gospel.[7] The result shows there is a total of

---

cpCP; 16.2 pcPCC; 18.11 paCPC; 22.58 pcPC; 24.52 pcPAA. The result of 1a(ambig.) is 22.54 p(C)P; 22.64 p(C)PA; 23.16 p(C)P, 22 p(C)P. Result of 1b is 1.63 pcP; 4.17 pcPC; 5.12 pcpaPC, 13 pcPC, 20 pcPC; 8.29 pcPAA; 9.47 pcPC; 10.25 cpCP; 18.18 cpCP; 19.41 pcPA; 22.41 pcP; 23.8 pcPA, 11pcPCA, 48 pcpcP; 24.23 pcP, 50 pcPC. Result of 1b(ambig.) is 8.15 Ap(C)P; 24.30 p(C)P. Result of 2a is 4.36 PApc; 7.4 PCApc, 30 CPApa; 8.21 PCpc, 38 PCpc; 9.19 PCpc; 10.25 PCpc; 18.16 PCpc, 18 PCpc; 19.6 PCp; 20.5 PCpc, 14 PCpc, 21 PCpc, 27 PCpc; 21.7 PCpc; 23.3 PCpc, 39 PCpc; 24.39 PCpc. Result of 2a(ambig.) is 20.10 P(C)p. Result of 2b is 1.24 PCApc; 6.1 PCpa; 7.16 PCpc, 29 PCpa; 10.34 PCpc; 15.13 PCpa; 17.13 PCpc; 18.13 PCpc; 23.5 PCpa, 47 PCpc. Result of 2b(ambig.) is 2.19 CPcpa or PCpa. Result of 3a is 2.48 pPC; 4.29 pPCA, 40 acpPC; 5.22 pPCC; 8.16 cpPCA, 21 pPCC, 24 pPC; 14.25 pPCC; 15.28 pPC; 20.3 pPCC. Result of 3a(ambig.) is 14.4 pP(C); 18.33 pP(C); 23.53 pP(C)A. Result of 3b is 3.18 cpPC; 5.2 apPC, 6 cpPC; 7.10 paPC; 8.8 pPC, 8 cpPC; 9.19 pPC, 20 pPC, 32 pPC; 10.27 pPC, 34 pPC; 11.13 cpPC; 14.28 apPC; 16.21 pPC; 18.8 pPC, 13 apPC, 43 pPCA; 19.1 pPC, 11 pPC, 30 ApPC; 23.47 pcPC, 56 pPC; 24.37 cpPC. There is no occurrence in 3b(ambig.).

3.   Complements are always located next to their corresponding predicates and form single units, thus the searched clause structures are typically something like PCpc, pPC or pcPC (all related predicates and complements are grouped as single unit such as PC or pc), and structures like CpP (where C and P are separated by p and do not form a single unit) or pPCc (where p and c are separated by PC and do not form a single unit) never occurs.

4.   14.4 pP(C); 18.33 pP(C) and 23.53 pP(C)A.

5.   The complements in these three instances are located next to the predicates of the indicative clauses and form single units with them, and thus the clause structures of these three instances can be written as 14.4 pPC; 18.33 pPC and 23.53 pPCA.

6.   There are two instances where the objects of participle and indicative are the same, and both of the complements are presented and located next to their corresponding predicates to form single units: 9.47 pcPC and 23.11 pcPCA.

7.   This time the search structure is participle + maximum of one interval word + dative case + maximum of one interval word + indicative, where the dative case can be a noun, a personal pronoun or a demonstrative pronoun.

four instances in which the direct objects (or indirect objects) of each of the participle and indicative are the same. That is, the dative case may contextually either belong to the participle or to the indicative. These are the four instances:

9.21 ὁ δὲ ἐπιτιμήσας αὐτοῖς παρήγγειλεν μηδενὶ λέγειν τοῦτο
20.17 ὁ δὲ ἐμβλέψας αὐτοῖς εἶπεν
23.3 ὁ δὲ ἀποκριθεὶς αὐτῷ ἔφη
23.40 ἀποκριθεὶς δὲ ὁ ἕτερος ἐπιτιμῶν αὐτῷ ἔφη

In the first instance (9.21), both the participle (ἐπιτιμήσας) and the indicative (παρήγγειλεν) usually take a dative as their complement,[8] and thus there is ambiguity in defining whether αὐτοῖς belongs to ἐπιτιμήσας or παρήγγειλεν. The second instance (20.17) is clear enough to define the role of the dative case (αὐτοῖς). The personal pronoun αὐτοῖς may possibly be linked to the participle (ἐμβλέψας) or to the indicative (εἶπεν) (either functioning as the direct object of ἐμβλέψας or as the indirect object of εἶπεν), but according to the occurrences of the two verbs in NT, it can be concluded that the pronoun αὐτοῖς is the complement of εἶπεν.[9] The third instance (23.3) has the participial form ἀποκριθεὶς used with the indicative ἔφη. It is very common (19x) in the Gospel to have the participial form ἀποκριθεὶς used with εἶπεν (a word which shares the same semantic domain with ἔφη); it is obvious in these 19 instances that ἀποκριθεὶς and εἶπεν have the same complement, and there is only one complement being presented in all these 19 cases, and each follows the indicative εἶπεν.[10] Since predicate and complement of each clause tend to be grouped as a single unit (as shown above), it can be seen that the complements in these 19 cases, which all follow the indicative verb, are all complements of the indicative verb; or it can be concluded that when the participle ἀποκριθεὶς is used as an adjunct with the predicate εἶπεν in a clause, the complement (either a dative noun/pronoun or a prepositional phrase with πρός) belongs to the predicate εἶπεν. Similar to λέγω,

---

8.   In NT, it is typical to have a dative as the complement of the verb ἐπιτιμάω. E.g. Mt. 8.26; 12.16; 17.18; 19.13; 20.31; Mk 1.25; 3.12; 4.39; 8.30, 33; 9.25; 10.13, 48; Lk. 4.35, 39; 8.24; 9.42, 55; 17.3; 18.15, 39; 19.39; Jude 1.9.

9.   In 20.17, εἶπεν typically takes a dative as an indirect object, where ἐμβλέψας typically takes an accusative as its complement. There are few occurrences of the word ἐμβλέπω in the NT. In taking a search of all the verbs with a root of βλέπω (that is, βλέπω, ἐμβλέπω, διαβλέπω, ἐπιβλέπω), the result is clear: almost all the verbs (42 out of 44x) with a root of βλέπω take an accusative as complement (Mt. 7.3; 13.17; 18.10; 24.2; Mk 5.31; 8.23, 24, 25; 13.2, 9; Lk. 6.41, 42; 7.44; 8.16; 10.23, 24; 11.33; 24.12; Jn 1.29; 5.19; 11.9; 20.1, 5; 21.9, 20; Acts 2.33; 9.8; Rom. 7.23; 8.24, 25; 1 Cor. 1.26; 10.18; 2 Cor. 10.7; 12.6; Phil. 3.2; Col. 4.17; Heb. 2.9; 10.25; 2 Jn 1.8; Rev. 11.9; 16.15; 18.19); there is only one occasion that may show ambiguity: Lk. 22.61 (καὶ στραφεὶς ὁ κύριος ἐνέβλεψεν τῷ Πέτρῳ) and one occasion of the verb takes a dative: Mk 10.21 (ὁ δὲ Ἰησοῦς ἐμβλέψας αὐτῷ).

10.   For the construction of ἀποκριθεὶς + εἶπεν + dative case noun or pronoun, the occurrences are 1.19, 35; 3.11; 4.8, 12; 7.22; 10.41; 11.45; 13.2, 8, 25; 15.29; for the construction of ἀποκριθεὶς + εἶπεν + πρός + accusative case of noun or pronoun, the occurrences are 5.22, 31; 7.40; 8.21; 14.3; 20.3; 24.18.

φημί takes a dative noun/pronoun or prepositional phrase with πρός as complement,[11] and thus it should also be the case that αὐτῷ belongs to ἔφη in Lk. 23.3 and 23.40.

In summary, based on the above discussions, it can be concluded that the personal pronoun αὐτόν in 23.16 and 23.22 belongs to the indicative ἀπολύσω, and thus it is a **CP** order.

---

11.   In NT, the occurrences of φημί + dative noun/pronoun are Mt. 4.7; 13.28; 17.26; 19.21; 21.27; 22.37; 25.21, 23; 26.34; 27.65; Mk 9.12, 38; 10.20; 12.24; 14.29; where dative noun/pronoun + φημί is Lk. 7.44; φημί + prepositional phrase beginning with πρός are Acts 10.28 and 16.37; prepositional phrase beginning with πρός + φημί are Lk. 22.70 and Acts 26.1, 32.

Chapter 7

TEMPORAL CLAUSE COMPLEXES
AND FOREGROUNDED MESSAGE IN LUKE 2

Luke 2 records the journey of Joseph and Mary to Bethlehem, and the birth narratives of Jesus. In Luke two, several human and supernatural participants besides Joseph's family have appeared throughout the episode and they have functioned as subjects in different occasions: Quirinius (2.2), shepherds (2.8), angels (2.9, 13), first group of people around (2.18), Simeon (2.25), Anna (2.36), and the second group of people around (2.47).

This chapter will show how Luke singles out Joseph's family as a focus of attention in this episode by using a series of six pairs of temporal clause complexes. The sixth temporal clause complex will be shown to be particularly significant by the consideration of a linguistic structure-theme-rheme consideration of the six pairs of temporal clause complexes. Other linguistic analyses including marked word order patterns will be employed to show the message which Luke wants to bring out as a foregrounded message: Jesus' parents' failure in understanding of Jesus' mission and his role.

The Six Pairs of Temporal Clause Complexes

There are a total of eight pairs of hypotactic enhancing temporal clauses throughout Luke 2.[1] Six of them are the ones which have been mentioned above, and these eight pairs are listed as follows:

2.2 αὕτη ἀπογραφὴ πρώτη ἐγένετο ἡ γεμονεύοντος τῆς Συρίας Κυρηνίου.

2.6 ἐγένετο δὲ ἐν τῷ εἶναι αὐτοὺς ἐκεῖ ἐπλήσθησαν αἱ ἡμέραι τοῦ τεκεῖν αὐτήν,

2.15a, b καὶ ἐγένετο ὡς ἀπῆλθον ἀπ' αὐτῶν εἰς τὸν οὐρανὸν οἱ ἄγγελοι, οἱ ποιμένες ἐλάλουν πρὸς ἀλλήλους·

2.21a καὶ ὅτε ἐπλήσθησαν ἡμέραι ὀκτὼ τοῦ περιτεμεῖν αὐτὸν καὶ ἐκλήθη τὸ ὄνομα αὐτοῦ Ἰησοῦς,

2.22-24 καὶ ὅτε ἐπλήσθησαν αἱ ἡμέραι τοῦ καθαρισμοῦ αὐτῶν κατὰ τὸν νόμον Μωϋσέως, ἀνήγαγον αὐτὸν εἰς Ἱεροσόλυμα ἀνήγαγον αὐτὸν εἰς Ἱεροσόλυμα παραστῆσαι τῷ κυρίῳ, καθὼς γέγραπται ἐν νόμῳ κυρίου ὅτι Πᾶν ἄρσεν διανοῖγον μήτραν ἅγιον τῷ κυρίῳ κληθήσεται, καὶ τοῦ δοῦναι θυσίαν κατὰ τὸ εἰρημένον ἐν τῷ νόμῳ κυρίου, ζεῦγος τρυγόνων ἢ δύο νοσσοὺς περιστερῶν.

---

1. For classifications of clause complex, see Halliday, *An Introduction to Functional Grammar*, pp. 215–39.

2.27b-28a καὶ ἐν τῷ εἰσαγαγεῖν τοὺς γονεῖς τὸ παιδίον Ἰησοῦν τοῦ ποιῆσαι αὐτοὺς κατὰ τὸ εἰθισμένον τοῦ νόμου περὶ αὐτοῦ καὶ αὐτὸς ἐδέξατο αὐτὸ εἰς τὰς ἀγκάλας καὶ εὐλόγησεν τὸν θεὸν καὶ εἶπεν·
2.39 καὶ ὡς ἐτέλεσαν πάντα τὰ κατὰ τὸν νόμον κυρίου, ἐπέστρεψαν εἰς τὴν Γαλιλαίαν εἰς πόλιν ἑαυτῶν Ναζαρεθ.
2.42-43 καὶ ὅτε ἐγένετο ἐτῶν δώδεκα, ἀναβαινόντων αὐτῶν κατὰ τὸ ἔθος τῆς ἑορτῆς καὶ τελειωσάντων τὰς ἡμέρας, ἐν τῷ ὑποστρέφειν αὐτοὺς ὑπέμεινεν Ἰησοῦς ὁ παῖς ἐν Ἰερουσαλήμ, καὶ οὐκ ἔγνωσαν οἱ γονεῖς αὐτοῦ.

In these eight pairs of clauses, six pairs out of them have one common feature: the members of Joseph's family are the subject of either the dependent or the independent clauses in these six pairs of temporal clause complexes (2.6; 2.21a; 2.22-24; 2.27b-28a; 2.39; 2.42-43); there are only two of the eight pairs of clauses carrying subjects who are not members of Joseph's family (2.2; 2.15a-b). In the birth narratives in Luke 2, eight different participants are major participants of different episodes throughout the story: Quirinius, Joseph's family, shepherds, angels, first group of people around, Simeon, Anna, second group of people around; among these only three of them are subjects in the eight pairs of temporal clauses, and in which six pairs of them are devoted to the members of Joseph's family, and the other two pairs are used to portray Caesar (2.2), the angels and the shepherds (2.15a-b). The six pairs of temporal clauses with the members of Joseph's family as subjects will be particularly studied in this chapter, which will be shown below.

The Temporal Clause Complexes and Reintroduction of Joseph's Family
The six pairs of temporal clauses about Joseph's family are mainly located at the occasions when the members of Joseph's family are reintroduced in the narrative after some other participants have participated as subject; that is, when they are back on 'stage', or the spotlight is back onto these members of Joseph's family,[2] where they participate as a subject or an actor in the story again. These reintroductions are typically begun by use of a temporal clause structure, which will be illustrated below. For the sake of convenience, these six pairs of temporal clause complexes will be abbreviated as TC in the rest of this chapter.

Augustus demanded the world to be registered in 2.1. It is then followed by a temporal clause (2.2), where Quirinius functions as the subject of the dependent temporal clause. Joseph, being a member of the family, is firstly reintroduced in 2.4; then the first TC occurs (2.6), in which Jesus' birth is introduced. 2.7 briefly narrates the process of Jesus' birth and his lying in a manger because of his parents' failure in finding a place for the birth. Joseph's family is then off the stage and the story is concentrated on the interactions between newly introduced shepherds and an angel (2.8-20). In 2.8-20, Mary has been reintroduced and a temporal clause has not been employed;[3] this is because a reduction is going to

---

2.   Here the term 'on stage' has been adopted by Levinsohn (*Discourse Features of New Testament Greek*, pp. 135, 141), which is also used by Martín-Asensio (*Transitivity-based Foregrounding in the Acts of the Apostles*, p. 95).
3.   Mary has already been introduced before 2.8-20 (2.5-7).

be made with another sentence later in the story, which will be discussed later in this chapter. This episode ends at 2.20 and a new episode begins at 2.21, where the members of Joseph's family function as central figures and the second TC is employed to do the reintroduction.[4] 2.22 starts another episode and it begins with the third TC, where Joseph's family is the subject of the action: bringing Jesus to Jerusalem and offering a sacrifice. 2.25 introduces a new major participant Simeon with the word ἰδού;[5] this Simeon is put on the stage with the spotlight being on him and 2.25-27a are devoted to narrate him. Joseph's family is back on the stage and they function as the subject in the event in 2.27b: bringing Jesus into the temple, and thus the fourth TC is employed. After the conversation between Simeon and Mary, Joseph's family is off the stage and the spotlight is switched to a newly introduced participant in 2.37-38: Anna. Joseph's family is then back on the stage in 2.39, where the fifth TC is employed. 2.41 begins a new episode and members of Joseph's family remain to be the central characters in the episode, where the spotlight remains on them, and thus the sixth TC is employed in 2.42-43b.

As it is shown above, the six TC structures typically occur when the members of Joseph's family are back on the stage-either the spotlight is switched back to them from the other participants, or a new episode begins where the members of Joseph's family are the central characters. These six TC structures, which all typically appeared under the above mentioned circumstances, eventually form cohesion ties. These cohesion ties focus attention onto the family of Joseph, whenever they are back on the stage and whenever the spotlight is focused back on them. These six repeated TCs cause Joseph's family to be singled out from the rest of the other participants and to be the focus of attention throughout the story, or a central character in the story.[6] This central character is accompanied by an emphasized message which is carried out by the six TCs; this message will be stated below.

Inter-Linguistic Relationships within the Six Pairs of Temporal Clause Complexes: Theme and Rheme
Theme-Rheme Structures in the Six TCs. In Hallidayan Functional Grammar, one of the three metafunctions is textual meaning. Textual meaning in a clause is mainly composed of two parts: theme and rheme. Theme is the element which functions as the point of departure or starting point of a message, it is what the

4. Although only Jesus has been mentioned in 2.21, the events described in 2.21 certainly involve other members of his family: the parents of Jesus, who apparently are also the ones who are involved in the circumcision and the naming of the baby.

5. The word ἰδού introduces a major participant; see Levinsohn, *Discourse Features of New Testament Greek*, p. 135.

6. Jesus and his birth may have been regarded as a central focus in Luke 2 rather than the whole family including Joseph and Mary, e.g., D. Ravens: 'In Luke 2 the attention is concentrated on Jesus and, to a lesser extent, on his family' (*Luke and the Restoration of Israel* [JSNTSup, 119; Sheffield: Sheffield Academic Press, 1995], p. 42). It is argued here that the entire family is actually being brought out as the central character in the story throughout the six pairs of temporal clause structures.

clause is going to be about, and can be incorporated with the three metafunctional elements and gives multiple themes: experiential (or topical), interpersonal and textual thematic elements. Rheme is the rest of the clause, it is the part of the message which the theme develops. Theme typically contains a piece of old or given information, which has been mentioned in other co-texts and is familiar to readers. Rheme typically contains new or unfamiliar information, it is a piece of new information about the point of departure. Based on this basic structure of theme and rheme, textual meaning is formed from 'given or familiar' to 'new or unfamiliar' information.[7]

This thematic organization also works in levels below and above clauses. In a clause complex, the entire dependent clause can function as the theme at the level of sentence; and the main clause can function as the rheme within the sentence.[8] This theme-rheme structure indeed occurs in the above six instances of clause complexes, which all begin with a dependent temporal clause.

In the above six clause complex structures, all dependent clauses serve as the themes and are typically placed at the front, and the main clauses serve as the rhemes and are all placed after the temporal clauses. The different themes and rhemes of these six clause complexes can be classified in the following table:

Table 7.1 *Theme-Rheme Structures of the Six Temporal Clause Complexes*

	Theme	Rheme
2.6	2.6a ἐγένετο δὲ ἐν τῷ εἶναι αὐτοὺς ἐκεῖ	2.6b ἐπλήσθησαν αἱ ἡμέραι τοῦ τεκεῖν αὐτήν
2.21a	2.21a (a) καὶ ὅτε ἐπλήσθησαν ἡμέραι ὀκτὼ τοῦ περιτεμεῖν αὐτόν[9]	2.21a (b) καὶ ἐκλήθη τὸ ὄνομα αὐτοῦ Ἰησοῦς
2.22-24	2.22a καὶ ὅτε ἐπλήσθησαν αἱ ἡμέραι τοῦ καθαρισμοῦ αὐτῶν κατὰ τὸν νόμον Μωϋσέως	2.22b-24 ἀνήγαγον αὐτὸν εἰς Ἱεροσόλυμα παραστῆσαι τῷ κυρίῳ, καθὼς γέγραπται ἐν νόμῳ κυρίου ὅτι Πᾶν ἄρσεν διανοῖγον μήτραν ἅγιον τῷ κυρίῳ κληθήσεται, καὶ τοῦ δοῦναι θυσίαν κατὰ τὸ εἰρημένον ἐν τῷ νόμῳ κυρίου, ζεῦγος τρυγόνων ἢ δύο νοσσοὺς περιστερῶν

7.   Halliday, *An Introduction to Functional Grammar*, pp. 37, 52-54; cf. Eggins, *An Introduction to Systemic Functional Linguistics*, pp. 271–75; cf. Butler, *Systemic Linguistics*, pp. 176–78; H. Gosden, *A Genre-based Investigation of Theme: Product and Process in Scientific Research Articles Written by NNS Novice Researchers* (MSL, 7; Nottingham: Department of English, University of Nottingham, 1996), pp. 66–69; Reed, 'Identifying Theme in the New Testament, pp. 75–101.

8.   Halliday, *An Introduction to Functional Grammar*, pp. 54–58; Eggins, *Systemic Functional Linguistics*, pp. 293, 305; cf. M. Ghadessy, 'Thematic Development and its Relationship to Registers and Genres', *OPSL* 7 (1993), p. 5; Grimes, *The Thread of Discourse*, p. 326.

9.   The phrase καὶ ὅτε occurs six times in Luke (2.21, 22, 42; 6.13; 22.14; 23.33), and two times in Acts (1.13; 22.20), and each one begins a new clause. In the six uses in Luke, three of

2.27b-28a	2.27b καὶ ἐν τῷ εἰσαγαγεῖν τοὺς γονεῖς τὸ παιδίον Ἰησοῦν τοῦ ποιῆσαι αὐτοὺς *κατὰ τὸ εἰθισμένον τοῦ νόμου περὶ αὐτοῦ*	2.28a καὶ αὐτὸς ἐδέξατο αὐτὸ εἰς τὰς ἀγκάλας καὶ εὐλόγησεν τὸν θεὸν καὶ εἶπεν
2.39	2.39a καὶ ὡς ἐτέλεσαν πάντα *τὰ κατὰ τὸν νόμον κυρίου*	2.39b ἐπέστρεψαν εἰς τὴν Γαλιλαίαν εἰς πόλιν ἑαυτῶν Ναζαρέθ
2.42-43	2.42-43a καὶ ὅτε ἐγένετο ἐτῶν δώδεκα, ἀναβαινόντων αὐτῶν *κατὰ τὸ ἔθος τῆς ἑορτῆς* καὶ <u>τελειωσάντων τὰς ἡμέρας</u>, ἐν τῷ ὑποστρέφειν αὐτούς	2.43b ὑπέμεινεν Ἰησοῦς ὁ παῖς ἐν Ἰερουσαλήμ, καὶ οὐκ ἔγνωσαν οἱ γονεῖς αὐτοῦ.

There are two groups of components of the above two categories being repeated throughout these six sentences. The first group contains the elements in underlined forms; the second group contains the elements in italics. The phrase ἐπλήσθησαν αἱ ἡμέραι occurs in the rheme of the first TC in 2.6b as a piece of new information. It appears again in 2.21a in the theme of the second TC as a piece of old information; it is then repeated in the theme of the third TC in 2.22a. The phrase κατὰ τὸ εἰρημένον ἐν τῷ νόμῳ κυρίου belongs to the rheme of the third TC in 2.22-24; it is then repeated twice in the themes of the fourth and the fifth TC (2.27b and 2.39a) as a piece of old information. These two repeated items are then repeated in a similar phrase and wording in the theme of the sixth TC in 2.42-43a as pieces of old information.

Thematic Progression in the Six TCs. F. Danes has introduced three main types of thematic progression.[10] The first one is theme progression with a continuous (constant) theme (or theme re-iteration), where the same element occurs regularly as theme; and thus the theme is being re-iterated. This keeps a text being focused and thus cohesion is formed. This can be summarized as follows:

them occur in these six TCs (2.21, 22, 42). R.E. Brown has wrongly counted the total occurrence of καὶ ὅτε structure: 'The pattern *kai hote* occurs twenty-two times in Luke/Acts and only three times elsewhere in the New Testament' (*The Birth of the Messiah: A Commentary on the Infancy Narratives in the Gospels of Matthew and Luke* [ABRL; London: Geoffrey Chapman, new updated version, 1993], p. 407), in fact, the total occurrence of this phrase in Luke and Acts is only nine times as stated above, and there are 17 other NT occurrences (Mt. 21.1; 27.31; Mk 4.6, 10; 7.17; 11.1; 15.20; Rev. 1.17; 5.8; 6.3, 5, 7, 9; 10.3, 4, 10; 12.13; 22.8), not three as Brown states. Plummer is right in counting the number of Lukan uses of the phrase; both Plummer and Nolland state this phrase is Lukan, but they may be wrong since the use of phrase is also common in Mark (5 times) and Revelation (11 times) (cf. Plummer, *Luke*, p. 61; Nolland, *Luke*, p. 110).

10. F. Danes, 'Functional Sentence Perspective and the Organization of Text', in *idem* (ed.), *Papers on Functional Sentence Perspective: First International Symposium* (JLSMin, 147; The Hague: Mouton, 1974), pp. 106–28, esp. 118–23; cf. S. Thomas and T. Hawes, *Theme in Academic and Media Discourse* (MSL, 8; Nottingham: Department of English Studies, University of Nottingham, 1997), pp. 9–15, 159–65 for discussion on these three types of thematic progression; and also cf. Eggins, *Systemic Functional Linguistics*, pp. 302–04; B.L. Dubois, 'A Reformation of Thematic Progression Typology', *Text* 7 (1987), pp. 89–116; Gosden, *A Genre-*

Figure 7.1 *Theme Re-iteration in Thematic Progression*

The next two are simple linear thematic progression (or thematic progression with linear thematization of rhemes, which may also be called a zig-zag thematic progression) and hypertheme (or may be called multiple themes). In the zig-zag pattern, an element in the rheme of a clause becomes an element of the theme of the next clause. This type of thematic progression creates cohesion by using pieces of information (rhemes) to accumulate thematic elements. This can be summarized in the following diagram:

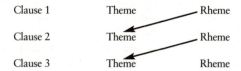

Figure 7.2 *Zig-Zag Pattern in Thematic Progression*

The other type of thematic progression is called multiple-theme pattern. In this pattern, several elements occur as the rheme of a clause; these different elements then become the themes of the subsequent clauses. This type of thematic progression is diagrammed as follows:

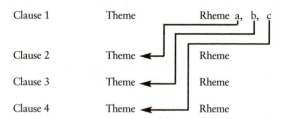

Figure 7.3 *Multiple Themes in Thematic Progression*

The above six instances of clause complexes are found to be a combination of the first two types of thematic development: theme re-iteration and zig-zag thematic progression; this is diagrammed as follows:

based *Investigation of Theme*, pp. 235–37; Vande Kopple, 'Given and New Information', pp. 89–92; and Martin, *English Text*, pp. 454–56.

The three types of theme progression can be summarized as follows: linear (Rheme A becomes Theme B, Rheme B becomes Theme C, and so on), constant (Theme A becomes Theme B, and then becomes Theme C, and so on) and hypertheme (Rheme A1 becomes Theme B, Rheme A2 becomes theme C, Rheme A3 becomes Theme D, and so on).

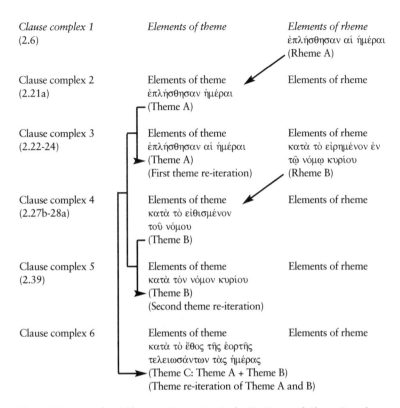

Figure 7.4 *Accumulated Thematic Progression in the Six Temporal Clause Complexes*

The phrase ἐπλήσθησαν αἱ ἡμέραι (Rheme A) is newly introduced as a part of the elements of the rheme in the first clause complex. It then becomes as a part of the elements of the theme (Theme A: ἐπλήσθησαν ἡμέραι) in the second clause complex; the similar phrase is then repeated in the third clause complex, it becomes a part of the elements of its theme (Theme A: ἐπλήσθησαν αἱ ἡμέραι). This repeated theme element functions as a kind of thematic progression: theme re-iteration. In the third clause complex, the phrase of κατὰ τὸ εἰρημένον ἐν τῷ νόμῳ κυρίου (Rheme B) is part of the elements in its rheme, it then becomes part of the elements of the theme in the fourth clause complex (Theme B: κατὰ τὸ εἰθισμένον τοῦ νόμου); a similar phrase is then repeated in the theme of the fifth clause complex (Theme B: κατὰ τὸν νόμον κυρίου). This becomes the second theme-reiteration in these six clause complexes. The elements of Theme A and B are then repeated in the theme of the sixth clause complex (κατὰ τὸ ἔθος τῆς ἑορτῆς and τελειωσάντων τὰς ἡμέρας);[11] this becomes the third theme re-iteration,

---

11. Although the phrase κατὰ τὸ ἔθος τῆς ἑορτῆς is not literally the same as 'according to Lord's Law' or 'according to what the Law says' in 2.27b and 2.39, semantically it is the same. It is clear that the usual practice of the Passover pilgrim feast is a command from God, and it is

which is an accumulated theme of Theme A and B (Theme C).[12] The theme (2.42-43a) of the sixth clause complex functions as the result of the accumulated thematic elements. This is the result of a zig-zag thematic progression pattern (Rheme A becomes theme A, and Rheme B becomes Theme B), and the thematic developments of the two different theme re-iterations (repeated Theme A and repeated Theme B): Themes A and B are then further repeated in 2.42-43a and form Theme C. This Theme C is the accumulated elements of the thematic developments throughout these six clause complexes. The temporal clause in 2.42-43a (Theme C, which is the accumulated result of a thematic development) functions as the theme in the sixth clause complex; it is the point of departure of the message in this clause complex. This Theme C (the accumulated thematic elements) is going to introduce a new message, which is contained in 2.43b as rheme: ὑπέμεινεν Ἰησοῦς ὁ παῖς ἐν Ἰερουσαλήμ, καὶ οὐκ ἔγνωσαν οἱ γονεῖς αὐτοῦ. The message 'Jesus stayed in Jerusalem, and his parents did not know' is the message which Luke ultimately wants to state by using the accumulated thematic developments (2.42-43a). The sixth TC is a place for the accumulated theme. This accumulated theme develops a message which Luke ultimately wants to bring out, which is the rheme (2.43b) of the sixth TC, and which is further developed in the rest of Luke 2. In fact, the sixth TC consists of different marked clause structures, both in the parts of the theme and the rheme; these marked clause structures are to be used to highlight the message at the end of these six TCs, and these will be discussed below respectively.

Foregrounded Message in Luke Two

As stated above, a sequence of six temporal clause complexes have been employed to give a multiple theme-rheme structure in Luke 2; the accumulated theme in the

recorded in the Law (Exod. 23.14-17), thus Lk. 2.42 'according to the custom of the festival' is semantically the same as 'according to Lord's words/commands' in 2.22, 27b and 39; cf. Johnson, *Luke*, p. 58; E. Schweizer, *The Good News According to Luke* (trans. D.E. Green; London: SPCK, 1984), p. 62.

12.   Although the multiple repetition of the wording 'according to...Law', in 2.22, 27 and 39 can easily be observed, few commentators and scholars have paid attention to them (e.g. Goulder only thinks the triple uses of the phrase 'emphasizes the piety of the family, and guarantees the factuality of the tale' [*Luke*, p. 255], and he fails to link these three to the fourth use of the phrase in 2.42 [p. 255]; Nolland only states '"according to the Law of Moses," is Lukan' [*Luke*, p. 117]). Most commentators and scholars either only pay little attention to these multiple uses of the phrase (e.g. M. Coleridge, *The Birth of the Lukan Narrative: Narrative as Christology in Luke 1-2* [JSNTSup, 88; Sheffield: Sheffield Academic Press, 1993], p. 158; Reiling and Swellengrebel have only observed the repetition of the phrase in 2.22 and 39 [*Handbook*, p. 144]; Fitzmyer observes 'the Law' is repeated in 2.22 and 27, and is then concluded in 2.39 [*Luke*, p. 421]; Bock only thinks the fulfillment of the Law is 'a continual emphasis of Luke 2' [*Luke*, p. 254]; Evans, *Luke*, p. 212; Soards, 'Luke 2.22-40', pp. 400–405), or don't even mention the multiple uses of the phrase (e.g. Marshall, *Gospel of Luke*, pp. 115–27; Plummer, *Luke*, pp. 62–75; Ellis, *Luke*, pp. 82–85; Easton, *Luke*, pp. 26–31; Creed, *Luke*, pp. 37–45; Manson, *Luke*, pp. 20–4; Brown, *The Birth of the Messiah*, pp. 412–73).

final TC is the point of departure of the message which Luke wants to bring out. The rheme (ὑπέμεινεν Ἰησοῦς ὁ παῖς ἐν Ἰερουσαλήμ, καὶ οὐκ ἔγνωσαν οἱ γονεῖς αὐτοῦ) of the final TC is the message which the theme has developed; this message is then further developed in the rest of Luke 2 (this will be discussed later in this chapter). This message 'Jesus stayed in Jerusalem, but his parents did not know' and its further developed elements is in fact a foregrounded message: not only is it brought out by an accumulated theme under the six temporal clause complexes, but also by a number of linguistic structures throughout 2.41-52 (including marked word order patterns and intratextual considerations of passages), which will be discussed below.

Marked Clause Structures in the Sixth Clause Complex
The sixth TC consists of a number of marked clause patterns. They are stated as follows:

Number of Temporal Clauses in the Theme of the Sixth TC. The theme, or the temporal clause (2.42-43a) in the sixth clause complex comes with a sequence of four different temporal clauses (ὅτε ἐγένετο ἐτῶν δώδεκα, ἀναβαινόντων αὐτῶν κατὰ τὸ ἔθος τῆς ἑορτῆς, τελειωσάντων τὰς ἡμέρας, and ἐν τῷ ὑποστρέφειν αὐτούς) to form an entire temporal clause. In Lukan temporal clause complexes, typically there is only one (or two in some events) temporal clause in one complex. It is certainly a marked clause type to have a sequence of four different temporal clauses to form one single temporal clause (2.42-43a).

Genitive Absolute Structures in the Sixth TC. The temporal clause consists of a sequence of two genitive absolute constructions. The first is ἀναβαινόντων αὐτῶν κατὰ τὸ ἔθος τῆς ἑορτῆς. The second is τελειωσάντων τὰς ἡμέρας, with a PC pattern with the ellipsis of its subject indicating the subject is the same as the one in the preceding clause. It is not common to have a double genitive absolute in the Gospel.[13]

---

13. The genitive absolute is very common in Luke, but they tend to occur only once in an occurrence, not twice. Brown notices the awkwardness of the first genitive absolute (2.42 ἀναβαινόντων αὐτῶν) being yoked to the second one in 2.43 (τελειωσάντων τὰς ἡμέρας). Brown wants to keep the sense of subordination expressed in the first genitive even though most modern translations have translated the participle into a finite verb (e.g. KJV, ASV, RSV, NRSV, NKJV; cf. Fitzmyer, *Luke*, p. 441); he thus suggests the awkward consequence of the subordinate clauses is to emphasize the finite clause 'Jesus stayed behind in Jerusalem' (*The Birth of the Messiah*, p. 473). This suggestion is echoed by Reiling and Swellengrebel: 'because Luke wants to focus all attention on the fact that Jesus stayed behind without his parents' knowledge, which is the basis for the subsequent narrative' (*Handbook*, p. 146). What is being argued here is Luke's emphasis is not only on 'Jesus stayed behind in Jerusalem' (2.43a), but in fact is also on 'his parents did not know it' (2.43b). This is based on the final rheme concluded from the analysis of the six TCs discussed before, and the marked structures which are being discussed in the chapter. This awkwardness is also recognized by other commentators (e.g. Marshall: 'The sentence is awkwardly expressed with a temporal clause, a lengthy genitive absolute phrase, and a temporal infinitive phrase before the main verb' [*Gospel of Luke*, p. 126]; and Plummer [*Luke*, p. 75]).

The Participial Clause τελειωσάντων τὰς ἡμέρας *in 2.43a.* This participial clause is in a PC order. PC order is the most common order in Luke, but it is not the case when the complement is the word ἡμέρα. This can be seen from the uses of the word in Luke's writings in the following table:

Table 7.2 *Uses of* ἡμέρα *in Luke's Writings*

ἡμέρα	in Luke	in Acts
Functioning as subject	18x[14]	12x[15]
Functioning as complement	3x[16]	6x[17]
Functioning as adjunct	61x[18]	72x[19]
Functioning as qualifier of a noun	1x[20]	2x[21]

In fact, this awkward use of the genitive absolutes can be observed by comparing with the other Lukan genitive absolutes. There is a total of 35 instances of having a single genitive absolute in the Gospel: Lk. 2.2; 4.2, 40, 42; 7.6, 24, 42; 8.23, 49; 9.34, 37, 42, 43, 57; 11.14, 29, 53; 12.1; 14.32; 15.14, 20; 17.12; 18.40; 19.11, 33, 36, 37; 20.45; 21.5, 28; 22.10, 47, 53; 23.45; 24.36; while there is only a total of nine instances having double genitive absolutes, two of them have two different subjects among the two genitive absolute structures (3.15-16; 8.4), the rest of them have only one subject, i.e., the subject of the first genitive absolute is also the subject of the second one, and thus the second one is always with an ellipsis of the subject (2.42; 3.21; 14.29; 20.1; 22.55 [the subject of this one has not been explicitly stated in the first genitive absolute structure]; 24.5, 41).

14.   Lk. 1.23 ἐπλήσθησαν αἱ ἡμέραι τῆς λειτουργίας αὐτοῦ; 2.6 ἐπλήσθησαν αἱ ἡμέραι, 21 ἐπλήσθησαν ἡμέραι ὀκτώ, 22 ἐπλήσθησαν αἱ ἡμέραι; 4.42 γενομένης δὲ ἡμέρας; 5.35 ἐλεύσονται δὲ ἡμέραι; 6.13 ἐγένετο ἡμέρα; 9.12 ἡ δὲ ἡμέρα ἤρξατο κλίνειν, 51 συμπληροῦσθαι τὰς ἡμέρας; 17.22 ἐλεύσονται ἡμέραι; 19.43 ἥξουσιν ἡμέραι; 21.6 ἐλεύσονται ἡμέραι, 34 ἐπιστῇ ἐφ᾽ ὑμᾶς αἰφνίδιος ἡ ἡμέρα ἐκείνη; 22.7 ἦλθεν δὲ ἡ ἡμέρα τῶν ἀζύμων, 66 ἐγένετο ἡμέρα; 23.29 ἔρχονται ἡμέραι, 54 ἡμέρα ἦν παρασκευῆς; 24.29 κέκλικεν ἤδη ἡ ἡμέρα.

15.   Acts 2.1 συμπληροῦσθαι τὴν ἡμέραν τῆς πεντηκοστῆς, 20 ἐλθεῖν ἡμέραν κυρίου; 9.23 ἐπληροῦντο ἡμέραι ἱκαναί; 12.18 γενομένης δὲ ἡμέρας; 16.35 ἡμέρας δὲ γενομένης; 21.27 ἔμελλον αἱ ἑπτὰ ἡμέραι συντελεῖσθαι; 23.12 γενομένης δὲ ἡμέρας; 24.11 οὐ πλείους εἰσίν μοι ἡμέραι δώδεκα; 25.13 ἡμερῶν δὲ διαγενομένων τινῶν; 27.29 ἡμέραν γενέσθαι, 33 ἡμέρα ἤμελλεν γίνεσθαι, 39 ἡμέρα ἐγένετο.

16.   Lk. 2.43 τελειωσάντων τὰς ἡμέρας; 21.22 ἡμέραι ἐκδικήσεως αὗταί εἰσιν; 24.21 τρίτην ταύτην ἡμέραν ἄγει.

17.   Acts 3.24 κατήγγειλαν τὰς ἡμέρας ταύτας; 12.3 ἦσαν δὲ [αἱ] ἡμέραι τῶν ἀζύμων; 17.31 ἔστησεν ἡμέραν; 21.5 ἡμᾶς ἐξαρτίσαι τὰς ἡμέρας; 27.33 τεσσαρεσκαιδεκάτην σήμερον ἡμέραν; 28.23 ταξάμενοι δὲ αὐτῷ ἡμέραν.

18.   Lk. 1.5, 7, 18, 20, 24, 25, 39, 59, 75, 80; 2.1, 36, 37, 46; 4.2, 2, 16, 25; 5.17; 6.12, 23; 8.22; 9.22, 23, 28, 36, 37; 10.12; 11.3; 12.46; 13.14, 16; 14.5; 15.13; 16.19; 17.4, 24, 26, 26, 27, 28, 29, 30, 31; 18.7, 33, 19.42, 47; 20.1; 21.6, 23, 37; 22.7, 53; 23.7, 12, 29; 24.7, 13, 18, 46

19.   Acts 1.2, 3, 5, 15, 22; 2.17, 18, 29, 41, 46, 47; 3.2; 5.36, 37, 42; 6.1; 7.8, 26, 41, 45; 8.1; 9.9, 19, 24, 37, 43; 10.30, 40, 48; 11.27; 12.21; 13.14, 31, 41; 15.7, 36; 16.5, 12, 13, 18; 17.11, 17, 31; 18.18; 19.9; 20.6, 16, 18, 26, 31; 21.4, 7, 10, 15, 26, 38; 23.1; 24.1, 24; 25.1, 6, 14; 26.7, 13, 22; 27.7, 20; 28.7, 12, 13, 14, 17

20.   Lk. 2.44

21.   Acts 2.15; 10.3

In Luke's writings, ἡμέρα is normally used as an adjunct in a clause (61x and 72x in Luke and Acts respectively), or as a subject (18x and 12x respectively). It is certainly not usual to have the word ἡμέρα functioning as the complement in a clause (there are only 3x and 6x of such in Luke and Acts respectively) and thus this word functioning as the complement of the clause in 2.43a is a marked pattern. The situation is not quite the same when the word ἡμέρα is replaced by a synonym or other word which shares the same semantic domains, as can be seen in the following tables:

Table 7.3 *Uses of the Synonyms of ἡμέρα in Luke's Writings*

ἔτος	Luke	Acts
Functioning as subject	0x	1x[22]
Functioning as complement	1x[23]	1x[24]
Functioning as adjunct	13x[25]	9x[26]
Functioning as qualifier of a noun	1x[27]	0x

καιρός	Luke	Acts
Functioning as subject	2x[28]	1x[29]
Functioning as complement	2x[30]	4x[31]
Functioning as adjunct	9x[32]	4x[33]
Functioning as qualifier of a noun	0x	0x

χρόνος	Luke	Acts
Functioning as subject	1x[34]	3x[35]
Functioning as complement	0x	5x[36]
Functioning as adjunct	6x[37]	9x[38]
Functioning as qualifier of a noun	0x	0x

22. Acts 7.30 πληρωθέντων ἐτῶν τεσσεράκοντα
23. Lk. 2.42 ἐγένετο ἐτῶν δώδεκα
24. Acts 4.22 ἐτῶν γὰρ ἦν πλειόνων τεσσεράκοντα
25. Lk. 2.36, 37, 41; 3.1, 23; 4.25; 8.43; 12.19; 13.7, 8, 11, 16; 15.29
26. Acts 7.6, 36, 42; 9.33; 13.20, 21; 19.10; 24.10, 17
27. Lk. 8.42 ἐτῶν δώδεκα
28. Lk. 21.8 ὁ καιρὸς ἤγγικεν, 24 πληρωθῶσιν καιροὶ ἐθνῶν
29. Acts 3.20 ἔλθωσιν καιροὶ ἀναψύξεως
30. Lk. 12.56 τὸν καιρὸν δὲ τοῦτον πῶς οὐκ οἴδατε δοκιμάζειν; 19.44 ἔγνως τὸν καιρὸν τῆς ἐπισκοπῆς σου
31. Acts 1.7 γνῶναι χρόνους; 14.17 διδοὺς καὶ καιροὺς καρποφόρους; 17.26 ὁρίσας προστεταγμένους καιρούς; 24.25 καιρὸν δὲ μεταλαβών
32. Lk. 1.20; 4.13; 8.13, 13; 12.42; 13.1; 18.30; 20.10; 21.36
33. Acts 7.20 ; 12.1; 13.11; 19.23
34. Lk. 1.57 ἐπλήσθη ὁ χρόνος
35. Acts 7.17 ἤγγιζεν ὁ χρόνος τῆς ἐπαγγελίας, 23 ἐπληροῦτο αὐτῷ τεσσερακονταετής χρόνος; 27.9 ἱκανοῦ δὲ χρόνου διαγενομένου
36. Acts 1.7 γνῶναι χρόνους ἢ καιρούς; 15.33 ποιήσαντες δὲ χρόνον; 17.30 τοὺς μὲν οὖν χρόνους τῆς ἀγνοίας ὑπεριδών; 18.23 ποιήσας χρόνον τινά; 19.22 αὐτὸς ἐπέσχεν χρόνον
37. Lk. 4.5 ; 8.27, 29; 18.4; 20.9; 23.8
38. Acts 1.6, 21; 3.21; 8.11; 13.18; 14.3, 28; 18.20; 20.18

The above tables show that ἡμέρα and its synonyms are mostly used as adjuncts in clauses. For the word ἡμέρα, it is also frequently used as a subject; three of these instances occur in Luke 2 and appear in the phrase ἐπλήσθησαν αἱ ἡμέραι, which functions as an element of the rheme in the first TC (2.6b) and the two theme reiterations in the next two TCs (2.21a, 22a). This phrase ἐπλήσθησαν αἱ ἡμέραι is obviously Lukan; there is no occurrence of such a phrase in the writings before Luke's Gospel in the entire TLG disc D, where documents are dated as early as the eighth century BCE. This phrase occurs three times in the first century CE, where are all from Luke,[39] and three times from the second century CE,[40] and ten times from the fourth century CE.[41] Luke uses his own unique wording of the phrase ἐπλήσθησαν αἱ ἡμέραι to bring out the thematic progression in the first three TCs; this element is then concluded as the accumulated theme in the final TC, which is also in Luke's own unique wording (the phrase τελειωσάντων τὰς ἡμέρας occurs only once in the entire TLG disc D, which is Lk. 2.43), and is appeared in a marked pattern. This marked pattern (in a PC order but with ἡμέρα as complement) comes with the other marked orders which have been discussed above; it also comes with other linguistic phenomena to bring forward the foregrounded message as prominence,[42] which is discussed below.

Prominence and Contrast: 2.48-50

Prominence and contrast (which will be discussed below) in the co-text (2.48-50) of the sixth TC is one of the major linguistic phenomena coming together with the marked clause structures (as mentioned above) in the sixth TC to highlight the foregrounded message in Luke 2. The prominence and contrast in 2.48-50 can be considered by the concept of coherence. The concept of coherence is here studied in the aspect of intratextuality.

---

39. Lk. 1.23; 2.6, 22; a total of three times, if the instance of 2.21a is not included, which has same wordings except the omission of the plural article αἱ (2.21).

40. The phrase ἐπλήσθησαν αἱ ἡμέραι occurs twice in Origen's *Fragmenta in Lucam* (56.3), both the two occurrences are quotations from Luke's Gospel; the third one is in Origen's work: *Scholia in Lucam* (17.317).

41. Gregory of Nyssa, *Contra Eunomium* (3.2.26.6) and *De occursu domini* (46.1169.10); Eusebius, *Framenta in Reges* (7.2.5.9); Athanasius, *Sermo de descriptione deiparae* (28.956.9) and *Homilia in occursum domini* (28.981.10); John Chrysostom, *In diem natalem* (49.354.20) and *In illud. Exiit edictum* (50.799.61); Amphilochius, *In natalitia domini* (102) and *In occursum domini* (39 and 42).

42. Grounding represents the choice of a speaker or writer of how and what to present to his listener/reader. A foregrounded message of a speaker represents the salient information which he wants to present to his listeners (by comparing with the background information) (cf. Hopper and Thompson's words: 'grounding itself reflects a deeper set of principles…relating to decisions which speakers make, on the basis of their assessment of their hearers' situation, about how to present what they have to say' ['Transitivity in Grammar and Discourse', p. 295]).

Intratextuality in Luke 2. C.J. Fillmore states that the coherence of a meaning-fully cohered text can be studied by the aspect of intratextuality.[43] Intratextuality allows coherence to be formed between pieces of a single text.[44] The coherence of two pieces of passage enables the first passage to function as an intratextual context to the other passage, and it provides internal semantic relationships between the two passages. They may have implicit or explicit interrelationship; thus an internal expectation is formed between the two passages. In fact, intra-textuality of Luke 2 can be studied by comparing its two pieces of passage (2.8-20 and 2.43-52). This intratextuality of the two passages is much related to the prominence and contrast mentioned above. This is shown below:

1. *P. Werth's Framework of Emphasis*: The prominence and contrast in 2.48-50 mentioned above can be considered by the theory proposed by P. Werth. Werth has proposed a framework of emphasis, which consists of two parts. The first is prominence (or focus), which is for material that stands out; the second is non-prominence, which is for recessive material. The framework is sketched as follows:[45]

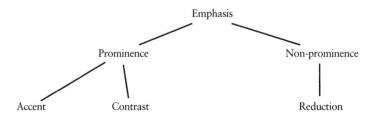

Figure 7.5 *Framework of Emphasis by P. Werth*

43. See C.J. Fillmore's definitions on the aspect of intratextuality: 'Intratextually, we have to do with relations between given pieces of a single text.' ('Linguistics as a Tool for Discourse Analysis', in T.A. van Dijk [ed.], *Handbook of Discourse Analysis*. I. *Disciplines of Discourse* [San Diego: Academic Press, 1985], pp. 11–39 [11]); and cf. A. Sharrock's words ('Intratextuality: Texts, Parts, and [W]holes in Theory', in A. Sharrock and H. Morales [eds.], *Intratextuality: Greek and Roman Textual Relations* [Oxford: Oxford University Press, 2000], pp. 1–39 [5-6]):

Reading intratextuality means looking at the text from different directions (backwards as well as forwards), chopping it up in various ways, building it up again, contracting and expanding its boundaries both within the *opus* and outside it... It is the hypothesis of intratextuality that a text's meaning grows not only out of the readings of its parts and its whole, but also out of readings of the relationships between the parts...

44. This includes anaphoric and cataphoric dependencies between given pieces of a text. Cf. Fillmore's words: 'With respect to intratextual relations, there are two possible directions of dependencies: "anaphoric", leading from a presented unit to something earlier in the text, and "cataphoric", leading from a presented unit to entities appearing later in the text.' ('Linguistics as a Tool for Discourse Analysis', p. 12).

45. P. Werth, *Focus, Coherence and Emphasis* (London: Croom Helm, 1984), p. 8 (cf. pp. 95, 109).

Reduction is an anaphoric operation, and belongs to non-prominence. It is associated with material which is repeated in a discourse and thus forms coherence, which can be lexical, semantic or grammatical. A reduced item is thus predictable from the common ground and can be described as a positive coherence.[46] Contrast is also anaphoric in nature, in which material would have a negative relationship with another piece of information in the discourse. Contrasting material implicitly makes it deny some other item(s) which is semantically or pragmatically linked with it in the discourse.[47] It can be described as a negative coherence or contrastive coherence,[48] and it belongs to prominence.

2. *Intratextuality and Prominence of the Two Passages (2.8-20 and 2.43-52):*[49] The narrative starting from 2.43 describing Jesus' parents' seeking him has indeed positive and negative coherence with another piece of narrative: the shepherds'

---

46.   As Werth states (*Focus, Coherence and Emphasis*, p. 9):
Reduction is associated with repeated semantic material, (which may be words, but need not be), when it is subsequently used with no special prominence, but merely, as it were, to keep the information in the 'current file'. Since in such cases there is a crucial link between a previous and a subsequent item. Reduction is an anaphoric operation. We shall also see that the information thus linked may be related in other ways than by straight identity.

47.   As Werth states (*Focus, Coherence and Emphasis*, p. 9) (cf. Givón, *Syntax*, vol. 2, pp. 699–715):
When an item has Contrast, we must assume that there is a previous piece of information which in some way has a negative relationship with the Contrasting item. Since, therefore, such items necessarily have an at least implicit connection with another piece of information in the discourse, they too, like Reduced items, are fundamentally anaphoric. This shared property will be seen to have important implication.

48.   Werth, *Focus, Coherence and Emphasis*, pp. 8–9, 95–96, 107–109.

49.   Coherence occurs between these two passages (this will be shown later). In fact, coherence also occurs within each of these two passages. Reiteration is the main phenomenon of this consideration:
(i) Reiteration in 2.8-20: The reiterations in 2.8-20 are mainly repetitions of lexical forms and synonyms (see M.A.K. Halliday and R. Hasan, *Cohesion in English* [London: Longman, 1976], pp. 277–79); this happens in the form of a single lexical item or an entire clause or phrase. Reiteration in single lexical items includes 'fearing' (2.9 ἐφοβήθησαν and 10 μὴ φοβεῖσθε), 'going' (2.15 διέλθωμεν, 16 ἦλθαν and 20 ὑπέστρεψαν), 'seeing' (2.15 ἴδωμεν, 17 ἰδόντες, 20 εἶδον), 'making known' (2.15 ἐγνώρισεν and 17 ἐγνώρισαν), 'being told' (2.17 λαληθέντος, 18 λαληθέντων, 20 ἐλαλήθη), 'hearing' (2.18 ἀκούσαντες and 20 ἤκουσαν). Reiteration of a clause or phrase includes 'finding a baby lying in a manger' (2.12 εὑρήσετε βρέφος...κείμενον ἐν φάτνῃ and 2.16 ἀνεῦραν... τὸ βρέφος κείμενον ἐν τῇ φάτνῃ), 'praising God' (2.13 αἰνούντων τὸν θεόν and 2.20 αἰνοῦντες τὸν θεόν). Reiterations in these two aspects demonstrate the internal coherence of the passage (2.8-20). They represent the attitudes and responses of the shepherds before and after the words of the angel spoken to them. Before hearing the words of the angel, the initial response of the shepherds of finding the glory of the Lord is 'fearing' (2.9). This is because of the sudden appearance of the divine power and they do not know and understand what is happening; after hearing the angel's words, their following response is 'going to seek Jesus'. After 'seeking Jesus' and 'seeing and hearing' everything happen, their response is exactly opposite to their initial response: they 'make known' the events and the words to the people around, and they 'praise God'. This implies their total understanding of the angel's words after seeing Jesus. The initial response of the shepherds is 'fearing, not knowing and not under-

seeking of Jesus and his parents (2.8-20). The coherence between the two is basically formed by lexical cohesions, which are mainly reiterations including repetitions of same words, synonyms (or near synonyms) and phrases.[50] This forms the intratextuality between the two passages (2.8-20 and 2.43-52).

Coherence of the two passages is formed by the repetitions of words, synonyms and phrases between them. The first passage functions as an intratextual context to the second one and thus internal expectations between the two are formed. The reiterations between the two are summarized as follows:

Table 7.4 *Intratextuality of the Two Passages (2.8-20 and 2.43-52)*

	Passage 1: 2.8-20	*Passage 2: 2.43-52*
Reduction 1 (near synonym)	Initial response of the shepherds: fearing, failure to understand (2.9 ἐφοβήθησαν φόβον μέγαν, 10 μὴ φοβεῖσθε)	Initial response of the parents: do not know (2.43 οὐκ ἔγνωσαν, 44 νομίσαντες)
Reduction 2 (synonyms with a same complement [Jesus])	Following action of the shepherds: seeking Jesus (2.12 εὑρήσετε βρέφος 2.16 καὶ ἦλθαν σπεύσαντες καὶ ἀνεῦραν τήν τε Μαριὰμ καὶ τὸν Ἰωσὴφ καὶ τὸ βρέφος κείμενον ἐν τῇ φάτνῃ)	Following action of the parents: seeking Jesus (2.44 ἀνεζήτουν αὐτόν, 45 καὶ μὴ εὑρόντες ὑπέστρεψαν εἰς Ἰερουσαλὴμ ἀναζητοῦντες αὐτόν, 46 καὶ ἐγένετο μετὰ ἡμέρας τρεῖς εὗρον αὐτὸν ἐν τῷ ἱερῷ καθεζόμενον ἐν μέσῳ τῶν διδασκάλων καὶ ἀκούοντα αὐτῶν καὶ ἐπερωτῶντα αὐτούς, 48 ὀδυνώμενοι ἐζητοῦμέν σε, 49 τί ὅτι ἐζητεῖτέ με)
Reduction 3 (synonyms and reiteration of clause)	Reaction of the people around: amazed (2.18 πάντες οἱ ἀκούσαντες ἐθαύμασαν)	Reaction of the people around: amazed (2.47 ἐξίσταντο δὲ πάντες οἱ ἀκούοντες)

standing'. After their sequent actions of 'hearing the words, going, seeking and seeing Jesus', their response is 'total understanding' of God's planning of salvation. These elements form an environment for understanding of the second passage (2.43-50) (this will be shown later).

(ii) Reiterations in 2.43-52: The reiterations in 2.43-52 are also mainly repetitions of lexical forms and synonyms including words and phrases. Reiterations on words and phrases include 'not knowing, not understanding' (4x) (2.43 οὐκ ἔγνωσαν, 44 νομίσαντες, 49 οὐκ ᾔδειτε, 50 οὐ συνῆκαν), 'seeking' (6x) (2.44 ἀνεζήτουν, 45 εὑρόντες, ἀναζητοῦντες, 46 εὗρον, 48 ἐζητοῦμεν, 49 ἐζητεῖτε). The first one occurs four times and the second one occurs six times in 2.43-52. These represent the major action of Joseph and Mary in the text: seeking Jesus; they also demonstrate the attitudes of Jesus' parents towards Jesus before and after the seeking of him. Before their seeking of Jesus, their attitude is 'do not know' (2.43); after the seeking, their attitude is still 'do not know, do not understand'.

50. Halliday and Hasan have classified lexical cohesion into two main categories: reiteration and collocation; reiteration includes repetition of the same word, synonym (or near synonym), superordinate and general word (e.g. vehicle is superordinate of car) (Halliday and Hasan, *Cohesion in English*, pp. 277–88).

Reduction 4 (synonyms and reiteration of clause)	Reaction of Mary: keeps the things in her heart (2.19 ἡ δὲ Μαριὰμ πάντα συνετήρει τὰ ῥήματα ταῦτα συμβάλλουσα ἐν τῇ καρδίᾳ αὐτῆς)	Reaction of Mary: keeps the things in her heart (2.51 ἡ μήτηρ αὐτοῦ διετήρει πάντα τὰ ῥήματα ἐν τῇ καρδίᾳ αὐτῆς)
Reduction 5 with Contrast 1 (repetition and collocation: near antonym)	The shepherds' reaction after seeing Jesus: understood (2.17 ἰδόντες δὲ ἐγνώρισαν)	The parents' reaction after seeing Jesus: astonished (2.48 ἰδόντες αὐτὸν ἐξεπλάγησαν)
Reduction 6 with Contrast 2 (repetition and collocation: near antonym)	The final description of the shepherds' reaction: praising God (understood) (2.20 οἱ ποιμένες δοξάζοντες καὶ αἰνοῦντες τὸν θεὸν ἐπὶ πᾶσιν οἷς ἤκουσαν καὶ εἶδον καθὼς ἐλαλήθη πρὸς αὐτούς)	The final description of the parents' reaction: do not understand (2.50 αὐτοὶ οὐ συνῆκαν τὸ ῥῆμα ὃ ἐλάλησεν αὐτοῖς)

Table 7.4 represents the coherence of the two passages formed by the repetitions of words and phrases between them (the corresponding repetitions between the two passages are in italics). The repetitions between the two eventually form a total of six reductions (as described above under Werth's proposal) which have been classified in Table 7.4.

In Reduction 1, the initial response of the shepherds and the parents are actually very similar: they do not know what is happening. Although the word used in Passage 1 is φοβέομαι (2.9, 10), which is not a synonym of the word used in passage 2 (2.43 γινώσκω), the effect is similar: they initially do not know and do not understand God's planning on salvation. The shepherds are scared when they see an angel of the Lord appearing to them; they are scared partly because of the sudden appearance of a divine power, and partly because they do not know what is happening and do not understand God's work. This is the same in Passage 2, Jesus' parents 'do not know' Jesus is not with them. They not only do not know Jesus is missing, but also do not know the reason for Jesus' absence. Jesus is staying in the temple and is fulfilling his mission (he must be in his father's house [2.49]);[51] this is what his parents do not understand. The similarities between the shepherds and Jesus' parents' failure in understanding of God's work form a repetition between the two passages, and this is Reduction 1.

In Reduction 2, the shepherds are asked to find the baby Jesus. They then go and find Jesus, and finally they successfully find Jesus and his parents. The same thing happens in Passage 2—the parents discover that Jesus is missing, they go and keep finding Jesus; finally they can successfully find Jesus. Repetitions of lexical items and synonyms are used in these two passages to make a reduction between the two passages: repetitions of lexical items (εὑρίσκω in 2.12 [Passage 1] and 2.45,

---

51. 2.49b ἐν τοῖς τοῦ πατρός μου δεῖ εἶναί με; for interpretation of the plural dative case, see D.D. Sylva, 'The Cryptic Clause *en tois tou patros mou dei einai me* in Lk. 2.49b', *ZNW* 78 (1987), pp. 132–40; cf. J.J. Kilgallen, 'Luke 2.41-50: Foreshadowing of Jesus, Teacher', *Bib* 66 (1985), pp. 553–59 (556–57).

46 [Passage 2]) and synonyms (2.12 εὑρήσετε, 16 ἀνεῦραν in Passage 1 and 2.44 ἀνεζήτουν, 45 εὑρόντες, 46 εὗρον, 48 ἐζητοῦμεν, 49 ἐζητεῖτε in Passage 2). Repetitions in grammatical patterns also occur in the two passages (2.12 εὑρήσετε βρέφος ἐσπαργανωμένον καὶ κείμενον ἐν φάτνῃ and 2.16 ἀνεῦραν τήν τε Μαριὰμ καὶ τὸν Ἰωσὴφ καὶ τὸ βρέφος κείμενον ἐν τῇ φάτνῃ in Passage 1 and 2.46 εὗρον αὐτὸν ἐν τῷ ἱερῷ καθεζόμενον ἐν μέσῳ τῶν διδασκάλων καὶ ἀκούοντα αὐτῶν καὶ ἐπερωτῶντα αὐτούς in Passage 2). In both cases, the complement (Jesus) comes with participles as its modifier: two in 2.12 (ἐσπαργανωμένον and κείμενον) and one in 2.16 (κείμενον), which makes a total of three in Passage 1; in Passage 2, a total of three participles as modifier of Jesus are also found in 2.46 (καθεζόμενον, ἀκούοντα and ἐπερωτῶντα). These repetitions between the two passages form the second reduction.

In Reduction 3, both passages have an insertion of a group of people and their response of what they have heard: being amazed. The repetition of the wording and order (2.18 πάντες οἱ ἀκούσαντες ἐθαύμασαν + adjunct in Passage 1 and 2.47 ἐξίσταντο δὲ πάντες οἱ ἀκούοντες αὐτοῦ + adjunct in Passage 2) with a synonym (2.18 ἐθαύμασαν and 2.47 ἐξίσταντο in Passage 2) forms the third reduction of the two passages.

Reduction 4 corresponds to the narrations of Mary's responses in the two events: keeping all the words into her heart. The similarity between the two passages in this event is clearly shown by the repetition of almost an entire clause (2.19 ἡ δὲ Μαριὰμ πάντα συνετήρει τὰ ῥήματα ταῦτα συμβάλλουσα ἐν τῇ καρδίᾳ αὐτῆς in Passage 1 and 2.51 ἡ μήτηρ αὐτοῦ διετήρει πάντα τὰ ῥήματα ἐν τῇ καρδίᾳ αὐτῆς in Passage 2).[52] This repetition of the entire clause forms Reduction 4.

Reduction 5 corresponds to the narrations of the shepherds and the parents' different responses when they have found Jesus in the two passages. In Reduction 5, the repetition occurs on a lexical item in aorist participial form (2.17 ἰδόντες in Passage 1 and 2.48 ἰδόντες in Passage 2). What is significant here is that this repetition comes with the first contrast: the contrasting responses of the shepherds and the parents immediately after seeing Jesus. In Passage 1, after seeing Jesus, the shepherds make known the words spoken to them; this implies their understanding of the angel's words. The immediate response of the shepherds is understanding—'making known the words'. What is totally different is the immediate response of Jesus' parent when they find him in Passage 2. The parents are 'astonished' immediately after seeking Jesus; this implies their failure in understanding (which is totally contrary to the shepherds' understanding). The repetition of the lexical item with the same grammatical form creates Reduction 5, but much more

---

52. All the major commentaries have failed to notice the many similarities (or the six reductions stated here) between 2.8-20 and 2.44-52; most of them can only easily recognize the similarity between 2.19 and 2.51 (e.g. Marshall, *Gospel of Luke*, p. 114, 130; Fitzmyer, *Luke*, p. 413; Reiling and Swellengrebel, *Handbook*, p. 154; Evans, *Luke*, p. 227; Goulder, *Luke*, p. 253; Creed; *Luke*, p. 46; Johnson, *Luke*, p. 51, 60; Godet, *Luke*, p. 93) (cf. Nolland, *Luke*, pp. 109–10; Bock, *Luke*, p. 273; Just, *Luke*, p. 128; Hendriksen, *Luke*, p. 186; Stein, *Luke*, p. 123).

important is the first contrast formed here. The two totally different responses of the shepherds and Jesus' parents after seeing Jesus form Contrast 1 between the two passages.

Reduction 6 is the narration of the final conclusions of the responses of the shepherds and Jesus' parents after seeing Jesus (2.20 and 2.50), which contains the repetitions of lexical items and near antonyms between the two verses (2.20 ἐπὶ πᾶσιν οἷς ἤκουσαν καὶ εἶδον καθὼς ἐλαλήθη πρὸς αὐτούς and 2.50 τὸ ῥῆμα ὃ ἐλάλησεν αὐτοῖς).[53] Like the case in Reduction 5, what is significant here is that this repetition in fact demonstrates a contrast—Contrast 2, which represents the two totally different responses (understanding and not understanding) between the shepherds and Jesus' parents after hearing the angels' and Jesus' words respectively. Contrast 1 in 2.17 and 2.48 demonstrates the contradictory responses of the shepherds and Jesus' parents after seeing Jesus. The degree of contrast between the responses of the two groups of participants actually increases in Contrast 2. In Contrast 2, on one hand the shepherds' understanding is further positively portrayed (from 'they made known the saying which had been told them' in 2.17 to 'glorifying and praising God for all they had heard' in 2.20); on the other hand the failure of the understanding of Jesus' parent is further negatively portrayed (from 'they were astonished' in 2.48 to 'they did not understand the saying' in 2.50). This increased contrast in Contrast 2 indicates the two totally different responses between the two parties: understanding and failure in understanding of God's work. The shepherds 'praise God' because they understand what has happened and the words spoken to them; on the contrary the parents of Jesus 'do not understand' the words of Jesus, which is totally contradictory to the shepherds' understanding of God's planned salvation.[54]

In summary, the six reductions formed by the repetitions provide connections between the two passages; and the two contrasts provide negative coherences between the two. These contrasts demonstrate prominence under Werth's model of emphasis. In other words, what is so significant here is that the two contrasts in the two passages discussed so far; they are representing a prominence which

53. See Halliday and Hasan, *Cohesion in English*, pp. 284–92.

54. Jesus' parents fail to understand Jesus' words and deeds even though they have listened to the angels' and Simeon's prophecies before (cf. Goulder, *Luke*, p. 266). Brown may be right in stating that Luke is drawing a sharp contrast between the parents' lack of understanding in 2.50 and Jesus' astounding understanding in 2.46-47 (Brown, *The Birth of the Messiah*, p. 477) (cf. the chiastic structure observed by de Jonge in 2.41-51a: A. Mary, Joseph and Jesus go to Jerusalem [2.41-42]; B. Jesus stays in Jerusalem, which is not noticed [2.43]; C. His parents seek and find him [2.44-46a]; X. Jesus among the doctors [2.46b-47]; C'. His parents, annoyed, reproach him [2.48]; B'. Jesus' reaction, which is not understood [2.49-50]; A'. Jesus, Mary and Joseph return to Nazareth [2.51a]; this proposed structure shows the central one [2.46b-47: Jesus among the doctors] as a climax) (H.J. de Jonge, 'Sonship, Wisdom, Infancy: Luke 2.41-51a', *NTS* 24 [1978], pp. 317–54 [339]; also cf. C.H. Talbert, *Reading Luke: A Literary and Theological Commentary on the Third Gospel* [New York: Crossroad, 1982], p. 37); in fact what is much more important here is the contrast between the responses of the shepherds in 2.8-20 and Jesus' parents in 2.44-52: one shows their understanding (2.20) and the other still shows their lack of understanding (2.50).

Luke indeed wants to bring out: Jesus' parents' failure in understanding of Jesus and God's planned salvation.

Summary. There are particularly two passages (2.8-20 and 2.43b-52) in Luke 2 illustrating the concept of intratextuality. Each of the two passages are well cohered within their own in the forms of reiterations of lexical items and phrases (as discussed above in a footnote). The first passage functions intratextually to the second and thus coherence is formed between the two passages. This coherence is mainly formed through the repetitions of lexical items and phrases (as discussed above), this includes six positive coherences (six reductions) and two negative coherences (two contrasts). According to Werth's classification as stated above, these eight instances can be classified as emphasis. The six reductions belong to non-prominence; and the two contrasts lead to prominence. This prominence indeed shows the foregrounded message which Luke wants to highlight: Jesus' parents' failure in understanding of his words and mission. In addition, this highlighted message (Jesus' parents' failure in understanding) is further enforced by a sequence of marked clause structures, which is stated below.

Marked Clause Structures in 2.43-52
2.43 καὶ οὐκ ἔγνωσαν οἱ γονεῖς αὐτοῦ. This clause is in a marked clause structure. This is a PS pattern, which only consists of a predicate (ἔγνωσαν) and its subject (οἱ γονεῖς αὐτοῦ). The complement of the predicate is elided but is anaphoric to the preceding clause: ὑπέμεινεν Ἰησοῦς ὁ παῖς ἐν Ἰερουσαλήμ. In Luke's writings, it is typical to have the content of the verb γινώσκω placed after the verb. This occurrence of γινώσκω in 2.43 with an ellipsis of its complement is a marked clause type;[55] in fact 28 out of the total 32x of γινώσκω in Luke's writings come with the content of the verb as complement.[56]

2.45 καὶ μὴ εὑρόντες ὑπέστρεψαν εἰς Ἰερουσαλὴμ ἀναζητοῦντες αὐτόν. 2.45 is a APAA pattern, where the final adjunct carries a purpose meaning in the form of a participial clause (ἀναζητοῦντες αὐτόν). This is a marked form since the usual

---

55. Reiling and Swellengrebel have noticed the absence of the object of γινώσκω: 'object of *egnosan* is, of course, the fact that Jesus stayed behind' (*Handbook*, p. 147).

56. γινώσκω is semantically mainly used to state a status of mental knowledge, which is usually translated as 'know', 'perceive' and 'understand' in mental processes (for mental process, see Halliday, *An Introducton to Functional Grammar*, pp. 112–19; Kress [ed.], *Halliday*, pp. 164–67; and M.A.K. Halliday and C.M.I.M. Matthiessen, *Construing Experience through Meaning. A Language-based Approach to Cognition* [London: Cassell, 1999], pp. 129–30, 137–39). In the total of 37x of γινώσκω in Luke and Acts, all but one are used to describe a status of mental knowledge (only 1.34 is used to state a physical sexual relationship); 32x of them are in an active voice, and 28x of them come with a complement which is either a direct object (with PC pattern: Lk. 1.18; 12.47; 16.15; 18.34; 19.42, 44; 24.18; Acts 8.30; with CP pattern: Lk. 12.46; Acts 19.15; 21.37) or a dependent clause stating the content of the verb (Lk. 7.39; 8.46; 10.11, 22; 12.39; 16.4; 19.15; 20.19; 21.20, 30, 31; Acts 2.36; 17.13; 19.35; 20.34; 21.24; 23.6) (in which more than half of them are introduced by the word ὅτι).

grammatical form used to express a purpose adjunct is an infinitival clause, rather than a participial clause.[57]

2.43b οὐκ ἔγνωσαν οἱ γονεῖς αὐτοῦ. The subject of this clause is stated explicitly: οἱ γονεῖς αὐτοῦ. This is not a usual practice in Luke's writing. This plural subject has already been introduced and stated explicitly in 2.41 (καὶ ἐπορεύοντο οἱ γονεῖς αὐτοῦ), which is then implicitly stated in 2.42 (ἀναβαινόντων αὐτῶν); it is then even an ellipsis in 2.43 (καὶ τελειωσάντων τὰς ἡμέρας).[58] T. Givón's theory of Topic Continuity is found to be helpful in interpreting the explicitly stated plural subject in 2.43b.[59] Based on this theory of Topic Continuity, S.H. Levinsohn classifies the scale of coding material in Koine Greek into zero anaphora, articular pronouns, independent pronouns and full noun phrases: the degree of topic continuity decreases, a higher scale of coding material is normally applied to a reintroduced participant.[60] For example, when a major participant is reintroduced

57.   In Luke, 52x of an infinitival clause are used to express a purpose adjunct (three are quotations from LXX: 4.18-19): 1.9, 17(2x), 19(2x), 54-55, 59, 69-75(3x), 76-77(2x), 78-79; 2.3, 4, 22-24(2x); 4.16, 18-19(3x), 34, 42; 5.15(2x), 17; 6.12; 8.35; 9.2, 16, 28, 51, 52; 12.49, 58; 14.17, 19; 15.1, 15; 17.31; 18.1, 10; 19.3, 10(2x), 12(2x); 21.38; 22.6; 23.26; 24.29, 45. On the contrary, there are only 9x of a participial clause used as a purpose adjunct: 2.45; 3.3; 7.3, 4; 13.6, 7; 16.20; 17.18-19; 19.48. Lk. 9.28 and 9.52 have a very similar pattern as the one in 2.45, both grammatically and semantically: 9.28 (παραλαβὼν Πέτρον καὶ Ἰωάννην καὶ Ἰάκωβον ἀνέβη εἰς τὸ ὄρος προσεύξασθαι) and 9.52 (πορευθέντες εἰσῆλθον εἰς κώμην Σαμαριτῶν ὡς ἑτοιμάσαι αὐτῷ); both 9.28 and 9.52 come with a APAA pattern: with an aorist participial clause as the first adjunct, then an aorist predicate plus a location adjunct, and then an infinitival clause as a purpose adjunct; the structure in 2.45 is in a similar pattern, except a participial clause (instead of using an infinitival clause) is used for the purpose adjunct.

58.   Fitzmyer has apparently noticed the awkwardness of the occurrence of the full noun phrase οἱ γονεῖς αὐτοῦ in 2.43b, he thus tries to reduce the difficulty 'for the sake of English' by transferring the subject 'his parent' to the preceding clause, which leads to a translation as 'when his parents started for home...but they did not know about it' (*Luke*, p. 441). Fitzmyer has only provided a smoother English translation instead of providing an explanation on the existence of the full noun phrase in 2.43b. A theory on topic continuity proposed by T. Givón is found to be indeed fruitful in tackling the problem, which will be discussed below.

59.   For the theory of Topic Continuity proposed by T. Givón, see *idem*, 'Topic Continuity in Discourse: The Functional Domain of Switch Reference', in J. Haiman and P. Munro (eds.), *Switch-Reference and Universal Grammar. Proceedings of a Symposium on Switch Reference and Universal Grammar, Winnipeg, May 1981* (Amsterdam: John Benjamins, 1983), pp. 51–82; and T. Givón, 'Topic Continuity in Discourse: An Introduction', in *idem* (ed.), *Topic Continuity in Discourse: A Quantitative Cross-Language Study* (Amsterdam: John Benjamins, 1983), pp. 1–41. For further discussions on Givón's theory of Topic Continuity and its applications on Lukan passages, see Chapter 8 of this work.

60.   Levinsohn classifies the scale of coding material in Koine Greek mainly based on the key concept of Givón's theory: the degree of topic continuity decreases, a higher scale of coding material is normally applied to a reintroduced participant (as Givón's words cited in Levinsohn's work: 'The more disruptive, surprising, discontinuous or hard to process a topic is, the more coding material must be assigned to it'. [*Discourse Features of New Testament Greek*, p. 135]) (cf. Reed, *A Discourse Analysis of Philippians*, p. 102, at which exactly the same sentence is also cited).

after an event in which he is absent, there is topic discontinuity and the reintro-duced participant would be referred with a full noun phrase (which carries with high scale of coding material).[61] However, a full noun phrase can also be employed if the sentence is to be highlighted, or the participant is salient, even though there is no discontinuity, or there is no disruption or surprise occurred in the event described; that is, if a sentence is highlighted, because the information concerned is important, a full noun phrase can be employed to highlight the sentence, to make the participant to be salient.[62] The discourse feature is particular helpful in inter-preting the full noun phrase in 2.43b (οὐκ ἔγνωσαν οἱ γονεῖς αὐτοῦ) by comparing the different coding materials employed onto the different participants in 2.41-52; which is classified as follows:

Table 7.5 *Coding Material Employed onto the Participants in 2.41-52*

No.	Verse	Subject	Coding material
1	2.41	Jesus' parents	full noun phrase (οἱ γονεῖς αὐτοῦ)
2	2.42a	Jesus	zero anaphora (ἐγένετο)
3	2.42b	Jesus' parents	zero anaphora (genitive absolute: ἀναβαινόντων αὐτῶν)[63]
4	2.43a	Jesus' parents	zero anaphora (genitive absolute: τελειωάντων)
5	2.43b	Jesus' parents	zero anaphora (articular infinitive: ὑποστρέφειν αὐτούς)[64]
6	2.43b	Jesus	full noun phrase ('Ιησοῦς ὁ παῖς)
7	2.43c	Jesus' parents	full noun phrase (οἱ γονεῖς αὐτοῦ)
8	2.44	Jesus' parents	zero anaphora (ἦλθον)
9	2.44	Jesus' parents	zero anaphora (ἀνεζήτουν)
10	2.45	Jesus' parents	zero anaphora (ὑπέστρεψαν)
11	2.46	Jesus' parents	zero anaphora (εὗρον)
12	2.47	people around	full noun phrase (πάντες οἱ ἀκούοντες αὐτοῦ)
13	2.48a	Jesus' parents	zero anaphora (ἐξεπλάγησαν)
14	2.48b	Mary	full noun phrase (ἡ μήτηρ αὐτοῦ)
15	2.49	Jesus	zero anaphora (εἶπεν)
16	2.50	Jesus' parents	independent pronoun (αὐτοὶ οὐ συνῆκαν)
17	2.51a	Jesus	zero anaphora (κατέβη)
18	2.51a	Jesus	zero anaphora (ἦλθεν)
19	2.51a	Jesus	zero anaphora (ἦν ὑποτασσόμενος)
20	2.51b	Mary	full noun phrase (ἡ μήτηρ αὐτοῦ)
21	2.52	Jesus	full noun phrase ('Ιησοῦς)

61. Levinsohn, *Discourse Features of New Testament Greek*, p. 136.

62. Levinsohn, *Discourse Features of New Testament Greek*, p. 136.

63. A personal pronoun is employed in 2.42b (ἀναβαινόντων αὐτῶν). The case is still considered to be a zero reference, since it is in the form of a genitive absolute (genitive absolute usually requires a personal pronoun to indicate its subject) (cf. Levinsohn, *Discourse Features of New Testament Greek*, pp. 136, 143).

64. A personal pronoun is employed in 2.43b (ὑποστρέφειν αὐτούς). The case is still considered to be a zero reference, since it is in the form of an infinitive and it functions as a dependent clause, which requires a personal pronoun to denote its subject).

2.41 starts a new episode. The parents of Jesus are back to the stage, they are re-introduced in a form of a full noun phrase (οἱ γονεῖς αὐτοῦ). Jesus is then re-introduced with a zero anaphora (ἐγένετο) in 2.42a (Jesus is usually re-introduced in the form of a zero anaphora in the Gospels).[65] After the full noun reference re-introduction in 2.41, Jesus' parents are then back to a sequence of two zero references in 2.42b (ἀναβαινόντων αὐτῶν) and in 2.43a (τελειωσάντων τὰς ἡμέρας), which are then followed by a full noun phrase reference of Jesus in 2.43b (Ἰησοῦς ὁ παῖς), and then a full noun phrase of Jesus' parents (2.43c οἱ γονεῖς αὐτοῦ).

From Table 7.5 at above, some of the participants are in full noun reference. There are at least a few reasons: (i) they are firstly introduced (no. 12 πάντες οἱ ἀκούοντες αὐτοῦ); (ii) they are re-introduced (no. 1 οἱ γονεῖς αὐτοῦ and no. 14 ἡ μήτηρ αὐτοῦ);[66] (iii) functioning as repetition to make reduction with a previously stated incident (no. 20 ἡ μήτηρ αὐτοῦ [2.51b] and no. 21 Ἰησοῦς [2.52]) and these reductions form coherences between texts,[67] and full noun phrases are used to make these reductions. It can be seen that in the rest of the table, the participants in 2.41-52 are mainly in zero references, because they have been re-introduced and they are already on the stage; and most importantly, they are in a continuing topic. In this text with a continuing topic, there are non-zero references employed to these participants besides the above three categories, which are 2.43b (Ἰησοῦς ὁ παῖς), 2.43c (οἱ γονεῖς αὐτοῦ) and 2.50 (αὐτοί). According to Givón's Topic Continuity stated above, these three incidents carrying a lot more coding materials than a zero reference in a continued topic is to state the importance of the sentence in which they are located; or the message which is being highlighted: Jesus' action (his staying in Jerusalem) and his parents' response (their failure of knowing his stay). This is the important message which the author wants to highlight: they not only fail to know Jesus' stay in Jerusalem, but also fail to understand his words after seeing and hearing him in the temple, even Jesus has explained the reason of his stay to them in 2.49. Their failure is again highlighted by another highly scaled coding of material in 2.50 (αὐτοί) (the so-called

---

65. Jesus is a central character in the Gospels, and thus his reference is always zero, even where there is topic discontinuity. As Levinsohn states: 'In the Gospels, Jesus is the global VIP. If we take the UBS paragraphing as an indication of the beginning of new narrative units, the norm there is for there to be no overt reference to Jesus (except in genitive absolute, where an independent pronoun is used), even when Jesus was not the subject of the previous clause.' (Levinsohn, *Discourse Features of New Testament Greek*, p. 143).

66. ἡ μήτηρ αὐτοῦ in 2.48 is different from οἱ γονεῖς αὐτοῦ (2.41); it is also a re-introduced participant, which has already been introduced in 2.33 (ἡ μήτηρ).

67. The occurrence of these two full noun phrases (2.51b and 2.52) is in fact employed for reductions and coherences between the two co-texts (2.8-20 and 2.43b-52) discussed above. As it has been stated above, 2.8-20 functions intratextually to 2.43b-52. The repetitions between 2.19 (ἡ δὲ Μαριὰμ πάντα συνετήρει τὰ ῥήματα ταῦτα συμβάλλουσα ἐν τῇ καρδίᾳ αὐτῆς) and 2.51 (ἡ μήτηρ αὐτοῦ διετήρει πάντα τὰ ῥήματα ἐν τῇ καρδίᾳ αὐτῆς) is a reduction of the two co-texts; 2.40 (τὸ δὲ παιδίον ηὔξανεν καὶ ἐκραταιοῦτο πληρούμενον σοφίᾳ, καὶ χάρις θεοῦ ἦν ἐπ ὸ αὐτό) and 2.52 καὶ Ἰησοῦς προέκοπτεν (ἐν τῇ) σοφίᾳ καὶ ἡλικίᾳ καὶ χάριτι παρὰ θεῷ καὶ ἀνθρώποις is another reduction of the two co-texts.

'redundant use of the personal pronoun'). In fact, a similar highlighted message occurs before 2.41-52 with highly scaled coding materials (full noun phrases). In 2.1-40, besides the uses on newly introduced and re-introduced participants, there is another incident of full noun phrases employed to Jesus' parents. In 2.33 (καὶ ἦν ὁ πατὴρ αὐτοῦ καὶ ἡ μήτηρ θαυμάζοντες ἐπὶ τοῖς λαλουμένοις περὶ αὐτοῦ),[68] the subject reference of Jesus' parents is in full noun phrases, even though it is in a continued topic of the interaction between Simeon and Jesus' parents (2.27b-35) after a full noun phrase participant re-introduction (2.27b εἰσαγαγεῖν τοὺς γονεῖς). This incident of the full noun phrases in 2.33 (ὁ πατὴρ αὐτοῦ καὶ ἡ μήτηρ) is in a high degree of coding material (two individual full noun phrases are employed here ['his father' and 'his mother'] instead of a single full noun phrase [e.g. 'his parents' as the other occurrences in the story]; here the degree of the coding material of a double full noun phrase is even much higher than the one of a single full noun phrase); it is to bring out the importance of the message: Jesus' parents' failure in understanding Simeon's words (2.29-32), or their failure in understanding God's plan of salvation and the mission of their son Jesus.[69]

In summary, the three uses of a full noun phrase as subject reference in 2.41-52, which are accompanied with another similar usage in 2.33, can be grouped as below:

2.43 ὑπέμεινεν Ἰησους ὁ παῖς ἐν Ἰερουσαλήμ, καὶ οὐκ ἔγνωσαν οἱ γονεῖς αὐτοῦ
2.50 καὶ αὐτοὶ οὐ συνῆκαν τὸ ῥῆμα ὃ ἐλάλησεν αὐτοῖς
2.33 καὶ ἦν ὁ πατὴρ αὐτοῦ καὶ ἡ μήτηρ θαυμάζοντες ἐπὶ τοῖς λαλουμένοις περὶ αὐτοῦ

These three verses, with the full noun phrases as subject references, all contribute to the prominence which Luke wants to highlight: the failure of Jesus' parents', their failure in knowing Jesus' mission and understanding God's planned salvation.

Conclusion
A sequence of six pairs of temporal clause complexes have been employed to introduce a thematic development in Luke 2, which leads to a theme which is employed to bring out a foregrounded message. This foregrounded message, which is brought out along with a sequence of marked orders and patterns, and the contrasts and prominence represented by the intratextuality of the two passages (2.8-20 and 2.43-52), represents a message which Luke wants to bring out as a highlighted prominence: the failure of Jesus' parents, their failure to understand Jesus' mission and God's planned salvation.

68. Cf. Reiling and Swellengrebel, *Handbook*, p. 137, at which their comment implies their observation of the unusual position of the third personal pronoun: 'αὐτοῦ goes with both ὁ πατήρ and ἡ μήτηρ'.
69. Cf. F.D. Weinert, 'The Multiple Meanings of Luke 2:49 and their Significance', *BTB* 13 (1983), pp. 19–22.

Chapter 8

GIVEN-NEW INFORMATION UNITS IN LUKE 22.24-38 AND ITS PROMINENT MESSAGE

Luke 22.24-38 is the narration about Jesus' conversation with his disciples. This conversation occurs after the Meal of Passover, which includes Jesus' predictions of Peter's failure and Jesus' suffering. In fact, this episode presents a prominent message which the author wants to bring out: Jesus is the one specified to face future sufferings; while Peter is the one specified for his future failure. This will be studied through two aspects: the theory of Topic Continuity and the framework of Given-New structures. This will be discussed in this chapter alongside significant word orders presented in the episode.

Topic Continuity and Discontinuity in Luke 22.24-38
Continuity and Discontinuity in Discourse

A meaningful text is a text which has its discourse units cohered together. These cohered discourse units eventually illustrate the topic continuity of the text. As it has been stated earlier in the work, T. Givón has proposed the theory of Topic Continuity. Givón suggests the concept of continuity includes three levels of discourse continuity: (i) thematic continuity, (ii) action continuity and (iii) topics/participants continuity.[1] Thematic continuity is more on a macro level; the thematic continuity of a thematic paragraph can show the smaller units of the paragraph are developing on the same theme. Action and topic/participant continuities are more on a micro level; they are commonly preserved in a thematic paragraph. Changes of action continuity are usually associated with circumstances such as spatial and temporal settings, and changes of topic/participant continuities are mainly results of theme/topic changes on sentence/clause level and changes of involved cast; changes in these two types of continuities on the micro level may not necessarily change the thematic continuity on the macro level.

---

1. Givón, 'Topic Continuity in Discourse: An Introduction', pp. 7–8; *idem*, 'Topic Continuity in Discourse: The Functional Domain of Switch Reference', p. 53; cf. *idem*, 'The Drift from VSO to SVO in Biblical Hebrew: The Pragmatics of Tense-Aspect', in C. Li (ed.), *Mechanisms of Syntactic Change* (Austin: University of Texas, 1977), pp. 182–254; also cf. his words on the aspect of Iconicity: 'less predictable information will be given more coding material' and 'more important information will be given more coding material' (*Syntax*, p. 969); and Vande Kopple, 'Given and New Information', pp. 97–102.

The conversations between Jesus and his disciples in Lk. 22.24-38 are tight-knit conversations. These tight-knit conversations occur mainly between two groups of participants (Jesus and his disciples); they do not have any interference from other participants and they represent continuity in the discourse.[2] These tight-knit conversations include the one regarding the dispute of the disciples and Jesus' prediction of Peter's denial (22.25-34), and the one regarding Jesus' prediction of his future suffering (22.35-38). Although tight-knit conversations represent continuities of a discourse, it is found that changes of continuities occur in the conversations between Jesus and his disciples in Lk. 22.25-34 and 22.35-38, and that is important for the foregrounded message discussed later in the work. The changes of continuities in the passage are discussed below.

Participant Switch and Change of Continuity in Luke 22.25-34
Luke 22.25-34 begins with a reported speech regarding an argument within the disciples. Jesus' response to this is a quoted direct speech preceded by a clause which begins with an article and a particle (ὁ δέ).[3] This articular pronoun (ὁ) is a small scale coding reference to the speaker Jesus in 22.25 and it represents the continuity of the discourse.[4] This is the same as the other coding references in the conversation, which is listed out as follows:

Table 8.1 *Coding References of the Speakers in Lk. 22.25-34*

Speech	Speaker	Coding reference of speaker	Addressee
22.25-32	Jesus	ὁ δὲ εἶπεν αὐτοῖς	disciples and then Peter
22.33	Peter	ὁ δὲ εἶπεν αὐτῷ	Jesus
22.34	Jesus	ὁ δὲ εἶπεν	Peter

The consequent uses of the three small scale coding references (with articular pronoun: ὁ δὲ εἶπεν αὐτοῖς, ὁ δὲ εἶπεν αὐτῷ, ὁ δὲ εἶπεν) in the above table represent a high degree of continuity in the tight-knit conversation in 22.25-34;

---

2.   A tight-knit conversation is a conversation occurring between two participants, in which the addressee of an initiative speech becomes speaker of the responding speech. The consecutive speeches are not interfered with by a new participant; and the narration of the conversation is not interrupted by the narrations of other events.

3.   Levinsohn has recognized that in a tight-knit conversation the default coding of reference to a speaker who was the addressee of a previous speech is an articular pronoun together with the developmental conjunction δέ. This developmental conjunction functions bi-directionally; this bi-directional function indicates the information which it is going to introduce builds on its preceding reported information, and it also creates new developments of the story which is being presented (Levinsohn, *Discourse Features of New Testament Greek*, pp. 218–20; for the particle δὲ, and the relationship with its surrounding developmental units, see also Levinsohn, *Textual Connection in Acts*, pp. 86–96; Black, *Sentence Conjunction in the Gospel of Matthew*, pp. 142–52.

4.   As Givón suggests: higher scale of coding material represents lower degree of continuity; while lower scale of coding material represents higher degree of continuity ('Topic Continuity in Discourse: The Functional Domain of Switch Reference', p. 53; *idem*, 'Topic Continuity in Discourse: An Introduction', pp. 7–8).

in addition, the constant involvement of same participants (with no interference from other participants) in the conversation also represents a high degree of continuity. In fact, the matter of continuity in the tight-knit conversation in 22.25-34 is actually a twofold matter. On one hand, the participants of the conversation are not changed and thus there is high degree of continuity; on the other hand, there is actually a certain degree of change of participants and thus that represents changes of continuity (as the third category suggested by Givón mentioned above). This can be seen from the change of addressee from 'you' (plural) (22.26) to 'Peter' (22.31) and the change of subject (the original addressee is 'you' [plural] in 22.30; while the subject in 22.33 is Peter instead of 'they').[5]

The reference to the apostles switched to the reference to Peter is switched from a more generalized reference (ὑμεῖς) to a much more specified reference: fully specified (from a generalized reference [you][plural] to a specified named reference [Simon]) and is directed (vocative showing the direct addressee: Simon [2x in 22.31]).[6] The original addressee of Jesus' response in 22.25 is the disciples, but this addressee is then switched from a collective, generalized one (a group of disciples) to a particular, specified one (Peter) at 22.31 and onwards.[7] This change from a collective addressee to a specified addressee from the previous collective addressee is the only occurrence throughout the Gospel of Luke (this is what is stated above: on the one hand the participant is not changed [still disciples; cf. the mentioning of the disciples 'you' (plural) in 22.31]; on the other hand the mentioning of the participant is actually switched to be 'Peter' [22.31, 32]['you' (singular)]); and more significantly, this change of addressee does not have any narration indicating the addressee has been switched in 22.31 (there is not wording like 'Jesus said to Peter' or 'Jesus turned to Peter').[8] The only indication

5.	Although the reference of addressee has been switched to Simon in 22.31, a second person plural personal pronoun ὑμᾶς is still used. Attention has been drawn to the plural form ὑμᾶς in 22.31; for example, as it is stated: 'Simon is being addressed as a representative of the group of the apostles' ('Peter in the Gospel of Luke', in R.E. Brown, K.P. Donfried and J. Reumann [eds.], *Peter in the New Testament: A Collaborative Assessment by Protestant and Roman Catholic Scholars* [New York: Paulist Press, 1973], p. 120) (this is a collection of discussions from a seminar; the section 'Peter in the Gospel of Luke' was led by M.M. Bourke).

6.	Cf. E. Ventola, *The Structure of Social Interaction: A Systemic Approach to the Semiotics of Service Encounters* (London: Frances Pinter, 1987), pp. 150–51.

7.	The addressee of Jesus' speech is originally his 12 apostles, but it then turns to a more specified one: Simon; while the content of the speech is still related to the others (the plural personal pronoun ὑμᾶς in 22.31 and τοὺς ἀδελφούς σου in 22.32) (Q. Quesnell unconvincingly suggests the plural forms represent more than the rest of the apostles: 'The Women at Luke's Supper', in R.J. Cassidy and P.J. Scharper [eds.], *Political Issues in Luke-Acts* [Maryknoll: Orbis Books, 1983], pp. 59–79 [64–65, 71], where Quesnell [p. 65 n. 39] has also wrongly cited H.F. Bayer's work [*Jesus' Predictions of Vindication and Resurrection: The Provenance, Meaning and Correlation of the Synoptic Predictions* (WUNT 2.20; Tübingen: J.C.B. Mohr, 1986) (p. 76) to support his theory]).

8.	A narration indicating a switch of addressee is a norm throughout the Gospel. Every time when the addressee of a speech is switched, it is shown by a noun phrase or a personal pronoun (the new addressees of speeches by the same speakers of previous speeches are shown in italics):

of showing the addressee has been changed is the double vocative in 22.31 (Σίμων Σίμων),[9] which shows the discontinuity.[10]

5.24 εἶπεν τῷ παραλελυμένῳ; 6.9 εἶπεν δὲ ὁ Ἰησοῦς πρὸς αὐτούς, 10 εἶπεν αὐτῷ; 7.24 ἤρξατο λέγειν πρὸς τοὺς ὄχλους περὶ Ἰωάννου, 48 εἶπεν δὲ αὐτῇ; 8.54 αὐτὸς δὲ κρατήσας τῆς χειρὸς αὐτῆς ἐφώνησεν λέγων; 9.59 εἶπεν δὲ πρὸς ἕτερον; 10.23 καὶ στραφεὶς πρὸς τοὺς μαθητὰς κατ᾽ ἰδίαν εἶπεν; 12.15 εἶπεν δὲ πρὸς αὐτούς; 14.12 ἔλεγεν δὲ καὶ τῷ κεκληκότι αὐτόν; 16.7 ἔπειτα ἑτέρῳ εἶπεν; 17.19 καὶ εἶπεν αὐτῷ (Jesus speaks to himself or to the people around in 17.17), 22 εἶπεν δὲ πρὸς τοὺς μαθητάς; 22.52 εἶπεν δὲ Ἰησοῦς πρὸς τοὺς παραγενομένους ἐπ᾽ αὐτόν. The missing of a narration stating the new addressee either in a form of noun phrase or personal pronoun (as stated above) has not drawn commentators' attention, though some recognize the speech strangely does not have a break between 22.30 and 22.31 (e.g. Plummer, *Luke*, p. 503; this difficulty may be reduced by an insertion of 'the Lord said' in some ancient manuscripts, cf. Fitzmyer, *Luke*, p. 1424 ; Marshall, *Gospel of Luke*, p. 802; Goulder, *Luke*, p. 736. The reading of a Chinese translation [Chinese Union Version] may also reflect this, which includes the phrase 'and the Lord said' [in Chinese] in its translation while indicating that it is not in the Greek text upon which the translation is based. This inclusion may reduce the difficulty of the missing break between 22.30 and 22.31, but it still does not solve the question of not mentioning the new addressee in the narrative in Lk. 22.31 as discussed above).

9.   Although vocatives show the identity of the addressee, speeches beginning with vocatives are still usually preceded by narrations showing addressee: 1.13 εἶπεν δὲ πρὸς αὐτὸν ὁ ἄγγελος, 30 καὶ εἶπεν ὁ ἄγγελος αὐτῇ; 2.28 καὶ εὐλόγησεν τὸν θεὸν καὶ εἶπεν, 48 καὶ εἶπεν πρὸς αὐτὸν ἡ μήτηρ αὐτοῦ; 3.7 ἔλεγεν οὖν τοῖς ἐκπορευομένοις ὄχλοις, 12 καὶ εἶπεν πρὸς αὐτόν; 5.12 πεσὼν ἐπὶ πρόσωπον ἐδεήθη αὐτοῦ λέγων; 6.42 πῶς δύνασαι λέγειν τῷ ἀδελφῷ σου; 46 τί δέ με καλεῖτε; 7.6 ἔπεμψεν φίλους ὁ ἑκατοντάρχης λέγων αὐτῷ, 40 εἶπεν πρὸς αὐτόν; 8.24 προσελθόντες δὲ διήγειραν αὐτὸν λέγοντες; 8.28 ἀνακράξας προσέπεσεν αὐτῷ καὶ φωνῇ μεγάλῃ εἶπεν, 48 ὁ δὲ εἶπεν αὐτῇ, 54 αὐτὸς δὲ κρατήσας τῆς χειρὸς αὐτῆς ἐφώνησεν λέγων; 9.33 εἶπεν ὁ Πέτρος πρὸς τὸν Ἰησοῦν, 37 συνήντησεν αὐτῷ ὄχλος πολύς; 10.25 ἐκπειράζων αὐτὸν λέγων, 41 ἀποκριθεὶς δὲ εἶπεν αὐτῇ ὁ κύριος; 11.1 εἶπέν τις τῶν μαθητῶν αὐτοῦ πρὸς αὐτόν, 45 ἀποκριθεὶς δέ τις τῶν νομικῶν κέγει αὐτῷ; 12.13 εἶπεν δέ τις ἐκ τοῦ ὄχλου αὐτῷ, 19 καὶ ἐρῶ τῇ ψυχῇ μου, 22 εἶπεν δὲ πρὸς τοὺς μαθητάς, 54 ἔλεγεν δὲ καὶ τοῖς ὄχλοις; 13.12 καὶ εἶπεν αὐτῇ, 15 ἀπεκρίθη δὲ αὐτῷ ὁ κύριος καὶ εἶπεν, 23 εἶπεν δέ τις αὐτῷ; 15.12 καὶ εἶπεν ὁ νεώτερος αὐτῶν τῷ πατρί, 18 καὶ ἐρῶ αὐτῷ, 21 εἶπεν δὲ ὁ υἱὸς αὐτῷ, 31 ὁ δὲ εἶπεν αὐτῷ; 17.37 καὶ ἀποκριθέντες λέγουσιν αὐτῷ; 18.18 καὶ ἐπηρώτησέν τις αὐτὸν ἄρχων λέγων; 19.5 ἀναβλέψας ὁ Ἰησοῦς εἶπεν πρὸς αὐτόν, 8 σταθεὶς δὲ Ζακχαῖος εἶπεν πρὸς τὸν κύριον, 17 καὶ εἶπεν αὐτῷ, 22 λέγει αὐτῷ, 25 καὶ εἶπαν αὐτῷ, 39 εἶπαν πρὸς αὐτόν; 20.21 καὶ ἐπηρώτησαν αὐτὸν λέγοντες, 27 ἐπηρώτησαν αὐτόν; 21.7 ἐπηρώτησαν δὲ αὐτὸν λέγοντες; 22.33 ὁ δὲ εἶπεν αὐτῷ, 48 Ἰησοῦς δὲ εἶπεν αὐτῷ; 23.28 στραφεὶς δὲ πρὸς αὐτὰς [ὁ] Ἰησοῦς εἶπεν.

There are several categories of speech involving a vocative to introduce a new addressee instead of narrating a new addressee by using a noun phrase or personal pronoun: (i) the new addressee actually appears within previous clauses (4.34, 5.5, 20; 7.14; 8.45; 9.49, 54, 59, 61; 10.17, 40; 12.14; 13.8, 25; 16.24; 17.13; 18.38, 39, 41;19.16, 18, 20; 22.49; 23.42); (ii) the narrative has already included something which relates to the addressee (5.8 προσέπεσεν τοῖς γόνασιν Ἰησοῦ λέγων. Peter starts a conversation with Jesus in 5.8. The speech begins with a vocative addressing Jesus, but the narrative itself does not show the speech is addressing Jesus. However, the narrative includes 'Peter falls to the feet of Jesus', which shows the addressee is Jesus); (iii) the occasions of prayers (10.21; 11.2; 18.11, 13; 22.42; 23.34, 46); (iv) the speech is addressing a very large group of people: a city, a country or even a generation (9.41; 10.13, 15; 13.34); (v) the addressee is the subject of the previous speech (12.41; 13.27; 14.22; 16.25, 27, 30; 20.39; 22.34, 38, 57, 58, 60). Lk. 22.25-32 does not belong to any of these five categories: the new addressee Peter does not appear in the preceding clauses (the last instance mentioning Peter is 22.8); the speech is not a prayer; and nothing related to Peter is mentioned here. 22.25-32 is the only speech in

Change of Continuity in Luke 22.35-38

The conversation between Jesus and his disciples in 22.35-38 is another tight-knit conversation. The discourse has a high degree of continuity and thus the participant references (both subjects and indirect objects) are all in small scale coding material (22.35a καὶ εἶπεν αὐτοῖς, 35b οἱ δὲ εἶπαν, 36 εἶπεν δὲ αὐτοῖς, 38 οἱ δὲ εἶπαν) (not full nouns). Like the situation in 22.25-34 as described above, the matter of continuity in the conversation is also a twofold matter. On the one hand, the discourse has a high degree of continuity; on the other hand, it also represents discontinuity. This can be particularly observed in 22.37, which will be shown below.

The speech of Jesus in 22.36-37 is a continuing utterance, which indicates a new proposal (or a counter-proposal).[11] The speech begins with a conjunction, ἀλλά; this indicates the speaker replies to the previous speaker with a new initiative, which may imply the decrease of the degree of continuity.[12] More significantly, the content of the speech recorded in 22.37 represents topic discontinuity, which is discussed below.

22.37 begins with the wording λέγω γὰρ ὑμῖν ὅτι to introduce the content of Jesus' speech. There are five other clauses with the same beginning wording in the

which the addressee is suddenly switched from the disciples to Peter without narrating the change of addressee. The identity of the new addressee can only be recognized by the presence of the vocative. The only other instance of sudden change of addressee is 1.67-79, which has its addressee being suddenly changed from God to baby John in 1.76. Like 22.31, 1.76 only has a vocative indicating the new addressee, but what is different is: 1.67-79 has mentioned the baby John many times in its previous clauses (1.57-66), and the speech starting from 1.67 is originally a prayer. These two features belong to two of the five categories mentioned above. Thus the changing of addressee with only a vocative in Lk. 22.31 is unique in Luke, and it shows discontinuity.

10. Change of subject represents a high degree of discontinuity (Givón, 'Topic Continuity in Discourse: The Functional Domain of Switch Reference', p. 57), thus the change of subject (from 'the disciple' to 'Peter' in 22.31) indeed represents a certain degree of discontinuity.

11. R.E. Longacre has proposed initiating utterance (IU), continuing utterance (CU) and resolving utterance (RU). IU and CU encode three notional units: question (Q), proposal (Pro) and remark (Rem); while RU encodes three notional units: answer, response and evaluation, which respectively resolve the structures initiated as a question, a proposal and a remark (*The Grammar of Discourse* [New York: Plenum Press, 1983], pp. 48–53). Continuing utterance may indicate that the second speaker does not like to accept the dialogue on the terms suggested by the first speaker, thus the three notional units of continuing utterance can also be named as counter-question, counter-proposal, and counter-remark (Longacre, *The Grammar of Discourse*, p. 51). Here Jesus' reply in 22.36-37 is a counter-proposal.

12. See Levinsohn's words on the effect of new initiative in a tight-knit conversation (Levinsohn, *Discourse Features of New Testament Greek*, p. 231):

...in a tight-knit conversation, the previous addressee takes up the topic of the exchange at the point at which the last speaker left off. However, the previous addressee may seek instead to take control of the conversation with an objection or new initiative that typically breaks the tight-knit nature of the exchange. This is reflected in the speech orienter, which often under such circumstances contains a form of ἀποκρίνομαι.

Gospel: Lk. 3.8; 10.24; 14.24; 22.16, 18.[13] All these five occurrences are used to show the content of a speech, and they all have a conjunction γάρ to function as a connector.[14] The connector γάρ usually represents a paratactic relation with its preceding clauses. What is significant here is, besides the incident in 22.37, the content of the speeches introduced by this wording (λέγω γὰρ ὑμῖν ὅτι) in the other five incidents (3.8; 10.24; 14.24; 22.16, 18) all have a common point: they contain information units which have already been mentioned in their preceding clauses. These repeated information units are either lexical-grammatical (3.8-9 τῷ Ἀβραάμ, ποιοῦν καρπόν; 10.24 ἃ ὑμεῖς βλέπετε; 14.24 τῶν κεκλημένων, τοῦ δείπνου; 22.16 φάγω αὐτό) or semantic (22.18 πίω, ἀπὸ τοῦ γενήματος τῆς ἀμπέλου).[15] These information units function as Given units, which have been mentioned before (in closing preceding co-texts) and are old information units. These can be illustrated as follows:

13. The ὅτι in 22.18 is missing in some ancient manuscripts. The other NT occurrences of this wording are Mt. 3.9; 5.20; 13.17; 18.10 and Mk 9.41.

14. For the role of conjunctions in continuity, see Martin, *English Text*, pp. 159–270; cf. Halliday and Hasan, *Cohesion in English*, pp. 226–73, for the role of conjunctions in coherence; and cf. Black, *Sentence Conjunctions in the Gospel of Matthew*, pp. 263–72.

15. In fact, other clauses in Luke with a similar beginning have a similar feature: containing information units which function as Given elements, which have been mentioned or can be recoverable in preceding clauses. For clauses beginning with λέγω ὑμῖν ὅτι, all ten such occurrences have this feature: Lk. 4.24 ἐν τῇ πατρίδι αὐτοῦ (23 ἐν τῇ πατρίδι σου); 10.12 τῇ πόλει ἐκείνῃ (8 πόλιν, 11 τῆς πόλεως ὑμῶν); 12.37 περιζώσεται, διακονήσει (35 περιεζωσμέναι, 37 οἱ δοῦλοι), 44 ἐπὶ πᾶσιν τοῖς ὑπάρχουσιν αὐτοῦ καταστήσει αὐτόν (42 ὃν καταστήσει ὁ κύριος ἐπὶ τῆς θεραπείας αὐτοῦ); 15.7 οὕτως χαρά (6 συγχάρητε); 18.8 ποιήσει τὴν ἐκδίκησιν αὐτῶν (7 ποιήσῃ τὴν ἐκδίκησιν τῶν ἐκλεκτῶν αὐτοῦ), 29 ἀφῆκεν οἰκίαν ἢ γυναῖκα ἢ ἀδελφοὺς ἢ γονεῖς ἢ τέκνα (28 ἀφέντες τὰ ἴδια); 19.26 δοθήσεται, ἀρθήσεται (24 ἄρατε, δότε); 21.3 ἡ χήρα αὕτη ἡ πτωχή, ἔβαλεν (2 τινα χήραν πενιχρὰν βάλλουσαν), 32 πάντα γένηται (31 ταῦτα γινόμενα). For clauses beginning with only λέγω and ὑμῖν, the great majority of them (21 out of 26x) have this feature: Lk. 4.25 Ἠλίου, 27 Ἐλισαίου τοῦ προφήτου (24 προφήτης); 7.9 τοσαύτην πίστιν (7 ἀλλὰ εἰπὲ λόγῳ, καὶ ἰαθήτω ὁ παῖς μου), 26b προφήτου (26a προφήτην), 28 Ἰωάννου (24 Ἰωάννου); 11.8 δώσει, φίλον (5 φίλε, 7 δοῦναι), 9 δοθήσεται (8 δώσει), 51 ἐκζητηθήσεται ἀπὸ τῆς γενεᾶς ταύτης (50 ἐκζητηθῇ, ἀπὸ τῆς γενεᾶς ταύτης); 12.5b φοβήθητε (5a φοβήθητε), 22 ψυχῇ (19 ψυχῇ, 20 ψυχήν), 27b ἓν τούτων (27a τὰ κρίνα), 51b διαμερισνόν (51a εἰρήνην and οὐχί); 13.3 ὁμοίως ἀπολεῖσθε (2 ταῦτα πεπόνθασιν), 5 ὡσαύτως ἀπολεῖσθε (4 ἀπέκτεινεν αὐτούς), 24b ζητήσουσιν εἰσελθεῖν (24a ἀγωνίζεσθε εἰσελθεῖν); 15.10 γίνεται χαρά (9 συγχάρητέ μοι); 16.9 τῆς ἀδικίας (8 τῆς ἀδικίας); 17.34 ταύτῃ τῇ νυκτί (31 ἐν ἐκείνῃ τῇ ἡμέρᾳ); 18.14 οὗτος, ἐκεῖνον (13 ὁ δὲ τελώνης, 11 ὁ Φαρισαῖος), 17 τὴν βασιλείαν τοῦ θεοῦ, παιδίον (16 ἡ βασιλεία τοῦ θεοῦ, τὰ παιδία); 19.40 κράξουσιν, οὗτοι (37 φωνῇ μεγάλῃ, 39 τοῖς μαθηταῖς σου); 20.8 ἐν ποίᾳ ἐξουσίᾳ ταῦτα ποιῶ (2 ἐν ποίᾳ ἐξουσίᾳ ταῦτα ποιεῖς); there are only five instances where clauses may not contain units which have been mentioned or can be recoverable from previous writings: Lk. 6.27; 9.27; 12.4, 8; 13.25. Three of them (Lk. 6.27; 12.4, 8) are instances at which new speeches begin, and this is probably the main reason no Given unit can be traced from previous writings, as Halliday states: 'discourse has to start somewhere, so there can be discourse-initiating units consisting of a New element only' (Halliday, *An Introduction to Functional Grammar*, p. 296), thus the only instances where no information unit can be recoverable from previous writings are Lk. 9.27 and 13.35.

Table 8.2 *Old Information Units in Luke 3.8; 10.24; 14.24; 22.16, 18*

	Old information units	Location of old information units in preceding clauses
Lk. 3.8c-9 λέγω γὰρ ὑμῖν ὅτι δύναται ὁ θεὸς ἐκ τῶν λίθων τούτων ἐγεῖραι τέκνα τῷ ᾿Αβραάμ. ἤδη δὲ καὶ ἡ ἀξίνη πρὸς τὴν ῥίζαν τῶν δένδρων κεῖται· πᾶν οὖν δένδρον μὴ ποιοῦν καρπὸν καλὸν ἐκκόπτεται καὶ εἰς πῦρ βάλλεται	8c τῷ ᾿Αβραάμ	3.8a μὴ ἄρξησθε λέγειν ἐν ἑαυτοῖς, Πατέρα ἔχομεν τὸν ᾿Αβραάμ
	9 *ποιοῦν καρπόν*	3.8b *ποιήσατε οὖν καρποὺς ἀξίους τῆς μετανοίας*
10.24 λέγω γὰρ ὑμῖν ὅτι πολλοὶ προφῆται καὶ βασιλεῖς ἠθέλησαν ἰδεῖν ἃ ὑμεῖς βλέπετε καὶ οὐκ εἶδαν, καὶ ἀκοῦσαι ἃ ἀκούετε καὶ οὐκ ἤκουσαν	24a ἃ ὑμεῖς βλέπετε	10.23b μακάριοι οἱ ὀφθαλμοὶ οἱ βλέποντες ἃ βλέπετε
14.24 λέγω γὰρ ὑμῖν ὅτι οὐδεὶς τῶν ἀνδρῶν ἐκείνων τῶν κεκλημένων γεύσεταί μου τοῦ δείπνου	24 *τῶν κεκλημένων γεύσεταί μου τοῦ δείπνου*	14.16-17 *ἄνθρωπός τις ἐποίει δεῖπνον μέγα, καὶ ἐκάλεσεν πολλοὺς καὶ ἀπέστειλεν τὸν δοῦλον αὐτοῦ τῇ ὥρᾳ τοῦ δείπνου εἰπεῖν τοῖς κεκλημένοις*
22.16 λέγω γὰρ ὑμῖν, ὅτι οὐ μὴ φάγω αὐτὸ ἕως ὅτου πληρωθῇ ἐν τῇ βασιλείᾳ τοῦ θεοῦ	16 οὐ μὴ *φάγω αὐτό*	22.15 τοῦτο τὸ *πάσχα φαγεῖν*
22.18 λέγω γὰρ ὑμῖν [ὅτι] οὐ μὴ πίω ἀπὸ τοῦ νῦν ἀπὸ τοῦ γενήματος τῆς ἀμπέλου ἕως οὗ ἡ βασιλεία τοῦ θεοῦ ἔλθῃ	18 οὐ μὴ *πίω ἀπὸ τοῦ νῦν ἀπὸ τοῦ γενήματος τῆς ἀμπέλου*	22.17a *καὶ δεξάμενος ποτήριον εὐχαριστήσας εἶπεν*

Table 8.2 above indicates that each of the five incidents has information units which have already been introduced in their preceding clauses. These introduced units repeated in their following clauses as Given units illustrate continuities in discourse. On the contrary, although the incident in 22.37 also begins with the formulaic wordings (λέγω γὰρ ὑμῖν ὅτι), the content of the speech in 22.37 does not contain any information unit which has already been introduced in its preceding clauses; here the incident of 22.37 represents topic discontinuity.

Summary

The conversations between Jesus and his disciples in Lk. 22.25-38 are tight-knit conversations and they represent topic continuity; however, changes of continuity occur in these tight-knit conversations. The first is at 22.31, where participant change occurs and the addressee of Jesus' speech is suddenly changed to be Simon, which causes the subject change from 'the disciple' to 'Peter' in 22.33. The one in the second tight-knit conversation is at 22.37; the content of the clauses in 22.37 functions as the 'reason' (as introduced by the conjunction γάρ) for their preceding clauses in 22.36. Being different from all the other five similar usages in the Gospel (3.8; 10.24; 14.24; 22.16, 18), the incident in 22.37 does not carry any old information which is recoverable from its preceding clauses. These two incidents (22.31 and 22.37) cause degrees of discontinuity which are related to thematization.[16] In fact, prominent messages are foregrounded at these two incidents (22.31-33 and 22.37); this can be studied through the linguistic framework of Given-New structures and related significant word order, which will be discussed below.

Given-New Structures in Luke 22.24-38

A piece of meaningful discourse is composed of different information units. A single information unit is made up of two functional units: Given and New. Interplay of Given and New units generates information in a discourse. Given is the unit representing what is known or predictable to the reader (or listener) of the discourse, which is recoverable, or has been mentioned before; New is the one representing what is new or unpredictable, which is information that is represented to the listener as unrecoverable, or is something that has not been mentioned before. New is important in an information unit, because it represents the information focus of the unit.[17] This framework of Given-New information units is found particularly helpful in studying the tight-knit conversations in Lk. 22.25-38, which is discussed below.

Given-New Structures in Luke 22.25-34

One easily observed feature in the tight-knit conversation in Lk. 22.25-34 is the numerous occurrences of redundant (or so called intensive use) personal pronouns. These redundant personal pronouns significantly occur throughout the tight-knit conversation, and they are typically first and second person personal pronouns. Although the frequent occurrences of the redundant personal pronouns in Jesus' speeches starting from 22.25 can be easily observed, only a few biblical scholars have commented on their significance in the discourse.[18] In fact, these

---

16. As R. Fawcett states: 'discontinuity is most frequently the result of various types of thematization' (*A Theory of Syntax for Systemic Functional Linguistics* [Amsterdam: John Benjamins, 2000], p. 262).

17. For the framework of Given-New information units and their functional contributions in language, see Halliday, *An Introduction to Functional Grammar*, pp. 296–98; *idem*, 'Notes on Transitivity and Theme in English, Part II', *J Ling* 3 (1967), pp. 199–244 (204–11); cf. O. Dahl, 'What is New Information', in Enkvist and Kohonen (eds.), *Reports on Text Linguistics*, pp. 37–50; Butler, *Systemic Linguistics*, pp. 177–78; and Kress (ed.), *Halliday*, pp. 174–88; also cf. R. Geluykens, 'Information Flow in English Conversation: A New Approach to the Given-New Distinction', in Ventola (ed.), *Functional and Systemic Linguistics*, pp. 141–67, for discussions of the aspect of 'Recoverability'.

18. Though many commentators have drawn attention to some particular instances of the redundant personal pronouns in Lk. 22.25-34 (their explanation on them are mostly giving contrast [e.g. Marshall, *Gospel of Luke*, p. 816; Reiling and Swellengrebel, *Handbook*, p. 695; Plummer, *Luke*, p. 504], correlation [e.g. Nolland, *Luke*, p. 1072] or emphasis [e.g. Reiling and Swellengrebel, *Handbook*, p. 693; Fitzmyer, *Luke*, p. 1418, 1425]), few have noticed or paid attentions to the overall intensive occurrences of these personal pronouns in the episode (e.g. Evans, *Luke*, p. 801, though he only mentioned the intensive occurrences in 22.31-34). P.K. Nelson has

redundant personal pronouns represent significant meanings through the framework of Given-New structures in the discourse (see below). The verses containing the redundant personal pronouns are listed as follows:

(1) 22.27b *ἐγὼ* δὲ ἐν μέσῳ *ὑμῶν* εἰμι ὡς ὁ διακονῶν

(2) 22.28 *ὑμεῖς* δέ ἐστε οἱ διαμεμενηκότες μετ' ἐμοῦ ἐν τοῖς πειρασμοῖς *μου*

(3) 22.29-30a *κἀγὼ* διατίθεμαι *ὑμῖν* καθὼς διέθετό μοι ὁ πατήρ μου βασιλείαν, ἵνα ἔσθητε καὶ πίνητε ἐπὶ τῆς τραπέζης μου ἐν τῇ βασιλείᾳ μου

(4) 22.32a *ἐγὼ* δὲ ἐδεήθην περὶ *σοῦ* ἵνα μὴ ἐκλίπῃ ἡ πίστις σου

(5) 22.32b καὶ σύ ποτε ἐπιστρέψας στήρισον τοὺς ἀδελφούς σου

It can be observed from the above that four (sentences [1] to [4]: 22.27b, 28, 29-30a, 32b) out of the five sentences come with another first or second person personal pronoun in close co-text (both of the two opposite personal pronouns [i.e. 'you' is opposite to 'I' or 'me'] are in the same clause) which is opposite to the redundant personal pronoun. For example, in sentence (1) there is a redundant first person personal pronoun (ἐγώ); this sentence comes with a second person personal pronoun (ἐν μέσῳ ὑμῶν) right after (in the same clause) the first person personal pronoun ἐγώ. All these redundant personal pronouns and their relative opposite personal pronouns in sentences (1) to (4) are distinguished in italic and underlined forms as shown above. In fact, within these four sentences a series of Given-New structures are illustrated through the presence of the opposite personal pronouns and the transitivities represented by them. These four sentences with their Given-New structures are listed as sentences (a) to (d) as follows:

Table 8.3 *Given-New Structures in Luke 22.25-34*

Sentence	Given	New
(a) 22.27b		Relational (Intensive: Identifying) Identified: speaker
(b) 22.28	Relational (Intensive: Identifying) Identified: addressee	Two circumstantial elements showing circumstantial relationship between speaker and addressee: a) accompaniment: comitation b) location: spatial
(c) 22.29-30a	Two circumstantial elements showing circumstantial relationship between speaker and addressee: a) location: spatial b) location: spatial	Role of participants between speaker and addressee in a material process: actor: speaker process: material beneficiary (recipient): addressee
(d)	Role of participants between	Information Focus

tried to tackle the matter and he argues that the uses of the redundant personal pronouns in v. 27-28 show a unifying feature of the passage (ἐγὼ δὲ...εἰμι...ὑμεῖς δέ ἐστε...in 22.27 and 22.28) ('The Unitary Character of Luke 22.24-30', *NTS* 40 [1994], pp. 609–19 [613–14]; cf. *idem, Leadership and Discipleship: A Study of Luke 22:24-30* [SBLDS, 138; Atlanta: Scholars Press, 1994], pp. 159ff.; and D. Lull, 'The Servant-Benefactor as a Model of Greatness [Luke 22.24-30]', *NovT* 28 [1986], pp. 289–305 [299–300]).

22.32a   speaker and addressee in a
material process:
actor: speaker
process: material
beneficiary (client): addressee

As shown in Table 8.3, sentence (a) consists of a Relational process, which demonstrates the function of identification (identifying Jesus).[19] This relational process sets up a relation between two entities: the Identified (ἐγώ: Jesus) and the Identifier (ὁ διακονῶν),[20] where the Identifier sets up a circumstantial relationship with the disciples (ἐν μέσῳ ὑμῶν); this Relational process (Intensive: Identifying) forms as the New unit in sentence (a); a similar Relational process (which also demonstrates the function of identification: identifying the apostles) happens in sentence (b) which then functions as the Given unit in the sentence. This time in sentence (b) the Identified is the disciples (ὑμεῖς), and the Identifier is οἱ διαμεμενηκότες, which shows the addressee (disciples) have two circumstantial relationships with the speaker (Jesus) (μετ᾽ ἐμοῦ and ἐν τοῖς πειρασμοῖς μου). These two circumstantial elements showing the circumstantial relationships between the disciples and Jesus form the New unit in sentence (b); another two circumstantial elements indicating the circumstantial relationships between the disciples and Jesus in sentence (c) then function as the Given unit in the sentence. In sentence (c), the Given is the addressee (disciples) having two circumstantial relationships with the speaker (Jesus) (ἐπὶ τῆς τραπέζης μου and ἐν τῇ βασιλείᾳ μου); the New unit is a Material process ('assigning'), where the role of Jesus (speaker) is the actor of the process, and the role of the disciples (addressee) is the beneficiary (recipient); another material process with the same participating roles in sentence (d) then functions as the Given unit in the sentence. In sentence (d), the Given unit is a material process with its participating roles the same as the ones in sentence (c); in sentence (d) the role of Jesus (speaker) is the still the actor of the material process, and the role of the beneficiary (client) is Peter (addressee). All these lead to the New unit of sentence (d), which functions as the Information Focus of the information unit: ἵνα μὴ ἐκλίπῃ ἡ πίστις σου.[21] This Information

---

19. Halliday has classified relational process into circumstantial, possessive and intensive; intensive consists of two types: attributive and identifying; identifying demonstrates the function of identification (e.g. He is a dentist; the boy is my son) (*An Introduction to Functional Grammar*, pp. 119–38; cf. R.P. Fawcett, 'The Semantics of Clause and Verb for Relational Process in English', in M.A.K. Halliday and R.P. Fawcett [eds.], *New Developments in Systemic Linguistics*. I. *Theory and Description* [London: Frances Pinter, 1987], pp. 136–38, 175–78; Halliday and Matthiessen, *Construing Experience through Meaning*, pp. 461–63).

20. Cf. Halliday, 'Notes on Transitivity and Theme in English, Part 2', pp. 223–36; cf. Kress (ed.), *Halliday*, pp. 182–88.

21. The importance of a New element in a communication is best explained in Thomas and Hawes' comments on J. Firbas' work (*Theme in Academic and Media Discourse*, pp. 7–9):

An element which is known/given information (retrievable from the immediate context), is less important, communicatively, than an element carrying new information. Thus, context-independent elements have relatively greater degrees of CD (Communicative Dynamism) than

Focus represents a message: Jesus' prediction about the future failure of Peter, which is already distinguished by the topic discontinuity as discussed above. In fact, this Information Focus coming with the topic discontinuity is to present a foregrounded message with other linguistic phenomena (see below). The Given-New interrelationship within sentences (a) to (d) is shown as follows:

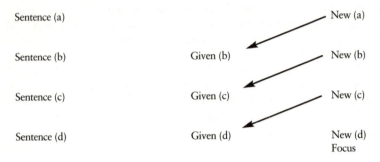

Figure 8.1 *Given-New Interrelationships within Sentences (a) to (d)*

Given-New Structure and Luke 22.37

The tight-knit conversation in Lk. 22.35-38 contains an incident of Jesus' prediction about his future sufferings (22.37); this incident in 22.37 is the final speech related to his suffering and death before his arrest in Luke 22.[22] Although biblical scholars and major commentaries generally agree that there are three instances (9.22, 44 and 18.31) of Jesus' prediction about his sufferings and death in the Gospel of Luke,[23] few have made a connection between the three passion

context-dependent elements because the former contribute to pushing the communication forward... At the same time, CD is said to be the extent to which an element pushes the communication forward. Logically, new information has a greater role in pushing the communication forward than old/given information. Thus new information can be equated with high degree of CD while old/given information has lower CD.

Cf. J. Firbas, 'On the Dynamics of Written Communication in the Light of the Theory of Functional Sentence Perspective', in Cooper and Greenbaum, *Studying Writing*, pp. 40–71; also cf. *idem*, 'On some basic problems of Functional Sentence Perspective', in M. Davies and L. Ravelli (eds.), *Advances in Systemic Linguistics: Recent Theory and Practice* (London: Pinter, 1992), pp. 167–88, for the discussion of Communicative Dynamism.

22. Cf. J.F. Gormley, 'The Final Passion Prediction: A Study of LK. 22.35-38' (PhD thesis, Fordham University, 1974), pp. 24, 30, where Gormley suggests a close relationship of this final passion prediction and the passion narratives which begin afterwards. Lk. 22.25-38 is the final speech relating to Jesus' death before his arrest; it may also have features of farewell addresses. See W.S. Kurz, 'Luke 22:14-38 and Greco-Roman and Biblical Farewell Addresses', *JBL* 104 (1985), pp. 251–68 (esp. pp. 262–63, for his comparisons of the passage with other biblical and Greco-Roman farewell speeches).

23. For example, W.R. Farmer, 'The Passion Prediction Passages and the Synoptic Problem: A Test Case', *NTS* 36 (1990), pp. 558–70; Bayer, *Jesus' Predictions of Vindication and Resurrection*, pp. 190–96; Fitzmyer, *Luke*, pp. 777–81, 812–14, 1207–12; Cunningham, *'Through Many Tribulations'*, pp. 80, 88, 116; Nolland, *Luke*, pp. 894–95; Manson, *Luke*, pp.

predictions and this incident in 22.37.[24] The incident in 22.37 not only is Jesus' final prediction about his sufferings; it is also the incident which carries high degrees of discontinuity as discussed above. In fact, the content of 22.37 (with change of continuity) is much related to the three previous predictions (9.22, 44 and 18.31) of Jesus' sufferings; they actually represent a series of Given-New structures within these four incidents of predictions.

Given-New Structures: Lexical Grammatical Approach. The Given-New structures of Jesus' predictions of his suffering are to be studied in two perspectives. The first one is the lexical-grammatical approach; that is, this is studied mainly

107, 116, 207; Creed, *Luke*, pp. 130, 137, 227; Easton, *Luke*, pp. xiv, 148, 274; J.T. Squires, *The Plan of God in Luke-Acts* (SNTSMS, 76; Cambridge: Cambridge University Press, 1993), pp. 140–41; and cf. O'Toole, 'Luke's Message in Luke 9.1-50', pp. 74–89. For scholars who hold slightly different views, see Evans, *Luke*, pp. 406, 424–25, 654–56, at which Evans states there are four passion predictions in Luke, which include Lk. 17.25; Ellis, *Luke*, p. 218, in which Ellis includes four other incidents and that makes the number of total predictions be seven (5.35; 9.22, 44; 12.50; 13.32; 17.25; 18.31-34).

24. C.H. Talbert has observed there are some significant parallelisms between Luke 9 and Luke 22-23 ('The Lukan Presentation of Jesus' Ministry in Galilee', *RevExp* 64 [1967], pp. 492–95; *idem*, *Literary Patterns, Theological Themes, and the Genre of Luke-Acts*, pp. 26–29). Talbert finds that a sequence of events in Luke 9 are either referred to or echoed in Lk. 22-23 (though they are not often in the same order). Although not all of them are convincing (e.g., it may not be very appropriate to make parallelism between 9.23-27 [Jesus says people need to take up their crosses daily if they want to follow him] and 22.28-30 [Jesus mentions the apostles have continued with him in his trials]), most of them offer significant parallelisms: (i) Jesus gives instructions to disciples on how to go preaching without necessity to prepare food and clothes for the journeys in Lk. 9.1-6, these are echoed in 22.35-38; (ii) Herod wants to meet Jesus because of the things he has done (9.7-9), which is echoed in 23.6-16; (iii) Jesus and his disciples are involved in a meal, with an action of breaking and passing the food (9.10-17 and 22.14-20); (iv) Peter makes a confession after the meal (9.20-22 and 22.31-34); (v) Jesus prays on a mountain while the disciples are sleepy beside him, and heavenly visitor(s) appear(s) (9.28-36 and 22.39-46); (vi) Jesus performs a miracle after the mountain scene, there is a sharp contrast drawn between Jesus and his disciples (9.37-43 and 22.47-53); (vii) there is a dispute on the topic of greatness (9.46-48 and 22.24-27); (viii) Jesus' prediction on his suffering and death (9.43-45) and this is echoed in 22.21-23. O'Toole generally agrees with what Talbert has observed (see O'Toole, 'Luke's Message in Luke 9.1-50', pp. 84–87), except he further recognizes the parallelism of the revelations of Jesus' Christological identifications (Jesus is revealed as the Christ of God through Peter's confession [9.20] and Son of God through God's direct revelation [9.35]; these two Christological identifications of Jesus are paralleled in 22.66-71, where Jesus is revealed as Christ [22.67] and Son of God [22.70]), which O'Toole thinks is 'the most important parallel that Luke 9.1-50 has with Luke 22-23' (p. 85). Talbert has observed a parallelism on Jesus' predictions of his suffering and death through the betrayals in 9.44 and 22.21-22; in fact, the number of correspondences is more than this, because the number of the predictions about Jesus' sufferings in Luke 9 is actually two (9.22 and 9.44), and the number of related correspondences in Luke 22 is at least three (22.14, 22 and 37). O'Toole has observed an important parallelism on the revelations of Jesus' Christological identifications; Talbert has observed the correspondence of Jesus' predictions of his sufferings (besides these, cf. Fitzmyer's observation on two similar uses of words in 18.31 and 22.37: 'fulfill' and 'written' [*Luke*, p. 1209]). In fact, there is also an important connection on the topic of revealing identification in the predictions of suffering between Luke 9 and Luke 22, which will be shown below in this chapter of the work.

on the repetitions of lexical items and grammatical matters within the incidents of Jesus' predictions. These are listed as follows:

Table 8.4 *Given-New Structures of Jesus' Predictions of His Sufferings: Lexical-Grammatical Approach*

Sentence	Given	New
(1) Lk. 9.22		New (1)
		9.22 εἰπὼν ὅτι δεῖ τὸν υἱὸν *τοῦ ἀνθρώπου* πολλὰ παθεῖν καὶ ἀποδοκιμασθῆναι ἀπὸ τῶν πρεσβυτέρων καὶ ἀρχιερέων καὶ γραμματέων καὶ ἀποκτανθῆναι καὶ τῇ τρίτῃ ἡμέρᾳ ἐγερθῆναι
(2) Lk. 9.44	Given (2)	New (2)
	9.44a ὁ γὰρ υἱὸς τοῦ ἀνθρώπου	9.44b μέλλει *παραδίδοσθαι* (with Son of Man as subject) εἰς χεῖρας ἀνθρώπων
(3) Lk. 18.31a-33	Given (3)	New (3)
		18.31a καὶ *τελεσθήσεται* πάντα τὰ γεγραμμένα διὰ τῶν προφητῶν τῷ υἱῷ τοῦ ἀνθρώπου
	18.32a *παραδοθήσεται* (with Son of Man as subject)	18.32b γὰρ τοῖς ἔθνεσιν καὶ ἐμπαιχθήσεται καὶ ὑβρισθήσεται καὶ ἐμπτυσθήσεται
		18.33 καὶ μαστιγώσαντες ἀποκτενοῦσιν αὐτόν, καὶ τῇ ἡμέρᾳ τῇ τρίτῃ ἀναστήσεται
(4) Lk. 22.37	Given (4)	New (4)
	22.37a *γεγραμμένον δεῖ τελεσθῆναι*	22.37b λέγω γὰρ ὑμῖν ὅτι τοῦτο τὸ γεγραμμένον δεῖ τελεσθῆναι ἐν ἐμοί, τὸ καὶ μετὰ ἀνόμων ἐλογίσθη· καὶ γὰρ τὸ περὶ ἐμοῦ τέλος ἔχει

The four incidents of Jesus' predictions of his sufferings are abbreviated as sentences (1) to (4) in Table 8.4. From the table, it can be seen that certain elements (the elements in italics are the New units in Table 8.4) from the New unit in each sentence are repeated in its following sentence to form the Given unit (which are also in italics in the table) of that following sentence. This situation consistently happens throughout the four sentences; this finally illustrates the New (4) (Information Focus) in 22.37b.

In sentence (1), this is the first instance of Jesus' prediction about his death, and the content of this prediction solely consists of a New information unit;[25] this is abbreviated as New (1). A lexical item ὁ γὰρ υἱὸς τοῦ ανθρώπου in sentence (2) has already been mentioned in New (1) (τὸν υἱὸν τοῦ ἀνθρώπου); it thus functions as the Given unit in sentence (2), which is then abbreviated as Given (2). The word

25. Although certain items have been mentioned in the Gospel before (such as Son of Man and scribes), these items are still treated as New here, since it is the first time to have them related to Jesus' death and suffering.

παραδοθήσεται is Given (3) in sentence (3), because it has already been mentioned in New (2) (παραδίδοσθαι); both of the two words have Jesus as their subject. Given (4) is γεγραμμένον δεῖ τελεσθῆναι; this lexical-grammatical structure has been mentioned in New (3) (τελεσθήσεται, γεγραμμένα) (both the words in New [3] and Given [4] are in the same tense [future and perfect] and same voice [passive]). This analysis is mainly based on the lexical and grammatical forms in these four sentences. These Given-New linguistic relationships of the four sentences ultimately illustrate the Focus information unit: New (4), which locates at 22.37b (ἐν ἐμοί, τὸ καὶ μετὰ ἀνόμων ἐλογίσθη· καὶ γὰρ τὸ περὶ ἐμοῦ τέλος ἔχει) (this New [4] indicates 'to whom' the OT writing is to be fulfilled-Jesus ['ἐν ἐμοί' and 'ἐμοῦ']). This Focus (New [4]) occurs immediately after the topic discontinuity (22.37 λέγω γὰρ ὑμῖν ὅτι... [as discussed before]) of the second tight-knit conversation. The situation is the same in the first tight-knit conversation in Lk. 22.25-34, where the Information Focus (Peter's future failure [at 22.32 as shown in Table 8.3]) occurs immediately after the topic discontinuity in 22.31 (the change of participant reference from 'you' to 'Simon'). This is important: both of the two Focuses discussed above occur immediately after the two topic discontinuities of the two tight-knit conversations. This is to present a foregrounded message (see below). The Given-New linguistic interrelationships within sentences (1) to (4) are shown as follows:

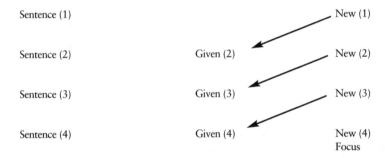

Figure 8.2 *Given-New Linguistic Interrelationships within Sentences (1) to (4)*

Given-New Structures: Functional Approach. This Given-New structure can also be analyzed functionally. This is mainly based on the considerations of the two material processes ('persecution' and 'fulfilment') of the four sentences. Three main elements of the first material process are actor, process and goal; the three main elements in the second material process are goal, process and recipient.[26] As it will be shown below, the main elements of these two processes compose the Given and New units throughout the four sentences.

---

26. Cf. M.A.K. Halliday, 'Notes on Transitivity and Theme in English, Part I', *J Ling* 3 (1967), pp. 37–81 (38–47).

Table 8.5 *Given-New Structures of Jesus' Predictions of His Sufferings: Functional Approach*

Sentence	Given	New
(1)		New (1)
		a) material process (persecution)
		Goal of material process: Son of Man
		b) material process (killing)
		Goal (Son of Man) + material process (killing)
(2)	Given (2)	New (2)
	Goal of material process (persecution): Son of Man	Material process (persecution)
		Revealing Actor of material process (persecution): human beings
(3)	Given (3)	New (3)
	Revealing Actor of material process (persecution)	Actor of material process (persecution): foreign human beings
		Content of material process (persecution): Six material processes: being delivered, mocking, shamefully treating, spitting, scourging, (killing)
		Material process (fulfilment) with goal (writing)
(4)	Given (4)	New (4): Focus
	Material process (fulfilment) with goal (writing)	Content of writing
		Revealing the identity of the recipient of the material process (fulfilment)

The Given-New structure of these four sentences can be analyzed based on their functional structures. Sentences (1) to (3) are Jesus' predictions about his sufferings and death. In fact, Jesus is facing persecution and this causes him many sufferings and finally his death.[27] The persecution which Jesus is going to face is a material process. Together with another material process (fulfillment), this material process and their main components (actor and goal) then form the Given-New functional structures throughout the four sentences. Sentence (1) reports a material process: a persecution.[28] This persecution consists of at least two material processes: rejection and killing. The actor of the 'rejection' process is revealed: religious leaders, but the actor of the 'killing' process is still not made known, and thus the actor of the persecution process is still not fully revealed. The goal of the persecution is clearly the Son of Man, since he is the one who 'is going to suffer many

27. Jesus is being handed over to human beings (9.44), the ones who hand him over are probably the tri-partite group in 9.22 (T.A. Friedrichsen, 'Luke 9.22–A Matthean Foreign Body?', *ETL* 72 [1996], pp. 398–407 (401)). The human beings who receive Jesus are the actors of the persecution process, who perform persecutions on him (e.g. mocking and scourging in 18.32-33).

28. For classifications of material processes, see Halliday, *An Introduction to Functional Grammar*, pp. 109–12; Eggins, *An Introduction to Systemic Functional Linguistics*, pp. 230–35.

things' (9.22a), and he is also the goal of both the 'rejection' and 'killing' processes. All these form part of the New unit in Sentence (1). Sentence (2) reports that the Son of Man is going to be delivered. The goal of this delivery is the Son of Man, who is actually the goal of the persecution process as already described in sentence (1); this forms Given (2), which has been mentioned in the New (1). The recipient of the 'delivery' process is human beings; this reveals the actor of the persecution which the Son of Man is going to face: they are human beings, not supernatural beings, which have not been revealed in Sentence (1); thus revealing the actor of the persecution process forms New (2). In Sentence (3), the actor of the persecution process is further revealed: they are not only human beings, but they are foreign human beings. This revealing of the actor of the persecution process is repeated; this forms Given (3). New (3) consists of a new material process (fulfilment) together with its goal (writing) revealed (all the writing by the prophets about the Son of Man). This process (fulfilment) completed with its goal (writing) is repeated in Sentence (4); this becomes Given (4), which then leads to New (4): revealing the identity of the recipient of the material process (the speaker of the speech: Jesus) as the Focus in these four consequent functional Given-New structures (see below). All these Given units and their corresponding elements in the New units of the four sentences are represented in italics in Table 8.5.

Summary
Given-New structures of the tight-knit conversation in Lk. 22.25-34 illustrate that Jesus' prediction of Peter's future failure (22.32) is the Information Focus. This Information Focus occurs immediately after the topic discontinuity (participant change [from 'you' to 'Simon'] in 22.31) of the tight-knit conversation. Given-New structures based on Jesus' final prediction of his future sufferings and his previous similar predictions are studied in two perspectives: lexical-grammatical and functional. The study of the Given-New structures based on the lexical-grammatical approach illustrates the destination of Jesus' prediction ('to whom' the OT writing is to be fulfilled: Jesus ['ἐμοί' and 'ἐμοῦ']) in 22.37b as the Information Focus. The study of Given-New structures based on the functional approach indicates the similar topic: the Focus is the identity of the material process (fulfilment) being revealed – Jesus. 22.37a has a topic discontinuity (λέγω γὰρ ὑμῖν ὅτι...as discussed before). The Information Focus at 22.37b occurs immediately after the topic discontinuity (λέγω γὰρ ὑμῖν ὅτι) in 22.37a. Both Information Focuses occur immediately after the topic discontinuity in each tight-knit conversation. All these are actually related to the contribution of representing the prominent message which is discussed below.

Less Specific-More Specific Semantic Relationship and the Foregrounded Message in Luke 22.24-38

As stated above, the results of the above analyses are actually related to the foregrounded message presented in Lk. 22.24-28. This prominent message can be analyzed by studying a kind of semantic relationship represented by the elements of the passages studied above (Lk. 22.24-38 and the other three incidents of Jesus' predictions of his sufferings): Less Specific-More Specific.[29] This is shown as follows:

The Tight-knit Conversation in Luke 22.25-34

The topic discontinuity in the first tight-knit conversation has generated a Less Specific-More Specific meaning. The addressee of Jesus' speech starting from 22.25 is originally a group of disciples (general or less specific), it is suddenly switched to Peter (more specific) as the addressee; this particularly named addressee (Simon) is much more specific than the original addressee (a group of disciples).

Jesus' Predictions of His Sufferings

Less-Specific-More Specific meaning is also generated through the four incidents of Jesus' predictions of his future sufferings. This can be considered from the New information units of the Functional analysis of the Given-New structures within the four sentences ([1] to [4]) discussed above. This is shown as below:

Table 8.6 *Less Specific-More Specific Semantic Relationship within Sentences (1) to (4)*

Sentence	Given	New
(1)		Process (persecution)
		Identity of Actor: Less/not Specific (unstated)
		Content of Process: Less Specific (generally stated: πολλὰ παθεῖν)
		Identity of Goal: Less Specific (τὸν υἱὸν τοῦ ἀνθρώπου)
(2)		Process (persecution)
		Identity of Actor: More Specific (εἰς χεῖρας ἀνθρώπων)
(3)		Process (fulfilment)
		Identity of Goal: Less Specific (πάντα τὰ γεγραμμένα)
		Identity of Circumstantial Element of Goal: Less Specific (τῷ υἱῷ τοῦ ἀνθρώπου)
		Identity of Recipient: Less Specific/not known
		Process (persecution)
		Identity of Actor: More Specific (τοῖς ἔθνεσιν)
		Content of Process: More Specific (ἐμπαιχθήσεται καὶ ὑβρισθήσεται καὶ ἐμπτυσθήσεται καὶ μαστιγώσαντες ἀποκτενοῦσιν αὐτόν)
(4)		Process (fulfilment)
		Identity of Goal: More Specific (τοῦτο τὸ γεγραμμένον. καὶ μετὰ ἀνόμων ἐλογίσθη)
		Identity of Circumstantial Element of Goal: More Specific (περὶ ἐμοῦ)
		Identity of Recipient: More Specific (ἐν ἐμοί)
		Process (persecution)
		Identity of Goal: More Specific (speaker of the speech)

29. While defining lexical cohesion, Halliday and Hasan have introduced three main semantic relationships: synonym, near synonym and superordinate (Halliday and Hasan, *Cohesion in English*, pp. 278–79, 285; cf. Halliday, *An Introduction to Functional Grammar*, p. 332; Halliday and Hasan, *Language, Context and Text*, pp. 80–81). Superordinate represents a

The semantic analysis of the consequent Given-New structures in the sentences (1) to (4) builds up a Less Specific-More Specific relationship between the main components of the processes throughout the four sentences: Actor, content, and goal of the process. All these Less Specific-More Specific relationships can be seen in all the four New units. In New (1), the material process is the persecution; the identity of the Goal is revealed as Son of Man, the content of the process is shown as 'suffering many things' and 'being rejected' and 'being killed', where the actor of the process is kept unknown.[30] In New (2), the identity of the actor of the persecution process has been revealed: human beings. The Son of Man is going to be delivered into men's hands. 'Human beings' is the one who is going to give Jesus many sufferings; here the actor 'human beings' of the material process (persecution) is more specific than the one in New (1) (which has not revealed who is the actor at all). In New (3), two processes are concerned: the 'persecution' process and the 'fulfilment' process. Sentence (3) tells the Son of Man is going to be delivered into foreigners' hands; this reveals the identity of the actor in the 'persecution' process and it becomes more specific than the one in New (2): not only are they human beings, but they are Gentiles. The content of the process is also revealed and it becomes more specific than the one in New (1). New (1) says the Son of Man is going to suffer 'many things'. New (3) makes it much more specific: the Son of Man is going to be mocked, shamefully treated and spit upon, scourged and killed. New (3) also portrays a new material process: 'fulfilment'. The goal of the process is revealed: all the writings by the prophets about the Son of Man.[31] The recipient

hyponymous relationship: specific and general (e.g. chair and furniture, boy and child, apple and fruit) (cf. R.A. Hudson, 'Constituency in a Systemic Description of the English Clause', in M.A.K. Halliday and J.R. Martin [eds.], *Readings in Systemic Linguistics* [London: Batsford Academic and Educational Ltd., 1981], pp. 103–21 (114–17) for his classification of 'specified' and 'unspecified'; and M.A.K. Halliday, *Explorations in the Functions of Language* [London: Edward Arnold, 1973], pp. 27–32 for 'general' and 'specific'; also Kress [ed.], *Halliday*, pp. 86–87; and Thomas and Hawes, *Theme in Academic and Media Discourse*, pp. 61–63 for 'General' and 'Particular'; also cf. Grimes, *The Thread of Discourse*, pp. 212–13). This general-specific semantic relationship is adopted and modified as less specific-more specific here, which is more applicable to the discussion below.

30.   Although it is known who reject the Son of Man, it is still not revealed who causes Jesus to suffer (since the Son of Man is supposed to 'suffer many things'); the identity of the one who is going to kill him is also not revealed.

31.   The writing τῷ υἱῷ τοῦ ἀνθρώπου is linked to πάντα τὰ γεγραμμένα rather than τελεσθήσεται (a majority of the major commentaries support this view; e.g. Marshall, *Gospel of Luke*, p. 690; Plummer, *Luke*, p. 428; Nolland, *Luke*, p. 895; Bock, *Luke*, p. 1496; Evans, *Luke*, p. 654; for different view, cf. Fitzmyer, *Luke*, p. 1029), thus it functions as a circumstantial element of the nominal group πάντα τὰ γεγραμμένα (all the writings *about*...), rather than as a recipient of the 'fulfilment' process. A majority of different Bible translations consider the phrase 'Son of Man' to be linked to the nominal group 'all the writings'. For example, KJV: 'everything that is written of the Son of Man by the prophets will be accomplished'; RSV: 'everything that is written of the Son of Man by the prophets will be accomplished'; NRSV: 'everything that is written about the Son of Man by the prophets will be accomplished'; NKJV: 'all things that are written by the prophets concerning the Son of Man will be accomplished'; TEV: 'everything the prophets

of the process has not been stated, thus the recipient of the process can be classified as 'unknown' or 'less specific' (since the identity of the recipient is not stated, it *may* imply that it is the Son of Man, because the writings are *about* the Son of Man). In New (4), the goal of the 'fulfilment' process is stated to be more specific; this time it is not a general term or a collective term (all the writings) as stated in New (3), but it is a much more specific item: a particular Old Testament writing is quoted (καὶ μετὰ ἀνόμων ἐλογίσθη).[32] The identity of the circumstantial element of the nominal group also becomes more specific: περὶ ἐμοῦ; this clearly states the identity: 'me', who is the speaker of the speech: Jesus. This is more specific than the one given in New (3) (Son of Man).[33] The recipient of the process is also stated to be much more specific than the one in New (3); this time it is clearly stated by using the phrase ἐν ἐμοί, which clearly indicates the recipient of the process is the speaker: Jesus. New (4) is the Focus of the consequent Given-New structures in the four sentences – it reveals the identity of the recipient of the 'fulfilment' process to be more specific (ἐν ἐμοί), it reveals the identity of the circumstantial element of the goal to be more specific (περὶ ἐμοῦ),[34] and it thus reveals the identity of the goal of the 'persecution' process to be more specific (the speaker: Jesus).

In summary, all the three main basic components of the two types of material process (actor, process and goal) demonstrate the Less Specific-More Specific semantic relationship within the above four sentences: they all become more and more specific all the way from sentence (1) to sentence (2), (3), then (4) (the Focus). The identity of the actor is originally not mentioned in New (1), but it is then made more specific and clearer in New (2) (human beings), and it is then made further specific in New (3) (Gentiles). The content of the process is originally stated as 'suffering many things' in New (1); it is then made much more specific (being

---

wrote about the Son of Man will come true'. The translations which hold the opposite view include NEB: 'all that was written by the prophets will come true for the Son of Man'; REB: 'Everything that was written by the prophets will find its fulfilment in the Son of Man'; ASV: 'all the things that are written through the prophets shall be accomplished unto the Son of Man'.

32.   This quotation in fact relates Jesus to his sufferings, or the persecution which he is going to face: he is going to be treated as a transgressor (Evans, *Luke*, p. 807), to be located among transgressors (cf. Lk. 23.33; Matera, *Passion Narratives and Gospel Theologies*, p. 166; and Fitzmyer, *Luke*, p. 1433), and to be mocked, scourged and killed.

33.   Although it is a common practice for Jesus to use a more generic term ('Son of Man') to refer to himself, it is much more specific here where Jesus directly refers to himself by using the word 'me' (which clearly states the speaker [Jesus] is exactly the one who is being referred to). Cf. Martin's classification of 'Generic Reference' and 'Specific Reference' in participant identification (*English Text*, pp. 103–11).

34.   The clause τὸ περὶ ἐμοῦ τέλος ἔχει indicates the fulfilment of Jesus' destined role; see G.W.H. Lampe, 'The Two Swords (Luke 22:35-38)', in Bammel and Moule (eds.), *Jesus and the Politics of His Day*, pp. 339, 350; the significance of this clause is marked by its word order (this is in SCP order; the number of SCP in independent clauses is 37x; while the number of SPC and PSC is 147x and 49x respectively) with an imperfective aspect ἔχει (cf. P.S. Minear, 'A Note on Luke xxii 36', *NovT* 7 [1964–65], pp. 128–34 (131), where Minear gives no explanation but strangely states the present tense is unusual: 'First is the worthy and unusual present tense in τέλος ἔχει').

delivered, mocked, shamefully treated, spit upon, scourged and killed) in New (3). The identity of the goal is originally stated as 'the Son of Man' in New (1) and (2); this is finally made more specific (me: the speaker of the speech, who is Jesus).[35] The situation in the other material process (fulfilment) is also the same. The identity of the goal becomes more specific from New (3) ('all the writings') to New (4) (the quotation of an OT writing); the recipient of the process also becomes more specific from New (3) (not stated) to New (4) (me: the speaker Jesus); and the identity of the circumstantial element of the goal also becomes more specific from New (3) (*about* the Son of Man) to New (4) (*about* me: the speaker Jesus). All these contribute to the Focus of the series of the Given-New Structures mentioned above,[36] which is the prominent message: Jesus is the one who is going to face the persecution and face the death. This is illustrated together with the other Focus in the first tight-knit conversation: Simon. Simon Peter is the one being specified (from less specific to more specific: from a general term 'you' to a much more specified participant 'Simon' [22.31]; from a general term 'you [ὑμᾶς-plural form]' to a much more specified term 'you [σοῦ-singular form]' [22.32]): he is the one who is predicted for his future failure; this occurs at the instance of the first topic discontinuity (22.31). Jesus is the other one being specified at the other Focus (also from less specific to more specific) at the other topic discontinuity: he is the one who is predicted for his future sufferings. Both of these two Focuses are obtained from a series of Given-New structures; they both occur at the point of topic discontinuity; they both have their participant (one is Peter; one is Jesus) being specified through the Less Specific-More Specific semantic

---

35. In fact, this is the first time that Jesus directly refers to himself as the object of the persecution. In all the previous instances that Jesus predicts his death, he uses a more generic term 'Son of Man' (a third person nominal group) to refer to himself more indirectly (cf. M. Casey, 'The Jackals and the Son of Man [Matt. 8.20 // Luke 9.58]', *JSNT* 23 [1985], pp. 3–22 (4–6); R. Bauckham, 'The Son of Man: "A Man in my Position" or "Someone"', *JSNT* 23 [1985], pp. 23–33 (27); C. Colpe, 'ὁ υἱὸς τοῦ ἀνθρώπου', *TDNT*, VIII, pp. 400–77 (401); for debates on the topic, see I.H. Marshall, 'Son of Man', in J.B. Green and S. McKnight [eds.], *Dictionary of Jesus and the Gospels* [Illinois: InterVaristy Press, 1992], pp. 775–81 (778–80); M. Casey, 'General, Generic and Indefinite: The Use of the Term "Son of Man" in Aramaic Sources and in the Teaching of Jesus', *JSNT* 29 [1987], pp. 21–56; B. Lindars, 'Response to Richard Bauckham: The Idiomatic Use of Bar Enasha', *JSNT* 23 [1985], pp. 35–41; *idem, Jesus Son of Man: A Fresh Examination of the Son of Man Sayings in the Gospels in the Light of Recent Research* [London: SPCK, 1983]; J.R. Donahue, 'Recent Studies on the Origin of "Son of Man" in the Gospels', *CBQ* 48 [1986], pp. 484–98; and cf. Smith, 'No Place for a Son of Man', pp. 93–96). Lk. 22.37 is the first time for Jesus to use a first person pronoun (I, me) to refer to himself as the object of the persecution; this is also the only occasion of Jesus to use such a first person pronoun (I, me) to refer to his suffering before his death.

36. This information focus, formed by a New element, functions as foregrounding information (Given material provides background information, where New material provides foreground information [M.A.K. Halliday and J.R. Martin, *Writing Science: Literary and Discursive Power* (London: Palmer Press, 1993), p. 64]), and the focusing device gives prominence (J. Taglicht, *Message and Emphasis: On Focus and Scope in English* [ELS, 15; London: Longman, 1984], p. 7).

relationship. This leads to the foregrounded message: Jesus is the one who is going to suffer; while Peter is the one who is going to fail. Peter's failure is being contrasted with Jesus: Peter is going to fail and lose his faith; while Jesus is bravely facing the persecution which is coming to him.

Significant Word Order in Luke 22.37

The foregrounded message discussed above (Peter's failure and Jesus' future sufferings) is re-enforced by another linguistic phenomenon: a marked word order pattern in Lk. 22.37. This marked word order pattern occurs at where the Focus and the topic discontinuity of the second tight-knit conversation locate.

Luke 22.37 introduces the content of Jesus' speech (τοῦτο τὸ γεγραμμένον δεῖ τελεσθῆναι ἐν ἐμοί, τὸ καὶ μετὰ ἀνόμων ἐλογίσθη). This is a clause with an infinitival clause functioning as the subject of the main clause, where the verb δεῖ functions as the predicate of the main clause. This embedded infinitival clause has its subject (τοῦτο τὸ γεγραμμένον) preceding the predicate (τελεσθῆναι), which is in the passive voice; the predicate (δεῖ) of the main clause is located between the subject (τοῦτο τὸ γεγραμμένον) and the predicate (τελεσθῆναι) of the infinitival clause.[37]

---

37.   The structure of the embedded infinitival clause can be abbreviated as SP(passive)AS, or S δεῖ P(passive)AS. When an infinitival clause functions as a subject, complement or circumstantial adjunct in a main clause, the usual pattern is to have the components of the infinitival clause grouped as one unit, but it is a common pattern to have the infinitival clause being interrupted by the predicate of the main clause when it is δεῖ or ἔδει; this is not only true in Luke (the instances of δεῖ or ἔδει used with an infinitival clause in Luke are 2.49 A δεῖ PS; 4.43 APS δεῖ C; 9.22 δεῖ SCP, P[passive]A, P[passive], AP[passive]; 11.42 C ἔδει P, CP; 12.12 C δεῖ P; 13.14 A δεῖ P, 16 S ἔδει P[passive]AA, 33 δεῖ SAP; 15.32 PP ἔδει; 17.25 δεῖ SCP, P[passive]A; 19.5 AA δεῖ SP; 21.9 δεῖ SPA; 22.7 A ἔδει P[passive]S, 37 S δεῖ P[passive]AS; 24.7 S ὅτι δεῖ P[passive]A, P[passive], AP, 26 C ἔδει PS, PA, 44 δεῖ P[passive]S; in these 17 instances there are only five which have a grouped or non-interrupted infinitival clause [9.22; 13.33; 17.25; 21.9; 24.44]; while the rest are all with an interrupted infinitival clause [three of them have a relative pronoun placed before δεῖ or ἔδει due to the tendency of a relative pronoun to appear at the front of a clause: 12.12; 13.14 and 22.7]), but it is also true in the other NT writings (the instances of δεῖ or ἔδει used with an infinitival clause in other NT books are Mt. 16.21 ὅτι δεῖ SAP, CPA, P[passive], AP[passive]; 17.10 ὅτι S δεῖ PA; 18.33 C ἔδει PS, PA; 23.23 C ἔδει P, CP; 24.6 δεῖ P; 25.27 ἔδει SPCC; 26.54 ὅτι A δεῖ P; Mk 8.31 ὅτι δεῖ SAP, P[passive]A, P[passive], AP; 9.11 ὅτι S δεῖ PA; 13.7 δεῖ P, 10 AA δεῖ PS; Jn 3.7 δεῖ SP[passive]A, 14 AP[passive] δεῖ S, 30 S δεῖ P; 4.4 ἔδει SPA, 20 AP δεῖ, 24 SA δεῖ P; 9.4 S δεῖ PC; 10.16 C δεῖ SP; 12.34 ὅτι δεῖ P[passive]S; 20.9 ὅτι δεῖ SAP; Acts 1.6 ἔδει P[passive]S; 3.21 C δεῖ SP; 4.12 A δεῖ P[passive]S; 5.29 P δεῖ C; 9.6 CS δεῖ P, 16 C δεῖ SAP; 14.22 ὅτι A δεῖ SPA; 15.5 ὅτι δεῖ P[passive]S, PC; 16.30 C δεῖ P; 17.3 ὅτι S ἔδει P, PA; 19.21 δεῖ SCP; 20.35 δεῖ PC; 23.11 S δεῖ AP; 24.19 S ἔδει AP, P; 25.10 AS δεῖ P; 27.24 AS δεῖ P, 26 A δεῖ SP; Rom. 12.3 C δεῖ P; 1 Cor. 8.2 δεῖ P; 11.9 δεῖ SAP; 15.25 δεῖ SP, 53 δεῖ SPC; 2 Cor. 2.3 A ἔδει SP; 5.10 SP δεῖ A; 11.30 P δεῖ; 12.1 P δεῖ; Eph. 6.20 δεῖ SP; Col. 4.4 δεῖ SP, 6 δεῖ SCP; 1 Thess. 4.1 δεῖ SP, PC; 2 Thess. 3.7 δεῖ PS; 1 Tim. 3.2 δεῖ SCP, 7 δεῖ CPA, 15 δεῖ AP; 2 Tim. 2.6 S δεῖ CP, 24 S δεῖ P; Tit. 1.7 δεῖ SCP, 11 C δεῖ P; Heb. 2.1 δεῖ APSA; 9.26 ἔδει SAPA; 11.6 P δεῖ SC; 2 Pet. 3.11 δεῖ PSA; Rev. 1.1 S δεῖ PA; 4.1 S δεῖ PA; 10.11 δεῖ SPA; 11.5 A δεῖ SP[passive]; 17.10 AS δεῖ P; 20.3 δεῖ P[passive]SA; 22.6 S δεῖ PA; 39 of these 71 incidents have interrupted infinitival clauses (components of the infinitival clauses are not grouped as a single unit), where 13 of

This infinitival clause comes with a passive predicate, which is located after its subject. In the infinitival clauses which contain subject and predicate, the number having the subject located before the predicate is 21x, in which 5x (12.50; 13.16, 33; 22.37; 24.7) are with passive predicate; there are also 21 instances of having the predicate located before the subject, in which 7x (2.21; 6.48; 9.7; 12.39; 16.22; 21.22; 22.7) are with passive predicate. What is significant here is a repetition of the subject (τὸ καὶ μετὰ ἀνόμων ἐλογίσθη) located after the phrase ἐν ἐμοί, which states the content of the subject τοῦτο τὸ γεγραμμένον; this is the only incident of an infinitival clause having a 'repeated' subject.[38] Moreover, when all these five incidents (subject of an infinitival clause precedes its passive predicate) are examined, it is interesting to find that all five incidents carry significant meaning, and three of them are the instances regarding Jesus' prediction of his sufferings.[39]

---

them have relative pronouns placed before δεῖ or ἔδει). For the Lukan use of δεῖ, see Coleridge, *The Birth of the Lukan Narrative*, p. 205 n. 1; Martín-Asensio, *Transitivity-based Foregrounding in the Acts of the Apostles*, pp. 76–77; and cf. Cunningham, 'Through Many Tribulations', pp. 82–83; C.H. Cosgrove, 'The Divine ΔΕΙ in Luke-Acts: Investigations into the Lukan Understanding of God's Providence', *NovT* 26 (1984), pp. 168–90, esp. pp. 169–72 for other studies related to the topic.

38. The significance of the infinitival clause at 22.37 can be seen by the double appearance of its subject (τοῦτο τὸ γεγραμμένον and τὸ καὶ μετὰ ἀνόμων ἐλογίσθη). In the entire Gospel, subject does not occur in embeddded infinitival clauses frequently (the majority of embedded infinitival clauses only consist of predicate, complement and adjunct [the total number of embedded infinitival clauses is 290, where only 42 come with their subjects; the rest are mainly different combinations of P, C and A]). Here the infinitival clause at 22.37 significantly has its subject appeared twice, and this is the only such example in the entire Gospel.

39. All five incidents carry significant meaning, which is very different from the seven instances which have the subject of an infinitival clause located after its passive predicate. Three (13.33; 22.37; 24.7) of the five incidents significantly describe Jesus' prediction of his sufferings (all these three are used with δεῖ); this may be best represented by the one in 24.7 (λέγω τὸν υἱὸν τοῦ ἀνθρώπου ὅτι δεῖ παραδοθῆναι εἰς χεῖρας ἀνθρώπων ἁμαρτωλῶν καὶ σταυρωθῆναι καὶ τῇ τρίτῃ ἡμέρᾳ ἀναστῆναι). 24.7 comes with an embedded infinitival clause which functions as a complement of the predicate (λέγων) of an embedded participial clause; the projected content of the verbal process is introduced by the word ὅτι. At this verse the subject (τὸν υἱὸν τοῦ ἀνθρώπου) of the infinitival clause not only precedes the word δεῖ, but also the word ὅτι; in fact, this is the only example among other similar instances in the NT where an element of an infinitival clause precedes the marker ὅτι which belongs to a preceding clause: all the other ten occurrences in the NT have δεῖ and all other elements of the infinitival clause placed after the word ὅτι (Mt. 16.21 ὅτι δεῖ SAP, CPA, P, AP; 17.10 ὅτι S δεῖ PA; 26.54 ὅτι A δεῖ P; Mk 8.31 ὅτι δεῖ SCP, PA, P, AP; 9.11 ὅτι S δεῖ PA; Jn 12.34 ὅτι δεῖ), P[passive]S ; 20.9 ὅτι δεῖ SAP ; Acts 14.22 ὅτι A δεῖ SPA; 15.5 ὅτι δεῖ P[passive]S, PC; 17.3 ὅτι S δεῖ P, PA). 24.7 is an instance to express the semantic weight: the necessity of the Son of Man to suffer (the other incidents include 12.50 βάπτισμα δὲ ἔχω βαπτισθῆναι, which is used with other marked word order patterns to express the foregrounded message as stated in Chapter 5 of this work; and the one in 13.16 [ταύτην δὲ θυγατέρα ᾿Αβραὰμ οὖσαν, ἣν ἔδησεν ὁ Σατανᾶς ἰδοὺ δέκα καὶ ὀκτὼ ἔτη, οὐκ ἔδει λυθῆναι ἀπὸ τοῦ δεσμοῦ τούτου τῇ ἡμέρᾳ τοῦ σαββάτου], where the subject [ταύτην δὲ θυγατέρα] of the infinitival clause precedes the passive predicate [it even precedes its preceding entire clause] to emphasize the woman: who is the one being healed by Jesus on the Sabbath; and the one in 22.37, which carries a prominent message as described above).

22.37 has an infinitival clause with its subject (τοῦτο τὸ γεγραμμένον) preceding its passive predicate (τελεσθῆναι). This infinitival clause has a repeated subject (τὸ καὶ μετὰ ἀνόμων ἐλογίσθη) stating the content of the 'writing' and it carries significant meaning with the prominent message which has been discussed above: Jesus is the one to suffer, which comes with the other message: Peter is the one to fail.[40]

Conclusion

Two topic discontinuities have been tackled in the tight-knit conversations in Lk. 22.24-38: the participant change of Peter and Jesus' speech in 22.37. Given-New structures have been studied within the first tight-knit conversation (22.25-34) and a series of Jesus' predictions of his sufferings. The analysis of the Given-New structures based on the concept of Less Specific and More Specific indicates the foregrounded message as Focus: Jesus is the one specified to face future sufferings; while Peter is the one specified for his future failure.

---

40. Peter's future failure can actually be much foreseen by the dispute in which he has involved; in fact, marked order is employed to highlight the dispute of the disciples. Lk. 22.24 (ἐγένετο δὲ καὶ φιλονεικία ἐν αὐτοῖς, τὸ τίς αὐτῶν δοκεῖ εἶναι μείζων) is in the order of PSAS. A very similar writing in 9.46 (εἰσῆλθεν δὲ διαλογισμὸς ἐν αὐτοῖς, τὸ τίς ἂν εἴη μείζων αὐτῶν) suggests φιλονεικία is the subject of ἐγένετο δέ in 22.24, rather than ἐγένετο δέ is the first clause and καὶ φιλονεικία ἐν αὐτοῖς is a copula clause with an ellipsis of its verb. The content of the subject (φιλονεικία) is then repeated in the following clause. This is not a very common pattern in Luke as there are only a total of four similar instances with a repeated subject stating its content (PSAS: 9.46; 22.24 and 23.38; ACSS: 1.43). The writing of ἐγένετο δέ occurs frequently in Luke; many times it is followed by an infinitival clause beginning with ἐν τῷ, which functions dependently (with logical semantic temporal meaning) to the clause which follows immediately (1.8; 2.6; 3.21; 5.1; 6.1; 6.6; 9.51; 11.27; 18.35). When the word ἐγένετο comes without δέ, usually it functions as the predicate of the subject which follows it (1.5, 44, 65; 2.2, 13; 3.2; 4.25, 36; 6.13, 49; 8.24; 9.34; 11.30; 15.14; 22.14, 44, 66) (or a few times the subject precedes ἐγένετο [6.16; 9.35; 10.21; 19.9; 23.44]). Here φιλονεικία functions as the subject of ἐγένετο with a δέ is a very unusual pattern; this is used to emphasize the content of the dispute among the disciples, which is indicated by the neuter article τό (τὸ τίς αὐτῶν δοκεῖ εἶναι μείζων) (besides the most common usage of τό as an article of a neuter noun, and an article of an articular infinitive construction [2.4; 5.17; 6.48; 8.6; 9.7; 11.8; 12.5; 18.1, 5; 19.11; 22.20; 23.8], τό is also used a few times to introduce the content of a projected speech: 1.62 τὸ τί ἂν θέλοι καλεῖσθαι αὐτό [this is actually the content of a non-verbal projection]; 22.4 τὸ πῶς αὐτοῖς παραδῷ αὐτόν; 22.23 τὸ τίς ἄρα εἴη ἐξ αὐτῶν ὁ τοῦτο μέλλων πράσσειν; the complement of a predicate: 22.2 τὸ πῶς ἀνέλωσιν αὐτόν; the content of a subject: 9.46 τὸ τίς ἂν εἴη μείζων αὐτῶν; 22.24 τὸ τίς αὐτῶν δοκεῖ εἶναι μείζων and 22.37 τὸ καὶ μετὰ ἀνόμων ἐλογίσθη).

CONCLUSION

This work has tried to study the topic through three different parts. Part I consists of surveying the recent studies in the area of word order studies and the methodological consideration of the present work. In surveying the recent works of the topic, Chapter 1 has tried to cover both the recent works in linguistic studies and the works in Classical and NT Greek. In the area of linguistic studies, authors have not only tried to explain word order universals implicationally, but also attempted to explain the causes behind the word order universals. Authors such as Greenberg, Lehmann, Vennemann and Hawkins have contributed much to the area and their works have stimulated many others' works in the area. A great number of scholars have tried to tackle Classical Greek word order. Many of their works devoted to the area are based on grammatical/syntactical approach or pragmatic approach; besides word order patterns, determinants which affect the Greek word order are also considered by scholars. A similar figure occurs in the studies of NT Greek word order. Works approach the matter either syntactically or pragmatically. Some of the works provide interaction with the results of modern linguistics on word order universals and try to propose explanations on word order patterns. Chapter 2 explains the methodological consideration of the present study. This work mainly classifies constituents of a clause functionally (subject, predicate, complement and adjunct) and studies their relative position. This study has classified all clauses of the Gospel of Luke into five main types (independent clauses, dependent clauses, infinitival clauses, participial clauses and embedded clauses) and the result of the study is presented in Part II.

Part II consists of Chapter 3 and 4. Chapter 3 gives figures of all the relative positions between three main constituents (subject, predicate and complement) in different categories: independent clauses, dependent clauses, infinitival clauses, participial clauses and embedded clauses. Chapter 4 particularly pays attention to the positions of different types of circumstantial adjuncts and their relative predicates. This is the first attempt to work on the topic with the inclusion of circumstantial adjuncts; it is also the first to put different tense forms of predicate into consideration. The result of the analyses in these two chapters gives figures of some unmarked orders and some usual syntactic and grammatical features associated with them in different types of Lukan clauses. These unmarked word order patterns provide a platform for studying marked word order patterns which are concerned in Part III of the work.

Part III has studied some marked word orders and the prominent messages associated with them. This part consists of four chapters. Through a series of indirect speech with imperfective aspect, a semantic chain of the disciples' failure in understanding of Jesus is formed in the study in Chapter 5. The components of this semantic chain and its surrounding related passages are packed with marked word order patterns to develop a foregrounded message: the disciples' failure in understanding of Jesus; this message is then further re-enforced by a series of Jesus' confrontations with his disciples which are also packed with marked word order patterns. This chapter illustrates the weakness of the disciples in the Gospel: their failure in understanding Jesus, which is always a topic of discussion in the Gospel of Mark,[1] but not in the third Gospel.[2]

1.   For example, J.B. Tyson, 'Blindness of the Disciples in Mark', *JBL* 80 (1961), pp. 261–68; D.J. Hawkin, 'Incomprehension of the Disciples in the Markan Redaction', *JBL* 91 (1972), pp. 491–500; W.H. Kelber, 'The Hour of the Son of Man and the Temptation of the Disciples (Mark 14:32-42)', in *idem* (ed.), *The Passion in Mark: Studies on Mark 14-16* (Philadelphia: Fortress Press, 1976), pp. 41–60, esp. pp. 47–56; E. Best, 'The Role of the Disciples in Mark', *NTS* 23 (1977), pp. 377–401; *idem, Disciples and Discipleship: Studies in the Gospel According to Mark* (Edinburgh: T&T Clark, 1986), pp. 98–130 (and cf. pp. 162–96); E.S. Johnson, 'Mark 10:46-52: Blind Bartimaeus', *CBQ* 40 (1978), pp. 191–204, esp. pp. 198ff.; *idem*, 'Mark VIII. 22-26: The Blind Man from Bethsaida', *NTS* 25 (1979), pp. 370–83, esp. pp. 374–75 and 379–83; N. Onwu, 'The Distorted Vision: Reinterpretation of Mark 8:22-26 in the Context of Social Justice', *WAR* 19 (1980), pp. 46–52; J.B. Gibson, 'The Rebuke of the Disciples in Mark 8.14-21', *JSNT* 27 (1986), pp. 31–47; F.J. Matera, 'The Incomprehension of the Disciples and Peter's Confession (Mark 6,14-8,30)', *Bib* 70 (1989), pp. 153–72; J.D. Kingsbury, *Conflict in Mark: Jesus, Authorities, Disciples* (Minneapolis: Fortress Press, 1989), pp. 89–103; M.R. Thompson, *The Role of Disbelief in Mark: A New Approach to the Second Gospel* (New York: Paulist Press, 1989), pp. 105–119.
    There are also numerous works which may not be directly focusing on the topic of the disciples' weaknesses and failures in Mark, but parts of their materials are very much related to the topic. For example, R.C. Tannehill, 'Disciples in Mark: The Function of a Narrative Role', *JR* 57 (1977), pp. 386–405; E. Best, 'Peter in the Gospel According to Mark', *CBQ* 40 (1978), pp. 547–58; S. Freyne, 'The Disciples in Mark and the *Maskilim* in Daniel', *JSNT* 16 (1982), pp. 7–23 (17–19); E.S. Malbon, 'Fallible Followers: Women and Men in the Gospel of Mark', *Semeia* 28 (1983), pp. 29–48, esp. pp. 31–32; *idem*, 'Disciples/Crowds/Whoever: Markan Characters and Readers', *NovT* 28 (1986), pp. 104–30, esp. pp. 114ff. (cf. *idem*, 'Text and Contexts: Interpreting the Disciples in Mark', *Semeia* 62 [1993], pp. 81–102 (87–88, 92–93)); A.T. Lincoln, 'The Promise and the Failure: Mark 16:7, 8', *JBL* 108 (1989), pp. 283–300, esp. pp. 294–95; C.D. Marshall, *Faith as a Theme in Mark's Narrative* (SNTSMS, 64; Cambridge: Cambridge University Press, 1989), pp. 208–24; B.M.F. Van Iersel, 'Failed Followers in Mark: Mark 13:12 as a Key for the Identification of the Intended Readers', *CBQ* 58 (1996), pp. 244–63, esp. pp. 248ff.; P. Danove, 'The Narrative Rhetoric of Mark's Ambiguous Characterization of the Disciples', *JSNT* 70 (1998), pp. 21–38 (28–36); J. M. Gundry-Volf, 'Between Text and Sermon: Mark 9:33-37', *Int* 53 (1999), pp. 57–61; T. Wiarda, 'Peter as Peter in the Gospel of Mark', *NTS* 45 (1999), pp. 19–37 (32–33).
    2.   The weakness of the disciples in Luke has not drawn scholars' attention; instead, some scholars would think Luke has positively portrayed the disciples in the Gospel; e.g., some of the negative portrayals in Mark are missed in Luke (e.g., the disciples' abandonment of Jesus in Mk 14.50, the rebuke of Peter as 'Satan' in Mk 8.33 and Jesus' prediction of the apostles' loss of faith and their scattering in Mk 14.27). There are certain events where the disciples are described positively in Luke, e.g., they are described as having remained with Jesus throughout his suffering (Lk. 22.28), and Peter's denial of Jesus during his arrest is described as Satan's work (22.31). Besides all these, the use of the word φιλονεικία in the disciples' dispute on greatness before Jesus'

Chapter 6 has concentrated its studies in the marked C(J)P clause type and the related cohesion chains in Lk. 23.1-25. There are three types of C(J)P in the Gospel: RSC(J)P, WSC(J)P and REJC(J)P. A study of Given-New structure illustrates that the first instance of REJC(J)P is marked with prominence and carries Information Focus. This Information Focus leads to the significance of Pilate's action of handing over Jesus. There are interactions between the chains of WSC(J)P and REJC(J)P, where Pilate has switched his attitude toward Jesus at the central token. Pilate's crime of handing over an innocent man is further re-enforced by a marked word order pattern in 23.25. This marked word order is used with the interactions of the C(J)P chains to highlight a prominent message about the degree of the seriousness of Pilate's crime that he has committed.

Six temporal clause complexes in Luke 2 are studied in Chapter 7. A study of Theme-Rheme structure in these six instances of clause complexes demonstrates that there are two types of thematic development: theme re-iteration and zig-zag thematic progression. These theme progressions illustrate a foregrounded message: Jesus' parents' failure of understanding Jesus. This foregrounded message is also brought out along with a sequence of marked orders and patterns, and the contrasts and prominence represented by the intratextuality of two passages (2.8-20 and 2.43-52). All these in Luke 2 represent one message that Luke wants to highlight: the failure of Jesus' parents—their failure of understanding Jesus' mission and God's planned salvation.

The analysis about the Topic Continuity and Given-New structures in the final chapter demonstrates a foregrounded message in Luke 22: Jesus is the one who is bravely going to face his sufferings; while Peter is the one who is going to fail in his faith. It is found that there is a topic discontinuity in each of the two tight-knit conversations in Lk. 24-38. Through a series of studying Given-New structure in Lk. 22.24-38 and other related passages in the Gospel, it is demonstrated that there is an Information Focus following each of the two cases of topic disconti-nuity. This is to bring out a foregrounded message with a significant word order in Lk. 22.37: Jesus is the one specified to face future sufferings; while Peter is the one specified for his future failure.

---

arrest in Lk. 22 has also been argued as carrying a neutral sense—which can be considered not as a morally unacceptable event, but as a more or less neutral exercise in the society (see F. Field, *Notes on the Translation of New Testament* [Cambridge: Cambridge University Press, 1899], pp. 75–76); cf. S. Brown, *Apostasy and Perseverance in the Theology of Luke*, pp. 62–74, where the perseverance of the apostles described in Lk. 22.28 is highly praised, and Peter's denial is not counted as a failure of faith; J.H. Neyrey, *The Passion According to Luke: A Redaction Study of Luke's Soteriology* (New York: Paulist Press, 1985), pp. 29–33; Tannehill, *The Narrative Unity of Luke-Acts*, pp. 262-63, where Tannehill admits on the whole the portrayal of the disciples in Luke is less negative than the one in Mark, except in the case of the passion narrative ('the portrait of the apostles in the passion narrative remains essentially negative, and Luke even has additional material which emphasizes the apostles' failure' [p. 262]; and cf. Onwu's words: 'Perhaps, we might add, it is because Mark relates the periscope [Mk 8.22-26] so closely to his presentation of the blindness of the disciples, a theme which Matthew and Luke did not develop' ('The Distorted Vision, p. 47).

This work has illustrated the word order of the Gospel with substantial data, and has analyzed the foregrounded messages associated with marked word order patterns in the Gospel.

Appendix

DISTRIBUTION OF THE WORD ORDERS IN LUKAN CLAUSES

This appendix represents the numeric data of the word order of Luke. This is done according to the different types of clause in the Gospel: independent clause, dependent clause, infinitival clause, participial clause, embedded clause and dependent clause of embedded clause. The distribution will be represented in two formats: the one including all clauses, and the one excluding the incidents of the verb εἰμί and οἶδα, the perfect passive form of γράφω and the citations of LXX.

Distribution of the Word Orders of Luke: Independent Clauses

	p	imf	f	a	pf	ppf	total
p	54	8	17	93			172
pa	21	19	12	71	1		124
paa	4	6	5	11			26
paaa		4	1	2			7
ap	19	2	10	28			59
apa	4	2	5	21			32
apaa	4	2		6			12
apaaa		1					1
aap	3	2		3			8
aapa			1	1			2
aapaa				1			1
aaapa				1			1
ps	15	15	5	25	11		71
psa	4	11	9	21			45
psas		1		2			3
psaa	2	5		6	2		15
psaaa		1		3			4
pas		1	3	7	1		12
pasa		2		1			3
paas				1			1
aps	4	1	4	1			10
apsa		1	2	6			9
apsaa				1			1
apsaaa				1			1
pc	87	35	33	140	9	2	306
pcc	51	16	11	89			167
pccc				3			3
pca	9	17	7	46			79
pcca				2	1		3

pcac			1				1
pcaa	1			7			8
pccaa		2					2
pcaaa				2	1		3
pcaaaa			1				1
pccacaaaa				1			1
pac	2	1	5	12			20
paca		1					1
apc	19	10	13	37	1	1	81
apcc	2	4	2	22			30
apccc				1			1
apca	6	1		15			22
apcca				2			2
apcaa				1			1
apaca				1			1
apacaa				1			1
aapc	1	3		5			9
aapcc			1	1			2
aapca			1	1			2
aaapcaa				1			1
pcs	4	6	1	13			24
pcsc	3	3	1	18			25
pcscc			1				1
pcsa	1	2	2	9			14
pcsaa				1			1
pcas		1					1
pacsc				1			1
apcs		2	1				3
apcsc				2			2
aapcsaa			1				1
psc	8	3	6	32			49
pscc		1		18			19
psca			2	1			3
pscca				1			1
psac				2			2
pasc				1			1
sp	31	9	14	8	2		64
spa	10	22	7	24			63
spaa	1	9	3	10	2		25
spaaa		3		1		1	5
spaaaa			1				1
sap	17	4	2	6			29
sapa	2	1	2	6			11
sapaa			1	1			2
saap	3	1					4
saaap				1			1
asp			6	3	3		12
aspa	1	2		3			6
aspaa				3			3
aspaaa				1			1
asap	2			2			4
aaspa				1			1
spc	47	25	14	55	5	1	147

	C1	C2	C3	C4	C5	Total
spcc	1	2	3	36		42
spca	5	4	3	8		20
spcac			1			1
spcaa		1		1		2
spac	1					1
sapc	7	7	2	15		31
sapcc	2			8		10
sapca	3		1	1		5
sapac				1		1
saapc				2		2
saapca				1		1
saaaapc				1		1
aspc	1	1		21		23
aspcc	1		2	16		19
aspca		2		4		6
asapc				2		2
asapcc		1		1		2
asaapca				1		1
scp	23	4	1	9		37
scpc	3		1	4		8
sccp	1		1			2
scpa	3		1	3		7
scap	1					1
sacp	2		1	2		5
sacpc				1		1
sacpa		1				1
saccpc		1				1
sc						41
scc						1
sca						5
sac						1
sa						20
saa						1
saaa						1
as						4
cp	39	3	18	17	1	78
cpc	8	1	2	6	1	18
cpcc	1					1
ccp	3			1		4
cpa	4	2	3	7		16
cpca	1					1
cpac			1	1		2
cpaa				1		1
cap			1	1		2
ccap				1		1
capa		1				1
acp	8	1	2	5		16
acpc	2			2		4
accp			1			1
acpa	1		1			2
acpac				1		1
acapa	1					1
cps	18	2	2	4	1	27

	p	imf	f	a	pf	ppf	total
cpcs			1				1
cpsa				1			1
cpsaa	1						1
acpsc				1			1
acpsaa				1			1
csp	7		2	1			10
cspc			1	1			2
cspa				1			1
cscp			2				2
cs							27
csa							1
acss							1
ca							5
caa							1
ac							2
total	590	303	267	1118	42	5	(2325)

Distribution of the Word Orders of Luke: Independent Clauses with Exclusions

	p	imf	f	a	pf	ppf	total
p	53	8	16	91			168
pa	19	15	11	69	1		115
paa	4	3	4	11			22
paaa		2	1	2			5
ap	16	2	10	28			56
apa	4	2	3	21			30
apaa	4	2		6			12
apaaa		1					1
aap	3	2		3			8
aapa			1	1			2
aapaa				1			1
aaapa				1			1
ps	12	10	5	25	5		57
psa	1	8	4	21			34
psas				2			2
psaa	2	4		6	2		14
psaaa		1		3			4
pas		1	2	7	1		11
pasa				1			1
paas				1			1
aps	2	1	1	1			5
apsa				6			6
apsaa				1			1
apsaaa				1			1
pc	80	30	30	138	1		279
pcc	51	16	11	89			167
pccc				3			3
pca	8	14	6	45			73
pcca				2	1		3
pcac		1					1
pcaa	1			7			8
pccaa		2					2

pcaaa				2			2
pcaaaa			1				1
pccacaaaa			1				1
pac	2	1	5	12			20
apc	17	10	12	36		1	76
apcc	2	4	2	22			30
apccc				1			1
apca	6	1		15			22
apcca				2			2
apcaa				1			1
apaca				1			1
apacaa				1			1
aapc	1	3		5			9
aapcc			1	1			2
aapca			1	1			2
aaapcaa				1			1
pcs	3	5		13			21
pcsc	2	3	1	18			24
pcscc			1				1
pcsa	1	2	1	9			13
pcsaa				1			1
pacsc				1			1
apcs		2	1				3
apcsc				2			2
aapcsaa			1				1
psc	8	1	1	31			41
pscc		1		17			18
psca			2	1			3
pscca				1			1
psac				2			2
pasc				1			1
sp	22	6	11	8	2		49
spa	7	10	6	23			46
spaa	1	4	3	10	2		20
spaaa		2		1		1	4
spaaaa			1				1
sap	11	1	2	6			20
sapa			2	6			8
sapaa			1	1			2
saap	2	1					3
saaap				1			1
asp			3	3	2		8
aspa	1	2		3			6
aspaa				3			3
aspaaa				1			1
asap	2			2			4
aaspa				1			1
spc	19	17	11	54	4		105
spcc	1	2	3	36			42
spca	5	4	3	8			20
spcac			1				1
spcaa		1		1			2
spac	1						1

sapc	7	7	2	15		31
sapcc	2			8		10
sapca	3		1	1		5
sapac				1		1
saapc				2		2
saapca				1		1
saaaapc				1		1
aspc	1	1		21		23
aspcc	1		2	16		19
aspca		2		4		6
asapc				2		2
asapcc		1		1		2
asaapca				1		1
scp	15	1		9		25
scpc	1		1	4		6
sccp	1					1
scpa			1	3		4
sacp				2		2
sacpc				1		1
sacpa		1				1
saccpc		1				1
sc						39
scc						1
sca						5
sac						1
sa						18
saa						1
saaa						1
as						4
cp	22	1	15	16	1	55
cpc	8		2	6		16
cpcc	1					1
ccp	3			1		4
cpa	3		3	7		13
cpca	1					1
cpac			1	1		2
cpaa				1		1
cap			1	1		2
ccap				1		1
capa		1				1
acp	7		2	5		14
acpc	2			2		4
accp			1			1
acpa	1					1
acpac				1		1
acapa	1					1
cps	1	1	2	4	1	9
cpcs			1			1
cpsa				1		1
cpsaa	1					1
acpsc				1		1
acpsaa				1		1
csp	1		1	1		3

	p	imf	f	a	pf	ppf	total
cspc			1	1			2
cspa				1			1
cscp			2				2
cs							25
csa							1
acss							1
ca							4
caa							1
ac							2
total	457	225	221	1104	23	2	(2032)

Distribution of the Word Orders of Luke: Dependent Clauses

	p	imf	f	a	pf	ppf	total
p	13	3	7	28			51
pa	7			19			26
paa	2			3			5
ap	9	1		14	1		25
apa				4			4
apaa				1			1
aap	2						2
ps	26	2	1	20	2		51
psa	8			14			22
psaa	3						3
psaaa				1			1
pas	2			3	2		7
paas				1			1
aps	2	2		4			8
apsaa	1						1
pc	22	2	4	51	3	2	84
pcc	1	1	1	8			11
pca	7	1		13			21
pcaa			1	2			3
pac				3			3
apc	2		2	5			9
pcs	2			4			6
pcsc				1			1
pccs				1			1
pcsa		1					1
pcasa				1			1
psc	9	2		4		1	16
pscc				2			2
psca	1			1			2
psac				1			1
psaac	1						1
apsc	1						1
sp	9		5	11	1		26
spa	5	2		8	1		16
spaa				1			1
sap	4	1		2			7
asp	3						3
sapa	2						2

	p	imf	f	a	pf	ppf	total
aspa				1			1
spc	12	1		7			20
spca	2	1		2			5
spac	1						1
sapc	4			1			5
aspc	1						1
aspac				1			1
scp	11	2					13
scpc	1		1				2
scpa	1		1	1			3
scpaa	1						1
scap	1			1			2
sc							1
sca							3
as							1
cp	19	1	1	17	2		40
cpc	2			2			4
cpa				3	1		4
cap				2			2
acp	2			4			6
acpc				1			1
acap				1			1
cps	7			2			9
cpsc			1				1
caps				1			1
csp	7						7
cspa	1						1
cs							1
total	218	21	27	273	13	3	(555)

Distribution of the Word Orders of Luke: Dependent Clauses with Exclusions

	p	imf	f	a	pf	ppf	total
p	13	1	7	28			49
pa	5			19			24
paa	2			3			5
ap	7	1		14	1		23
apa				4			4
apaa				1			1
aap	1						1
ps	26		1	20	2		49
psa	7			14			21
psaa	2						2
psaaa				1			1
pas	2			3			5
paas				1			1
aps				4			4
apsaa	1						1
pc	20	2	4	49		1	76
pcc		1	1	7			9
pca	7	1		12			20
pcaa			1	2			3

pac				2			2
apc	2		2	5			9
pcs	2			4			6
pcsc				1			1
pccs				1			1
pcasa				1			1
psc	6	1		4			11
pscc				2			2
psca	1			1			2
psac				1			1
psaac	1						1
apsc	1						1
sp	7		5	11			23
spa	3			6			9
spaa				1			1
sap	2	1		2			5
asp	3						3
sapa	2						2
aspa				1			1
spc	4		1	7			12
spca	2		1	2			5
spac	1						1
sapc	4			1			5
aspc	1						1
aspac				1			1
scp	2						2
scpc	1		1				2
scpa			1	1			2
scpaa	1						1
scap				1			1
sc							1
sca							3
as							1
cp	11		1	17	2		31
cpc	2			2			4
cpa				3	1		4
cap				2			2
acp	2			4			6
acpc				1			1
acap				1			1
cps	3			2			5
cpsc			1				1
caps				1			1
csp	4						4
cs							1
total	161	8	27	271	6	1	(474)

Distribution of the Word Orders of Luke: Infinitival Clauses

	p	*f*	*a*	*pf*	*total*
p	20		27		47
pa	9		15		24

	p	f	a	pf	total
paa	1		2		3
ap	2		7	1	10
aap	1				1
ps	4		6		10
psa			1		1
psaa			1		1
pas	1				1
pasaa			1		1
aps	1		1		2
pc	27		45		72
pcc	7		7		14
pca	2		9		11
pcca	1		2		3
pcac	2		1		3
pcaaa	1				1
pac			3		3
apc			3		3
apcc			1		1
apcaaa	1				1
pccs	1				1
psc	1				1
psac			1		1
sp			8		8
spa			3		3
spas			1		1
spaa	1				1
sap	2		2		4
asp	1				1
aasp			1		1
spc	1				1
scp			1	1	2
sccp			1		1
cp	12		23		35
cpc	1				1
cpcc	1				1
ccp	1		2		3
cpa	1		4		5
cpaa			1		1
acp			1	1	2
cps	1		1		2
cpsc			1		1
total	104		183	3	290

Distribution of the Word Orders of Luke: Infinitival Clauses with Exclusions

	p	f	a	pf	total
p	20		27		47
pa	9		15		24
paa	1		2		3
ap	2		7	1	10
aap	1				1
ps	4		6		10

psa		1		1
psaa		1		1
pas	1			1
pasaa		1		1
aps	1	1		2
pc	23	43		66
pcc	6	7		13
pca	2	7		9
pcca	1	2		3
pcac	2	1		3
pcaaa	1			1
pac		3		3
apc		3		3
apcc		1		1
apcaaa	1			1
pccs	1			1
psc	1			1
psac		1		1
sp		8		8
spa		3		3
spas		1		1
spaa	1			1
sap	1	2		3
asp	1			1
aasp		1		1
scp		1	1	2
sccp		1		1
cp	12	23		35
cpc	1			1
cpcc	1			1
ccp	1	2		3
cpa	1	4		5
cpaa		1		1
acp		1		1
cps		1		1
cpsc		1		1
total	96	178	2	276

Distribution of the Word Orders of Luke: Participial Clauses

	p	*f*	*a*	*pf*	*total*
p	89	1	151	45	286
pa	56		63	13	132
paa	8		4	3	15
paaa			1		1
ap	15		13	3	31
apa	4		1	1	6
aap	1				1
ps				1	1
psaa	1				1
pas				1	1
pc	203		101	11	315

pcc	8	2		10
pca	13	12	2	27
pcaa	1	1		2
pac	3	3	1	7
apc	4	2		6
apca	1			1
cp	21	18		39
cpc	1			1
cpa	2			2
cap	1			1
acp	1			1
total	433	1	372	81	887

Distribution of the Word Orders of Luke: Participial Clauses with Exclusions

	p	*f*	*a*	*pf*	*total*
p	88	1	151	42	282
pa	52		62	13	127
paa	7		4	1	12
paaa			1		1
ap	13		13	2	28
apa	4		1	1	6
aap	1				1
pc	199		101	8	308
pcc	8		2		10
pca	13		12	2	27
pcaa	1		1		2
pac	3		3	1	7
apc	4		2		6
apca	1				1
cp	20		18		38
cpc	1				1
cpa	2				2
cap	1				1
acp	1				1
total	419	1	371	70	861

Distribution of the Word Orders of Luke: Embedded Clauses

	p	*imf*	*f*	*a*	*pf*	*ppf*	*total*
p	2	1		1			4
pa	2			1			3
ap	8	1	1	5		1	16
psa	1						1
aps	2			1	1	1	5
apsa			1	3			4
pc	2	2		1			5
pca				1			1
apc	2						2
aapc			1				1
pcs			1				1

psc	1						1
sp	3	1	3	5			12
spa	3	3	3	2			11
spaa		1					1
sap	1						1
saap	1						1
saapa				1			1
saaap	1						1
asp	1			3		2	6
aspa				2			2
spc	11	6	3	6			26
spca	1	4	2	5			12
spac		2					2
sapc	1			1			2
scp	2		1	1			4
sc							1
sa							1
cp	9	4		18	1		32
cpc			2	2		1	5
ccp				2			2
cpa	1			1			2
ccpa				1			1
cpcac				1			1
cpaa	1						1
cap				1			1
cps	1	1		5			7
cpcs				1			1
ccps				1			1
cpsa				1			1
cpsaa			1				1
csp	2						2
cspc				1			1
cspa				1			1
casp			2				2
csc							1
total	59	26	21	75	2	5	(188)

Distribution of the Word Orders of Luke: Embedded Clauses with Exclusions

	p	*imf*	*f*	*a*	*pf*	*ppf*	*total*
p	2	1		1			4
pa	2			1			3
ap	8	1	1	5		1	16
psa	1						1
aps	2			1		1	4
apsa			1	3			4
pc	2	2		1			5
pca				1			1
apc	2						2
aapc			1				1
pcs			1				1
psc	1						1

	p	imf	f	a	pf	ppf	total
sp	3		3	5			11
spa	2		2	2			6
sap	1						1
saap	1						1
saapa				1			1
saaap	1						1
asp	1			3		2	6
aspa				2			2
spc	9	3	2	6			20
spca		3	1	5			9
sapc	1			1			2
scp	2		1	1			4
sc							1
sa							1
cp	9	4		18	1		32
cpc			2	2		1	5
ccp				2			2
cpa	1			1			2
ccpa				1			1
cpcac				1			1
cpaa	1						1
cap				1			1
cps		1		4			5
cpcs				1			1
ccps				1			1
cpsa				1			1
cpsaa			1				1
csp	2						2
cspc				1			1
cspa				1			1
casp			2				2
csc							1
total	54	15	18	74	1	5	(167)

Distribution of the Word Orders of Luke: Dependent Clauses of Embedded Clauses

	p	imf	f	a	pf	ppf	total
p				2			2
pa	1						1
ap	1						1
ps	1			2			3
aps	1			1			2
pc	1			2			3
apc				1			1
psc	1		1				2
sp	1			1			2
spa				2			2
spc	1						1
scp	3						3
cp	1				1		2
acp		1					1
total	12	1	1	11	1		26

Distribution of the Word Orders of Luke: Dependent Clauses of Embedded Clauses with Exclusions

	p	*imf*	*f*	*a*	*pf*	*ppf*	*total*
p				2			2
pa	1						1
ps	1			2			3
aps	1			1			2
pc				2			2
apc				1			1
psc	1						1
sp				1			1
spa				2			2
cp	1				1		2
acp		1					1
total	5	1		11	1		18

BIBLIOGRAPHY

Achtemeier, P.J., 'The Lukan Perspective on the Miracles of Jesus: A Preliminary Sketch', in C.H. Talbert (ed.), *Perspective on Luke-Acts* (Edinburgh: T&T Clark, 1978), pp. 153–67.

Aitchison, J., 'The Order of Word Order Change', *TPS* (1979), pp. 43–65.

Alexander, L., *The Preface to Luke's Gospel: Literary Convention and Social Context in Luke 1.1-4 and Acts 1.1* (SNTSMS, 78; Cambridge: Cambridge University Press, 1993).

Amman, H., 'Wortstellung und Stilentwickelung', *Glotta* 12 (1922), pp. 107–11.

—'Untersuchungen zur homerischen Wortfolge und Satzstruktur', *IF* 42 (1924), pp. 149–78, 300–322.

Andersen, H., 'Markedness Theory – the First 150 Years', in O.M. Tomic (ed.), *Markedness in Synchrony and Diachrony* (TILSM, 39; Berlin: Mouton de Gruyter, 1989), pp. 11–46.

Andersen, P.K, 'On Universal 22', *J Ling* (1982), pp. 231–43.

—*Word Order Typology and Comparative Constructions* (ASTHLS, 4; CILT, 25; Amsterdam: John Benjamins, 1983).

Angel, G.T.D., 'ἐπιτιμάω', in NIDNTT, I, p. 572.

Ard, J., 'Word Order Templates in Ergative Languages', *Ling Inq* 9 (1978), pp. 297–99.

Argyle, A.W., 'The Greek of Luke and Acts', *NTS* 20 (1973–74), pp. 441–45.

Bammel, E., 'The Trial before Pilate', in Bammel and Moule (eds), *Jesus and the Politics of His Days*, pp. 415–51.

Bammel, E., and C.F.D. Moule (eds), *Jesus and the Politics of His Days* (Cambridge: Cambridge University Press, 1984).

Banker, J., 'The Position of the Vocative *adelphoi* in the Clause', *START* 11 (1984), pp. 29–36.

Battistella, E.L., *Markedness: The Evaluative Superstructure of Language* (Albany: State University of New York Press, 1990).

—*The Logic of Markedness* (Oxford: Oxford University Press, 1996).

Bauckham, R., 'The Son of Man: "A Man in My Position" or "Someone"', *JSNT* 23 (1985), pp. 23–33.

Bauer, W., *A Greek-English Lexicon of the New Testament and other Early Christian Literature* (rev. and ed. F.W. Danker; Chicago: University of Chicago Press, 3rd edn 2000).

Bayer, H.F., *Jesus' Predictions of Vindication and Resurrection: The Provenance, Meaning and Correlation of the Synoptic Predictions* (WUNT, 2.20; Tübingen: J.C.B. Mohr, 1986).

Beattle, A.J., '"Greek Word Order"', *CRNS* 12 (1962), pp. 234–38.

Beck, B.E., '"Imitatio Christi" and the Lukan Passion narrative', in W. Horbury and B. McNeil (eds), *Suffering and Martyrdom in the New Testament. Studies Presented to G.M. Styler by the Cambridge New Testament Seminar* (Cambridge: Cambridge University Press, 1981), pp. 28–47.

Bergson, L., *Zur Stellung des Adjektivs in der älteren griechischen Prosa* (Acta Universitatis Stockholmiensis, SGS, I; Stockholm: Almqvist & Wiksell, 1960).

Berkowitz, L., and K.A. Squitier, *Thesaurus Linguae Graecae: Canon of Greek Authors and Works* (Oxford: Oxford University Press, 3rd edn 1990).

Bertram, G., 'ἄφρων', in TDNT, IX, p. 230.

Best, E., 'The Role of the Disciples in Mark', *NTS* 23 (1977), pp. 377–401.

—'Peter in the Gospel According to Mark', *CBQ* 40 (1978), pp. 547–58.

—*Disciples and Discipleship: Studies in the Gospel According to Mark* (Edinburgh: T&T Clark, 1986).

Bishop, C.E., 'The Greek Verbal in TEO: Part III', *AJP* 20 (1899), pp. 241–53.

Black, D.A., 'The Article, Conjunctions and Greek Word Order', *BR* 9.5 (1993), pp. 23, 61.

Black, M., *An Aramaic Approach to the Gospels and Acts* (Oxford: Clarendon Press, 3rd edn 1967).

— '"Not Peace but a Sword": Matt. 10.34ff; Luke 12.51ff', in Bammel and Moule (eds), *Jesus and the Politics of His Days*, pp. 287–94.

Black, S.L., *Sentence Conjunction in the Gospel of Matthew: καί, δέ, τότε, γάρ, οὖν and Asyndeton in Narrative Discourse* (JSNTSup, 216; SNTG, 9; Sheffield: Sheffield Academic Press, 2002).

Blass, F., and A. Debrunner, *A Greek Grammar of the New Testament and Other Early Christian Literature* (trans. and rev. R.W. Funk; Chicago: University of Chicago Press, 1961).

Blomqvist, J., *Greek Particles in Hellenistic Prose* (Lund: Berlingska Boktryckeriet, 1969).

Bock, D.L., *Luke* (BECNT, 3A and 3B; Grand Rapids: Baker Books, 1994–96).

Bornkamm, G., G. Barth and H.J. Held, *Tradition and Interpretation in Matthew* (London: SCM Press, 1960).

Brodie, T.L., 'Luke 7.36-50 as an Internalization of 2 Kings 4.1-37: A Study in Luke's Use of Rhetorical Imitation', *Bib* 64 (1983), pp. 457–85.

—'Animadversiones: The Departure for Jerusalem (Luke 9.51-56) as a Rhetorical Imitation of Elijah's Departure for the Jordan (2 Kgs 1.1-2.6)', *Bib* 70 (1989), pp. 96–109.

Brody, J., 'Some Problems with the Concept of Basic Word Order', *Ling* 22 (1984), pp. 711–36.

Brown, R.E., 'Gospel Infancy Narrative Research from 1976 to 1986: Part II (Luke)', *CBQ* 48 (1986), pp. 660–80.

—*The Birth of the Messiah: A Commentary on the Infancy Narratives in the Gospels of Matthew and Luke* (ABRL; London: Geoffrey Chapman, new updated version 1993).

—*The Death of the Messiah: A Commentary on the Passion Narratives of the Four Gospels* (2 vols.; ABRL; London: Geoffrey Chapman, 1994).

Brown, R.E., K.P. Donfried and J. Reumann (eds), *Peter in the New Testament: A Collaborative Assessment by Protestant and Roman Catholic Scholars* (New York: Paulist Press, 1973).

Brown, S., *Apostasy and Perseverance in the Theology of Luke* (Analecta Biblica, 36; Rome: Pontifical Biblical Institute Press, 1969).

Bruce, F.F., *The Acts of the Apostles: The Greek Text with Introduction and Commentary* (Grand Rapids: Eerdmans, 3rd rev. edn 1990).

Buck, E., 'The Function of the Pericope "Jesus before Herod" in the Passion Narrative of Luke', in W. Haubeck and M. Bachmann (eds), *Wort in der Zeit* (Leiden: E.J. Brill, 1980), pp. 165–78.

Burton, E.D., *Syntax of the Moods and Tenses in New Testament Greek* (Edinburgh: T&T Clark, 3rd edn 1898).

Butler, C.S., 'Discourse Systems and Structures and their Place within an Overall Systemic Model', in J.D. Benson and W.S. Greaves (eds), *Systemic Perspectives on Discourse* (Norwood: Ablex Publishing Company, 1985), I, pp. 213–28.

—*Systemic Linguistics: Theory and Application* (London: Batsford Academic & Educational, 1985).

—'Communicative Function and Semantics', in M.A.K. Halliday and R.P. Fawcett (eds), *New Developments in Systemic Linguistics. I. Theory and Description* (London: Frances Pinter, 1987), pp. 212–29.

—'Politeness and the Semantics of Modalised Directives in English', in J.D. Benson,
     M.J. Cummings and W. Greaves (eds), *Linguistics in a Systemic Perspective* (ASTHLS,
     4; CILT, 39; Amsterdam: John Benjamins, 1988), pp. 119–53.
Butts, J.R., 'The Voyage of Discipleship: Narrative, Chreia, and Call Story', in C.A. Evans
     and W.F. Stinespring (eds), *Early Jewish and Christian Exegesis: Studies in Memory
     of William Hugh Brownlee* (Atlanta: Scholars Press, 1987), pp. 199–219.
Byrskog, S., 'Jesus the Only Teacher', *TB* 45 (1994), pp. 413–14.
—*Jesus the Only Teacher: Didactic Authority and Transmisson in Ancient Israel, Ancient
     Judaism and the Matthean Community* (CBNTS, 24; Stockholm: Almqvist & Wiksell,
     1994).
Cadbury, H.J., *The Style and Literary Method of Luke* (HTS, 6; Cambridge: Harvard
     University Press, 1920).
—'Some Lukan Expressions of Time (Lexical Notes on Luke-Acts VII)', *JBL* 82 (1963),
     pp. 272–78.
—'Four Features of Lukan Style', in L.E. Keck and J.L. Martyn (eds), *Studies in Luke-
     Acts* (Nashville: Abingdon Press, 1966), pp. 87–102.
Callow, J., 'Word Order in New Testament Greek, Part I', *START* 7 (1983), pp. 3–50.
—'Word Order in New Testament Greek, Part II, III', *START* 8 (1983), pp. 3–32.
—'Constituent Order in Copula Clauses: A Partial Study', in D.A. Black and D.S.
     Dockery (eds), *Linguistics and New Testament Interpretation* (Grand Rapids: Zondervan,
     1991), pp. 68–89.
Callow, K., *Discourse Considerations in Translating the Word of God* (Grand Rapids:
     Zondervan, 1974).
Carroll, J.T., 'Luke's Portrayal of the Pharisees', *CBQ* 50 (1988), pp. 604–21.
Casey, M., 'The Jackals and the Son of Man (Matt. 8.20 // Luke 9.58)', *JSNT* 23 (1985), pp. 3–22.
—'General, Generic and Indefinite: The Use of the Term "Son of Man" in Aramaic Sources
     and in the Teaching of Jesus', *JSNT* 29 (1987), pp. 21–56.
Catchpole, D.R., 'The Centurion's Faith and its Function in Q', in Segbroeck, Tuckett, Belle and
     Verheyden (eds), *The Four Gospels 1992*, I, pp. 517–40.
Cervin, R.S., 'On the Notion of "Second Position", in Greek', *SLSc* 18 (1988), pp. 23–39.
—'Word Order in Ancient Greek: VSO, SVO, SOV, or All of the Above?' (PhD thesis
     University of Illinois at Urbana-Champaign, 1990).
—'A Critique of Timothy Friberg's Dissertation: New Testament Greek Word-Order in
     Light of Discourse Consideration', *JOTT* 6 (1993), pp. 56–85.
Cheng, L.L.S., *On the Typology of Wh-Questions* (ODL; New York: Garland, 1997).
Cheung, P.W., 'Revisiting the Case of an Infinitive with Two Substantival Accusatives',
     JD 13 (1999), pp. 69–101.
Coakley, J.F., 'The Anointing at Bethany and the Priority of John', *JBL* 107 (1988), pp.
     241–56.
Coleridge, M., *The Birth of the Lukan Narrative: Narrative as Christology in Luke 1-2*
     (JSNTSup, 88; Sheffield: Sheffield Academic Press, 1993).
Collison, F.J.G., 'Linguistic Usages in the Gospel of Luke' (PhD thesis Southern
     Methodist University, 1977).
Colpe, C., 'ὁ υἱὸς τοῦ ἀνθρώπου', *TDNT*, VIII, pp. 400–77.
Comrie, B., *Language Universals and Linguistic Typology: Syntax and Morphology* (Oxford:
     Basil Blackwell, 2nd edn 1989).
Congdon, R.D., 'Did Jesus Sustain the Law in Matthew 5?', *BibSac* 135 (1978), pp. 117–25.
Conrad, C.W., *From Epic to Lyric: A Study in the History of Traditional Word-Order in
     Greek and Latin Poetry* (HDC; New York: Garland, 1990).
Conzelmann, H., *The Theology of St. Luke* (trans. G. Buswell; London: Faber & Faber,
     1960).
Cooper, C.R., and S. Greenbaum (eds), *Studying Writing: Linguistics Approaches* (WCA, 1;
     Beverly Hills: Sage Publications, 1986).

Corner, N., and H. van Riemsdijk (eds), *Studies on Scrambling: Movement and Non-Movement Approaches to Free Word-Order Phenomena* (SGG, 41; Berlin: Mouton de Gruyter, 1994).

Cosgrove, C.H., 'The Divine ΔEI in Luke-Acts: Investigations into the Lukan Understanding of God's Providence', *NovT* 26 (1984), pp. 168–90.

Costelloe, M., 'K.J. Dover, Greek Word Order', *CB* 38 (1962), p. 46.

Cotterell, F.P., 'The Nicodemus Conversation: A Fresh Appraisal', *ExpTim* 96 (1985), pp. 237–42.

Creed, J.M., *The Gospel According to St. Luke: The Greek Text with Introduction, Notes, and Indices* (London: Macmillan, 1965).

Cristofaro, S., 'Grammaticalization and Clause Linkage Strategies: A Typological Approach with Reference to Ancient Greek', in A.C. Ramat and P.J. Hopper (eds), *The Limits of Grammaticalization* (TSL, 37; Amsterdam: John Benjamins, 1998), pp. 59–88.

Croft, W., 'Review of "Basic Word Order: Functional Principles", by Russell S. Tomlin', *Ling* 26 (1988), pp. 892–95.

—*Typology and Universals* (CTL; Cambridge: Cambridge University Press, 1990).

Crossan, J.D., 'Parable and Example in the Teaching of Jesus', *Semeia* 1 (1974), pp. 63–104.

Cunningham, S., *'Through Many Tribulations': The Theology of Persecution in Luke-Acts* (JSNTSup, 142; Sheffield: Sheffield Academic Press, 1997).

Dahl, O., 'What is New Information', in Enkvist and Kohonen (eds), *Reports on Text Linguistics*, pp. 37–50.

Danes, F., 'Functional Sentence Perspective and the Organization of Text', in *idem* (ed.), *Papers on Functional Sentence Perspective: First International Symposium* (JLSMin, 147; The Hague: Mouton, 1974), pp. 106–28.

Danove, P.L., *The End of Mark's Story: A Methodological Study* (BIS, 3; Leiden: E.J. Brill, 1993).

—'The Theory of Construction Grammar and its Application to New Testament Greek', in Porter and Carson (eds), *Biblical Greek Language and Linguistics*, pp. 119–51.

—'The Narrative Rhetoric of Mark's Ambiguous Characterization of the Disciples', *JSNT* 70 (1998), pp. 21–38.

—'Verbs of Experience: Toward a Lexicon Detailing the Argument Structures Assigned by Verbs', in Porter and Carson (eds), *Linguistics and the New Testament*, pp. 144–205.

—*Linguistics and Exegesis in the Gospel of Mark: Applications of a Case Frame Analysis* (JSNTSup, 218; SNTG, 10; Sheffield: Sheffield Academic Press, 2001).

Davies, D., 'The Position of Adverbs in Luke', in Elliot (ed.), *Studies in New Testament Language and Text*, pp. 106–22.

Davies, M., and L. Ravelli (eds), *Advances in Systemic Linguistics: Recent Theory and Practice* (London: Pinter, 1992).

Davison, M.E., 'A Computer-Assisted Analysis of Word Order in the Greek New Testament' (MA thesis, The Queen's University of Belfast, 1987).

—'New Testament Greek Word Order', *LLC* 4 (1989), pp. 19–28.

—'Object Position in Herodotus', *Glotta* 74 (1997–98), pp. 146–58.

Decker, R.J., *Temporal Deixis of the Greek Verb in the Gospel of Mark with Reference to Verbal Aspect* (SBG, 10; New York: Peter Lang, 2001).

Denaux, A., 'The Delineation of the Lukan Travel Narrative within the Overall Structure of the Gospel of Luke', in C. Focant (ed.), *The Synoptic Gospels: Source Criticism and the New Literary Criticism* (BETL, 110; Leuven: Leuven University Press, 1993), pp. 357–92.

Denniston J.D., 'Review of "H. Frisk, Studien zur griechischen Wortstellung"', *CR* 47 (1933), pp. 18–20.

—*Greek Prose Style* (Oxford: Oxford University Press, 1952).

—*The Greek Particles* (Oxford: Oxford University Press, 2nd edn 1954).

Derbyshire, D.C., 'Word Order Universals and the Existence of OVS Languages', *Ling Inq* 8 (1977), pp. 590–99.

Derrett, D.M., 'Three Shorter Contributions: Christ's Second Baptism (Lk. 12.50; Mk. 10.38-40)', *ExpTim* 100 (1988–89), pp. 294–95.

Dezsó, L., *Studies in Syntactic Typology and Contrastive Grammar* (trans. I. Gombos and B. Hollósy; JLSM, 89; The Hague: Mouton, 1982).

Dik, H., *Word Order in Ancient Greek: A Pragmatic Account of Word Order Variation in Herodotus* (ASCP, 5; Amsterdam: J.C. Gieben, 1995).

Dik, S.C., *Functional Grammar* (Dordrecht: Foris, 1978).

—*The Theory of Functional Grammar*. I. *The Structure of the Clause* (Dordrecht: Foris, 1989).

Donahue, J.R., 'Recent Studies on the Origin of "Son of Man" in the Gospels', *CBQ* 48 (1986), pp. 484–98.

Donaldson, T.L., *Jesus on the Mountain: A Study in Matthean Theology* (JSNTSup, 8; JSOT Press, 1985).

Dover, K.J., 'Review of: "L. Bergson, Zur Stellung des Adjectives, Stockholm, 1960"', *Gnomon* 33 (1961), pp. 831–37 (reprinted in Dover, *Greek and the Greeks*, pp. 67–69).

—*Greek Word Order* (Cambridge: Cambridge University Press, 2nd edn 1968).

—'Some Types of Abnormal Word Order in Attic Comedy', *CQNS* 35 (1985), pp. 324–43 (reprinted in Dover, *Greek and the Greeks*, pp. 43–66).

—*Greek and the Greeks: Collected Papers*. I. *Language, Poetry, Drama* (Oxford: Basil Blackwell, 1987).

Downing, P., and M. Noonan (eds), *Word Order in Discourse* (TSL, 30; Amsterdam: John Benjamins, 1995).

Dressler, W., 'Markedness and Naturalness', in Tomic (ed.), *Markedness in Synchrony and Diachrony*, pp. 111–20.

Droge, A., 'Call Stories in Greek Biographies and the Gospels', *SBLSP* (1983), pp. 245–57.

Dryer, M., 'Siewierska: Word Order Rules', *Lang* 65 (1989), p. 678.

Dubois, B.L., 'A Reformation of Thematic Progression Typology', *Text* 7 (1987), pp. 89–116.

Dunn, G., 'Syntactic Word Order in Herodotus' (PhD thesis, University of Canterbury, 1981).

—'Ancient Greek Order and the Lehmann Hypothesis', *TR* 28 (1985), pp. 81–94.

—'Syntactic Word Order in Herodotean Greek', *Glotta* 66 (1988), pp. 63–79.

—'Enclitic Pronoun Movement and the Ancient Greek Sentence Accent', *Glotta* 67 (1989), pp. 1–19.

—'Greek Word Order: Three Descriptive Models', *TR* 33 (1990), pp. 57–63.

Easton, B.S., *The Gospel According to St. Luke: A Critical and Exegetical Commentary* (Edinburgh: T&T Clark, 1926).

Ebeling, H.L., 'Some Statistics on the Order of Words in Greek', in *Studies in Honor of Basil L. Gildersleeve* (no stated editor; Baltimore: The Johns Hopkins Press, 1902), pp. 229–40.

Eckman, F.R., E.A. Moravcsik and J.R. Wirth (eds), *Markedness* (New York: Plenum Press, 1986).

Eggins, S., *An Introduction to Systemic Functional Linguistics* (London: Pinter, 1994).

Elliott, J.K., 'The Anointing of Jesus', *ExpTim* 85 (1973–74), pp. 105–07.

—'The Position of Causal ὅτι Clauses in the New Testament', *FN* 3 (1990), pp. 155–57.

Elliott, J.K. (ed.) *Studies in New Testament Language and Text: Essays in Honour of George D. Kilpatrick on the Occasion of his Sixty-fifth Birthday* (NovTSup, 44; Leiden: E.J. Brill, 1976).

Ellis, E.E., *The Gospel of Luke* (NCBC; Grand Rapids: Eerdmans, rev. edn 1974).

—'The Composition of Luke 9 and the Sources of its Christology', in G.F. Hawthorne (ed.), *Current Issues in Biblical and Patristic Interpretation: Studies in Honor of Merrill C. Tenny Presented by his Former Students* (Grand Rapids: Eerdmans, 1975), pp. 121–27.

Enkvist, N.E., 'Prolegomena to a Symposium on "The Interaction of Parameters Affecting Word Order"', in Enkvist and Kohonen (eds), *Reports on Text Linguistics*, pp. 51–74.

Enkvist, N.E., and V. Kohonen (eds), *Reports on Text Linguistics: Approaches to Word Order* (Abo: Text Linguistic Research Group, 1976).

Evans, C.A., 'Luke's Use of the Elijah/Elisha Narratives and the Ethic of Election', *JBL* 106 (1987), pp. 75–83.

—*Life of Jesus Research: An Annotated Bibliography* (NTTS, 24; Leiden: E.J. Brill, rev. edn 1996).

Evans, C.F., *Saint Luke* (TPI New Testament Commentaries; London: SCM Press, 1990).

Fanning, B.M., *Verbal Aspect in New Testament Greek* (Oxford: Clarendon Press, 1990).

Farmer, W.R., 'The Passion Prediction Passages and the Synoptic Problem: A Test Case', *NTS* 36 (1990), pp. 558–70.

Farris, S., *The Hymns of Luke's Infancy Narratives: Their Origin, Meaning and Significance* (JSNTSup, 9; Sheffield: JSOT Press, 1985).

Fawcett, R.P., 'The Semantics of Clause and Verb for Relational Process in English', in M.A.K. Halliday and R.P. Fawcett (eds), *New Developments in Systemic Linguistics*. I. *Theory and Description* (London: Frances Pinter, 1987), pp. 130–83.

—'The English Personal Pronouns: An Exercise in Linguistic Theory', in J.D. Benson, M.J. Cummings and W.S. Greaves (eds), *Linguistics in a Systemic Perspective* (Amsterdam: John Benjamins, 1988), pp. 185–220.

—*A Theory of Syntax for Systemic Functional Linguistics* (Amsterdam: John Benjamins, 2000).

Field, F., *Notes on the Translation of the New Testament* (Cambridge: Cambridge University Press, 1899).

Fillmore, C.J., 'Linguistics as a Tool for Discourse Analysis', in T.A. van Dijk (ed.), *Handbook of Discourse Analysis*. I. *Disciplines of Discourse* (San Diego: Academic Press, 1985), pp. 11–39.

Finer, D.L., *The Formal Grammar of Switch-Reference* (New York: Garland, 1985).

Firbas, J., 'On the Dynamics of Written Communication in the Light of the Theory of Functional Sentence Perspective', in Cooper and Greenbaum (eds), *Studying Writing*, pp. 40–71.

—'On some basic problems of Functional Sentence Perspective', in M. Davies and L. Ravelli (eds), *Advances in Systemic Linguistics: Recent Theory and Practice* (London: Pinter, 1992), pp. 167–88.

Fischer, P., 'Zur Stellung des Verbums im Griechischen', *Glotta* 13 (1924), pp. 1–11, 189–205.

Fitzmyer, F.A., 'The Composition of Luke, Chapter 9', in C.H. Talbert (ed.), *Perspectives on Luke-Acts* (Edinburgh: T&T Clark, 1978), pp. 139–52.

—*The Gospel According to Luke* (AB, 28 and 28A; New York: Doubleday, 2nd edn 1981–1985).

Fleddermann, H.T., 'Demands of Discipleship: Matt. 8.19-22 Par. Luke 9.57-62', in Segbroeck, Tuckett, Belle and Verheyden (eds), *The Four Gospels 1992*, I, pp. 540–61.

Flynn, M.J., *Structure Building Operations and Word Order* (New York: Garland, 1985).

Ford, J.M., 'Reconciliation and Forgiveness in Luke's Gospel', in R.J. Cassidy and P.J. Scharper (eds), *Political in Luke-Acts* (Maryknoll, Orbis Books, 1983), pp. 80–98.

Foster, J.F., and C.A. Hofling, 'Word Order, Case and Agreement', *Ling* 25 (1987), pp. 475–99.

France, R.T., *Matthew: Evangelist and Teacher* (Exeter: The Paternoster Press, 1989).

Fraser, B.L., 'Word Order, Focus, and Clause Linking in Greek Tragic Poetry' (PhD thesis, University of Cambridge, 1999).

Freyne, S., 'The Disciples in Mark and the *Maskilim* in Daniel', *JSNT* 16 (1982), pp. 7–23.

Friberg, B., and T. Friberg (eds), *Analytical Greek New Testament* (2 vols.; Grand Rapids: Baker Book House, 1991).

Friberg, B., T. Friberg and N.F. Miller (eds), *Analytical Lexicon of the Greek New Testament* (Grand Rapids: Baker Book House, 2000).

Friberg, T., 'New Testament Greek Word Order in Light of Discourse Considerations' (PhD thesis; University of Minnesota, 1982).

Friedrich, P., *Proto-Indo-European Syntax: The Order of Meaningful Elements* (JIESM, 1; Washington: The Institute for the Study of Man, 1975).

Friedrichsen, T.A., 'Luke 9.22–A Matthean Foreign Body?', *ETL* 72 (1996), pp. 398–407.

Frischer, B.D., *et al.*, 'Word-Order Transference between Latin and Greek: The Relative Position of the Accusative Direct Object and the Governing Verb in Cassius Dio and Other Greek and Roman Prose Authors', *HSCP* 99 (1999), pp. 357–90.

Frisk, H., *Studien zur griechischen Wortstellung* (GHA, 39.1; Göteborg: Wettergren & Kerbers Förlag, 1933).

Gabr, M.Y., 'Philological Studies on the Coptic Versions of the Gospel of John' (PhD thesis; University of Liverpool, 1990).

Gagnon, R.A.J., 'Statistical Analysis and the Case of the Double Delegation', *CBQ* 55 (1993), pp. 709–31.

—'Luke's Motives for Redaction in the Account of the Double Delegation in Luke 7.1-10', *NovT* 36 (1994), pp. 122–45.

Garrett, S.R., 'Exodus from Bondage: Luke 9.31 and Acts 12.1-24', *CBQ* 52 (1990), pp. 656–80.

Gaston, L., 'The Messiah of Israel As Teacher of the Gentiles: The Setting of Matthew's Christology', *Int* 29 (1975), pp. 24–40.

Geldenhuys, N., *Commentary on the Gospel of Luke* (London: Marshall, Morgan & Scott, 1950).

Geluykens, R., 'Information Flow in English Conversation: A New Approach to the Given-New Distinction', in Ventola (ed.), *Functional and Systemic Linguistics*, pp. 141–67.

Gench, F.T., 'Luke 7.36-50', *Int* 46 (1992), pp. 285–90.

Gergely, G., *Free Word Order and Discourse Interpretation* (Budapest: Akadémiai Kiadó, 1991).

Ghadessy, M., 'Thematic Development and its Relationship to Registers and Genres', *OPSL* 7 (1993), pp. 1–25.

Giblin, C.H., '"The Things of God" in the Question Concerning Tribute to Caesar', *CBQ* 33 (1971), pp. 510–27.

Gibson, J.B., 'The Rebuke of the Disciples in Mark 8.14-21', *JSNT* 27 (1986), pp. 31–47.

Giseke, B., 'Über die Wortstellung in abhängigen Sätzen bei Homer', *JCP* 31 (1861), pp. 225–32.

Givón, T., 'The Drift from VSO to SVO in Biblical Hebrew: The Pragmatics of Tense-Aspect', in C. Li (ed.), *Mechanisms of Syntactic Change* (Austin: University of Texas, 1977), pp. 182–254.

—'The Binding Hierarchy and the Typology of Complements', *SL* 4 (1980), pp. 333–77.

—'Topic Continuity in Discourse: The Functional Domain of Switch Reference', in J. Haiman and P. Munro (eds), *Switch-Reference and Universal Grammar: Proceedings of a Symposium on Switch Reference and Universal Grammar, Winnipeg, May 1981* (Amsterdam: John Benjamins, 1983), pp. 51–82.

—'Topic Continuity in Discourse: An Introduction', in *idem* (ed.), *Topic Continuity in Discourse: A Quantitative Cross-Language Study* (Amsterdam: John Benjamins, 1983), pp. 1–41.

—'Beyond Foreground and Background', in R.S. Tomlins (ed.), *Coherence and Grounding in Discourse* (Amsterdam: John Benjamins, 1987).

—*Syntax: A Functional-Typological Introduction* (2 vols.; Amsterdam: John Benjamins, 1984–1990).

Givón, T. (ed.), *Topic Continuity in Discourse: A Quantitative Cross-Language Study* (TSL, 3; Amsterdam: John Benjamins, 1983).

Godet, F.L., *Commentary on Luke* (KRL; Grand Rapids: Kregel, 1981).

Goodell, T.D., 'The Order of Words in Greek', *TAPA* 21 (1890), pp. 5–47.

Gormley, J.F., 'The Final Passion Prediction: A Study of LK. 22:35-38' (PhD thesis, Fordham University, 1974).

Gosden, H., *A Genre-based Investigation of Theme: Product and Process in Scientific Research Articles Written by NNS Novice Researchers* (MSL, 7; Department of English, University of Nottingham, 1996).

Goulder, M.D., *Luke: A New Paradigm* (JSNTSup, 20; Sheffield, Sheffield Academic Press, 1989).

Grassi, J.A., 'The Five Loaves of the High Priest', *NovT* 7 (1964–65), pp. 119–122.

Green, S.G., *Handbook to the Grammar of the Greek Testament. Together with Complete Vocabulary and an Examination of the Chief New Testament Synonyms* (London: The Religious Tract Society, rev. edn 1912).

Greenbaum, S., 'Syntactic Frequency and Acceptability', in T.A. Perry (ed.), *Evidence and Argumentation in Linguistics* (Berlin: Walter de Gruyter, 1980), pp. 301–14.

Greenberg, J.H., 'Some Universals of Grammar with Particular Reference to the Order of Meaningful Elements', in *idem* (ed.), *Universals of Language* (Cambridge: MIT Press, 2nd edn 1966), pp. 58–93.

—*Language Universals: With Special Reference to Feature Hierarchies* (JLSMin, 59; The Hague: Mouton, 1966).

—'Language Universals', in C.A. Ferguson *et al.* (eds), *Theoretical Foundations* (CTIL, 3; The Hague: Mouton, 1966), pp. 61–112.

—*Language Typology: A Historical and Analytic Overview* (JLSMin, 184; The Hague: Mouton, 1974).

Grimes, J.E., *The Thread of Discourse* (JLSMin, 207; The Hague: Mouton, 1975).

Grimes, J.E., (ed.), *Sentence Initial Devices* (SILPL, 75; Dallas: Summer Institute of Linguistics, 1986).

Gundry-Volf, J.M., 'Between Text and Sermon: Mark 9:33-37', *Int* 53 (1999), pp. 57–61.

Gvozdanović, J., 'Defining Markedness', in O.M. Tomic (ed.), *Markedness in Synchrony and Diachrony* (TILSM, 39; Berlin: Mouton de Gruyter, 1989), pp. 47–66.

Hagner, D.A., 'Balancing the Old and the New: The Law of Moses in Matthew and Paul', *Int* 51 (1997), pp. 20–30.

Hahn, E.A., *Subjunctive and Optative: Their Origin as Futures* (New York: American Philological Association, 1953).

Hall, S., 'Synoptic Transfigurations: Mark 9.2-10 and Partners', *KTR* 10 (1987), pp. 41–44.

Halliday, M.A.K., 'Notes on Transitivity and Theme in English, Part I', *J Ling* 3 (1967), pp. 37–81.

—'Notes on Transitivity and Theme in English, Part II', *J Ling* 3 (1967), pp. 199–244.

—'Notes on Transitivity and Theme in English, Part III', *J Ling* 4 (1968), pp. 179–215.

—*Explorations in the Functions of Language* (London: Edward Arnold, 1973).

—'Language As Code and Language As Behaviour: A Systemic-functional Interpretation of the Nature and Ontogenesis of Dialogue', in R.P. Fawcett *et al.* (eds), *Language as Social Semiotic* (SCL, 1; London: Frances Pinter, 1984), pp. 3–35.

—*An Introduction to Functional Grammar* (London: Edward Arnold, 2nd edn 1994).

Halliday, M.A.K., and R. Hasan, *Cohesion in English* (London: Longman, 1976).

—*Language, Context, and Text: Aspects of Language in a Social-Semiotic Perspective* (Oxford: Oxford University Press, 2nd edn 1989).

Halliday, M.A.K., and J.R. Martin, *Writing Science: Literary and Discursive Power* (London: Palmer Press, 1993).

Halliday, M.A.K., and C.M.I.M. Matthiessen, *Construing Experience through Meaning: A Language-based Approach to Cognition* (London: Cassell, 1999).

Halpern, A.L., 'Topics in the Placement and Morphology of Clitics (Slavic, Greek, Sanskrit)' (PhD thesis, Stanford University, 1992).

Hamitouche, F., 'Studies in Word Order, A Functional Pragmatic Approach' (PhD thesis, University of Essex, 1988).

Hammond, M., E.A. Moravcsik and J.R. Wirth (eds), *Studies in Syntactic Typology* (TSL, 17; Amsterdam: John Benjamins, 1988).

Harder, M.A., R.F. Regtuit and G.C. Wakker (eds), *Hellenistica Groningana II: Theocritus* (Groningen: Frosten, 1996).

Harm, H., 'Word Order in Jude', *START* 8 (1983), pp. 32–39.

Hasan, R., 'Coherence and Cohesive Harmony', in J. Flood (ed.), *Understanding Reading Comprehension: Cognition, Language, and the Structure of Prose* (Newark: International

Reading Association, 1984), pp. 181–219.

Hatina, T.R., 'The Perfect Tense-Form in Recent Debate: Galatians as a Case Study', *FN* 8 (1995), pp. 3–22.

—'The Perfect Tense-Form in Colossians: Verbal Aspect, Temporality and the Challenge of Translation', in S.E. Porter and R.S. Hess (eds), *Translating the Bible: Problems and Prospects* (JSNTSup, 173; Sheffield: Sheffield Academic Press, 1999), pp. 224–52.

—*In Search of a Context: The Function of Scripture in Mark's Narrative* (JSNTSup, 232; SSEJC, 8; Sheffield: Sheffield Academic Press, 2002).

Hawkin, D.J., 'Incomprehension of the Disciples in the Markan Redaction', *JBL* 91 (1972), pp. 491–500.

Hawkins, J.A., 'Implicational Universals as Predicators of Word Order Change', *Lang* 55 (1979), pp. 618–648.

—'On Implicational and Distributional Universals of Word Order', *J Ling* 16 (1980), pp. 193–235.

—*Word Order Universals* (QALS, 3; New York: Academic Press, 1983).

—'Modifier-Head or Function-Argument Relations in Phrase Structure?', *Lingua* 63 (1984), pp. 107–38.

—'Implicational Universals as Predictors of Language Acquisition', *Ling* 25 (1987), pp. 453–73.

—'On Generative and Typological Approaches to Universal Grammar', in Hawkins and Holmback (eds), *Papers in Universal Grammar*, pp. 85–100.

—'Explaining Language Universals', in J.A. Hawkins (ed.), *Explaining Language Universals* (Oxford: Basil Blackwell, 1988), pp. 3–28.

—'A Parsing Theory of Word Order Universals', *Ling Inq* 21 (1990), pp. 223–61.

—*A Performance Theory of Order and Constituency* (CSL, 73; Cambridge: Cambridge University Press, 1994).

Hawkins, J.A., and A. Cutler, 'Psycholinguistic Factors in Morphological Asymmetry', in J.A. Hawkins, (ed.), *Explaining Language Universals* (Oxford: Basil Blackwell, 1988), pp. 280–317.

—'Heads, Parsinga and Word Order Universals', in G.G. Corbett *et al.* (eds), *Heads in Grammatical Theory* (Cambridge: Cambridge University Press, 1993), pp. 231–65.

Hawkins, J.A., and G. Gilligan, 'Prefixing and Suffixing Universals in Relation to Basic Word Order', in Hawkins and Holmback (eds), *Papers in Universal Grammar*, pp. 219–59.

Hawkins, J.A., and H.K. Holmback (eds), *Papers in Universal Grammar: Generative and Typological Approaches* (*Lingua* 74 [special issue]; Amsterdam: Elsevier, 1988).

Headlam, W., 'The Transposition of Words in MSS', *CR* 16 (1902), pp. 243–56.

Heimerdinger, J., 'Word Order in Koine Greek: Using a Text-Critical Approach to Study Word Order Patterns in the Greek Text of Acts', *FN* 9 (1996), pp. 139–80.

—*The Bezan Text of Acts: A Contribution of Discourse Analysis to Textual Criticism* (JSNTSup, 236; Sheffield: Sheffield Academic Press, 2002).

Heimerdinger, J.-M., *Topic, Focus and Foreground in Ancient Hebrew Narratives* (JSOTSup, 295; Sheffield: Sheffield Academic Press, 1999).

Hendriksen, W., *Exposition of the Gospel According to Luke* (NTC; Grand Rapids: Baker Book House, 1978).

Hess, H.H., 'Dynamics of the Greek Noun Phrase in Mark', *OPTAT* 4 (1990), pp. 353–69.

Hobart, W.K., *The Medical Language of St. Luke: A Proof from Internal Evidence That "The Gospel According to St. Luke" and "The Acts of the Apostles" Were Written by the Same Person, and that the Writer was a Medical Man* (DUPS; London: Longmans, Green, 1882).

Hoehner, H.W., 'Why Did Pilate Hand Over Jesus to Antipas?', in E. Bammel (ed.), *The Trial of Jesus: Cambridge Studies in Honour of C.F.D. Moule* (SBTSS, 13; London: SCM Press, 1970), pp. 84–90.

Holst, R. 'The One Anointing of Jesus: Another Application of the Form-Critical Method', *JBL* 95 (1976), pp. 435–46.

Hopper, P.J., and S.A. Thompson, 'Transitivity in Grammar and Discourse', *Lang* 56 (1980), pp. 251–99.

Horrocks, G., *Greek: A History of the Language and its Speakers* (London: Longman, 1997).

Houben, J.L., 'Word-Order Change and Subordination in Homeric Greek', *JIES* 5 (1977), pp. 1–8.

Householder, F.W., and G. Nagy, *Greek: A Survey of Recent Work* (JLSP, 211; The Hague: Mouton, 1972).

Hudson, R.A., 'Constituency in a Systemic Description of the English Clause', in M.A.K. Halliday and J.R. Martin (eds), *Readings in Systemic Linguistics* (London: Batsford Academic and Educational, 1981), pp. 103–21.

Jacobson, A.D., 'Divided Families and Christian Origins', in R.A. Piper (ed.), *The Gospel behind the Gospels: Current Studies on Q* (NovTSup, 75; Leiden: E.J.Brill, 1995), pp. 360–80.

Jannaris, A., *An Historical Greek Grammar Chiefly of the Attic Dialect* (London Olms, Hidlesheim, 2nd edn 1897).

Janse, M., 'Convergence and Divergence in the Development of the Greek and Latin Clitic Pronouns', in R. Sornicola *et al.* (eds), *Stability, Variation and Change of Word-Order Patterns over Time* (Amsterdam: John Benjamins, 2000), pp. 231–58.

Jeffers, R., 'Review of Lehmann: Proto-Indo-European Syntax', *Lang* 52 (1976), pp. 982–88.

Jepson, J., 'Holistic Models of Word Order Typology', *Word* 40 (1989), pp. 297–314.

Johnson, A.F., 'Jesus and Moses: Rabbinic Backgrounds and Exegetical Concerns in Matthew 5 as Crucial to the Theological Foundations of Christian Ethics', in M. Inch and S.J. Schultz (eds), *The Living and Active Word of God* (Winona Lake, IN: Eisenbrauns, 1983), pp. 85–108.

Johnson, E.S., 'Mark 10:46-52: Blind Bartimaeus', *CBQ* 40 (1978), pp. 191–204.

—'Mark VIII. 22-26: The Blind Man from Bethsaida', *NTS* 25 (1979), pp. 370–83.

Johnson, L.T, *The Gospel of Luke* (SPS, 3; Collegeville: The Liturgical Press, 1991).

de Jonge, H.J., 'Sonship, Wisdom, Infancy: Luke 2:41-51a', *NTS* 24 (1978), pp. 317–54.

Jordaan, G.J.C., 'The Word-Order Differences between the Greek and the Latin Text in Codex Bezae', in J.H. Petzer and P.J. Hartin (eds), *A South African Perspective on the New Testament: Essays by South African New Testament Scholars Presented to Bruce Manning Metzger during his Visit to South Africa in 1985* (Leiden: E.J. Brill, 1986), pp. 99–111.

Just, A.A., *Luke* (CC; 2 vols.; Saint Louis: Concordia, 1996–97).

Karali, M., 'Aspects of Delphic Word Order' (DPhil thesis, University of Oxford, 1991).

Kelber, W.H., 'The Hour of the Son of Man and the Temptation of the Disciples (Mark 14:32-42)' in *idem*, (ed.), *The Passion in Mark: Studies on Mark 14-16* (Philadelphia: Fortress Press, 1976), pp. 41–60.

Kerr, A.J., 'No Room in the Kataluma', *ExpTim* 103 (1991), pp. 15–16.

Kieckers, E., *Die Stellung des Verbs im griechischen und in den verwandten Sprachen* (Strassburg: K.J. Trübner, 1911).

—'Die Stellung der Verba des Sagens in Schaltesätzen im Griechischen und in den indogermanischen Sprachen', *IF* 30 (1912), pp. 145–90.

Kilgallen, J.J., 'Luke 2.41-50: Foreshadowing of Jesus, Teacher', *Bib* 66 (1985), pp. 553–59.

—'John the Baptist, the Sinful Woman, and the Pharisee', *JBL* 104 (1985), pp. 675–79.

—'The Sadducees and Resurrection from the Dead: Luke 20.27-40', *Bib* 67 (1986), pp. 478–95.

—'A Proposal for Interpreting Luke 7.36-50', *Bib* 72 (1991), pp. 305–30.

—'Jesus, Saviour, the Glory of Your People Israel', *Bib* 75 (1994), pp. 305–28.

—'The Plan of the 'ΝΟΜΙΚΟΣ' (Luke 10:25-37)', *NTS* 42 (1996), pp. 615–19.

Kilpatrick, G.D., 'The Order of Some Noun and Adjective Phrases in the New Testament', *NovT* 5 (1962), pp. 111–14.

Kim, K.J., *Stewardship and Almsgiving in Luke's Theology* (JSNTSup, 155; Sheffield: Sheffield Academic Press, 1998).

Kingsbury, J.D., *Matthew As Story* (Philadelphia: Fortress, 2nd edn 1988).
—*Conflict in Mark: Jesus, Authorities, Disciples* (Minneapolis: Fortress Press, 1989).
Kitzberger, I.R. 'Love and Footwashing: John 13.1-20 and Luke 7.36-50. Read
          Intertextuality', *BI* 2 (1994), pp. 190–206.
Knowles, M., *Jeremiah in Matthew's Gospel: The Rejected Prophet Motif in Matthean
          Redaction* (JSNTSup, 68; Sheffield: Sheffield Academic Press, 1993).
Kodell, J., 'Luke and the Children: The Beginning and End of the Great Interpolation
          (Luke 9:45-56; 18:9-23)', *CBQ* 49 (1987), pp. 415–30.
Kress, G.R. (ed.), *Halliday: System and Function in Language* (Oxford: Oxford
          University Press, 1976).
Kuno, S., 'The Position of Relative Clauses and Conjunctions', *Ling Inq* 5 (1974), pp. 117–36.
Kurz, W.S., 'Luke 22:14-38 and Greco-Roman and Biblical Farewell Addresses', *JBL* 104
          (1985), pp. 251–68.
Lampe, G.W.H., 'The Two Swords (Luke 22:35-38)', in Bammel and Moule (eds), *Jesus
          and the Politics of His Days*, pp. 335–51.
Lampe, G.W.H. (ed.), *A Patristic Greek Lexicon* (Oxford: Oxford University Press, 1961).
Larkin, W.J., 'Luke's Use of the Old Testament in Luke 22-23' (PhD thesis, Durham
          University, 1974).
Larsen, I., 'Word Order and Relative Prominence in New Testament Greek', *NOT* 5 (1991),
          pp. 29–34.
Lehmann, W.P., 'Converging Theories in Linguistics', *Lang* 48 (1972), pp. 266–75.
—'A Structural Principle of Language and its Implications', *Lang* 49 (1973), pp. 47–66.
—*Proto-Indo-European Syntax* (Austin: University of Texas Press, 1974).
—'A Discussion of Compound and Word Order', in Li (ed.), *Word Order and Word Order
          Change*, pp. 149–62.
—'From Topic to Subject in Indo-European', in Li (ed.), *Subject and Topic*, pp. 447–56.
—'The Great Underlying Ground-Plans', in Lehmann (ed.), *Syntactic Typology*, pp. 1–55.
—*Historical Linguistics* (London: Routledge, 3rd edn 1992).
Lehmann, W.P. (ed.), *Syntactic Typology: Studies in the Phenomenology of Language*
          (Sussex: The Harvester Press, 1978).
Levinsohn, S.H., 'Initial Elements in a Clause or Sentence in the Narrative of Acts',
          START 4 (1981), pp. 2–23.
—*Textual Connections in Acts* (SBLMS, 31; Altanta: Scholars Press, 1987).
—'Phrase Order and the Article in Galatians: A Functional Sentence Perspective Approach',
          OPTAT 3 (1989), pp. 65–82.
—'A Discourse Study of Constituent Order and the Article in Philippians', *NOT* 8 (1994),
          pp. 25–26.
—'A Discourse Study of Constituent Order and the Article in Philippians', in Porter and
          Carson (eds), *Discourse Analysis and Other Topics in Biblical Greek*, pp. 60–74.
—*Discourse Features of New Testament Greek: A Coursebook on the Information
          Structure of New Testament Greek* (Dallas: SIL International, 2nd edn 2000).
Li, C.N. (ed.), *Word Order and Word Order Change* (Austin: University of Texas Press, 1975).
—*Subject and Topic* (New York: Academic Press, 1976).
Liddell, H.G., and R. Scott, *A Greek-English Lexicon* (rev. H.S. Jones *et al*; Oxford:
          Clarendon Press, 9th edn with a supplement 1968).
Lightfoot, D., 'Abstract Verbs and the Development of the Greek Mood System', in L.
          Heilmann (ed.), *Proceedings of the Eleventh International Congress of Linguistics*.
          (Bologna: Societa editrice il Mulino, 1974), II, pp. 549–56.
—*Natural Logic and the Greek Moods: The Nature of the Subjunctive and Optative in
          Classical Greek* (JLSP, 230; Paris: Mouton, 1975).
Lincoln, A.T., 'The Promise and the Failure: Mark 16:7, 8', *JBL* 108 (1989), pp. 283–300.
Lindars, B., *Jesus Son of Man: A Fresh Examination of the Son of Man Sayings in the
          Gospels in the Light of Recent Research* (London: SPCK, 1983).

—'Response to Richard Bauckham: The Idiomatic Use of Bar Enasha', *JSNT* 23 (1985), pp. 35–41.

Loepfe, A., *Die Wortstellung im griechischen Sprechsatz, erklärt an Stücken aus Platon und Menander* (Paulusdruckerei: Freiburg in der Schweiz, 1940).

Longacre, R.E., *The Grammar of Discourse* (New York: Plenum Press, 1983).

Louw, J.P., 'Macro Levels of Meaning in Lk 7:36-50', in Petzer and Hartin (eds), *A South African Perspective on the New Testament*, pp. 128–35.

Louw, J.P., and E.A. Nida, *Greek-English Lexicon of the New Testament Based on Semantic Domains* (2 vols.; New York: United Bible Society, 2nd edn 1989).

Lull, D., 'The Servant-Benefactor as a Model of Greatness (Luke 22:24-30)', *NovT* 28 (1986), pp. 289–305.

Luraghi, S., 'The Pragmatics of Verb Initial Sentences in Some Indo-European Languages', in P. Downing and M. Noonan (eds), *Word Order in Discourse* (TSL, 30; Amsterdam: John Benjamins, 1995), pp. 355–86.

Lyons, J., *Semantics* (2 vols.; Cambridge: Cambridge University Press, 1977).

Malbon, E.S., 'Fallible Followers: Women and Men in the Gospel of Mark', *Semeia* 28 (1983), pp. 29–48.

—'Disciples/Crowds/Whoever: Markan Characters and Readers', *NovT* 28 (1986), pp. 104–30.

—'Text and Contexts: Interpreting the Disciples in Mark', *Semeia* 62 (1993), pp. 81–102.

Mallinson, G., and B.J. Blake, *Language Typology: Cross Linguistic-Studies in Syntax* (Amsterdam: North Holland, 1981).

Manson, W., *The Gospel of Luke* (MNTC; London: Hodder & Stoughton, 1930).

Marquis, G., 'Word Order as a Criterion for the Evaluation of Translation Technique in the LXX and the Evaluation of Word-Order Variants as Exemplified in LXX-Ezekiel', *Textus* 13 (1986), pp. 59–84.

Marshall, C.D., *Faith as a Theme in Mark's Narrative* (SNTSMS, 64; Cambridge: Cambridge University Press, 1989).

Marshall, I.H., *The Gospel of Luke: A Commentary on the Greek Text* (NIGTC; Exeter: The Paternoster Press, 1978).

—'Son of Man', in J.B. Green and S. McKnight (eds), *Dictionary of Jesus and the Gospels* (Downers Grove: InterVarsity Press, 1992), pp. 775–81.

Marshall, M.H.B., *Verbs, Nouns and Postpositives in Attic Prose* (SCS, 3; Edinburgh: Scottish Academic Press, 1987).

Martin, J.R., *English Text: System and Structure* (Amsterdam: John Benjamins, 1992).

Martín-Asensio, G., 'Participant Reference and Foregrounded Syntax in the Stephen Episode', in S.E. Porter and J.T. Reed (eds), *Discourse Analysis and the New Testament: Approaches and Results* (JSNTSup, 170; SNTG, 4; Sheffield: Sheffield Academic Press, 1999), pp. 235–57.

—*Transitivity-based Foregrounding in the Acts of the Apostles: A Functional-Grammatical Approach to the Lukan Perspective* (JSNTSup, 202; SNTG, 8; Sheffield: Sheffield Academic Press, 2000).

Matera, F.J., *Passion Narratives and Gospel Theologies: Interpreting the Synoptics through their Passion Stories* (New York: Paulist Press, 1986).

—'The Incomprehension of the Disciples and Peter's Confession (Mark 6,14-8,30)', *Bib* 70 (1989), pp. 153–72.

—'Jesus' Journey to Jerusalem (Luke 9.51-19.46): A Conflict with Israel', *JSNT* 51 (1993), pp. 57–77.

Matthiessen, C.M.I.M., and J.A. Bateman, *Text Generation and Systemic-Functional Linguistics: Experience from English and Japanese* (London: Pinter, 1991).

McDonald, J.I.H., 'Rhetorical Issues and Rhetorical Strategy in Luke 10.25-37 and Acts 10.1-11.18', in S.E. Porter and T.H. Olbricht (eds), *Rhetoric and the New Testament: Essays from the 1992 Heidelberg Conference* (JSNTSup, 90; Sheffield: Sheffield Academic Press, 1993), pp. 59–73.

McGing, B.C., 'Pontius Pilate and the Sources', *CBQ* 53 (1991), pp. 416–38.

McGregor, W., 'The Concept of Rank in Systemic Linguistics', in Ventola (ed.), *Functional and Systemic Linguistics*, pp. 121–38.

—'The Place of Circumstantials in Systemic-functional Grammar', in Davies and Ravelli (eds), *Advances in Systemic Linguistics*, pp. 136–49.

McKay, K.L., *A New Syntax of the Verb in New Testament Greek: An Aspectual Approach* (SBG, 5; New York: Peter Lang, 1994).

Michaelson, S., and A.Q. Morton, 'Positional Stylometry', in R.W. Bailey and H. Smith (eds), *The Computer and Literary Studies* (Edinburgh: The University Press, 1973).

Middleton, T.F., *The Doctrine of the Greek Article: Applied to the Criticism and Illustration of the New Testament* (rev. J. Scholefield; Cambridge: J. & J.J. Deighton, 2nd edn 1828).

Milden, A.W., *The Limitations of the Predicative Position in Greek* (Baltimore: John Murphy, 1900).

Minear, P.S., 'A Note on Luke xxii 36', *NovT* 7 (1964–65), pp. 128–34.

—'Luke's Use of the Birth Stories', in L.E. Keck and J.L. Martyn (eds), *Studies in Luke-Acts: Essays Presented in Honor of Paul Schubert, Buckingham Professor of New Testament Criticism and Interpretation at Yale University* (Nashville: Abingdon Press, 1966), pp. 111–130.

Mitchell, D., 'Lehmann's Use of Syntactic Typology', in C.F. Justus and E.C. Polomé (eds), *Language Change and Typological Variation: In Honor of Winfred P. Lehmann on the Occasion of his 83rd Birthday. II. Grammatical Universals and Typology* (JIESM, 31; Washington: Institute for the Study of Man, 1999), pp. 437–43.

Mithun, M., 'Is Basic Word Order Universal?', in R.S. Tomlin (ed.), *Coherence and Grounding in Discourse* (Amsterdam: John Benjamins, 1987), pp. 281–328.

Moeller, H.R., and A. Kramer, 'An Overlooked Structural Pattern in New Testament Greek', *NovT* 5 (1962), pp. 25–35.

Moessner, D.P., 'Luke 9:1-50: Luke's Preview of the Journey of the Prophet like Moses of Deuteronomy', *JBL* 102 (1983), pp. 575–605.

—'"The Christ Must Suffer": New Light on the Jesus-Peter, Stephen, Paul Parallels in Luke-Acts', *NovT* 28 (1986), pp. 220–56.

Monro, D.B., *A Grammar of the Homeric Dialect* (Oxford: Clarendon Press, 2nd edn 1891).

Moorhouse, A.C., *Studies in the Greek Negatives* (Cardiff: University of Wales Press, 1959).

—*The Syntax of Sophocles* (MnemosyneSup, 75; Leiden: E.J. Brill, 1982).

Moravcsik, E., and J. Wirth, 'Markedness: An Overview', in Eckman, Moravcsik and Wirth (eds), *Markedness*, p. 3.

Morpurgo-Davies, A., 'Article and Demonstrative: A Note', *Glotta* 46 (1968), pp. 77–85.

Morrell, K.S., 'Studies on the Phrase Structure of Early Attic Prose' (PhD thesis, Harvard University, 1990).

Morris, L., *The Gospel According to St. Luke: An Introduction and Commentary* (London: Inter-Varsity Press, 1974).

Morris, R.L.B., 'Why AUGOUSTOS? A Note to Luke 2.1', *NTS* 38 (1992), pp. 140–42.

Moule, C.F.D., *An Idiom Book of New Testament Greek* (Cambridge: Cambridge University Press, 2nd edn 1959).

Muraoka, T., 'The Use of ὡς in the Greek Bible', *NovT* 7 (1964–65), pp. 51–72.

Neale, D.A., *None but the Sinners: Religious Categories in the Gospel of Luke* (JSNTSup, 58; Sheffield: Sheffield Academic Press, 1991).

Neirynck, F., 'Minor Agreements Matthew-Luke in the Transfiguration Story', in P. Hoffmann (ed.), *Orientierung an Jesus: Zur Theologie der Synoptiker* (Freiburg: Herder, 1973), pp. 253–66.

Nelson, P.K., 'The Flow of Thought in Luke 22: 24-27', *JSNT* 43 (1991), pp. 113–23.

—*Leadership and Discipleship: A Study of Luke 22:24-30* (SBLDS, 138; Atlanta: Scholars Press, 1994).

—'The Unitary Character of Luke 22:24-30', *NTS* 40 (1994), pp. 609–19.

Nesbitt, C., and G. Plum, 'Probabilities in a Systemic-functional Grammar: The Clause Complex in English', in R.P. Fawcett and D. Young (eds), *New Developments in Systemic Linguistics*. I. *Theory and Application* (London: Pinter, 1988), pp. 6–38.

Neyrey, J.H., *The Passion According to Luke: A Redaction Study of Luke's Soteriology* (New York: Paulist Press, 1985).

Nolland, J., *Luke* (WBC, 35A, 35B and 35C; Dallas: Word Books, 1989–1993).

Nuyts, J., and G. de Schutter (eds), *Getting One's Words into Line: On Word Order and Functional Grammar* (FGS, 5; Dordrecht: Foris, 1987).

Olofsson, S., 'Studying the Word Order of the Septuagint: Questions and Possibilities', *SJOT* 10 (1996), pp. 217–37.

Onwu, N., 'The Distorted Vision: Reinterpretation of Mark 8:22-26 in the Context of Social Justice', *WAR* 19 (1980), pp. 46–52.

O'Toole, R.F., 'Luke's Message in Luke 9:1-50', *CBQ* 49 (1987), pp. 74–89.

Ottey, J.L., 'In a Stable Born our Brother', *ExpTim* 98 (1986), pp. 71–73.

Owen-Ball, D.T., 'Rabbinic Rhetoric and the Tribute Passage (Mt. 22.15-22; Mk. 12.13-17; Lk. 20.20-26)', *NovT* 35 (1993), pp. 1–14.

Paffenroth, K., *The Story of Jesus According to L* (JSNTSup, 147; Sheffield: Sheffield Academic Press, 1997).

Palek, B. (ed.), *Proceedings of LP'94. Proceedings of the Conference: Item Order in Natural Languages* (Prague: Charles University Press, 1995).

Parker, F., 'Typology and Word Order Change', *Ling* 18 (1980), pp. 269–88.

Patterson, S.J., 'Fire and Dissension. Ipsissima Vox Jesu in Q 12.49, 51-53', *Forum* 5 (1989), pp. 121–39.

Payne, D.L., 'Hawkins: Word Order Universals', *Lang* 61 (1985), pp. 462–66.

Payne, D.L. (ed.), *Pragmatics of Word Order Flexibility* (TSL, 22; Amsterdam: John Benjamins, 1992).

van Peer, W., *Stylistics and Psychology: Investigation of Foregrounding* (London: Croom Helm, 1986).

Perry, T.A. (ed.), *Evidence and Argumentation in Linguistics* (Berlin: Walter de Gruyter, 1980).

Perysinakis, I.N., 'Herodotus Grammarized', *CRNS* 47 (1997), pp. 346–48.

Pierpont, W.G., 'Studies in Word Order: Personal Pronoun Possessives in Nominal Phrases in the New Testament', *START* 15 (1986), pp. 3–25.

Plummer, A., *A Critical and Exegetical Commentary on the Gospel According to St. Luke* (ICC; Edinburgh: T&T Clark, 5th edn 1922).

Porter, S.E., *Verbal Aspect in the Greek of the New Testament, with Reference to Tense and Mood* (SBG, 1; New York: Peter Lang, 1989).

—'Word Order and Clause Structure in New Testament Greek: An Unexplored Area of Greek Linguistics Using Philippians as a Test Case', *FN* 6 (1993), pp. 177–205.

—*Idioms of the Greek New Testament* (BLG, 2; Sheffield: Sheffield Academic Press, 2nd edn 1994).

—'Discourse Analysis and New Testament Studies: An Introductory Survey', in Porter and Carson (eds), *Discourse Analysis and Other Topics in Biblical Greek*, pp. 14–35.

Porter, S.E., and D.A. Carson (eds), *Biblical Greek Language and Linguistics: Open Questions in Current Research* (JSNTSup, 80; Sheffield: Sheffield Academic Press, 1993).

—*Discourse Analysis and Other Topics in Biblical Greek* (JSNTSup, 113; Sheffield: Sheffield Academic Press, 1995).

—*Linguistics and the New Testament: Critical Junctures* (JSNTSup, 168; SNTG,5; Sheffield: Sheffield Academic Press, 1999).

Poythress, V.S., 'The Use of the Intersentence Conjunctions DE, OUN, KAI, and Asyndeton in the Gospel of John', *NovT* 26 (1984), pp. 312–40.

Quesnell, Q., 'The Women at Luke's Supper', in R.J. Cassidy and P.J. Scharper (eds), *Political Issues in Luke-Acts* (Maryknoll: Orbis Books, 1983), pp. 59–79.

Quirk, R., and S. Greenbaum, *A University Grammar of English* (London: Longman, 1973).

Quirk, R., S. Greenbaum and G. Leech (eds), *A Grammar of Contemporary English* (London: Longman, 1972).

Radics, K., *Typology and Historical Linguistics: Affixed Person-Marking Paradigms* (SUA, 24; Szeged: Attila József University Press, 1985).

Radney, J.R., 'Some Factors That Influence Fronting in Koine Clauses', *OPTAT* 2 (1988), pp. 1–79.

Ransom, E.N., *Complementation: Its Meanings and Forms* (TSL, 10; Amsterdam: John Benjamins, 1986).

Ravens, D.A.S., 'The Setting of Luke's Account of the Anointing: Luke 7.2-8.3', *NTS* 34 (1988), pp. 282–92.

—'Luke 9:7-62 and the Prophetic Role of Jesus', *NTS* 36 (1990), pp. 119–29.

—*Luke and the Restoration of Israel* (JSNTSup, 119; Sheffield: Sheffield Academic Press, 1995).

Reed, J.T., 'The Infinitive with Two Substantival Accusatives: An Ambiguous Construction?', *NovT* 33 (1991), pp. 1–27.

—'Cohesive Ties in 1 Timothy: In Defense of the Epistle's Unity', *Neot* 26 (1992), pp. 131–47.

—'Identifying Theme in the New Testament: Insights from Discourse Analysis', in Porter and Carson (eds), *Discourse Analysis and Other Topics in Biblical Greek*, pp. 75–101.

—*A Discourse Analysis of Philippians: Method and Rhetoric in the Debate over Literary Integrity* (JSNTSup, 136; Sheffield: Sheffield Academic Press, 1997).

—'Discourse Analysis', in S.E. Porter (ed.), *Handbook to Exegesis of the New Testament* (NTTS, 25; Leiden: Brill, 1997), pp. 189–217.

Reed, J.T., and R.A. Reese, 'Verbal Aspect, Discourse Prominence, and the Letter of Jude', *FN* 9 (1996), pp. 181–99.

Reiling, J., and J.L. Swellengrebel, *A Translator's Handbook on the Gospel of Luke* (Leiden: E.J. Brill, 1977).

Renkema, J., *Discourse Studies: An Introductory Textbook* (Amsterdam: John Benjamins, 1993).

Resseguie, J.L., 'Automatization and Defamiliarization in Luke 7.36-50', *JLT* 5 (1991), pp. 137–50.

Rijkhoff, J., 'Word Order Tendencies in Two Prefield Subtypes', in Nuyts and de Schutter (eds), *Getting One's Words into Line*, pp. 1–15.

Rijksbaron, A., *The Syntax and Semantics of the Verb in Classical Greek: An Introduction* (Amsterdam: J.C. Gieben, 2nd edn 1994).

Rijksbaron, A., (ed.), *New Approaches to Greek Particles. Proceedings of the Colloquium Held in Amsterdam, January 4-6, 1996, to Honour C.J. Ruijgh on the Occasion of his Retirement* (ASCP, 7; Amsterdam: J.C. Gieben, 1997).

Rijksbaron, A., H.A. Mulder and G. Wakker (eds), *In the Footsteps of Raphael Kühner. Proceedings of the International Colloquium in Commemoration of the 150th Anniversary of the Publication of Raphael Kühner's Ausführliche Grammatik der griechischen Sprache. II. Theil: Syntaxe. Amsterdam, 1986* (Amsterdam: J.C. Gieben, 1988).

Ringe, S.H., 'Luke 9:28-36: The Beginning of an Exodus', *Semeia* 28 (1983), pp. 81–99.

Robbins, V.K., 'The Woman Who Touched Jesus' Garment: Socio-Rhetorical Analysis of the Synoptic Accounts', *NTS* 33 (1987), pp. 502–15.

Roberts, J.R., 'The Syntax of Discourse Structure', *NOT* 11 (1997), pp. 15–34.

Roberts, W.R., 'A Point of Greek and Latin Word-Order', *CR* 26 (1912), pp. 177–79.

Robertson, A.T., *A Grammar of the Greek New Testament in the Light of Historical Research* (Nashville: Broadman Press, 1934).

Robinson, B.P., 'The Place of the Emmaus Story in Luke-Acts', *NTS* 30 (1984), pp. 481–97.

Rosenbaum, P.S., *The Grammar of English Predicate Complement Construction* (Cambridge, MA: MIT Press, 1967).

Ross, J.R., 'Gapping and the Order of Constituents', in M. Bierwisch and K.E. Heidolph (eds), *Progress in Linguistics: A Collection of Papers* (JLSMaj, 43; The Hague: Mouton, 1970), pp. 249–59.

Roth, S.J., *The Blind, the Lame, and the Poor: Character Types in Luke-Acts* (JSNTSup, 144; Sheffield: Sheffield Academic Press, 1997).

Saldarini, A.J., *Matthew's Christian-Jewish Community* (Chicago: University of Chicago Press, 1994).

Schmidt, D., 'Luke's "Innocent" Jesus: A Scriptural Apologetic', in R.J. Cassidy and P.J. Scharper (eds), *Political Issues in Luke-Acts* (Maryknoll: Orbis Books, 1983), pp. 111–21.

Schneider, G., 'The Political Charge against Jesus (Luke 23:2)', in Bammel and Moule (eds), *Jesus and the Politics of His Days*, pp. 403–14.

Schriefers, H.J., *On Semantic Markedness in Language Production and Verification* (Druck: Stichting Studentenpers Nijmegen, 1985).

Schwartz, A., 'The VP-Constituent of SVO Languages', in Heilmann (ed.), *Proceedings of the Eleventh International Congress of Linguistics*, II, pp. 619–37.

Schwartz, L.J., 'Syntactic Markedness and Frequency of Occurrence', in Perry (ed.), *Evidence and Argumentation in Linguistics*, pp. 315–33.

Schweizer, E., *The Good News According to Luke* (trans. D.E. Green; London: SPCK, 1984).

Segbroeck, F.V. (ed.), *The Gospel of Luke: A Cumulative Bibliography 1973–1988* (Leuven: Leuven University Press, 1989).

Segbroeck, F.V., C.M. Tuckett, G. Belle and J. Verheyden (eds), *The Four Gospels 1992*, ICBETL, 100; Leuven: Leuven University Press, 1992).

Senior, D., *The Gospel of Matthew* (Nashville: Abingdon Press, 1997).

Sharrock, A., 'Intratextuality: Texts, Parts, and (W)holes in Theory', in A. Sharrock and H. Morales (eds), *Intratextuality: Greek and Roman Textual Relations* (Oxford: Oxford University Press, 2000), pp. 1–39.

Short, C., 'The Order of Words in Attic Greek Prose: An Essay', in C.D. Yonge, *An English Greek Lexicon: With Many New Articles, an Appendix of Proper Names, and Pillon's Greek Synonyms* (ed. H. Drisler; New York: Harper & Brothers, 1870), pp. i–cxv.

Siewierska, A., *Word Order Rules* (New York: Croom Helm, 1988).

Smith, M.H., 'No Place for a Son of Man', *Forum* 4 (1988), pp. 83–107.

Smith, N.V., 'Constituency, Markedness and Language Change: On the Notion "Consistent Language"', *J Ling* 17 (1981), pp. 39–54.

Smith, R.E., 'The Unmarked Order of Pronominal Objects and Indirect Objects', *START* 12 (1984), pp. 24–26.

—'Recognizing Prominence Features in the Greek New Testament', *START* 14 (1985), pp. 16–52.

Snodgrass, K., 'Matthew and the Law', in D. R. Bauer and M.A. Powell (eds), *Treasures New and Old: Recent Contributions to Matthean Studies* (Altanta: Scholars Press, 1996), pp. 99–127.

Soards, M.L., *The Passion According to Luke: The Special Material of Luke 22* (JSNTSup, 14; Sheffield: Sheffield Academic Press, 1987).

—'Luke 2.22-40', *Int* 44 (1990), pp. 400–405.

Squires, J.T., *The Plan of God in Luke-Acts* (SNTSMS, 76; Cambridge: Cambridge University Press, 1993).

Stein, R.H., *Luke* (NAC, 24; Nashville: Broadman Press, 1992).

Steinhauser, M.G., 'Putting One's Hand to the Plow: The Authenticity of Q 9.61-62', *Forum* 5 (1989), pp. 151–58.

Sterling, G.E., 'Jesus as Exorcist: An Analysis of Matthew 17.14-20; Mark 9.14-29; Luke 9.37-43a', *CBQ* 55 (1993), pp. 467–93.

Stirling, L., *Switch-Reference and Discourse Representation* (Cambridge: Cambridge University Press, 1993).

Suggs, M.J., *Wisdom, Christology, and Law in Matthew's Gospel* (Cambridge, MA: Harvard University, 1970).

Sylva, D.D., 'The Cryptic Clause *en tois tou patros mou dei einai me* in Lk. 2.49b', *ZNW* 78 (1987), pp. 132–40.

Taglicht, J., *Message and Emphasis: On Focus and Scope in English* (ELS, 15; London: Longman, 1984).

Talbert, C.H., 'The Lukan Presentation of Jesus' Ministry in Galilee', *RevExp* 64 (1967), pp. 492–95.

—*Literary Patterns, Theological Themes, and the Genre of Luke-Acts* (SBLMS, 20; Missoula, MT: Scholars Press, 1974).

—*Reading Luke: A Literary and Theological Commentary on the Third Gospel* (New York: Crossroad, 1982).

Talbert, C.H. (ed.), *Perspective on Luke-Acts* (Edinburgh: T&T Clark, 1978).

Talbert, C.H., and J.H. Hayesm, 'A Theology of Sea Storms in Luke-Acts', in D.P. Moessner (ed.), *Jesus and the Heritage of Israel: Luke's Narrative Claim upon Israel's Legacy* (LII, 1; Harrisburg: Trinity International, 1999), pp. 267–83.

Tannehill, R.C., 'Disciples in Mark: The Function of a Narrative Role', 57 (1977), pp. 386–405.

—*The Narrative Unity of Luke-Acts: A Literary Interpretation. I. The Gospel According to Luke* (Philadelphia: Fortress Press, 1986).

—*Luke* (ANTC; Nashville: Abingdon Press, 1996).

Taylor, A., 'Clitics and Configurationality in Ancient Greek' (PhD thesis, University of Pennsylvania, 1990).

—'The Change from SOV to SVO in Ancient Greek', *LV&C* 6 (1994), pp. 1–37.

—'A Prosodic Account of Clitic Position in Ancient Greek', in A.L. Halpern and A.M. Zwicky (eds), *Approaching Second: Second Position Clitics and Related Phenomena* (Stanford: Centre for the Study of Language and Information, 1996), pp. 477–503.

Taylor, V., *The Passion Narrative of St. Luke: A Critical and Historical Investigation* (SNTSMS, 19; Cambridge: Cambridge University Press, 1972).

Thesleff, H., *Studies on Intensification in Early and Classical Greek* (CHL, 21.1; Helsingfors: Centraltryckeriet, 1954).

Thibeaux, E.R., '"Known to Be a Sinner": The Narrative Rhetoric of Luke 7:36-50', *BTB* 23 (1993), pp. 151–60.

Thomas, S., and T. Hawes, *Theme in Academic and Media Discourse* (MSL, 8; Nottingham: Department of English Studies, University of Nottingham, 1997).

Thompson, G., 'The Postponement of Interrogatives in Attic Drama', *ClQ* 33 (1939), pp. 147–52.

—'On the Order of Words in Plato and Saint Matthew', *Link* 2 (1939), pp. 7–17.

—'Simplex Ordo', *CQNS* 15 (1965), pp. 161–75.

Thompson, M.R, *The Role of Disbelief in Mark: A New Approach to the Second Gospel* (New York: Paulist Press, 1989).

Thrall, M.E., *Greek Particles in the New Testament* (NTTS, 3; Leiden: E.J. Brill, 1962).

Tobin, Y., *Invariance, Markedness and Distinctive Feature Analysis: A Contrastive Study of Sign Systems in English and Hebrew* (CILT, 111; Amsterdam: John Benjamins, 1994).

Tomlin, R.S., 'Foreground-Background Information and the Syntax of Subordination', *Text* 5 (1985), pp. 85–122.

—*Basic Word Order: Functional Principles* (CHLS; London: Croom Helm, 1986).

Tomlin, R.S., (ed.), *Coherence and Grounding in Discourse* (Amsterdam: John Benjamins, 1987).

Trainor, M., 'The Begetting of Wisdom: The Teacher and the Disciples in Matthew's Community', *Pacifica* 4 (1991), pp. 148–64.

Trites, A.A., 'The Transfiguration in the Theology of Luke: Some Redactional Links', in L.D. Hurst and N.T. Wright (eds), *The Glory of Christ in the New Testament: Studies in Christology, in Memory of George Bradford Caird* (Oxford: Oxford University Press, 1987), pp. 71–81.

Trudinger, L.P., 'No Room in the Inn: A Note on Luke 2.7', *ExpTim* 102 (1991), pp. 172–73.

Tucker, G., 'An Initial Approach to Comparatives in a Systemic Functional Grammar', in Davies and Ravelli (eds), *Advances in Systemic Linguistics*, pp. 150–65.

Turner, N., *Syntax* (J.H. Moulton, *A Grammar of New Testament Greek*, III; Edinburgh: T&T Clark, 1970).

—*Style* (J.H. Moulton, *A Grammar of New Testament Greek*, IV; Edinburgh: T&T Clark, 1976).

—'The Quality of the Greek of Luke-Acts', in Elliot (ed.), *Studies in New Testament Language and Text*, pp. 387–400.

Tweedie, F.J., and B.D. Frischer, 'Analysis of Classical Greek and Latin Compositional Word-Order Data', *JQL* 6 (1999), pp. 85–97.

Tyson, J.B., 'Blindness of the Disciples in Mark', *JBL* 80 (1961), pp. 261–68.

—'Jews and Judaism in Luke-Acts: Reading as a Godfearer', *NTS* 41 (1995), pp. 19–38.

Vaage, L.E., 'Q1 and the Historical Jesus: Some Peculiar Sayings (7.33-34; 9.57-58, 59-60; 14.26-27)', *Forum* 5 (1989), pp. 159–76.

Vachek, J., *The Linguistic School of Prague: An Introduction to its Theory and Practice* (Bloomington, IN: Indiana University Press, 1966).

Van Iersel, B.M.F., 'Failed Followers in Mark: Mark 13:12 as a Key for the Identification of the Intended Readers', *CBQ* 58 (1996), pp. 244–63.

Vande Kopple, W.J., 'Given and New Information and Some Aspects of the Structures, Semantics, and Pragmatics of Written Texts' in Cooper and Greenbaum (eds), *Studying Writing*, pp. 72–111.

Vennemann, T., 'Analogy in Generative Grammar: The Origin of Word Order', L. Heilmann (ed.), *Proceedings of the Eleventh International Congress of Linguistics*, II, pp. 79–83.

—'Topics, Subjects and Word Order: From SXV to SVX via TVX', in J.M. Anderson and C. Jones (eds), *Historical Linguistics*, I. *Syntax, Morphology, Internal and Comparative Reconstruction. Proceedings of the First International Conference on Historical Linguistics, Edinburgh 2–7 September 1973* (NHLS, 12a; Amsterdam: North Holland, 1974), pp. 339–76.

—'An Explanation of Drift', in Li (ed.), *Word Order and Word Order Change*, pp. 269–306.

Ventola, E., *The Structure of Social Interaction: A Systemic Approach to the Semiotics of Service Encounters* (London: Frances Pinter, 1987).

Ventola, E., (ed.), *Functional and Systemic Linguistics: Approaches and Uses* (TILSM, 55; Berlin: Mouton de Gruyter, 1991).

Via, E.J., 'According to Luke, Who Put Jesus to Death', in R.J. Cassidy and P.J. Scharper (eds), *Political Issues in Luke-Acts* (Maryknoll: Orbis Books, 1983), pp. 122–145.

Votaw, C.W., *The Use of the Infinitive in Biblical Greek* (Chicago: Published by the Author, 1896).

Wagner, G. (ed.), *An Exegetical Bibliography of the New Testament: Luke and Acts* (Macon, GA: Mercer University Press, 1985).

Wagner, U., *Der Hauptmann von Kafarnaum (Mt. 7.28a; 8.5-10, 13 par Lk. 7.1-10): Ein Beitrag zur Q-Forschung* (WUNT, 2; Tubingen: Mohr, 1985).

Wakker, G.C., 'Purpose Clauses in Ancient Greek' in Nuyts and Schutter (eds), *Getting One's Words into Line*, pp. 89–101.

—'Purpose Expressions in Homeric Greek', in Rijksbaron, Mulder and Wakker (eds), *In the Footsteps of Raphael Kühner*, pp. 327–44.

—*Conditions and Conditionals: An Investigation of Ancient Greek* (ASCP, 3; Amsterdam: J.C. Gieben, 1994).

Wallace, D.B., 'The Relation of Adjective to Noun in Anarthrous Constructions in the New Testament', *NovT* 26 (1984), pp. 128–67.

—'The Semantics and Exegetical Significance of the Object-Complement Construction in the New Testament', *GTJ* 6 (1985), pp. 91–112.

Watt, J.M., *Code-Switching in Luke and Acts* (BILS, 31; New York: Peter Lang, 1997).

Weil, H., *The Order of Words in the Ancient Languages Compared with that of the*

Modern Languages (ASTHLS, I; ACL, 14; Amsterdam: John Benjamins, new and reprint edn 1978).

Weinert, F.D., 'The Multiple Meanings of Luke 2:49 and their Significance', *BTB* 13 (1983), pp. 19–22.

Werth, P., *Focus, Coherence and Emphasis* (London: Croom Helm, 1984).

Whaley, L.J., *Introduction to Typology: The Unity and Diversity of Language* (Thousand Oaks: Sage, 1997).

Wiarda, T., 'Peter as Peter in the Gospel of Mark', *NTS* 45 (1999), pp. 19–37.

Wieand, D.J., 'Subject Verb Object Relationship in Independent Clauses in the Gospels and Acts' (PhD thesis, University of Chicago, 1946).

Wills, J., 'Homeric Particle Order', *HS* 106 (1993), pp. 61–81.

Winer, G.B., *A Treatise on the Grammar of New Testament Greek* (trans. W.F. Moulton; Edinburgh: T&T Clark, 9th English edn 1882).

Wright, B.G., *No Small Difference: Sirach's Relationship to its Hebrew Parent Text* (SBLSCS, 26; Atlanta: Scholars Press, 1989).

York, J.O., *The Last Shall Be First: The Rhetoric of Reversal in Luke* (JSNTSup, 46; Sheffield: Sheffield Academic Press, 1991).

Young, D.J., *The Structure of English Clauses* (London: Hutchinson, 1980).

Young, R.A., *Intermediate New Testament Greek: A Linguistic and Exegetical Approach* (Nashville: Broadman & Holman, 1994).

Zubizarreta, M.L., *Prosody, Focus, and Word Order* (LIM; Cambridge, MA: MIT Press, 1998).

INDEXES

INDEX OF REFERENCES

1.45	89, 143	2.4	37, 60, 74,	2.21	82, 84, 87,	2.38	68, 76, 87
1.46	129		78, 152,		153–55,	2.39	82, 152,
1.47	73		170, 196		160, 162,		153, 155,
1.48	67	2.5-7	152		195		157, 158
1.49	56	2.5	85	2.21a	151, 152,	2.39a	155
1.51	71	2.6	115, 151,		154, 155,	2.39b	155
1.53	71, 76		152, 154,		157, 162	2.40	69, 87,
1.54-55	58, 74, 84,		157, 160,	2.21a (a)	154		172
	170		162, 196	2.21a (b)	154	2.41-52	159,
1.57-66	178	2.6a	154	2.22-24	74, 151,		171–73
1.57	75, 161	2.6b	154, 155		152, 154,	2.41-51a	168
1.58	56	2.7	36, 78,		155, 157,	2.41-42	168
1.59	67, 74,		129, 152		170	2.41	41, 67,
	160, 170	2.8-20	152, 163,	2.22	82, 146,		153, 161,
1.60	68		164,		153–55,		170–72
1.61	91		167–69,		158, 160,	2.42-43b	153
1.62	55		172, 173,		162	2.42-43a	155, 158,
1.63	68, 69,		199	2.22a	154, 155		159
	148	2.8	69, 87,	2.22b-24	154	2.42-43	152, 155
1.64	67, 69		151	2.23	39, 78,	2.42	71, 77,
1.65	66, 196	2.9	34, 71,		146		154, 155,
1.66	69, 76		151,	2.23 LXX	49		158–61,
1.67-79	178		164–66	2.24	59, 86, 87,		170
1.67-75	74	2.10	46, 49, 50,		143	2.42a	172
1.67	69, 71,		60, 69,	2.25-27a	153	2.42a	171
	178		164–66	2.25	151, 153	2.42b	171
1.68	56	2.11	60, 78, 79	2.26	48, 49, 77,	2.43-52	163, 165,
1.69-75	75, 170	2.12	87, 129,		129, 143		199
1.69-70	49		164, 165,	2.27	73, 81, 86,	2.43	115, 159,
1.69	129		167		115, 129,		160,
1.70	79, 80	2.13	69, 71, 76,		158		164–66,
1.73-74	58		151, 164,	2.27b	153, 155,		169, 170,
1.73	60		196		157, 158,		173
1.74-75	84, 85	2.15	50, 60, 78,		173	2.43a	161, 171
1.74	87, 129		164	2.27b-28a	152, 155,	2.43b	155, 158,
1.75	160	2.15a	151		157		159,
1.76-77	74, 170	2.15a-b	152	2.27b-35	173		170–72
1.76	178	2.15b	151	2.28	129, 177	2.43b-52	169, 172
1.77	58, 84	2.16	71, 87,	2.28a	155	2.43c	171, 172
1.78-79	73–75, 170		129, 164,	2.29-32	173	2.44-52	167, 168
1.79	84, 87		165, 167	2.29	47, 67, 77	2.44-46a	168
1.80	67, 160	2.17	68, 76, 87,	2.31	60, 90	2.44	67, 68,
2	151, 153,		89, 164,	2.32	146		160, 165,
	158, 159,		166, 168	2.33	76, 89,		167, 171
	163, 169,	2.18	37, 76,		173	2.45	72, 74,
	173, 199		151, 164,	2.34	74		165, 167,
2.1-40	173		165, 167	2.35	56		169–71
2.1	67, 152,	2.19	69, 87,	2.36	67, 87, 88,	2.46-47	168
	160		148, 166,		146, 151,	2.46	67, 87,
2.2	53, 151,		167, 172		160, 161		129, 160,
	152, 160,	2.20	60, 69, 89,	2.37-38	153		167, 171
	196		153, 164,	2.37	60, 87, 91,	2.46b-47	168
2.3	73, 170		166, 168		160, 161		

Ref		Ref		Ref		Ref	
14.4	68, 148	15.2	69	16.5	49, 50, 68	17.9	49
14.5	50, 66, 67, 71, 160	15.3	50	16.6	47, 50, 68, 88	17.10	55
14.6	51, 76	15.4	55, 73, 75	16.7	40, 47, 50	17.11	78, 115
14.7	50, 59, 67, 69, 92	15.5	68, 69	16.8	50, 79, 80, 179	17.12	53, 60, 78, 90, 160
14.8	46, 56, 78, 83, 143	15.6	47, 59, 68, 69, 87	16.9	47, 50, 55, 56, 71, 74, 78, 179	17.13	47, 69, 148, 177
14.9	37, 47, 50, 51, 68, 74, 76	15.7	60, 66, 72, 73, 179			17.14	47, 50, 54, 68, 115
14.10	46, 56, 68	15.8	56, 71	16.10	76	17.15	68, 69, 87
14.12	47, 55, 56, 177	15.9	47, 60, 68, 69, 179	16.11	49, 82	17.16	69, 129
14.13	47, 55	15.10	73, 179	16.12	49, 82	17.17	69, 177
14.14	49, 50, 55, 67	15.12	47, 50, 177	16.13	51	17.18-19	170
14.15	50, 56, 60, 68, 90, 129	15.13	66–68, 71, 88, 148, 160	16.15	87, 169	17.18	58, 76
14.16-17	180	15.14	51, 53, 160, 196	16.17	48, 49	17.19	46, 68, 177
14.16	50	15.15	68, 74, 170	16.18	87, 143		
14.17	46, 58, 67, 74, 170	15.16	51, 60, 84	16.19	69, 87, 88, 160	17.20	68, 76, 89, 92
14.18	47, 50, 51, 84	15.17	66, 68, 73, 87	16.20	69, 74, 170	17.22	55, 160, 177
14.19	170	15.18	68, 177	16.21	59, 68, 84, 148	17.23	46
14.20	51, 73	15.19	47, 72	16.22	48, 49, 84, 86, 195	17.24	67, 87, 160
14.21	46, 48, 50, 68, 71	15.20	54, 68, 78, 160	16.23	68, 87, 88	17.25	71, 86, 185, 194
14.22	60, 177	15.21	50, 177	16.24	47, 55, 69, 78, 80, 177	17.26	67, 79, 160
14.23	35, 46, 47, 50, 51, 56	15.22	47, 50, 71	16.25	47, 66, 67, 177	17.27	90, 160
14.24	179, 180	15.23	46, 47, 71	16.26	56, 66, 78, 84	17.28	67, 160
14.25-26	50, 68	15.24	51	16.27	55, 78, 177	17.29	67, 90, 160
14.25	129, 148	15.25	78, 79	16.28	55, 56, 78	17.30	67, 77, 90, 160
14.26	78	15.26	68, 104	16.29	47	17.31	60, 67, 74, 90, 160, 170, 179
14.27	51, 60, 90	15.27	50	16.30	56, 78, 177		
14.28	59, 82, 87, 148	15.28	51, 68, 148	16.31	56, 78	17.32	47
14.29-30	55, 56, 79	15.29	50, 56, 67, 68, 82, 149, 161	16.70	50	17.33	60
14.29	53, 55, 160			17.1	48, 49, 91	17.34	67, 179
14.30	51	15.30	74, 88	17.2	55, 72, 78	17.35	69, 88
14.31	59, 68, 84, 87, 88	15.31	42, 50, 177	17.3	47, 56, 149	17.37	50, 66, 68, 177
14.32	54, 71, 74, 78, 160	15.32	37, 48, 49, 194	17.4	56, 78, 79, 160	18.1	50, 69, 74, 170, 196
14.33	38, 51, 60	16.1	60	17.5	47, 50, 129	18.2	69
14.34	56, 70, 71	16.2	47, 50, 51, 68, 91, 148	17.6	46, 80	18.3	47, 70
14.35	66, 88	16.3	40, 50, 51, 78	17.7	46, 50, 68, 87	18.4	67, 161
15.1	74, 129, 170	16.4	55, 56, 78, 169	17.8	47, 55, 56, 68	18.5	55, 58, 73, 80, 87, 196
						18.6	47
						18.7	87, 160, 179

11.20	110	7.36	161	16.13	160	24.24	160
11.30	110	7.41	160	16.18	160	24.25	161
12.18	110	7.42	161	16.30	194	25.1	160
12.34	194, 195	7.45	160	16.35	160	25.6	160
20.1	149	8.1	160	16.37	150	25.10	194
20.5	149	8.11	161	17.3	194, 195	25.13	160
20.9	194, 195	8.30	169	17.11	160	25.14	160
21.9	149	9.6	194	17.13	169	26.1	150
21.20	149	9.8	149	17.17	160	26.7	160
		9.9	160	17.26	161	26.13	160
Acts		9.16	194	17.30	161	26.18	143
1.2	160	9.19	160	17.31	160	26.22	160
1.3	160	9.23	160	18.18	160	26.32	150
1.5	160	9.24	160	18.20	161	27.7	160
1.6	161, 194	9.33	161	18.23	161	27.9	161
1.7	161	9.37	160	19.9	160	27.20	160
1.13	154	9.43	160	19.10	161	27.24	194
1.15	160	10.3	160	19.15	169	27.26	194
1.21	161	10.17	143	19.21	194	27.29	160
1.22	160	10.28	150	19.22	161	27.33	160
2.1	160	10.30	160	19.223	161	27.39	160
2.15	160	10.33	143	19.35	169	28.7	160
2.16	143	10.40	160	20.6	160	28.12	160
2.17	160	10.41	143	20.16	160	28.13	160
2.18	160	10.42	143	20.18	160, 161	28.14	160
2.20	160	10.48	160	20.22	143	28.17	160
2.22	143	11.11	143	20.26	160		
2.29	160	11.27	160	20.31	160	*Romans*	
2.33	149	12.1	161	20.34	169	7.23	149
2.36	169	12.3	160	20.35	194	8.24	149
2.41	160	12.6	143	21.4	160	8.25	149
2.46	160	12.18	160	21.5	160	12.3	194
2.47	160	12.21	160	21.7	160		
3.20	143, 161	13.11	161	21.10	160	*1 Corinthians*	
3.21	160, 161, 194	13.14	160	21.15	160	1.26	149
		13.18	161	21.24	169	4.8	25
3.24	160	13.20	161	21.26	160	4.8b RSV	25
4.12	143, 194	13.21	161	21.37	169	4.9 RSV	25
4.22	161	13.29	143	21.38	160	4.10 RSV	26
4.27	143	13.31	160	22.3	143	5.2	25
5.23	143	13.40	143	22.5	143	8.2	194
5.29	194	13.41	160	22.20	154	10.18	149
5.36	160	14.3	161	23.1	160	11.9	194
5.37	160	14.17	161	23.6	169	15.25	194
5.42	160	14.22	194, 195	23.11	194	15.53	194
6.1	160	14.28	161	23.12	160		
7.6	161	15.5	194, 195	24.1	160	*2 Corinthians*	
7.8	160	15.7	160	24.8	143	2.3	194
7.17	161	15.33	161	24.10	161	5.10	194
7.20	161	15.36	160	24.11	160	10.7	149
7.23	161	16.4	143	24.14	143	11.30	194
7.26	160	16.5	160	24.17	161	12.1	194
7.30	161	16.12	160	24.19	194	12.6	149

Index of Authors